Causes of Supply Chain Disruptions

Verena Brenner

Causes of Supply Chain Disruptions

An Empirical Analysis in Cold Chains for Food and Pharmaceuticals

Springer Gabler

Verena Brenner
Hannover, Germany

Dissertation Jacobs University Bremen, 2014, Germany

ISBN 978-3-658-08661-9 ISBN 978-3-658-08662-6 (eBook)
DOI 10.1007/978-3-658-08662-6

Library of Congress Control Number: 2015930260

Springer Gabler

Printed on acid-free paper

Springer Gabler is a brand of Springer Fachmedien Wiesbaden
Springer Fachmedien Wiesbaden is part of Springer Science+Business Media
(www.springer.com)

Preface

How can wasteful handling of such precious goods as food and pharmaceuticals be reduced between production and consumption?

This was the key question at the beginning of this research project. Having witnessed vivid and frank discussions between logistics experts from all segments of the cold chain in conferences and workshops during my work for the Cool Chain Association (CCA), I became increasingly curious and involved in the search for solutions. To prevent massive losses of nutritious food and life-saving pharmaceuticals caused by supply chain disruptions is one of the main goals of this association and its members. However, I realized that a more systematic and academic way of addressing the problem would be required.

During my search for cooperation partners from the scientific world, Professor Hülsmann offered me a position as PhD student and Research Associate in his workgroup "Systems Management" at Jacobs University Bremen. Hence, I took the opportunity to analyze causes of supply chain disruptions in more depth by linking scientific and industrial perspectives.

In the following years, research projects in logistics and supply chain management as well as scientific seminars and conferences broadened my horizon and deepened my insights into cold chain logistics, but also into scientific research methods and systematic analyses. Furthermore, discussions with my research colleagues, but also my former boss and colleagues from the CCA reinforced my motivation and determination to find out why supply chain disruptions occur.

These efforts led to the absolute highlight of this project, namely the empirical survey among cold chain managers from around the world. Their interest and willingness to support my research was amazing and showed how relevant the topic is for the industry. In the future, the results will hopefully be starting points for further research and will be considered in the design of supply chain partnerships.

These years of research were incredibly tough, challenging and rewarding. To all the people who guided and supported me as well as this project: thank you very much!

Verena Brenner

Preface

Table of Contents

List of Figures

List of Tables

List of Abbreviations

AHP	Analytic Hierarchy Process
A/N	Author's Note
AVE	Average Variance Extracted
BOL	Bill of Lading
BRC	British Retail Consortium
CAPA	Corrective and Preventive Action
CBL	Dutch Food Retail Association
CCQI	Cool Chain Quality Indicator
CFSAN	Center for Food Safety and Applied Nutrition
CM	Category Management
DC	Distribution Centre
EC	European Commission
ECR	Efficient Consumer Response
EDI	Electronic Data Interchange
EU	European Union
ECSLA	European Cold Storage and Logistics Association
FAO	Food and Agriculture Organization of the United Nations
FEFO	First-Expired-First-Out
FoB	Free-on-Board
FPEF	Fresh Produce Exporter's Forum
GoF	Goodness of Fit
HACCP	Hazard Analysis and Critical Control Points
IATA	International Air Transport Association
Incoterms	International Commercial Terms
IFS	International Food Standard
JIT	Just in Time
KPI	Key Performance Indicator
LOSA	Line Operations Safety Audits
LSP	Logistics Service Provider
MCAR	Missing Completely at Random
MOR	Modulus of Rupture
MAUT	Multi Attribute Utility Theory
MIMIC	Multiple Indicators Multiple Cause
NAT	Normal Accident Theory
PLS	Partial Least Squares
QAA	Quality Assurance Agreement

QS	Quality System
RFID	Radio Frequency Identification
RH	Relative Humidity
SCOR	Supply Chain Operations Reference Model
SCRQ	Supply Chain Relationship Quality
SEM	Structural Equation Modelling
SME	Small and Medium-Sized Enterprises
SOP	Standard Operating Procedures
TI	Transfrigoroute International
USDA	United States Department of Agriculture
VIF	Variance Inflation Factor
WFO	World Farmers' Organization
WHO	World Food Organization

1 Introduction

1.1 Problem: Can Organizational Designs Impact on the Susceptibility to Disruptions?

Why do systems fail? Many researchers have investigated this question in areas such as nuclear power plants, air flight operations, or manufacturing plants.[1] The approach to investigate failures in an industry-specific context seems to be useful, since causes may be dependent on parameters, which may differ between industries.[2] A reason for selecting the industries above as fields of research is their complexity,[3] which makes the identification of causes of failures and the correct evaluation of critical situations more difficult (Perrow 1999). As another example, Dörner (1992) names the criticality of these systems, which means that accidents might cause death and/or severe harm to many people. Hence, on the one hand, causes of failures may differ from industry to industry, and on the other hand, the negative effects of errors differ in form and magnitude.

According to Helmreich, Klinect & Wilhelm (2001), the purpose of research on such failures is to enhance the robustness of systems. For such an analysis, Woolthuis, Lankhuizen & Gilsing (2005) suggest to make a distinction between failures due to the rules of the system and failures by humans, as humans cannot only cause failures but also resolve them. Additionally, Cook, Woods & McDonald (1991) stress the importance of differentiating between process and outcome since a defect might still be resolved if discovered before a shift to negative consequences occurs. This understanding implies that in case of undiscovered defects, a performance failure results, thus the actual outcome is different from the intended outcome, yet that it could have been prevented.

Analyses of failures in different industries resulted in the perception that even though the specific failures might have been different between several accidents, the patterns leading to the negative consequences of errors were similar. For example, frequently not only one defect occurred, nor were the failure-causing factors attributable to being either purely human, or technological. Furthermore, these failures occurred repeatedly in situations, were the system state and the normal workflow was amended (e.g. for maintenance) (Dörner 1992; Reason 1995; Perrow 1999). Thus, failures seem to occur more frequently when the system shows vulnerabilities in its processes.

Another industry, which reveals considerable criticality and complexity in its systems, is the food industry. Especially cold chains for temperature-sensitive products have been identified as incorporating a significant complexity (Trienekens & Zuurbier 2008; Vega 2008; Fritz &

---

1 E.g. Rasmussen & Vicente (1989); Reason (1990); Dörner (1992); Reason (1995); Misumi, Wilpert & Miller (1998); Kletz (1998); Perrow (1999); Klinect, Wilhelm & Helmreich (1999); Helmreich (2000); Kjellen (2000); Helmreich, Klinect & Wilhelm (2001); Ornitz & Champ (2002); Dhillon (2007); Clarke et al. (2008).

2 For some examples see: Reason (1990) and Reason (1995).

3 Complexity in this context refers to the large number of agents in a system and the number of relations between these agents; see e.g. Dörner (1992); Hülsmann et al. (2007).

Schiefer 2009). In today's cold chains, the contamination of food at one production stage can be critical to many people, as the market, especially in developed countries, is highly centralized and dominated by a few multinational food producers (Lyson & Raymer 2000). Their products are distributed to many retailers in different regions and countries, extending the radius of damage. Therewith, failures in the system of one food manufacturer can harm many people. Additional challenges arise in the case of temperature-sensitive products, such as fruit, vegetables, but also vaccines, as variations in temperature during transport can have significant negative effects on the products transported (Bogataj, Bogataj & Vodopivec 2005).

Furthermore, similar to other critical industries, as for example the pharmaceutical industry (Backhaus 1983), the food industry involves a broader class of stakeholders, including regulatory bodies and security agencies. According to the failure classification framework by Woolthuis, Lankhuizen & Gilsing (2005), thereby also the probability of failures is enhanced, simply because a wider range of rules exist. Furthermore, even though there are some major players in food production and retail, many actors are involved along the cold chain, due for example to the globalization of sourcing of food products and ingredients. This has transformed food supply chains to interconnected systems with a multitude of complex relationships (Trienekens & Zuurbier 2008).

In addition, food products increase the complexity of the systems due to their special characteristics. Among these are the heterogeneity of packaging and transport requirements of products, the huge variety in shipping volumes, due to e.g. seasonal variation, the continuous decay of quality attributes, which also depends on the applied processes, as well as the interaction between food compounds, packaging and equipment (Luning & Marcelis 2006). Therefore, food supply chains and especially cold chains can be considered as critical and complex systems, but do they also have industry-specific causes of failures and can negative outcomes be considered as failures?

In order to answer this question, in the following, three examples of deviations from planned outcomes will be described and analyzed.[4] For better comparability, they all refer to cases in the food industry.

Example 1: Specific causes of failures in global food systems

A recent study conducted for the Food and Agricultural Organization of the United Nations (FAO), revealed that approximately one-third of all food produced for human consumption is lost or wasted along the supply chain (Gustavsson et al. 2011). According to this study, food losses refer to "*... the decrease in edible food mass throughout the part of the supply chain that specifically leads to edible food for human consumption*" (Gustavsson et al. 2011, p. 2).

[4] According to Yin (2009), case studies are useful if phenomena shall be investigated, which take place in large systems of great complexity, where rules are continuously and rapidly changing. Furthermore, according to Kromrey (2009) such qualitative studies are useful for exploratory research as is conducted here.

Especially fresh fruits and vegetables are susceptible to such losses (Parfitt, Barthel & Macnaughton 2010), which can be attributed to the following reasons: firstly, fruits and vegetables are of a perishable nature, which implies that shelf life is limited by **time** and may be further reduced by exposing the fruit or vegetable to wrong **temperatures** (Nunes et al. 2009). Furthermore, fruits and vegetables are also sensitive towards the **relative humidity** (RH) of the surrounding air, which should be kept high in order to avoid moisture losses and wilding of the produce (Zhang 1997). However, not only the environmental conditions play a role in the maintenance of shelf life, but also the **physical handling**, as waste due to mechanical injuries may be a large contributor to the entire food waste (Nunes et al. 2009). These and other factors have to be considered during handling of fruits and vegetables in the entire food system. If the system does not comply with these constraints, major losses may occur.

The FAO study estimated food losses for several agricultural food commodities in different regions of the world. On average, the following loss rates for fruits and vegetables could be observed for each step of the commercial food system:

Figure 1: Global average losses of fruits and vegetables from farm to fork

Agricultural production	Postharvest handling and storage	Processing and packaging	Distribution	Consumption
10-20%	4-10%	2-25%	8-17%	5-28%

Source 1: own illustration; data from Gustavsson et al. (2011)

The types of losses or waste are grouped according to the part of the food supply chain in which they occur, hence agricultural production, postharvest handling or storage, processing, distribution (supermarket retail) and consumption.

Regarding the findings of the FAO study, it becomes obvious that there are significant losses of fruits and vegetables in the food system. These occur not only in some parts of the supply chain, but in all parts. Nevertheless, there are considerable differences between loss rates for the same stage of the food system in different regions of the world. The differing loss rates could be an indicator for a varying degree of efficiency in the food system and therewith for potential loss reductions. For example, fruits and vegetables losses in processing and packaging in developed countries are estimated by Gustavsson et al. (2011) to amount to only 2%, whereas in developing countries in Asia or Africa, about 20-25% of the harvest is lost in this part of the chain.

Furthermore, the study provides information about the causes of food waste, which are for example:

- Inadequate forecasting of demand
- Poor storage facilities

- Lack of infrastructure
- Errors during processing
- Damaged packaging
- Damage during loading, transport and storage
- Rough handling
- Unsanitary conditions
- Lack of processing facilities (Gustavsson et al. 2011, pp. 10–14)

Regarding the numerous causes of food waste, it becomes obvious that a significant amount is lost not only because of natural and unavoidable decay, but due to errors occurring along the supply chain. This implies also economic losses for the parties in the food system, as for instance in the US, food waste from farm to fork amount to about US$ 90 to US$ 100 billion per year (Williams 2004). Several other studies support these findings, indicating that firstly, the amount of food waste is substantial in all segments of the supply chain, and secondly that a considerable part of these losses could be prevented by adequate food supply chain management.[5] Subsuming this example, causes of defects are quite specific due to the nature of the products. However, the reasons why defects amounted to failures cannot be analyzed based on this example as the level of abstraction precludes this information, wherefore it will be analyzed in the next example.

Example 2: Vulnerability of processes in food systems

Fraud is a frequent and sensitive issue in the food industry. On the one hand, cases of fraud are published every year (BWV 2011), and on the other hand, the loss of trust by consumers may have a significant negative impact on sales and reputation of companies (Luo 2010), even though the case might have been committed somewhere else in the food supply chain, or even in other food systems.

One example is the dioxin scandal in Germany at the beginning of 2011. Back then, a producer of ingredients for animal feed illicitly mixed its feed fat with fatty acid in order to cut costs (Brandt et al.). This fatty acid was, according to its supplier, a biodiesel producer, only dedicated for technical utilization purposes and was found later on to be contaminated with dioxin (Marquart 2011). Even though the producer effected in 2010 three self monitoring tests, where the legal threshold for dioxin was breached every time, the contamination of the animal feed was not reported to the authorities, nor the deliveries to the customers stopped (Brandt et al. n.d.). In consequence, about 3,000 tonnes of dioxin contaminated feed fat was delivered to about 25 producers of animal feed in eight federal states in Germany, which led to the contamination of 150,000 tonnes of animal feed (Marquart 2011). After feeding the animal feed to pigs, chicken and turkey, dioxin contaminated meat and eggs got into the human food chain.

---

5 E.g. Ward (1996) cited in: Cheke & Ward (1998); Engström & Carlsson-Kanyama (2004); Nunes, Emond & Brecht (2006); Vermeulen et al. (2006); Nunes et al. (2009).

This caused losses of billions of Euro, because several hundred thousand eggs had to be destroyed, consumers avoided buying animal products, and 5.000 farms were temporarily closed (Der Spiegel n.d.).

That the transaction between the producer of biodiesel and the producer of feed fat has not been noted, even though the producer was a member of a private quality control system (QS), has several reasons: first of all, the transaction was effected indirectly through a Dutch trader, who deals with animal fat as well as fatty acids. This indirect trade obscured the relation between the two companies, who would normally not work in the same system. Secondly, producers of ingredients for animal feed were the first link of the controlled food system, thus no attention was paid to their suppliers. This means that inadequate products could enter the food system without notice. Thirdly, the company was audited only once by QS during the year 2010. So, whereas the company was certified as being compliant with QS, little attention was paid to control this statement.

That the contamination has not been detected earlier is also due to the regulatory structure of the food sector in general. For example, there is no standardized list of allowed ingredients in animal feed across Europe (El-Sharif 2011). In consequence, some ingredients might be allowed in some countries, while being forbidden in others. Since supplies can be purchased worldwide and animal feed supply chains are highly complex with a multitude of actors involved (Marquart 2011), the possibilities to control the entire supply chain by local authorities and to assure the quality of the end product is limited. Furthermore, according to Brandt et al., companies involved in feed production tend to diversify their business and transport units are also used for other products, the animal feed supply chain is prone to contamination, resulting in contaminated food destined for human consumption. And finally, up to the dioxin scandal the audits of the responsible German authorities were mainly concerned with food production plants and not with animal feed production plants (Brandt et al.).

Thus, even though there are private quality control systems as well as official regulations, audits, and laws in place to assure the innocuousness of human food, the planned flows in the food system can be breached without notice, resulting in highly vulnerable processes. Furthermore, it is the complex interaction of several defects, which result in the negative shift in consequences, what Cook, Woods & McDonald (1991, p. 15) call a "*going sour incident*". How critical such failures in food systems can become shows the next example.

Example 3: System failures

An example for a recent food scandal without obvious intentional fraud was the outbreak of enterohaemorrhagic Escherichia coli (EHEC) in Germany in May 2011. This case represented a major challenge, not only to German authorities, but also to European ones. First of all, this was the first outbreak of this particular germ, so very little information regarding its resistance and behaviour was available. EHEC is a bacterium, which normally resides in the intestinal of humans and animals, and which can be conferred via contaminated food (BfR 2011). However, it was not possible to trace back the source of contamination, where the planned product flow had been breached. Secondly, the product is part of a multitude of food products, such as salads (RKI 2011), spices, and food additives (BfR 2011). In consequence, it took a lot of time and effort to trace back the EHEC infections to their origin.

Within two months, approx. 3.850 people were infected and about 53 patients died (RKI 2011). During several weeks, information on which food product caused the disease as well as on the origin of the contaminated product varied. After having firstly accused cucumbers from Spain being the cause of the epidemic, finally fenugreek seed scions from Egypt were identified as the germ carrier (Kwasniewski 2011). In all, 37 tonnes of potentially contaminated fenugreek seeds had been exported to Germany and from there been distributed to at least 14 other states (BfR 2011).

The outbreak of EHEC had considerable implications for farmers across Europe, seed producers in Egypt, but also for consumers in Germany. European farmers are claiming more than 210 million Euros of losses, due to the preventive destruction of food products and the slump in demand of many different kinds of vegetables (Kwasniewski 2011). The European Union banned all Egyptian seeds as well as beans to prevent further outbreaks and consumers in Germany were unsettled, not only because of the risk of infection, but also because of the inferior crisis management and communication by official authorities (Teevs 2011).

The detection of the source of infection was complicated by several factors. First of all, the product was only causing infections as raw scions, which are frequently used in mixed salads. The mix of different vegetables from different countries and suppliers made the detection of the source of infections considerably more difficult. Furthermore, the breeding from a seed to a scion provided a different end product, which was only in its raw estate damaging to human health. This implies that products from the same charge may have caused harm to humans or not, depending on their final state, which is intended to make the food system safe and transparent. Thus, the complexity of the supply chain, caused for example by the number of potential infection sources, the number of agents involved, the different authorities involved, and the different processing stages of the product, resulted in the inefficiency of the traceability system for food products. Hence, food systems can be considered as critical systems, since the effects of errors can be devastating, even though they differ in form and magnitude.

Synopsis of the Examples

The examples given above highlight the diversity of issues which may occur in supply chains vital for the society. These concern for instance the type of product affected (animal product or plant product) and the type and severity of negative outcome (economic losses or health risk). Nevertheless, the three examples also show some similarities regarding how the failures evolved. In the FAO study for example, frequent causes for food waste are mentioned. These failures did not only occur in one food system, but repetitively re-occur in many food systems all around the world. So, whereas the negative results as well as the causing defects are known, these defects are not eliminated. Also the other two cases show some similarities regarding the types of defects. In both cases, food products were contaminated, showing a lack of protection. Additionally, the lack of information collection within the supply chain was a major contributor to the negative outcome and occurred repetitively, i.e. at more than one node in the system. So, even though the situation and the system were different from each other, the same types of defects occurred repetitively.

From what has been learned from other industries, an error committed by one person frequently does not lead directly to a consequential negative outcome. For example, Flin, O'Connor & Mearns (2002) state that accidents in surgical medicine are frequently due to the communication and teamwork, thus due to interaction. They also cite an example from the aviation industry, where a crash could have been prevented, if the pilot would have been informed appropriately by the crew about a technical error. In both cases, the negative outcome is due to some kind of multi-causal interaction, and is only indirectly caused by the original technical or human error. However, what all these cases have in common is the negative effect of errors, which significantly decrease the performance of the system.

In the literature on supply chain management, such failures are also known as supply chain disruptions (e.g. Wagner & Bode 2008). Disruptions are a phenomenon, which is increasingly gaining attention in the literature, as will be shown in 2.2.2. As a consequence of such disruptions, the achievement of the main logistics objectives[6] is imperilled. In the context of food supply chains for perishables, hence time and temperature sensitive products, the provision of the right quantity and the right quality of products is directly related to the maintenance of optimal conditions from farm to fork. Thus, disruptions do not only occur by delaying, destroying or impeding the product and information flow, but also by interrupting the temperature maintenance, also known as cold chain ruptures (Coton et al. 2011). In consequence, disruptions may also be caused by failures to maintain surrounding conditions as required.

The occurrence of disruptions can also be seen in the three examples above. In all three cases, some defects caused destruction or contamination of products, and/or the information flow was impeded. In the first example, defects in checking products and providing information led to contamination of products and lack of information flow. This could only be realized as adequate quality control procedures within the company, but also at its customers were lacking. In the second example, errors led to food wastage due to some kind of wrong handling, combined with the lack of adequate protection of the product and suitable infrastructure. In the third example, the contamination of seeds may also only lead to the negative consequences, as apparently suitable quality controls are lacking. Hence, it seems as if the negative effects of errors are only realized, if their occurrence interacts with some vulnerable organization of the processes concerned with the product or information flow, which then leads to the disruption.

6 The 7Rs of logistics are: right product, right quantity, right quality, right time, right costs, right place, right knowledge (e.g. Jetzke 2007; Ross 2011).

In summary, there is a practical need to analyze the occurrence of disruptions in supply chains. As Chmielewicz (1979) asserts, research is always a combination of theoretical and practical purposes, wherefore also the relevancy of the research question has to be shown for both perspectives. Therefore, section 1.2 will focus on the theoretical relevance.

1.2 Relevance: Theoretical Gaps on Organizational Design and Disruptions

In order to show the theoretical relevance of the research question, the related research in the fields of failures/disruptions, and organizational design has to be illustrated, to reveal its limitations in explaining the causal relation between the variables. Thereby, the contributions are structured according to the focus of investigation into three categories, namely organizations in general, supply chains, and food systems.

Organizational Design

According to Ansoff & Brandenburg (1971), organizational design is the decision making by companies on their organizational structure under considerations of the organizational strategy and environmental constraints. This contingent optimality of organizational structures has been taken up in empirical research, but led also to the theoretic stream known as contingency theory (e.g. Wolf 2008; Kieser & Ebers 2006).

In a comparative analysis of six organizations, Lawrence & Lorsch (1967) tried to assess the effect of organizational design on economic performance. They come to the conclusion that those organizations where integration and differentiation of the organizational structure fit the requirements by their respective environments performed better.

Based on data from 34 medium-sized firms, Gordon & Narayanan (1984) tested whether information systems and organizational structure are affected by environmental constraints. They conclude that those companies facing higher environmental uncertainty tend to seek increasingly more information from outside the company, transforming the company structure more and more into an organic structure. Hence, in these two examples, evidence is found for the influence by the environmental conditions on the organizational design.

The same can be reasoned for the influence of organizational strategy, as the next two examples indicate. In an empirical analysis of the effects of the kind of technology used on the organizational structure, Hickson, Pugh & Pheysey (1969) come to the conclusion that the technology only has an influence on those organizational variables, which are concerned with the workflow. The extent of effects was found to differ considerably with different sizes of companies and different ratios of employee-manager relations.

In a survey in the savings and loans industry, Jennings & Seaman (1994) aimed for answering the question, how the choice of a strategy and structure affects performance of companies. They found evidence for a better performance if companies chose a static structure when a defender strategy was followed or a dynamical structure when a prospector strategy was followed.

These findings indicate that firstly, organizational structure depends on constraints, and secondly, organizational design has an impact on performance. However, the unit of analysis in this research is mainly a single company. The question, how the organizational design that includes several companies affects the performance has therewith not been answered, yet.

This topic is part of the **supply chain** management literature. Wathne & Heide (2004) for instance assess the governance of relationships in supply chain networks of the fashion apparel industry. Based on transaction cost theory, they build a theoretic framework for how to deal with uncertainties in vertical relationships. Furthermore, they argue based on network literature that the need for flexibility or relationship modification of a manufacturer in his relation to retailers does not only depend on the governance of this relationship, but also on how the relationship towards its suppliers is designed. In order to allow for flexibility of the arrangements with suppliers, two governance mechanisms were identified: the choice of suppliers shall be based on formal supplier qualification programs, and the incentive structure shall be based on long-term gains instead of short-term profit payoffs of potential opportunism. They come to the conclusion that firstly, relationships and the ability to adapt to uncertainties are indeed interdependent in larger networks, and that the governance is far more complex, as to be managed by the two mechanisms identified. Therefore, they call for additional research into the properties and effects of alternative mechanisms of relationship governance in supply chain networks.

Fynes, Voss & de Burca (2005) examine the impact of supply chain relationship quality on quality performance. Based on several theoretical frameworks, [7] and different research streams,[8] they come to the conclusion that paradigms to explain the nature of supply chain relationships converge to some common components. These components, namely trust, adaptation, communication, dependence and interdependence, commitment and co-operation are combined to what they refer to as supply chain relationship quality (SCRQ). They come to the conclusion, that the SCRQ indeed has a positive impact on quality, and that in order to enhance it companies should focus on the management of supply chain relationships. Thus, the kind of relationship was found to have an impact on quality performance, yet based on an eclectic approach.

The role of organizational design has also been studied in the context of **food systems**. Loader (1997) for example bases his analysis on transaction cost theory. He stipulates that the configuration of exchange relationships is determined by the nature of transaction (i.e. standardized, occasional non-standardized, or recurring non-standardized) and the characteristics of investments (non-dedicated, dedicated, or input characteristics mixed). Based on the two criteria, he differentiates between market-based, trilateral, and bilateral/unified governance of the exchange relationship. He applies this framework to an international supply chain of fresh products and comes to the conclusion that due to asset specificity and uncertainty prevalent in

7 For instance transaction cost theory, political economy theory, and social exchange theory.

8 Such as relationship marketing, operations management, supply chain management and logistics.

this supply chain, a vertical integration can be observed. In consequence, the nature or type of transaction seems to have an effect on the organizational structure of exchange relationships.

The role of asset specificity in the design of food systems has been affirmed by Ménard & Klein (2004), who compare network designs for different agricultural products. Based on data from Europe and the US, they observe that during the last century, the production, processing and distribution of food as been significantly consolidated, even though farming remains a mainly family-owned business. The structure of the food sector, together with the requirements for vertical coordination and quality control has led to a shift away from spot-market exchanges, to more vertical integration and long-term contracting. However, numerous forms of vertical coordination exist, which, according to the authors, can be explained by transaction cost considerations. Food products, which are subjects to mechanization, quality standards, and physical asset specificity, as well as site and temporal specificity, are controlled more closely than others. Thus, the degree of processing, the criticality to health, and the product characteristics such as its perishability all seem to play a role in the design of the food systems.

However, all these examples are rather concerned with how partners cooperate with each other on a rather abstract level. The question, how the organizational structure can be related to the occurrence of disruptions as therewith not been answered, yet.

In summary, the relation between interface design and performance has been studied in detail in the literature in general, as well as in supply chain management literature, and even in the context of food systems. However, a connection to the phenomenon of disruptions and systematic errors is lacking. Furthermore, the analyses mainly remain on a relatively abstract level and employ case-study research.

System failures

The research on failures has developed as a research discipline of its own, even though up to now, a discipline-encompassing and thorough illustration of perspectives and results of the research, as well as a general taxonomy, is lacking (Weingardt 2004). On the **organizational level**, different research disciplines analyzed causes for break-downs, catastrophes and accidents (Kletz 1998; Kjellen 2000; Ornitz & Champ 2002; Perrow 2006; Dhillon 2007; Hofmann 2008). Perrow (1999) for example analyzes accidents in large scale process plants. Based on his observations, he comes to the conclusion that accidents happen due to the complexity of interactions and the tight coupling of elements in complex systems. Furthermore, he acknowledges the impact of systematic barriers and organizational design on the creation of poor performance in complex systems, such as air transport systems or marine transport systems.

Dörner (1992) comes to a similar conclusion in his analysis of a reactor catastrophe. Additionally, he stresses the fact that the explosion was not due to only one defect, but due to a series of interconnected errors. He argues that the unintended secondary effects of actions were not observable and that their joint occurrence led to a chain reaction of wrong decisions and system changes, which finally resulted in the catastrophe.

In the analysis of major oil spills and resulting natural catastrophes, Ornitz & Champ (2002) estimate that in the end about 80% of these spills were due to human error. However, as root cause, they also name other causes, such as lack of maintenance of ships, lack of training, and reduction of workforce. Hence, human errors have been found to be the ultimate cause of such catastrophes, but their occurrence was already inherent in the systems.

The human factor is also widely studied and centralized around the study of human beings and their interaction with products, environments, and equipment in performing tasks and activities (Czaja & Nair 2006). Research is based on a multidisciplinary approach comprising psychology, engineering, information science, social science and economics (Badke-Schaub, Hofinger & Lauche 2008). Since this field of research encompasses many different disciplines, in the following some aspects from different fields will be highlighted.

A person-focused approach to explain errors and consequential failures originates from **psychology** (Reason 1995). In cognitive psychology, many errors are explained by the wrong retrieval of information, which has been obtained earlier, and which had been stored in the subconscious till it is needed. Since experiences and knowledge are not stored exactly as they are, friction losses occur which might lead to wrong actions when, based on this information, activities are executed later in time (Spencer 2000). Human errors are also analyzed for example in the error-mode-and-effect-analysis, which classifies human errors into: errors related to learning and adaptation, interference among competing cognitive control structures, lack of resources, and intrinsic human variability (Rasmussen & Vicente 1989). In the context of human errors, the systematic occurrence has been already observed as early as 1926, when Weimer (1926) stated that errors are not random, but are indicators for more deeply rooted defects. Hence, even though the human being is the one to commit an error, systematic errors do have a causal explanation.

Errors are also closely investigated in **engineering** for the optimal design of human-machine interfaces (e.g. Vicente & Rasmussen 1992; Vicente 2002; Wilson 2000). For example, in the air flight industry, human errors in cockpits have been studied closely in order to prevent accidents. Klinect, Wilhelm & Helmreich (1999) for instance analyzed data from the Line Operations Safety Audits (LOSA) of different airlines and divide errors of flight crews into intentional non-compliance, procedural errors, communication errors, proficiency errors and operational decision errors. They come to the conclusion that not all errors result in consequential negative outcomes, that they have different frequencies of occurrence, and that different airlines tend to be unequally exposed to errors. Thus, the amount and magnitude of causes of errors seems to depend on the specific organization, resulting in different degrees of susceptibility to errors. Furthermore, even though errors were committed by people, the data revealed different levels of vulnerability, hence the extent of damage caused by errors. These findings support the argument of other authors, who argue that the underlying system structure should be designed in such a way, as to prevent the negative outcome of human errors (Rasmussen & Vicente 1989; Reason 2000; Thomeczek & Ollenschläger 2006).

According to Reason (1990), a person's active failure only results in a negative outcome, if the system design, consisting of the layers humans, technologies and organization, are arranged in such a way that latent error provoking conditions of all three components overlap each other so that all safety mechanisms fail. This so-called Swiss cheese model has been applied to many different systems, such as in anaesthesia, nuclear power plants or air traffic control centres (e.g. Reason 2000; Grube, Schaper & Graf 2002). Reason (1997) comes to the conclusion that an effective safety culture needs to be based on reports, fairness, flexibility and a willingness to learn.

The importance of system's design for the occurrence of human errors is also supported by other authors. For example, Dörner (1992) presents some simulation cases, in which the behaviour and decision making of testing groups during the management of fictive villages was analyzed. He observes that errors in the decision making of humans were mainly caused by the inability to capture the complex interactions of causal relations, and the neglect of signs which were indicating effects that did not fit the assumptions of participants on causal relations. Hence, error prevention involves a temporal dimension, namely to learn from past errors and to use this knowledge for an active error prevention and mitigation of effects. Furthermore, human error and system defects seem to reinforce each other and jointly lead to failures. Therefore, also both should be considered in the analysis of failures.

In the area of **supply chain** management research, interest in failures or, more specifically, disruptions is still relatively young but on the rise, as can be seen in Figure 2.

Figure 2: Evolution of publications on supply chain disruptions

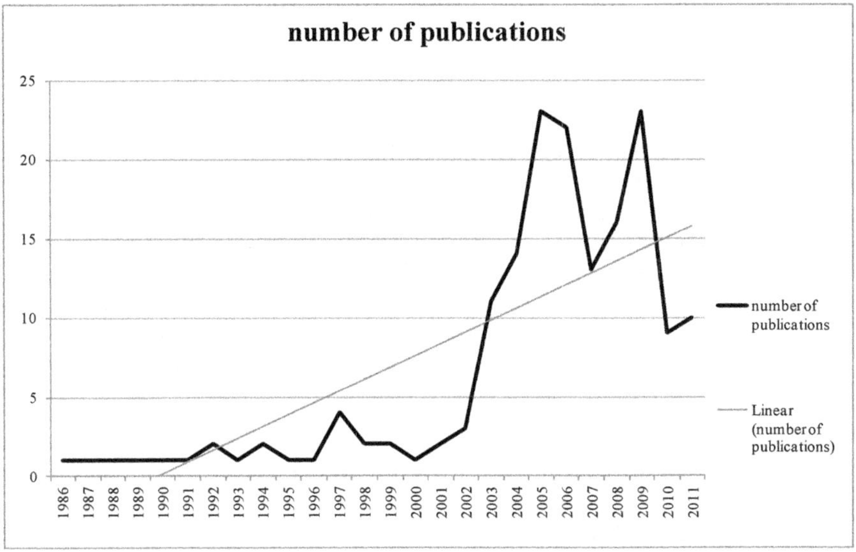

Source 2: own illustration; for further details on the review see section 2.2

According to Stevens (1989), who investigates supply chains in the manufacturing industry, the scope of a supply chain begins at the source of supply and ends at the final point of consumption. It comprises not only the physical movement of goods, but also relates to other activities, like supplier management, purchasing, materials management, customer service and information flow. Furthermore, Stevens points out that all these activities are interdependent and that if one of them fails, the supply chain is disrupted, which creates poor performance and jeopardizes the effectiveness of the supply chain. In order to avoid such disruptions he suggest that the partners in the supply chain should work together in a closely manner, to create an integrated supply chain.

This view on supply chain disruptions and solutions is also issued by Geary, Childerhouse & Towill (2002, p. 53) who aim for "*the seamless supply chain*", which is constituted by a perfect flow of information and materials, and all supply chain partners thinking and acting as one single entity. Based on their research on supply chains in the automotive industry, they come to the conclusion that safety mechanisms have to be established to protect the supply chain. These safety mechanisms are ultimately trying to tackle the uncertainty related to potential disruptions. In order to reduce uncertainty in the areas of process, demand, supply, and control, supply chain partners shall strive for the integration of the entire supply chain.

Based on a cross-sector empirical study and on systems theory, Peck (2005) argues that in order to reduce the vulnerability of a supply chain to risks, functional goals of supply chain management have to be linked to decisions on the organizational design and business strategy. She cites many causes for supply chain disruptions, stemming from company-specific, supply chain specific or industry specific sources. However, the understanding of disruptions is again reduced to a disruption in supply, without considering any other kind of disruptions, and without any further harmful effects outside of the companies in the supply chain.

While the understanding of supply chain disruptions from the sources above is still more related to balancing supply and demand, other authors are explicitly addressing the possible intervention of some external incidences or operational contingencies as causes for supply chain disruptions. Paul (2008) for instance names as causes for supply chain disruptions three major classes of risks, being operational contingencies such as equipment failures, natural hazards, and terrorism or political instability. He suggests that in order to manage these risks managers first need to identify the vulnerabilities of their company.[9] However, given the aim to derive general assumptions on causal relations, the focus will be narrowed down to a specific industry to learn more about its vulnerabilities do disruptions.

A meta-analysis of research on causes for disruptions by Hülsmann & Brenner (2011) reveals many contributions dealing with disruptions in **temperature-sensitive food supply chains**. These papers indicate that disruptions occur quite often in cold chains, and that their negative effects are substantial. Thereby, the lack of transparency, a multitude of actors along the supply chain and differing requirements by products, but also by regulations are frequently cited system defects causing disruptions. At the same time, the lack of staff, lack of education of staff and carelessness by employees is frequently cited as human errors causing disruptions. However, they mostly report results of case studies and do not analyze in detail the causal relations between the disruption and the cited errors causing this disruption.

Nevertheless, many authors confirm the important role of the supply chain design and especially of the interfaces in the diminution of disruptions in the information, product and temperature flows. Examples for disruptions at interfaces are for instance the exposure of fruits and vegetables to ambient temperatures during loading and unloading, or the delay of information forwarding to the customer. Such delays or the refusal of information forwarding has also been observed in the examples above, while the loading process has also been mentioned as cause of disruptions by Gustavsson et al. (2011).

In summary, the interdependence between system design and the occurrence of failures has been recognized in the literature. Also disruptions are an important topic and their reasons have been investigated in many different settings. The role of interface design as a contributing factor to disruptions is also acknowledged. This includes for instance tight coupling of processes, complex interactions, and uncertainty during decision making. However, research on disruptions seems to either focus on a specific case, where insights are gained on the actual evolvement of one disruption. Or research is on a very abstract level, where generic insights

9 For a detailed overview on understandings of disruptions see section 2.2.2.

are gained, yet where the process remains a black box. Therewith, no general causal relations between the interface design and the occurrence of disruptions can be deduced.

According to Chmielewicz (1979), information content of research results varies in two aspects, namely regarding the universality of statements, and their precision. There are therefore two options to increase information content of research, either by increasing the universality of statements, or by increasing their preciseness. Trying to increase both at the same time will is however limited, as therewith also the risk of false statements rises (Chmielewicz 1979). In the case of failure research in general, already a wide body of insights has been gained, which are generic and explain the evolvement of failures. However, in this case, a single company or even department or team stands in the focus of research, which might be more homogenous in the set of rules as when transaction partners are evolved. Hence, an extension of analysis regarding interaction effects is currently still required, to be able to explain failures in more settings. Therefore, this research will try to bridge the gap between case study-based precision of causes for failures, and general applicability of insights on optimality of organizational design.

Therefore, there is a need to identify, describe and explain causal relations between interface designs and the occurrence of disruptions in supply chains and to show starting points for their improvement.

An overview on contributions in the related research areas, and the identified research gap can be found in Figure 3.

Figure 3: Overview on relevant literature and current research gaps

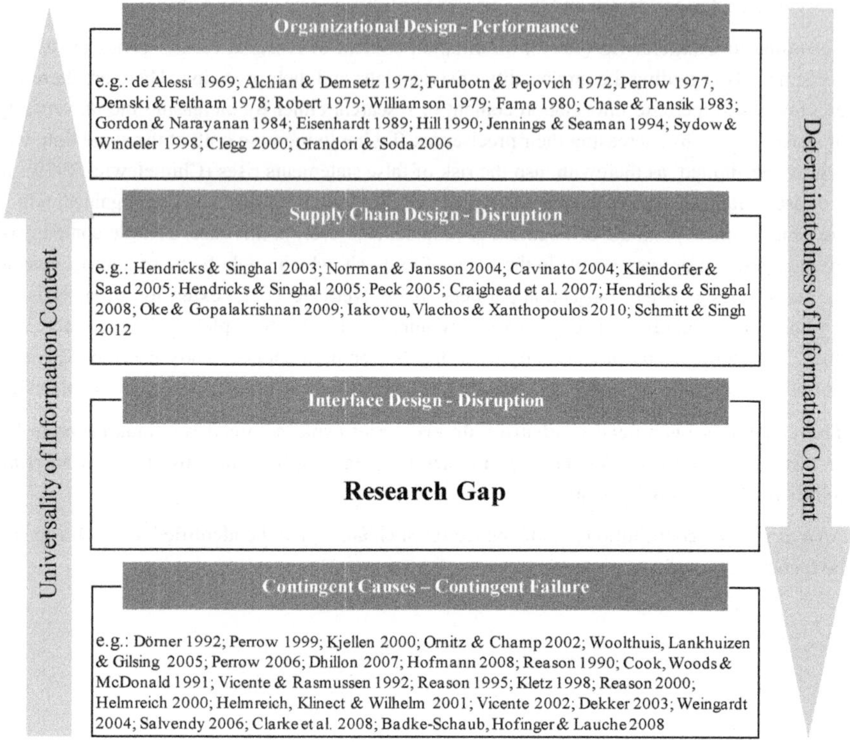

1.3 Aims: Explaining the Occurrence of Disruptions Based on Organizational Design

As has been highlighted in the previous sections, the susceptibility of supply chains to disruptions seems to differ depending on their configuration, indicating potential for a reduction of disruptions. Nevertheless, up to now, research on disruptions and their causes in temperature-sensitive supply chains, such as food chains is scarce.[10] Therefore, based on the assumptions stipulated in section 1, the overarching objective of this thesis is to identify, describe and explain causes of disruptions at interfaces for the example of cold chains.

According to Bea & Haas 2001, scientific research in the field of business economics has the purpose to develop tools that help to describe, explain and design companies in the context of

---

10 See section 2.2 and 2.3.

their environment. Following this understanding, the overarching objective of this thesis can be divided into descriptive, analytic and pragmatic sub-objectives.[11]

Descriptive Objectives

Before starting to analyze potential causal relations, first of all, the real-world phenomena have to be defined, and their major characteristics described, to unambiguously link these phenomena to the terms used in research (Chmielewicz 1979). Therefore, the elements of interface design (i.e. constraints and structure) and disruptions have to be defined and described for the subsequent use. Additionally, the descriptive objectives include the dimensional analysis of research objects, which can be used to narrow down the focus on relevant aspects and the comparison of effects (Kromrey 2009). Hence, the main variables will be decomposed to gather further insights on their interlocking and resulting changes in the overall construct. Thereby, disruptions will be further specified to ensure unambiguous identification of the phenomenon compared to similar constructs, and will therefore also be concretized in an industry-specific context, namely in food supply chains.

Analytic Objectives

The analytic objective is to explain causal relations between the design of interfaces and the occurrence of disruptions in supply chains. Therefore, it has to be analyzed how interfaces are designed by partners in the supply chain, how the resulting interface structure affects the susceptibility to errors and defects, and how these errors may lead to supply chain disruptions. As a case of illustration and to gain more insights on the phenomenon of disruptions, the specific context of food supply chains will be used to explore causal relations.

This implies that first of all, the constraints under which partners agree on an interface structure are analyzed regarding their impact on the resulting interface structure. Secondly, this implies that the effect of this interface structure on disruptions is analyzed. The causal relations will be integrated in a causal model, based on the chain of argumentation. In order to build the structural equation model, the causal models will be combined with the measuring models of the relevant dimensions identified for each variable. The achievement of these objectives will show whether there are any causal relations between the elements and how the elements affect each other. This helps to understand how different interface designs may enhance or reduce the occurrence of different types of disruptions.

Pragmatic Objectives

The pragmatic objective is to derive suggestions on how to design interfaces in such a way that disruptions can be prevented and/or mitigated. Therewith, a decision basis shall be provided for the management of supply chains, to support the design of robust processes and to avoid preventable waste. Furthermore, a tool shall be developed which allows the measure-

11 For other differentiations of the scientific research objectives, see e.g. Chmielewicz (1979); Kosiol (1964); Hill, Fehlbaum & Ulrich (1994).

ment of disruptions in supply chains, to identify disruptions, but also to measure the effects of changes in the interface design on supply chain performance. Thus, this thesis shall facilitate the identification, monitoring, and controlling of disruptions in supply chains and the choice of the adequate interface design. Wherever possible, reference will be made to a specific type of supply chain, namely cold chains, to derive more precise statements and assure applicability of results.

1.4 Proceeding: Theories, Terminology, Research Methods and Outline

The structure of this thesis is based on the previously defined descriptive, analytical and pragmatic objectives. In the following, the tasks and methods for each section will be presented and explained. An overview on the structure of the thesis and the functional tasks and purposes of each section can be found in Figure 4.

Figure 4: Course of research followed in this thesis

	Task	Purpose
Section 1: Introduction	▪ Specification of the Topic ▪ Illustration of the Relevancy ▪ Presentation of the Proceeding	Overview on the Thesis
Section 2: Problem	▪ Literature Review on Disruptions ▪ Provision of Definition, Classification, & Measurement Tool for Disruptions	▪ Terminological & Taxonomical Framework for Disruptions ▪ Identification of Research Gap
Section 3: Solution Approach	▪ Provision of Theoretic & Conceptual Organizational Background ▪ Deduction of Hypotheses & Combination	▪ Terminological Framework for Interface Design ▪ Two-Tier Causal Model
Section 4: Discussion	▪ Operationalization of the Structural Equation Model ▪ Pre-tests & Execution of the Main Survey	▪ Validation of Measurements ▪ Validation of Hypotheses
Section 5: Conclusion	▪ Discussion of Contributions & Limitations ▪ Identification of Future Research Opportunities	Summary & Outlook

The thesis will be structured in five main sections. In section 1, an overview on the topic is provided. This includes the introduction to the topic, the illustration of the relevancy, and the structure of the sections. The fundamental basis of research in this thesis is the ontological imperative, which follows the critical rationalism stipulated by Popper (1973). According to Chmielewicz (1979), the purpose of theoretic sciences is to derive general statements and rules with a maximal area of validity. With reference to Popper, he states that the transference of inductive statements from a specific context to general relationships bears the risk of premature judgment and is therefore not a logically created conclusion, but only a situation-specific statement, which has to be tested regarding its applicability to a general circumstance. Therefore, the only way to approach the truth is to falsify hypotheses which intent to state general causal relations (Chmielewicz 1979).

Section 2 will be focused around the introduction of the terminological and taxonomical bases and the identification of the research gap to investigate causal relationships between designs of interfaces, interface structure, and disruptions in (food) supply chains. **Section 2.1** will give an overview about the content, objectives, and structure of section 2. **Section 2.2** will depict the status-quo of research on disruptions and lay the terminological foundations on which this thesis is based. In **section 2.3**, the phenomenon of disruptions will be further scrutinized regarding typologies of disruptions encountered in the literature, and a framework for the classification of disruptions developed. This framework is required for the systematic decomposition of disruptions and the deduction of hypotheses on causal relations between interface design and types of disruptions. In **section 2.4**, this descriptive basis will be used to develop a tool for the measurement of disruptions. The intention thereby is to bridge the gap between a systematic, conceptual identification of disruptions and their actual measurement in practice. In **section 2.5**, the literature review will be extended regarding findings on causes of disruptions in general, and in food supply chains in particular to identify the research gap and starting points for analysis. Finally, **section 2.6** summarizes the contributions of section 2 to the achievement of the overall research objective.

In **section 3**, the role of interface design as cause of disruptions is put into focus. Firstly, **section 3.1** provides an overview on the section, its structure and the objectives followed. In **section 3.2**, the theoretical foundation of the thesis will be deduced and illustrated. The assumptions of new institutional economics will be used to explain and compare different designs of interfaces. The focus of decision theory in turn is the individual, and can be used to explain the occurrence of errors, which result in inferior process performance. In **section 3.3** the concept of interface structure is depicted theoretically and conceptually, to provide a systematic basis for the following deduction of hypotheses. To this purpose, the understanding of organizational design, organizational structure and of interfaces will be illustrated. From management theory, a methodology for the description and differentiation of organizational designs will be selected and adapted to the designs of interfaces in supply chains. **Section 3.4** aims at the deduction of causal relationships between interface designs and disruptions in supply chains. The creation of hypotheses will be based on the theoretical approaches presented in section 3.2 and the literature review in section 2.5. By analyzing the potential causal relationships between different elements of interface design and the occurrence of disruptions, it shall be understood, how different design options in combination with different transaction types affect the susceptibility of supply chains to disruptions. **Section 3.5** will aggregate the findings of the previous sections and combine the hypotheses in a two-tier structural equation model. Therewith, the empirical analysis of causal relations between interface design and disruptions will be prepared and the results of all previous sections condensed. **Section 3.6** summarizes the findings of the third section.

The fourth section aims at the empirical testing and validation of the hypotheses, as well as the modification of the structural equation model for further research. Therewith, **section 4** intents to satisfy the empirical-analytic and pragmatic objectives of this thesis. **Section 4.1** again provides an overview on the structure of the following sections and the topics to be discussed. Then, in **section 4.2**, different options for the testing and validation will be presented and, based on previously established criteria, the most appropriate method selected. Furthermore, the elements of interface design and disruptions will be operationalized taking into account the method selected. **Section 4.3** describes the empirical analyses to be carried out, which involves firstly, pretesting and adaptation of indicators in expert panels, and secondly the main survey. In **section 4.4**, the data of the main investigation will be illustrated and summarized, to provide an overview on the sample and descriptive results. Based on analytical statistics, the causal relations will in turn be discussed in **section4.5**, where falsified hypotheses will be eliminated from the causal explanation model and the model adapted. Finally, **section 4.6** summarizes the results and findings of section 4.

Section 5 is dedicated to the critical reflection of the thesis. In **section 5.1**, the main findings of the thesis will be illustrated and summarized, to provide an overview on the contributions to research on supply chain disruptions. **Section 5.2** in turn provides a critical reflection of this thesis, by depicting the limitations regarding proceeding and results. This is followed in **section 5.3** by theoretical and practical implications of the findings. Recommendations for the design of interfaces will be derived depending on different purposes. Finally, in **section 5.4**, based on findings and limitations, starting points for future research will be derived. A summary of the aims, methods, and theories of this thesis can be found in Figure 5.

Figure 5: Theories and methods applied in this thesis

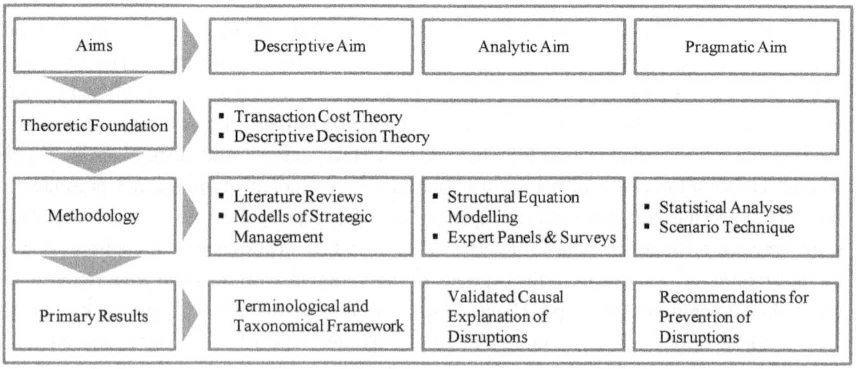

2 Phenomena of Disruptions in Supply Chains

2.1 Introduction to the Section

The research process in social sciences firstly requires the specification of the research subject and the development of a conceptual system (e.g. Chmielewicz 1979; Hill, Fehlbaum & Ulrich 1994; Kromrey 2009). This includes according to Kromrey (2009) a specification of terms by a semantic and a dimensional analysis, the elaboration of the status of research related to these terms, as well as related to potential causal relations. Therefore, in section 2, a deeper understanding of disruptions in general and supply chain disruptions in particular shall be provided. Based on the understanding to be developed, the focus will be narrowed down afterwards to the identification and analysis of causes of disruptions in food supply chains. How these research objectives will be pursued is depicted in the following paragraphs.

Firstly, the term "disruption" has to be specified and distinguished from similar concepts, to concretize the research focus. Therefore, section 2.2 creates first of all the terminological basis by a semantic analysis. Section 2.2.1 aims at the specification of the understanding of disruptions, which currently still diverges considerably not only regarding content, but also regarding terms used. Because of this variation, not only the term "disruption" will be analyzed, but also the term "rupture", as both terms find application in the literature and partly are used to describe the same phenomena. Based on the semantic analysis of the terms rupture and disruptions in research disciplines such as medicine, physics, and sociology, the understanding and terminology used in the rest of this thesis is chosen, to avoid confusion with similar constructs from other disciplines. Apart from the specifying the understanding of disruptions based on the research discipline, in section 2.2.2, the focus is narrowed down to the actual research field. The status-quo of research concerned with disruptions in supply chains is illustrated, to provide an overview on already existing insights on causal relationships, as well as on common understandings of disruptions in this context. Thereby, not only encountered definitions will be depicted and compared, but also their conformity with requirements of philosophy of science analyzed, to assess their suitability and explanatory power for the purpose of this thesis. Based on the previous considerations, section 2.2.3 develops an own understanding and definition of disruptions in supply chains. Thereby, quality criteria of philosophy of science will be considered as well as the previously illustrated definitions, to increase its explanatory power as well as convenience for purpose. Therewith, assertiveness of the definition as demanded by Chmielewicz (1979) shall be increased.

However, before being able to develop hypotheses on causal relations, the semantic analysis of disruptions has to be followed by a dimensional analysis, to understand the construct in its entirety (Kromrey 2009). Therefore, the construct disruption is decomposed into its elements and related dimensions, which can then be used to build typologies of disruptions, to facilitate the deduction of hypotheses (Hill, Fehlbaum & Ulrich 1994). Current literature on disruptions in supply chains identified or mentions implicitly different dimensions of reality, which are part of disruptions. For the empirical analysis of disruptions it is important, which dimensions are involved, to what extent these dimensions can be grouped, or whether they need consideration by choosing specific indicators (Kromrey 2009). Therefore, the dimensional analysis and construction of typologies is the purpose of section 2.3.

To this purpose, section 2.3.1 will provide the dimensional analysis of supply chain disruptions. Therewith relevant dimensions of reality shall be illustrated, the construct decomposed, and causal connections between dimensions identified. Section 2.3.2 will asses already existing typologies of disruptions encountered in the literature review. Such typologies may help to describe conditions for the validity of stipulated hypotheses in a shortened form (Hill, Fehlbaum & Ulrich 1994). Based on the deficits of typologies of disruptions encountered in the literature, in section 2.3.3, a terminological decomposition of supply chain disruptions will be executed, which aims at a complete and comprehensive decomposition of the construct. Based on the hitherto developed understanding of disruptions, their semantic content, dimensional characteristics and causal relations, a systematic classification will be developed, which is conceptual and multidimensional in nature. In order to identify and measure empirically occurring disruptions with statistical analyses however, quantitative indicators have to be attributed to the different theoretical categories (Bailey 1994). Therefore, this conceptual classification has to be integrated in a tool for the systematic operationalization of indicators and measurement of disruptions.

This tool will be developed in section 2.4 and serves as a starting point for the identification and development of indicators for disruptions in food supply chains. Section 2.4.1 provides the logical basis, on which the tool can be developed under consideration of the definition and prevalent dimensions of disruptions. At the end of this section, a framework will be offered, which allows for a systematic deduction of indicators for disruptions in food supply chains. How these indicators can be developed is part of section 2.4.2. In this section, specifications will be made based on the terminological decomposition of disruptions from section 2.3.3, for the deduction and prioritization of indicators. Therewith, the abstract phenomenon is already concretized, but still lacks rules for operationalization, which is done in section 2.4.3. In order to increase its general usability, a guideline for the deduction of indicators and measures will be developed. At the end of this section, a scoring model will be provided which may help to analyze disruptions in food supply chains.

However, before starting the analysis, the status-quo of research on causal explanations of disruptions in supply chains has to be depicted, to avoid redundancies and facilitate the concretization of the research question. Therefore, section 2.5 is concerned with depicting the status-quo of research on potential causal relationships of disruptions. To this purpose, section 2.5.1 will depict firstly the status of research on causes and effects of disruptions in supply chains, to identify already empirically tested causes of disruptions for the use in subsequent investigations, and to avoid redundancies. Therewith, the preliminary understanding of causes of disruptions shall be enhanced, assumptions on causal relationships reconsidered, and the research gap outlined. The research field will be further concretized in section 2.5.2. Therefore, an overview on characteristics of food supply chains in general, as well as on challenges reported in the literature will be provided, to identify potential starting points of analysis. Furthermore, the objective is thereby to deepen the understanding in the context of this thesis, as well as its practical relevancy. This end is further pursued in section 2.5.3, which will highlight potential causes of disruptions in food supply chains. Based on a content analysis of the status-quo of research in food supply chains, insights will be grouped schematically into different aspects of supply chains, to identify core areas of potential causes. Therewith, starting points for the development of hypotheses on causes of disruptions shall be provided.

Finally, section 2.5 summarizes the findings of section 2, giving a short overview on tasks and results of each section. Based on these terminological and conceptual results, section 3 can then start to pursue the analytical objectives of this thesis.

2.2 Deficits in Understandings and Definitions of Disruptions

2.2.1 Untangling "Ruptures" and "Disruptions"

The purpose of this section is to provide an overview on use of the terms disruptions and ruptures in general. Therewith, a better understanding of the phenomenon and its theoretical context shall be achieved, which is indispensable for a subsequent empirical testing of hypotheses (Kromrey 2009). The reason why both terms will be investigated is that with reference to cold chains, industrial associations as well as official authorities[12] use the expression "cold chain *rupture*", whereas in the general supply chain literature, the term "supply chain *disruption*" is used (see section 2.2.2). Since this thesis will focus on the intersection between both research fields, both terms will be included to avoid the omission of important aspects.

For the collection of relevant literature, the database Business Source Premier by EBSCO has been chosen, since it is used in business-related industries and research in such fields as marketing, finance, management, accounting and economics and offers more than 2,300 journals, of which 1,100 are peer-reviewed (Oulanov 2008). In order to assure that the papers considered dispose a certain quality, only those papers were considered, which were published in academic peer-reviewed journals.

The search for the term "rupture" yielded 296 results, whereas for "disruption", 1,405 results were found. For the review of the terms in general, the first 150[13] search results on each term have been assessed regarding the understanding and contextual embeddedness of the phenomenon. Additionally, for the review of disruptions and ruptures in a supply chain management context, the database Google Scholar has been used to double check and extent the results obtained in Business Source Premier. Out of the 1,405 results on disruptions in Business

12 E.g. Cool Chain Association (www.coolchain.org) or reports in the European Commission's database RASFF (http://ec.europa.eu/food/food/rapidalert/index_en.htm).

13 This threshold assures that at least 10% of the publications encountered have been included in the general overview on the terms.

Source Premier, 113 dealt with the phenomenon in a supply chain context and were therefore assessed in detail. In Google Scholar, 84 additional papers were identified of which 60 were included in the review after deletion of duplicates. An overview on the findings will be provided in the next paragraphs, as well as in sections 2.2.2 and 2.5.1.

The first time when the term "disruption" in Business Source Premier was mentioned dates back to 1938, when it was used to describe *family disintegration* processes. Mowrer (1938) understands a disruption as being the climax of a conflict between family members, when a drastic change becomes inevitable, such as a divorce. Furthermore, he notes that up to the point of a disruption, even though existing, the conflict might be ignored. In the following years, the term has been repeatedly used to describe *social disintegration*, either in the contexts of communities, or families (Elliott 1941), societies as a whole (Buckley 1958), or habits and status (Holt 1940). Thereby, the discontinuous character of disruptions has been highlighted, with conflicts or changes evolving over time up to the point of no return.

The abstract nature of disruptions is also highlighted in other application fields. For example, in *psychology* it often means the disturbance of a train of thought or of the execution of a task by background noises or irrelevant speech, which has been a widely studied phenomenon (e.g. Banbury & Berry 1998; Larsen & Baddeley 2003; Bridges & Jones 1996; Jones, Macken & Mosdell 1997; MaCken et al. 1999). Instead of disrupting the link between two or more different elements however, these disruptions take place internally in a human being. Thus, the disruption occurs in cognitive processes caused by some external stimuli.

In the area of *ecology*, a disruption is concerned with pollution and depletion of natural resources, which lead to considerable changes of the environment (e.g. Embrey, Remais & Hess 2012; Driesen & Popp 2010; Leontief 1977). Again, the lack of some kind of resources is stressed, which is caused by complex interactions of multiple and diverse reasons. The cause and its effect may thereby be temporally and spatially apart, so that it might not be clear what caused the observed negative effect.

A variety of applications can be found in fields of study concerned with economics and management. For instance, "disruption" describes the introduction of an innovative technology in the market, which leads to substantial adjustments of this market (e.g. Cochran, Patz & Rowe 1978; Ash & Smith-Daniels 2004). Lam et al. (2010, p. 128) for instance define market disruptions as "*major events occurring in the market that threaten customer–brand relationships*". However, not in every case, such a disruption is necessarily understood as something negative, but also as a creative process, an entrepreneurial ability, and as the start of something new (Vedres & Stark 2010). Therewith, a disruption is understood as an important and necessary event to foster evolution of markets and becomes similar to the creative destruction that is at the core of the theory of economic development by Schumpeter (1947). Nevertheless, it implies substantial adaptation and re-alignment of strategies and production plans to a new situation and may result in concurrency (Cochran, Patz & Rowe 1978) or competitive advantage (Vedres & Stark 2010).

In *international trade*, the use of the term is related to the termination of supply of critical resources (e.g. petrol, copper, etc.) between states or regions (e.g. Glick & Taylor 2010; Lindsey 1989; Dean 1995), which can again be linked to the depletion of resources in ecology. However, in this case, not only commercial interests play a role, but also political factors (Glick & Taylor 2010), whereby the termination of supply is not seen as the final effect, but as a side effect or as a mean to achieve another ultimate goal. Thereby, the complexity and need for contextual interpretation of disruptions is stressed.

Closely related to international trade is the topic field of *finance*, where a disruption is for example understood as periodic misalignments of price and income, stressing its potentially repeated occurrence (Nourse 1960). Its unintended nature is additionally stressed by Williamson (1945), who uses the term to describe economic crises in the United States caused by bank failures and lacking governmental control of banks. He stresses thereby the complexity and multi-causality of what he terms "*serious disruption of economic affairs*" (Williamson 1945, p. 217). These two examples understand disruptions as a temporal lack of purchasing power, either by increase of prices or loss of capital due to multiple causes and their complex interactions.[14]

One last example stems from the literature on construction claims (e.g. Ibbs & Liu 2005; Norfleet 2005; Braimah & Ndekugri 2006). Here, disruption claims occur, if during the construction process, the plans are changed by the customer, so that the constructor has to change the planned workflow, which results in additional costs. Frequently, those costs are substantially higher than the directly change-related costs, difficult to estimate and to trace for external parties. In this context, "disruption" is understood similarly to "ripple effects", "knock-on impacts", "secondary effects", "impact on unchanged work", and "lost productivity" (Cooper, Reichelt & Moore 2004, p. 1). Again, the difficulty to identify causes for a disruption becomes obvious, as well as the limited control over its inducing events, and its process characteristics.

In summary of the literature depicted above, a disruption seems to involve multiple causes, which cannot necessarily be identified as such, as firstly, their complex interaction causes the disruption, and/or secondly, they occur at remote places, and/or thirdly with a considerable time span in between. This highlights the abstract nature of disruptions, as well as the need for at least two elements, which are involved in some kind of relationship. Additionally, a disruption and its causes might only be observable ex-post. Furthermore, the causes might not be in control of those experiencing the disruption, which is in the majority of cases a negative and substantial effect. The question arising is now, whether the term "rupture" is similarly used, which is analyzed next.

---

14 A similar understanding can be found for example in Hall (1997), Moskow (2000), Elifoglu, Fitzsimons & Lange (2010), and Sufian & Habibullah (2012).

In comparison to the term "disruption", the first mentioning of the term "rupture" in the literature provided by Business Source Premier was later, namely in 1953. Also this term is applied in an abstract context, namely discontinuity of evolutionary processes (Geiger 1953). The author argues that any event is always embedded in a multitude of causes on the one hand and being a cause itself for future events on the other hand. Additionally, it is used in relation with economic structure, to describe the growing inadequacy of a traditional market organization to new requirements, (Lodge 1966) or the end of an economic union between two countries (Moes 1966). Comparing the two terms, it can be noted that both terms are used in similar contexts (social and economic ones), and describe the same type of events. Thus, it seems as if their meaning coincides. However, later on the meanings of both terms begin to differentiate more.

"Rupture" is used frequently in *medicine*, where it describes the bursting of a structure, such as an aneurysm (e.g. Chien et al. 2008; Helderman et al. 2008; Neugebauer et al. 2009). Again, the term is used to describe a negative outcome, but yet its occurrence can be predicted more easily, as the existence of the aneurysm can be taken as an indicator.

Another prominent application of the term is in *mechanics*, where it is used to describe how a material bursts under the influence of mechanical pressure (e.g. Yang Zhang & Zhiming Yu 2011; Gupta, Yan & Feng 2011; Olorunnisola, Pitman & Mansfield-William 2005). Many papers have been written on the "modulus of rupture" (MOR), which seems to be an established term on its own (e.g. Mao, Shi & Steele 2011; Yafang Yin et al. 2011; Dian-Qing Yang, Xiang-Ming Wang & Hui Wan 2010; Juwan Jin & Chunping Dai 2010; Hegazy & Aref 2010). To test the elasticity of materials, they are exposed to static bending till the point of rupture of the material (Ayarkwa, Hirashima & Sasaki 2001). In contrast to the hitherto developed understanding of disruptions, such ruptures are thus purposefully induced under controlled conditions and their causes can be identified and quantified.

Nevertheless, also in sociology the term is still frequently used, when certain historically grown social structures are substantially changed (e.g. Palazuelos & García 2008; Waldheim & Berger 2008; Young 2002). However, in the case of ruptures, the structural perspective seems to play a larger role than the process-related perspective.

Comparing the use of both terms, a "rupture", at least in its application in medicine and mechanics, seems to be more an observable event at a determined point in time, where by force and external pressure, a structure is changed in such a way that it cannot return to its previous form. The causal relationships as well as the effects seem to be clearer, with fewer directly influencing parameters. The specification of these parameters can be measured more easily, as for example the amount of force necessary to break lumber (e.g. Cheng Piao & Groom 2010; Lebow, Lebow & Nelson 2010). However, when the term is used in sociological contexts, these characteristics do not apply anymore and it becomes more similar to the use of "disruption".

The following figure shall illustrate the perceived similarities and differences between the use of the two terms and their meanings.

Figure 6: Interpretations of disruption and rupture based on the literature review

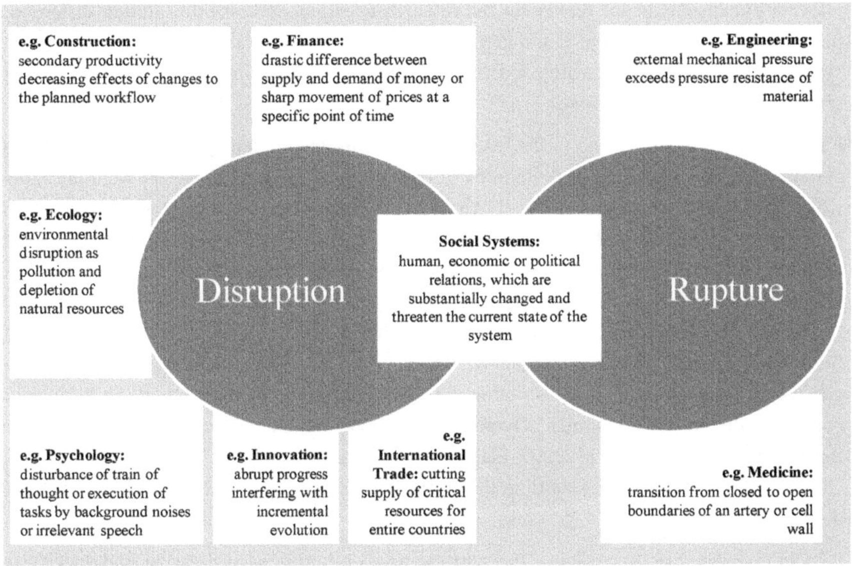

In sum of the first and second part of the literature review, a complete separation of the two terms is not possible, since the term "rupture" as used in sociology seems to imply the same as "disruption". The reason why in the case of cold chains the term "rupture" prevails at least in some parts of the literature, could be that a cold chain rupture is observable and measurable (e.g. by temperature tags), which makes it more tangible than a "disruption" in social systems. Furthermore, a cold chain rupture involves the exchange of cold and warm air, which is subject to the laws of thermodynamics. These laws are closely associated with statistical mechanics (e.g. Ramsey 1956; Lubliner 1972; Curado & Tsallis 1991), which in turn, and as illustrated above, refer to "ruptures" when something is broken instead of "disruptions".

However, whereas in cold chains the term is used, the two databases revealed no mentioning of the term "rupture" in the context of the literature on supply chains or production systems in general. Since both terms are used interchangeably in certain contexts, and since cold chains can be seen as a specific type of supply chains, a cold chain rupture is therefore understood as being one special case of supply chain disruptions. Therefore, the following paragraphs will only focus on disruptions of supply chains and production systems.

2.2.2 Contextual Shortcomings of Definitions of Disruptions

According to Kromrey (2009), the research process starts in general with the clarification of the research context, which contains the identification of already existing suitable definitions, relevant dimensions of the reality for the research question, and potential further differentiations of dimensions. Therefore, the literature on disruptions in supply chains and production systems was assessed regarding existing definitions, dimensions of disruptions, and approaches to classify disruptions.

First of all, the contributions to the research on disruptions of supply chains and production systems revealed a scarcity of definitions of disruptions. In total, 173 papers were identified, which deal with disruptions in a supply chain or production system context. Of those, 160 papers did not provide any definition of disruptions. This scarcity of definitions can be partly attributed to the fact that not all of the papers encountered put a focus on disruptions, but mentioned it as a side issue. However, even the majority of papers dealing primarily with disruptions did not provide a definition (e.g. Kleindorfer & Saad 2005; Qi, Shen & Snyder 2009; Schaefer et al. 2005; Ratick, Meacham & Aoyama 2008). A reason could be that there exists a general consistency on what a disruption means. If this would be the case, all definitions encountered should be very similar. Overall, thirteen publications outlined an understanding of the term (e.g. Craighead et al. 2007; Gaonkar & Viswanadham 2004; Wagner & Bode 2008), which have to be evaluated regarding their ability to describe and specify the phenomenon of disruptions.

As Chmielewicz (1979) explains, the purpose of a definition is to describe and specify the phenomena encountered, in order to allow for the development of theories and the discussion of research results to be based on a common understanding. If different terms are used for the same phenomenon, the comprehensibility of the results is imperilled and may lead to wrong conclusions. Therefore, he advocates for evaluating definitions based on certain quality criteria.

Criteria to evaluate the quality of definitions are according to Chmielewicz (1979, pp. 59–64):

- usefulness (1)
- unambiguousness (2)
- preciseness (3)
- non-redundancy (4)

These criteria can be used to determine, whether a definition fulfils the basic scientific requirements and shall therefore also be used here to evaluate the definitions encountered in the literature. The criterion of *usefulness* means that the definition has to be suitable for the purpose of research (Chmielewicz 1979). Considering that the purpose of this thesis is to causally explain the occurrence of disruptions in supply chains and production systems, it shall be assessed, whether the definition explains, **what** a supply chain disruption is.

Unambiguousness implies according to Chmielewicz (1979) that the term defined (i.e. definiendum) cannot be used to describe different things and vice versa. For example, Hendricks & Singhal (2005a) use the term "glitches", whereas in Hendricks & Singhal (2005b) the same phenomenon is called "disruptions", to circumscribe a firm's inability to match supply and demand. This ambiguousness could lead for instance to significant ascertainment errors, if the phenomenon is not adequately explained (Kromrey 2009).

According to Chmielewicz (1979), *preciseness* of a definition is primarily a matter of discretion, since every definition includes further terms, which would require a definition themselves. However, to avoid confusion and reliance on basic non-defined terms, the attempt should be to use terms, which specify the definiendum instead of keeping the definition at the surface. This also implies the avoidance of abstract and vague terms to define the term in question. In this context, Kornmeier (2007) suggests the use of technical terms, if possible.

Finally, *non-redundancy* implies that the definiendum is not repeated in the definiens (Chmielewicz 1979). For example, if risk would be defined by risky behaviour, no further insights into the meaning of risk would be gained, since the term remains unexplained by this repetition. An overview on the definitions of disruptions encountered, and their assessment according to the quality criteria, can be found in Table 1.

Table 1: Definitions of disruptions and assessment for this thesis

Source	Definition	Breached Criteria
Albino, Garavelli & Okogbaa 1998	"any event that causes variations in the expected behaviour of a production system" (p. 3057)	3: no clear identification of disruptions possible
Rosenberger et al. 2002	"an event that prohibits an airline from operating as scheduled" (p. 357)	1: reduction of focus on airline industry excludes other areas
Gaonkar & Viswanadham 2004	"occurs when the structure of the supply chain system is radically transformed, through the non-availability of certain production, warehousing and distribution facilities or transportation options due to unexpected events caused by human or natural factors" (p. 2700)	3: by naming kinds of causes others might be excluded
Hendricks & Singhal 2005b	"a firm's inability to match demand and supply" (p. 35)	3: separation of disruptions from other issues impossible
Wagner & Bode 2006	"an unintended, untoward situation, which leads to supply chain risk" (p. 303)	3: risk exists before something occurs[15]
Dorndorf et al. 2007	"a situation, in which one or more activities in one or more key areas [...] have deviated from the resource plan. Subsequent activities in the affected lines of work either cannot start on time, or can start on time, but only after controller intervention" (p. 94)	1: reduction of focus on airline industry excludes other areas
Craighead et al. 2007	"unplanned and unanticipated events that disrupt the normal flow of goods and materials within a supply chain and, as a consequence, expose firms within the supply chain to operational and financial risks." (p. 132)	2: goods and materials are overlapping 3: normal is an elastic term 4: repetition of disrupt
Wagner & Bode 2008	"the combination of (1) an unintended, anomalous triggering event that materializes somewhere in the supply chain or its environment, and (2) a consequential situation which significantly threatens normal business operations of the firms in the supply chain" (p. 309)	3: significance and normal business operations are elastic terms, making separation difficult
Berman, Krass & Menezes 2009	"periodic failures, rendering them [*service facilities*] temporarily unable to provide service" (p. 845)	1: focus on service facilities excludes other areas
Parmar et al. 2010	"During this entire process of transforming specifications to finished deliverables, things often do not go as planned. This is what is commonly referred to as an exception or a disruption [...]" (p. 3803)	3: specification of „things" is lacking 3: specification of extent of deviation from plan is lacking
Yang & Yang 2010	"a failure at a supplier facility that results in the inability of the purchasing company to meet its customers' demands" (p. 1906)	3: only failures at suppliers considered
Cole 2010	"the unprotected losses for an activity" (p. 255)	2: only consideration of unprotected losses 1,3: not precise enough for purpose

15 Risk can be defined as "*the chance, in quantitative terms, of a defined hazard occurring*" Parkinson (1992, p. 4).

Desai 2011	"transient occurrences that are difficult to foresee and whose impacts on organizations are potentially inimical" (p.264)	1,3: not precise enough for purpose

Based on one example, the potential shortcomings of a definition in the context of this research shall be illustrated.

Craighead et al. (2007, p. 132) for instance define supply chain disruptions as "*unplanned and unanticipated events that disrupt the normal flow of goods and materials within a supply chain and, as a consequence, expose firms within the supply chain to operational and financial risks.*" First of all, in the definition the verb "disrupt" is used to explain disruptions. However, therewith the definiens only repeats the definiendum, since the term disruption is not further specified, but only repeated, which contradicts the criterion of non-redundancy. Then, the flow which is disrupted is described as "normal". Yet it remains unclear what the authors perceive as being "the normal flow", which can therefore not be separated from the flow during or after a disruption. Furthermore, the objects of the flow are specified, namely "goods" and "materials". However, a clear distinction between goods and materials is not provided and may depend on the point of view, as a supplier may consider his output as a good, whereas his customer may regard the same product as material. Consequently, this definition is in parts redundant, relatively broad, and ambiguous, which does not allow for a meaningful and precise explanation of disruptions.

In all, thirteen definitions of disruptions were found in the literature review. The reasons for why they are deemed inappropriate for this purpose are dispersed among the quality criteria, yet with a focus on the preciseness of the definition. The advantage of less precise definitions is that the definition may apply to more observed phenomena, thus the universal validity of the definition might be enhanced. At the same time, with less preciseness, less precise consequences can be derived from research on disruptions, and in consequence the information content of conclusions is reduced.[16] As this research aims for a definition applicable to supply chains in general, the universality should be larger regarding the application field in comparison to some of the definitions. At the same time, as the conclusions should support supply chain managers in their decision making (see the pragmatic aims in section 1.3), they have to be sufficiently precise, which requires a more precise definition than for example those provided by Albino, Garavelli & Okogbaa (1998), Cole (2010), or Desai (2011). Nevertheless, the majority of definitions share some common points, which may serve as a basis for the development of a synoptic definition. This attempt will be pursued in the next section.

2.2.3 Development of a Definition of Disruptions

The first commonality can be found regarding the nature of a disruption, hence the **subject**. Here, the majority of authors explicitly mention that a disruption is an "*event*" (Albino, Garavelli & Okogbaa 1998, p. 3057; Rosenberger, Johnson & Nemhauser 2003, p. 357; Gaonkar & Viswanadham 2004, p. 2700; Craighead et al. 2007, p. 132; Wagner & Bode 2008, p. 309). According to Collins English Dictionary (2000, p. 572) an event is "*anything that takes place or happens, esp[*ecially, A/N*] something important*". Furthermore, it is regarded as "*a bare instant of space-time as contrasted with an object which fills space and has endurance*" (Collins English Dictionary 2000). Terming a disruption an event implies thus that it has a temporal and a spatial dimension, which is in conformance with the analysis of the term in section 2.2.1.

However, other authors term it as a "*situation*" (Wagner & Bode 2006, p. 303; Dorndorf et al. 2007, p. 94), which is a more static term as it is not actively taking place, but rather passively existing (see also: Hülsmann 2005). Also the term "*failure*" (Berman, Krass & Menezes 2009, p. 845; Yang & Yang 2010, p. 1906) is more static as it describes rather an effect and therewith might be enduring as opposed to an event. However, the failure observed can be considered as the outcome of an event. The connection of the event and a consequential threatening situation is especially highlighted by Wagner & Bode 2008, p. 309, who states that a disruption is "*the combination of (1) an unintended, anomalous triggering event that materializes somewhere in the supply chain or its environment, and (2) a consequential situation which significantly threatens normal business operations of the firms in the supply chain.*" The cause-and-effect relation as part of the definition can also be found in the majority of other definitions (Albino, Garavelli & Okogbaa 1998, p. 3057; Gaonkar & Viswanadham 2004, p. 2700; Wagner & Bode 2006, p. 303; Desai 2011, p. 264) as well as in the general use of the term shown in section 2.2.1. This understanding implies that a disruption is a process, which starts with one or more events (i.e. cause) and ends with a supply chain-related effect.

However, whereas some definitions refer to a single cause (Albino, Garavelli & Okogbaa 1998, p. 3057; Rosenberger et al. 2002, p. 357; Wagner & Bode 2006, p. 303), the majority of definitions consider the possibility of more than one event as the cause (e.g. Gaonkar & Viswanadham 2004, p. 2700; Craighead et al. 2007, p. 132; Desai 2011, p. 264). As with the general use of the term, this is pointing again at complex interactions and causal relations, which might only be observable ex-post.

The dynamic development of a disruption is also highlighted by such formulations as "*variation in expected behaviour*" (Albino, Garavelli & Okogbaa 1998, p. 3057), "*deviated...resource plan*" (Dorndorf et al. 2007, p. 94), "*not go as planned*" (Parmar et al. 2010, p. 3803), or "*prohibits operating as scheduled*" (Rosenberger, Johnson & Nemhauser 2003, p. 357). Therewith, it seems that a disruption possesses rather a continuum of potential shapes, which might change from one moment to the next or between one disruption and another. Furthermore, a disruption is apparently only observable as the difference between plans and

[16] For a more detailed analysis of the connection between universality, preciseness and information content

actual performance, which supports the impression that disruptions might to some degree only be observable ex-post.

The majority of definitions also mention the **effect** direction of a disruption. This is indicated by formulations such as "*structure radically transformed...non-availability*" (Gaonkar & Viswanadham 2004, p. 2700), "*inability to match demand and supply*" (Hendricks & Singhal 2005b, p. 35), "*unintended, untoward...risk*" (Wagner & Bode 2006, p. 303), "*unplanned, unanticipated...risks*" (Craighead et al. 2007, p. 132), "*unintended, anomalous...threatens*" (Wagner & Bode 2008, p. 309), "*periodic failures...unable to provide service*" (Berman, Krass & Menezes 2009, p. 845), "*inimical*" (Desai 2011, p. 264), "*failure...inability to meet customer demands*" (Yang & Yang 2010, p. 1906) and "*unprotected losses*" (Cole 2010, p. 255). Additionally, from the contextual use of disruptions, this negative deviation can be assumed to be significant. This is also highlighted by some of the definitions encountered, which speak for instance of "*significant threats*" (Wagner & Bode 2008, p. 309) or "*radical transformations*" (Gaonkar & Viswanadham 2004, p. 2700). Therewith, a disruption involves a significant negative deviation from the plans, which cannot be attributed to common fluctuations, but which is exceptional.

Regarding the question, which plans are affected by a disruption, thus the **object** of disruptions, the definitions refer to the "*production system*" (Albino, Garavelli & Okogbaa 1998, p. 3057), "*structure of the supply chain system*" (Gaonkar & Viswanadham 2004, p. 2700), "*supply chain*" (Wagner & Bode 2006, p. 303; Wagner & Bode 2008, p. 309), "*key areas...lines of work*" (Dorndorf et al. 2007, p. 94), "*flows of goods and materials within a supply chain*" (Craighead et al. 2007, p. 132), "*service facilities*" (Berman, Krass & Menezes 2009, p. 845), "*supplier facility*" (Yang & Yang 2010, p. 1906), and "*activity*" (Cole 2010, p. 255). What these definitions have in common is the focus on the operational process level of supply chains, which is also supported by Parmar et al. (2010) with the reference to the transformation processes and by the operations mentioned by Rosenberger et al. (2002). Additionally, the focus is thereby not restricted to company boundaries, but rather spans the processes along the entire supply chain. These supply chain processes can be defined with Cooper, Lambert & Pagh (1997 p. 5) as "*specific ordering of work activities across time and place, with a beginning, an end, and clearly identified inputs and outputs, a structure for action*" that "*can cross intra-and inter-organizational boundaries*". Hence, a disruption would imply that the actual work activities, their sequence, the inputs, and/or the outputs would deviate negatively from what has been planned by one or several organizations.

Consequently, with recourse to the definitions of disruptions encountered in the literature, a supply chain disruption can be understood as follows:

Supply chain disruptions are unexpected significant negative deviation(s) from process plans caused by one or more temporal events

see: Chmielewicz (1979 pp. 123-129).

As already pointed out above, a disruption is thus an **interference process** with causing events (or a causing event) and as a consequence, a negative deviation, or several deviations. Accordingly, the supply chain disruption can only be observed ex-post, since the entire process of triggering event(s) and negative deviation(s) has to take place. This process may be described for instance in analogy to the logical-analytic process of crises by Krystek (1987), who also understands crises as an interference process.[17] He divides the process of crisis into potential crisis, latent crisis, acute manageable crisis, and acute non-manageable crisis (Krystek 1987, p. 29 based on von Löhneysen 1982, p. 102). In analogy, the process of supply chain disruptions could be distinguished and described as follows:

- phase of potential disruption
- phase of latent disruption
- phase of acute manageable disruption and
- phase of acute non-manageable disruption.

Thereby, in the phase of potential disruption, none of the causing events has occurred, yet. However, for prevention purposes, the predisposition of the supply chain to the occurrence of disruptions can be assumed. In the second phase, the development of a disruption has already begun, as at least one event already occurred. However, this event or these events did not lead to the exceptional negative deviation yet, as initial negative deviations could be observed and an aggravation prevented. Hence, at this point, there is still the possibility to prevent the negative deviation from the plans if the accumulation of events and their effects can be hindered. This is changed in the acute manageable disruption phase, where the disruption becomes obvious in the deviation from the process plans and where its destructive power increases. Simultaneously, time pressure and decision making pressure increases as the containment of the disruption still is possible, even though it requires more resources to counteract the progress of negative deviations. Finally, in the phase of acute non-manageable disruption, the supply chain processes are restricted in such a way, that the planned output cannot be realized anymore. Alternatives for counteracting the development of the disruption do not exist anymore and the efforts have to be concentrated on reducing the impact of the disruption on the system to avoid further negative impacts. Either the system is able to resume work, or it has been changed in such a way that also following processes cannot proceed as planned.[18] However, this strict separation of phases of disruption is an idealized case, whereas in reality, such distinctions might be difficult to make. Furthermore, nothing can be said regarding the temporal duration of the phases, due to their individual development.

---

[17] However, whereas a crisis refers to existential threats to socio-technical systems Krystek (1987), disruptions refer to deviations on the process level, which are not necessarily threatening the existence of the entire system as such.

[18] For the description of the phases of a crisis see Krystek (1987, pp. 29–32). For a similar description of the process phases of a crisis, see e.g. Hülsmann (2005), Krystek (1980), and von Löhneysen (1982).

As shown in Figure 7, the differentiation between single and multiple **events** leads to four classes of processes, namely a single event causing a single negative deviation, a single event causing multiple negative deviations, multiple events causing a single negative deviation and multiple events causing multiple negative deviations.

Figure 7: Possible combinations between triggering events and negative outcomes

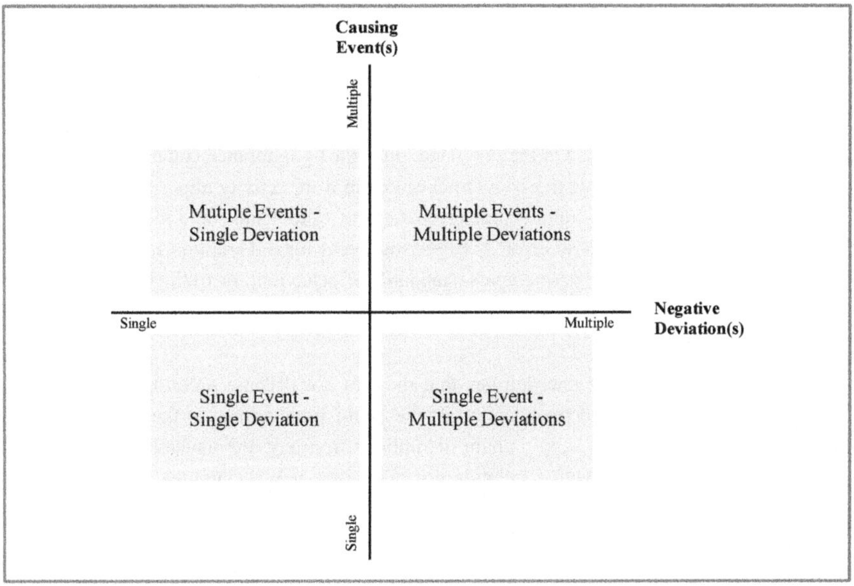

As has been observed in general failure research, the classes with multiple causes may occur more frequently, but are more difficult to analyze (White 1995). One reason is that in these classes, events may occur all simultaneously, or include time shifts, but are in combination necessary for causing the negative deviation. Additionally, they may all be causing the negative deviation to a differing degree, where some may have stronger influences, and others less. Only once the negative deviation has been observed, it may be traced back to the events, which were in combination causing the deviation. This differentiation also implies that whereas in some cases, there is one event with such a high impact that it may cause a negative deviation alone, in other cases, various events each with relatively low impact have to occur jointly to cause the negative deviation. This is also reflected by e.g. Cole (2010), who notes that potential causing events range on a continuum between everyday small events, and unusual as well as infrequent events. Hence, regarding the number of events contributing to the negative deviation, as well as the number of levels of cause-and-effect relations to be observed, a demarcation problem arises, or, put differently, there is a need to make a decision regarding what is considered for triggering a negative deviation.

The **unexpectedness** of disruptions leaves room for two possible reasons: either they are unexpected because the triggering events stem from *outside of the supply chain*, hence the event is extraordinary so that the potential of occurrence and its potential impact on the supply chain is neglected (e.g. natural disasters or regional power outages (Hale & Moberg 2005)). In this case, their avoidance might not be in the power of the supply chain actors or that improbable that the costs for prevention would outweigh the benefits. Or they are unexpected because a factor *within the supply chain processes* was neglected or not in the condition as defined during planning. Hence, they are unexpected, because the expected input or work activity in the supply chain process is different from the realized work activity. Such an unintended deviation can be understood according to Hofmann & Frese (2011) as an error, either by ignorance, or by inability. On the one hand, an error by ignorance could be for instance a wrong decision by an individual on how to execute the work activity imposed. An unintended deviation from the specified input characteristics on the other hand could result in an error by inability. However, whereas an error as triggering event for a disruption implies already an unintended deviation from external goals, standards of behaviour, or truth (Hofmann & Frese 2011), it does not necessarily have such an impact, that a negative deviation from operational planning is unavoidable.

Next, the **temporality** of events implies that they do not become a constant in the supply chain, which would result in the adaption of the entire supply chain to their existence. This understanding differentiates supply chain disruptions from e.g. the understanding of disruptions in the context of innovative technologies, where the new technology leads to a disruption of the existing one (e.g. Ash & Smith-Daniels 2004; Cochran, Patz & Rowe 1978). However, temporality is still an elastic term, since it may include a ten-minute fire outbreak at a supplier facility (Norrman & Jansson 2004), as well as leaving perishables during two hours on a hot apron (Nunes, Emond & Brecht 2006). Furthermore, as the event can at least theoretically be measured regarding its duration, it implies that the event has a start and an end, which can be identified compared to the situation before and after. However, its observation might be complicated by e.g. the complexity of supply chain processes. In this case, its occurrence may be frequently observed ex-post, after the effects become obvious. In consequence, corrective action could be taken, to prevent further damage. Therewith, the disruption becomes avoidable which helps to explain, why the same event in one case may lead to a disruption, while in the other case, the disruption does not occur. Thus, temporal and unexpected events only increase the probability of disruptions, but do not lead automatically to a disruption as corrective action is possible.

The **negative deviation** from the plans excludes the consideration of "*happy disasters*" (Wagner & Bode 2008, p. 309) as types of disruptions. If deviations could also be positive, then one would have to differentiate between these classes on the level of pragmatic objectives, when e.g. recommendations for the management of disruptions are derived. Furthermore, in general, the literature on supply chain disruptions refers to negative impacts, so that positive deviations do not seem to constitute a characteristic of disruptions (e.g. Sheffi 2005; Hendricks & Singhal 2005b; Smith et al. 2007; MacPherson 2008). However, the necessary extent of negativity of deviation is not determined per se, but has to be concretized based on the specific context of analysis. For instance, whereas the shift of production from machine A to machine B might constitute a deviation from the process plan, it might not be a significant negative deviation, if everything else remains equal. However, if transportation has to shift from sea freight to air freight, the deviation might be significantly negative, as normally shipping costs for air freight are by far higher than for sea freight (Vega 2008). Furthermore, as the negative deviation juxtaposes plans and reality, it becomes observable as an inferior performance in comparison to the plans. Therewith, it also becomes measurable as deviation from the plans.[19]

According to Frese, Graumann & Theuvsen (2012), organizational plans consist of a system of sub-plans, with interdependencies and mutual influences on planning decisions on different planning levels. However, disruptions do not imply necessarily a deviation from the strategic plans, which are, according to Remer (2004), the chain of strategic sub-goals of an organization. Hence, from this point of view, plans provide the decision-framework in which forthcoming activities should take place (Remer 2004). In contrast to the understanding of organizational crisis (see e.g. Hülsmann 2005), the long-term strategic goals of the organization or the supply chain partners are not necessarily directly affected by the occurrence of a disruption. This does not exclude the possibility that the strategic goals of organizations are imperilled, since the occurrence of disruptions may also force companies out of the market (Manuj & Mentzer 2008). Nevertheless, in general, disruptions are threatening normal business operations (Wagner & Bode 2008; Dorndorf et al. 2007; Rosenberger et al. 2002). Therefore, the reference object for identifying and measuring a disruption are the **process plans** or, how Remer (2004) terms it, the operational plans, which can be understood in analogy to the strategic plans as the chain of operational sub-goals of an organization.

These plans are plans for action, and are therefore more concrete, execution-oriented, functional and short-termed than strategic plans (Remer 2004). Theoretically, a deviation from process plans might also occur, because the plans were not realistic. In such cases, disruptions would be due to poor planning or inaccurate forecasting (Hendricks & Singhal 2008). However, unrealistic plans do not fit the definition of unexpected events, as they only provide the framework for decision making, but do not fulfil the requirement of "*taking place or happening*", which constitute an event (see: Collins English Dictionary 2000, p. 572). Hence, they cannot cause a disruption alone – as they have to be executed, whereby one could realize that they cannot be met and adapt them. Therefore, they might be one contributing cause, but not a unique cause for a disruption.

---

19 A proposal for how to measure supply chain disruptions is provided in section 2.4.

From the findings above, it becomes apparent that the type of events to be considered in this thesis still has to be specified. On the one hand, this is necessary to allow for a deeper analysis of potential causes. On the other hand it is necessary, to be able to derive recommendations, as different events might require different prevention strategies. Apart from determining the phenomenon by a suitable definition, Kromrey (2009) suggests therefore the specification of the research focus by identifying the dimensions of reality which are affected by the object of research. In order to further enhance the understanding of a disruption and its implication for supply chains, in the next section, the phenomenon shall be therefore regarded from different perspectives. The intention is thereby to establish filters, which help to differentiate and cluster disruptions, and which help to identify possible theoretical explanations of disruptions in a later step.

2.3 Deficits in Classifying Disruptions

2.3.1 Multidimensional View on Disruptions

According to Zetterberg (1973), Kromrey (2009), and others, the descriptive research aims in social science do not only encompass the definition of relevant terms, but also a dimensional analysis of the research object to provide an orientation framework. Dimensions are thereby understood as "*characteristics of reality (hence of the research object to be investigated)*" (Kromrey 2009, p. 110). Such a dimensional analysis shall be executed in the following to assess what dimensions are addressed with the term disruption and to enhance the understanding of the phenomenon.

Apart from the descriptive quality of the definitions encountered in the literature, different dimensions of disruptions in supply chains are put into focus. Besides many similarities, it becomes clear that partly different dimensions – as for example the radical changes of the **structure** stipulated by Gaonkar & Viswanadham (2004, p. 2700), or the unplanned changes in the **process** by Parmar et al. (2010, p. 3803) – stand in the focus of interest. Such general dimensions have the purpose to describe a wide array of phenomena, which are used to analyze "*dimensions of nature*" from the perspective of a specific discipline, such as for example sociology (Zetterberg 1973, p. 105). Since supply chains consist of organizations (Vonderembse et al. 2006) dimensions used to describe such organizations will be taken as a basis to analyze supply chain disruptions in more detail.

Thereby, organizational dimensions frequently used in the literature are the functional, institutional (e.g. Hill, Fehlbaum & Ulrich 1994; Staehle 1999; Scherm & Pietsch 2007), structural, and process-related (Kosiol 1962; Frese 1992; Macharzina 2010) perspective. How supply chain disruptions might be described along these four dimensions will be illustrated in the following. First of all, a disruption in a supply chain can be understood as already pointed out above, as a process, with one or more causing events, and one or more consequential deviations from the supply chain process plans. However, as the events leading to a negative deviation might only be traced ex-post or some might even remain unidentified due to the complexity of interaction, it seems to be more straightforward to start the dimensional analysis of disruptions from the negative deviations. This procedure also allows for avoiding to narrow down the focus of causal analysis at this point, as no research results can be obtained on those dimensions now eliminated (Kromrey 2009).

The first dimension to be addressed when analyzing deviations from process plans is the **process dimension** as the realized process determines the existence and extent of a disruption. According to Schulte-Zurhausen (2010, p. 41), a process *"includes the creation of goods or services, or the adaptation of an object by a sequence of logically interconnected activities"*. Kosiol (1962, p. 187) specifies that these activities are subject to a detailed spatiotemporal structuring. Furthermore, they can be distinguished into transformation and transport activities (Hill, Fehlbaum & Ulrich 1994). For the execution of these activities, humans and materials (e.g. machines or input factors) are combined (Kosiol 1962, p. 185), and relevant information for the specific activity is provided (Schulte-Zurhausen 2010, pp. 51–61). This is also consistent with the understanding of processes in the supply chain management literature, as illustrated by the definition of Cooper, Lambert & Pagh (1997) in section 2.2.3. Additionally, in the supply chain management literature, processes are further differentiated into flows of materials and information (e.g. Douglas J. Thomas & Paul M. Griffin 1996; Sarathy 2006; Tang 2006; Bode et al. 2011). Thus, in the case of a disruption, and with reference to the definitions of disruptions encountered in the literature (e.g. Dorndorf et al. 2007; Parmar et al. 2010), these logically interconnected activities in the material or information flow are not effected as planned.

A second dimension is the **structural dimension**, where the physical representation, or according to Frese (1992) the infrastructure, of the process plans is put into focus (e.g. Craighead et al. 2007; Gaonkar & Viswanadham 2004; Wagner & Bode 2008). On a higher level, such a physical representation of supply chain process plans can be seen as a network of nodes connected by arch, or facilities of suppliers and customers connected by communication channels and transport modes (Craighead et al. 2007). More specifically, the infrastructure has to be related to the achievement of the process plans, as for example a disruption due to machine breakdown (Subramaniam, Raheja & Rama Bhupal Reddy 2005). Hence, all the materials required for executing the activities to transform or transport goods or services (including humans) could deviate from what has been specified or supposed by the process plans. In this context, a disruption could be seen as the unavailability or break down of infrastructure at one node anywhere in the geographically dispersed network, which would also have a disrupting impact on the rest of the network (Blackhurst et al. 2005). Thus, apart from disruptions occurring to process plans inside a company or node, a disruption might involve process plans at adjacent nodes (i.e. inter-organisational), or even of the entire network (i.e. intra-supply chain).

The structural and processual dimensions are closely related to each other. This is because the infrastructure is required to realize the processes and determines in part, how and which processes will be effected (e.g. differences in loading processes of ships or airplanes).The relationship is consequently the same as for single organizations, where organizational structure provides a system of rules, in which human and mechanical task completion processes take place (Grochla & Welge 1978).

The tasks to be completed lead over to the **functional dimension**, which can be understood as the task or performance dedicated to achieve a specific organizational goal (Staehle 1999; Hill, Fehlbaum & Ulrich 1994). If a disruption occurs, this task is not be completed as postulated, leading for example to financial risk (Craighead et al. 2007), losses (Cole 2010), or destruction of products (Qi, Shen & Snyder 2009). However, a disruption can then only occur, if a certain outcome has been specified in the process plans or is expected implicitly. This requires thus some kind of quantification of expected outcomes. Considering the supply chain management literature, there is a multitude of potential performance measures to be used to assess the adherence to process plans. Beamon (1999) for instance names costs, fill-rate, profits, on-time delivery, backorders, and customer responsiveness as being frequently used to measure performance. However, it depends on individual choices and strategies of companies, which of these specific measures are relevant. Thus, a focus on more general measures assures the coverage of more supply chains. According to Porter & Millar (1985), p. 150, the ultimate goal of companies is to obtain a competitive advantage, either by lower cost or by differentiation. In this understanding, a disruption of the supply chain would imply a deviation from the cost-optimal output (e.g. excessive use of material vs. resource efficiency), or the non-realisation of an expected competitive advantage (e.g. delays in transport vs. faster supply).

Finally, there is the **institutional dimension** of disruptions in supply chain processes which is addressed by references to noncompliance with legal, regulatory and bureaucratic requirements during production and exchange processes (e.g. Hendricks & Singhal 2005b; Yang & Yang 2010; Desai 2011). According to Wolf (2008, pp. 526), the term institution includes all interaction-controlling phenomena, no matter if they are constituted in between organizations or externally. These interactions are thus based on rules, laws and norms which form the basis of exchanging products between suppliers and customers. For example, Bakshi & Kleindorfer (2009) argue that disruptions can occur, because quality standards have not been applied to the entire system, or because agreements on investments in enhanced (technological) infrastructure could not be reached. This position is shared by Holl, Pardo & Rama (2010), who state that in Just-in-Time production systems, exchange relationships between suppliers and customers are highly institutionalized, as disruptions would substantially increase transaction costs. As such, a disruption could be described as the violation of one or more components of the legal, regulatory, and bureaucratic rule base.

Considering the variety of dimensions of supply chain disruptions, it becomes clear that the examination of disruptions has many different starting points. Furthermore, the point of view might lead to significant differences in observations and conclusions whereby the comparability of research results is imperilled (Kromrey 2009). Therefore, in order to reduce the complexity of the phenomenon under study, it seems useful to follow a prioritization approach (Schulte-Zurhausen 2010). The hitherto provided research insights and terminological foundations of disruptions indicate that such a prioritization should start from the process dimension due to the following reasons:

Firstly, a disruption implies a discontinuity, which in turn favours a dynamic perspective. Even though a disruption might have *structural* implications, the focus is on the linking aspect between structures, thus on the processes, which have not been decomposed for different structural elements (such as positions, see e.g. Kosiol 1962; Remer 2004), yet. *Secondly*, as a disruption involves an event and a consequential negative deviation, the *functional* perspective is only affected subsequently to the processes. This view on the functional perspective is also supported by Hülsmann (2002), who highlights its logical succession of the other dimensions. Therefore, the process dimension will be regarded as the primary dimension, which allows for the identification of disruptions.

Based on such a dimensional analysis, Hill, Fehlbaum & Ulrich (1994) suggest the development of types, which can be used to facilitate the deduction of hypotheses in preparation of the empirical analysis. This could be necessary for instance, if different types of disruptions require different prevention and mitigation strategies. The development of types can be either based on empirically observed types or theoretically defined types (Hill, Fehlbaum & Ulrich 1994; Bailey 1994; Kromrey 2009). Therefore, in the next section, types of disruptions stemming from observation in the literature shall be presented, to assess to what extent they could be used to describe and cluster disruptions for the subsequent deduction of hypotheses. Thus, in the following section, classification frameworks of supply chain disruptions shall be identified from the literature, and their suitability for the purpose of this thesis assessed.

2.3.2 Incomplete Classification Frameworks in the Literature

Research in a new field should start according to Popper (1973) and Chmielewicz (1979) with the attempt to gather as much new information as possible. A potential issue is thereby the selection of aspects, which could, if selected without caution, eliminate causal relations between real world phenomena (Kromrey 2009). One method supporting the study of relationships and even the specification of hypotheses regarding these relationships is to build classifications (Bailey 1994). According to Oke & Gopalakrishnan (2009, p. 169), "*pioneering research in any field often starts with identifying and defining concepts and developing categories or taxonomies*". Such taxonomies can basically be understood as empirical classifications of phenomena under study. Conceptual classifications in turn, can be formed without empirical data and are, according to Bailey (1994), referred to as typologies.

Especially for such rich phenomena as disruptions, building a classification framework seems to have many advantages. For instance, it allows for the reduction of complexity, the identification of similarities and differences, which in turn lead to different types, and the comparability of types (Kromrey 2009). Furthermore, it is versatile and can be adapted to the specific focus of study (Bailey 1994). Based on the literature review, several taxonomies of disruptions in supply chains were identified. As with the definitions of disruptions, also for the classification frameworks different dimensions of disruptions were observed. An overview is provided by Table 2.

Table 2: Taxonomies of disruptions and implied dimensions

Source	Types of Disruptions	Dimensions
Rice & Caniato 2003a	Supply; transportation; production facilities; communications; human resources	Process & Structure
Chopra & Sodhi 2004	Supplier-related; internal; customer-related	Institution
Gaonkar & Viswanadham 2004	Strategic; tactical; operational	Structure
Christopher & Peck 2004	Internal; external to the firm but internal to the supply chain network; environmental	Structure & Institution
Norrman & Jansson 2004	Severe; major; minor; negligible	Function
Cavinato 2004	Physical; financial; informational; relational; innovational	Process
Sarathy 2006	Manufacturing locations; goods; supply chain partners and intermediaries; transportation nodes and carriers; people; information	Process, Structure & Institution
Smith et al. 2007	Organizational; network; environmental	Structure & Institution
Wagner & Bode 2008	Demand-side; supply-side; regulatory, legal and bureaucratic; infrastructure; catastrophic	Process, Structure, Function & Institution
Shah 2009a	Supply-side; demand-side	Structure
Shah 2009b	Supplier; geo-political; logistics; commercial	Process, Function & Institution
Parmar et al. 2010	Input related; process related; output related	Process

As can be seen by the dates of publication, such typologies of supply chain disruptions are relatively recent, with the first classification being from 2003. However, even though since then many authors classified disruptions, some of these classifications are both, similar to each other, and similar or identical to classification frameworks of supply chain risks.[20]

This highlights firstly that supply chain risks and supply chain disruptions are overlapping concepts, where either supply chain risk is seen as a determinant of disruptions (e.g. Kleindorfer & Saad 2005; Manuj & Mentzer 2008; Huang, Chou & Chang 2009), or as an effect of disruptions (e.g. Wagner & Bode 2006). Secondly, it highlights that during building taxonomies for measuring disruptions, many authors do not differentiate between causes (risks) and effects (disruptions).[21] Furthermore, with recourse to the dimensions of disruptions identified in section 2.3.1, it seems obvious that the classification of supply chain disruptions followed different dimensions.

Thereby, these classifications of disruptions bear some content-wise inconsistencies, as well as incomplete classes. For example, Rice & Caniato (2003b, p. 26) name supply, transportation, production facilities, communications, and human resources for locations of disruptions. However, the question arises, how to classify for instance a disruption in communication during transport, or a disruption of supply at a production facility. Such cases reveal that the classes are not disjoint and might result in inconsistent classifications of the same phenomenon by different researchers. Furthermore, whereas the localization of the disruption is more or less identified, it does not become clear, what other characteristics the disruption has. How long was the disruption, what exactly has been disrupted (e.g. product or information flow), and to what extent? These questions cannot be answered in detail and reduce the expressiveness of classifying disruptions following this approach.

All four of the dimensions identified were addressed in one publication, namely by Wagner & Bode (2008). According to them, disruptions can be classified in either being on the demand-side or supply-side of production (process-related), regulatory, legal and bureaucratic (institutional dimension), infrastructure (structural dimension), and catastrophic disruptions (functional dimension). However, these classes do not seem to characterise disruptions sufficiently, since for example in the process-related dimension, no disruptions in different flows are considered, nor would is supply-side and demand-side unambiguous. Additionally, the consideration of infrastructure on the structural level, does not seem to adequately capture the numerous facets of potential structural disruptions, nor are all classes free of overlaps due to the focus on different dimensions.

Considering these and the other attempts to classify disruptions, it becomes clear that in order to better understand and differentiate disruptions, a more systematic approach is required. In

---

20 Even though it is not always stated clearly, whether authors refer to typologies or taxonomies, from the context of most publications it becomes clear that the majority speaks of taxonomies based on prominent disruptions observed.

21 This has also been observed by Smith et al. (2007) in the case of taxonomies built for measuring supply chain risk.

principle, different approaches for classifying disruptions could be used, as will be illustrated in the following.

Firstly, the classification could be done by choosing typical parameters of supply chains or classes of observed disruptions, as is the case for most examples. However, such taxonomies have some disadvantages, as accuracy relies heavily on correct identification of the phenomenon (Wing & Greenwood 1993), assuring that criteria are on the same level of generalization is at least questionable (Marradi 1990), and might not tab the roots of observed configurations (Miller 1996). Furthermore, as taxonomies are based on empirical data (Bailey 1994), this approach is deemed unsuitable for this relatively young research area.[22]

Another possibility would be secondly, to build classes following a certain theoretical perspective. A frequently used approach for describing supply chains is systems theory for the structural perspective (e.g. Blackhurst, Dunn & Craighead 2011; Zsidisin, Melnyk & Ragatz 2005; Murray, Matisziw & Grubesic 2008; Müller & Gaudig 2011), or the resource-based view for the functional perspective (e.g. Bode et al. 2011; Blackhurst et al. 2005; Kovács & Tatham 2009). However, even though selecting a general framework may prevent omission of important aspects,[23] the examples cited above may be too focused on one perspective to unambiguously identify and classify disruptions. Combining several theoretic approaches instead for larger specificity, bears risks of incommensurability.[24]

Thirdly, there is the possibility to use general descriptive frameworks, which have for instance been developed in organization theory. The advantage is that due to their general character, they can be adapted and applied to many different kinds of organizations. Furthermore, due to their descriptive nature, incommensurability can be avoided, since they are based on theory-neutral facts. Therefore, in the following, a conceptual classification framework for disruptions will be developed, based on the dimensions of disruptions, as well as the classifications encountered in the literature.

2.3.3 Development of a Classification Framework of Disruptions

One conceptual framework, which aims for the general, consistent, and coherent description of social systems, is the management system by Remer (2004).[25] According to him, a management system can be defined as "*a quantity of managerial elements, with relations between them*" (p. 2). The four basic management elements that influence each other reciprocally are policy (e.g. strategic goals), organization (e.g. leadership structure), potential (e.g. personnel), and planning (e.g. distribution strategy) (see Figure 8). This description can also be adapted to the management of supply chains, which is understood as the approach to de-

---

22 See figure Figure 2 in section 1.

23 Kromrey (2009, p. 71) speaks in this context of "*exclusion by definition*".

24 According to Chalmers (2007, p. 125), incommensurability describes the relation between two theories or paradigms, which cannot be compared logically due to a lack of theory-neutral facts.

25 For alternatives to describe social systems holistically, see e.g. Hill, Fehlbaum & Ulrich (1994) or Grochla & Welge (1978).

sign, organize, and execute activities along the entire value chain (Vonderembse et al. 2006). From this perspective, the entire supply chain might be regarded as a management system, which could be decomposed and described along the four elements policy, organization, potential, and planning. However, since the focus here is on disruptions, the following description will concentrate on planning.

Figure 8: The management system between ideas and reality

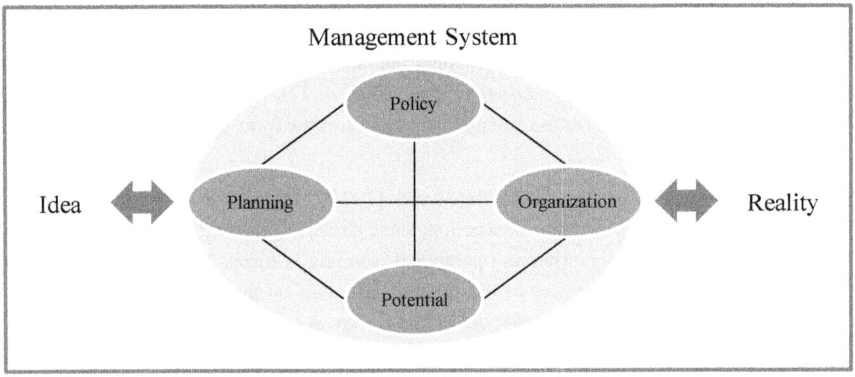

Source 3: Own illustration based on Remer (2004 p. 3)

In order to systematically describe the four elements used above, Remer (2004) decomposes each element by *object*, *dimension*, and *direction*. Furthermore, each element and their sub-elements are described by the characteristics *type*, *degree*, *form*, *standardization,* and *formalization*.[26] Therewith, consistency is not only enhanced on the same level, but also across levels of analysis.

According to Staehle (1999), planning is thereby the centre of the management process and determines the perception of all other management functions. As developed in section 2.2.2, a disruption is defined as a negative deviation from the process plans. This implies a mismatch of what has been planned and what has been realized. Consequently, the determination of a disruption according to the framework by Remer (2004) would be the observable gap between outcome and process planning. Depending on how and in which respects the processes failed to achieve the plans, different types of disruptions can be identified and grouped into classes. To this purpose, the process plan needs to be systematically decomposed in general elements, so that disruptions can be concretized. Therefore, in the following, the element planning will be further described and decomposed for the classification of disruptions.

---

26 This terminological concept was first developed by Remer (1989) for the description of organizational structures in organizations theory, before later on it was applied to the description of the entire management system destined for management science.

In general, planning can be understood as the anticipation of activities under uncertainty and incomplete information (Staehle 1999, p. 539). Remer (2004) understands hereby a company not as a combination of humans and objects, but rather as a conjunction of processes or activities. In order to differentiate planning from politics, Remer (2004) specifies that politics represent the overarching objective of the organization, whereas plans indicate the way to achieve this objective. Consequently, he defines planning as "*the conception of input-, transformation-, and output-processes*" (p. 26).[27] He differentiates planning further into strategic and operational planning. Whereas strategic planning refers to the "*relatively abstract strategic decision premise*", operational planning is "*the concrete realization premise for the (immediately following) action*" (Remer 2004, p. 37). As such, operational plans incorporate the concrete realization premises for how to transform or transport goods or services.

With reference to the planning literature, Remer (2004) suggests the separation of strategic and operational planning for their conception, since strategic planning is focused on the general design of the company, whereas operational planning is focused on the action level. As disruptions occur in the processes of the supply chain, thus on the action level and since the purpose here is to use this terminological model for the description and classification of disruptions, the following explanations will be focused on operational planning.

The task of operational planning is to translate the strategic planning into executable prescriptions in the different functional areas, such as finance or human resources (Remer 2004). In a supply chain context, operational planning involves the coordination of flows of goods and materials, as well as the connected storage and transport decisions of all actors in the supply chain bearing in mind expected demand and available resources during the next weeks or next few months (Zäpfel 2004). Thus, considering a disruption to be a deviation from the planned outcome, there seem to be many possible ways for disruptions to occur.

In order to reduce the complexity of the variable under study, Remer (1989) suggests that before starting to describe the elements based on the characteristics presented above, a systematic de-composition should be effected, based on the criteria *object*, *dimension*, and *direction*. As already indicated above, operational planning involves the assignment and disposition of resources dependent on strategic targets and operational constraints (Remer 2004). The criterion *object* helps thereby to answer the question, what kind of activities, resources etc. have to undergo operational planning (Remer 2005). These activities can thus be seen as *objects* of operational planning, which may differ depending on the context observed, and for which operational planning may differ. However, some of the basic features of supply chain processes seem to be identical across supply chains, namely the basic activities executed. In this context, Remer (2004) speaks of input, transformation and output processes, Kosiol (1978) of activi-

---

27 Remer (2004) stresses the point that input in this definition does not comprise employees, which are regarded to be on the same level as planning and therewith an own element of the management system, namely potential (p. 26).

ties concerned with changing the condition or position of a product, Seuring 2009 refers to production and logistics, while Hill, Fehlbaum & Ulrich (1994) only speak of transformation and transportation processes, which is also supported by Williamson (1981). As input and output processes can only be determined by a company perspective (Porter & Millar 1985), *transformation* and *transportation* are used here as basic objects of operational planning.

In the context of the element organization, Remer (1989) differentiates the objects further by the *direction* of differentiation, arguing that it is the most frequently named criterion for differentiation. Even though he does not apply it to the sub-elements of planning, a further distinction of sub-elements also seems to be appropriate here, to further specify types of transformation and transportation processes. A criterion frequently used to differentiate processes in supply chains is the distinction of primary and supportive activities, as for example in the value chain model by Porter (1998). Thereby, normally the flow of products is differentiated from the flow of information, which is necessary to coordinate the product flow (e.g. Seuring 2009; Albino, Garavelli & Okogbaa 1998; Cooper, Lambert & Pagh 1997; Alfred Dupont Chandler 1977). Hence, whereas the primary objective is to bring the products to the market (i.e. the material flow), coordination along the supply chain has to take place facilitate the seamless flow of products (i.e. the information flow) (Stevens 1989). Therewith, instead of speaking of *directions* as in the case of organizational structures, rather different process *levels* seem to be addressed by operational planning. To avoid omission of certain flows (e.g. financial flows), these are termed in the following *material* and *immaterial* flows to distinguish between primary operational processes and supportive operational processes.

The final distinction made by Remer (1989) deals with the four *dimensions qualitative*, *quantitative*, *temporal*, and *spatial*. As in the case of organizational differentiation, these four dimensions do not have to be determined all to the same extent (Remer 2005). However, in the case of supply chains, where the ultimate goal is to provide the right product, in the right quantity and quality, at the right time and place (e.g. Jetzke 2007; Ross 2011), these dimensions are of critical importance to achieve the overarching goals. A disruption in product arrival could for example be due to damage, delay, wrong location, or wrong weight. In consequence, this further differentiation seems to be useful for the creation of classes of disruptions.

Figure 9 shall serve as an overview on all considered modes of describing operational planning.

Figure 9: Sub-objects for the description of operational planning

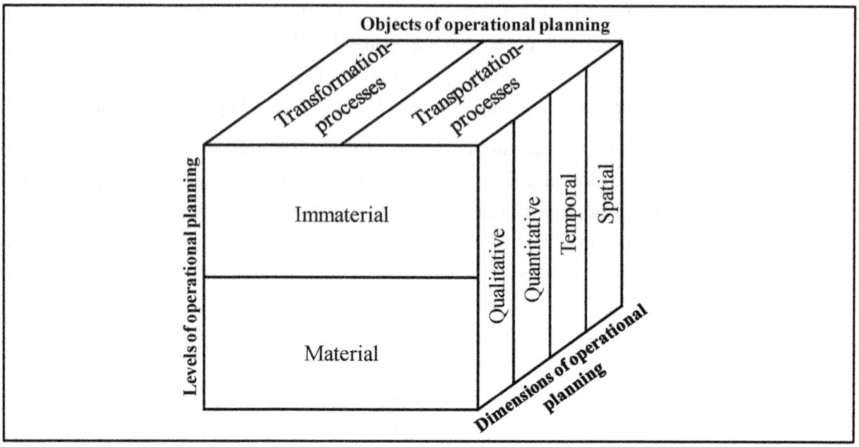

Source 4: own illustration based on Remer (1989) and Remer (2004)

Now that operational planning has been further specified regarding objects, directions, and dimensions, the resulting sub-objects could be described by the characteristics type, degree, form, standardization, and formalization in more detail. However, the specification of disruptions based on characteristics of operational planning will not be pursued here. The reason for excluding the characteristics for the classification of disruptions can be illustrated for the characteristic *type*, according to which operational plans are allocated on a continuum between *functional* or *optimal* planning (Remer 2004). An optimal plan for the qualitative product flow in a food supply chain could for instance be the exact determination of the temperature (e.g. 7 degree) at which the product has to be transported. In this case, a deviation by one degree could already be a disruption, even though the product does not have to be negatively affected. A functional plan in turn would state that the product has to arrive in the right condition, allowing the temperature to be maintained in a certain range (e.g. 7-12 degrees). Therewith, certain disruptions might already be avoided by changing the type of planning.

Additionally, the categorization of a specific configuration is not necessarily intersubjectively unambiguous. When is planning functional, when is it optimal? When is the degree of planning high, when is it low? These and other questions emerge, and the answers might depend on the point of view. Furthermore, also the focus of operational planning is rather oriented towards the functionality of the system, and less towards the optimal execution of tasks (Remer 2004). Therefore, Remer (2004) assigns operational planning rather a pragmatic function, and less a configurative function, as opposed to strategic planning. Hence, the importance of configuration possibilities is considered to be comparatively low. Considering that *firstly*, optimality of operational planning is less important than functionality (Remer

2004) and that *secondly*, scalability and inter-subjectively unambiguous identification of characteristics of disruptions might not be possible, these characteristics will not be included in the classification framework. In consequence, disruptions can be identified by their deviation from the quantitative, qualitative, temporal, or spatial planning of immaterial and material transportation or transformation processes (see Figure 10).

Figure 10: Classification framework of supply chain disruptions

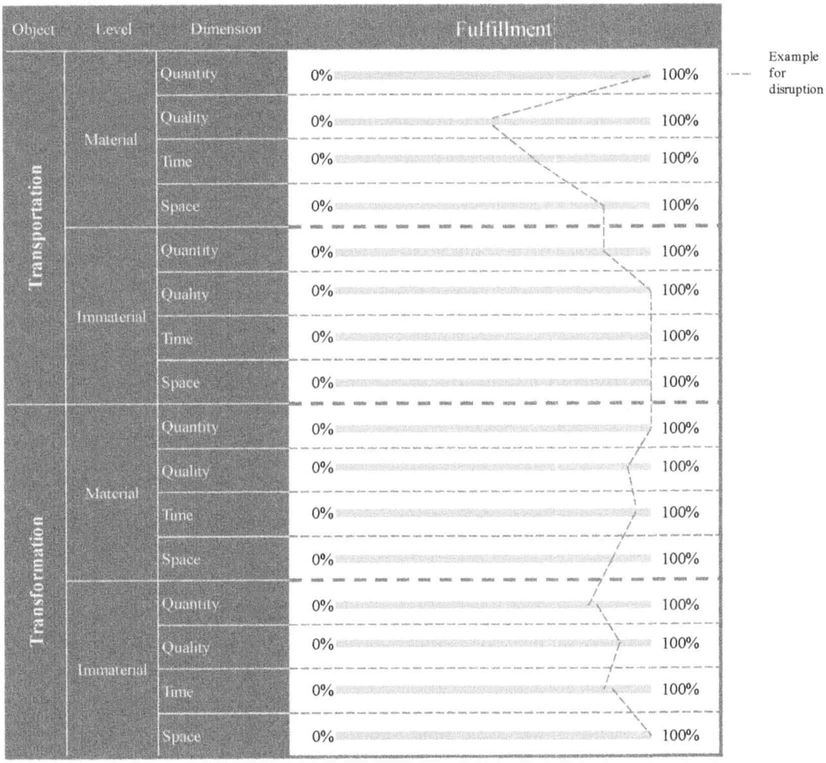

Therewith, this systematic classification approach includes more general dimensions and comprises logically derived manifestations as opposed to empirical ones, which shall reduce the risks of redundancy and omission. Furthermore, classes may be aggregated or further differentiated according to the requirements during practical use, following the stringent logical structure of classes. Therewith, a semantic decomposition of operational plans as a basis for the identification of supply chain disruptions has been conducted, which needs according to Kromrey (2009) a further specification for empirical investigations. The development of such a model will be subject to section 2.4. Sections 2.4.1 to 2.4.3 have thereby to a great extent already been published by Brenner, Hülsmann & Cordes (2013).

2.4 Development of a Scoring Model for Disruptions in Food Supply Chains

2.4.1 Exploration of Disruptions as Object of Investigation

As the preceding already indicated, a disruption is a construct, which is not directly observable in reality. Kromrey (2009) states that such phenomena only can be traced indirectly via indicators and measures. However, before starting to identify, classify and measure disruptions, one has to make sure that indicators and measures are valid and reliable. Therefore, indicators shall not be picked at random, but deduced from the object of research in a systematic and logical process (Kromrey 2009). In consequence, a scoring model will be developed, to assure the quality of indicators and measures which can be used to identify, measure and analyze supply chain disruptions.

For the development of the scoring model, the constitutive characteristics of the phenomenon have to be defined (Hülsmann et al. 2006). As a supply chain disruption is basically understood as a deviation from the process plans, these process plans need further specification to be able to identify any deviation thereof. However, the combinatorial possibilities and content of process plans might differ substantially between supply chains and even companies, which reduces either the specificity of information or the range of possible applications of the scoring model (Chmielewicz 1979). Therefore, process plans need to be further decomposed to obtain general classes from which indicators can be deduced.

If the plans are feasible, the process should be a reflection of the plans. Processes in turn, as specified in section 2.3.3, are the transformation and transportation activities of products or information. To allow for a concretization of process plans, while maintaining its general applicability, they cannot only be specified regarding the activities, but also regarding the products subject to these activities. The two basic elements of process plans can thus be seen as being the planned products (in any processing stage, thus with differing characteristics) and the planned activities, which in combination concretize the process plan further to derive indicators and measures. However, one has to make sure that indicators measuring different aspects do not overlap, while at the same time, the operationalization is complete (Kromrey 2009). To derive indicators systematically, again, a classification approach can be used.

For the creation of classes, Bailey (1994) stresses that they must be exhaustive and mutually exclusive. However, he continues that during research the number of different classes can be overwhelming, wherefore frequently only some classes are used, depending on their relevancy for the research question. For reasons of practicality, the scoring model will be developed with a focus on the primary function of supply chains, hence on the product flow, considering the information flow only in a subsequent step. Therefore, the following deduction of classes of process plans will focus on those activities and product characteristics deemed most relevant by the existing literature.

In the case of food products, there are numerous classifications of product characteristics (e.g. Pennington 1993; Szczesniak 1962; Cardello 1995). Depending on the scope of analysis, these might comprise many different aspects, as for example nutritional characteristics, appearance, or microbiological characteristics, even though they might all be designed to investigate food quality (Engelhardt 2005). The question is thus which characteristics are relevant for the description of product characteristics in a supply chain context.

Firstly, the classes should comprise characteristics, which are critical for the realization of process plans. Any case, where the food is deemed inappropriate for its intended use, process plans are not met. Secondly, the classification should be easily accessible, usable and widely applicable, to increase the number of users of the scoring model and the comparability of results. Therefore, the classification by LanguaL™ Food Product Indexer is chosen, as it is based on a free access software tool, with a classification originating from international standards, as those set by the United States Department of Agriculture (USDA), and is widely recognized in research on food products (Pennington 1993; Cardello 1995). Additionally, it does not only help to describe the product itself but also refers to further information relevant in food supply chains, as for example the nature of the packaging, the preservation method and the region of origin. Thereby, more information can be gathered to specify the process plans based on a systematic approach.

The term LanguaL stands for "Langua aLimentaria" meaning language of food. It was created in the late 1970's by the Center for Food Safety and Applied Nutrition (CFSAN) of the USDA as a method to automatically describe, capture, and retrieve data about food products. Since then, it has been constantly refined and applied to more food products, as well as other geographical regions. The thesaurus provides a standardized language which is intended to systematically describe any food product by a combination of characteristics. These are in turn structured into different viewpoints and coded for computer processing. These codes can be used to retrieve information on specific food products from external databases, in which up to date, already 35.000 food products have been classified.[28]

The major classes, which are further specified into sub-classes, and where every characteristic has a unique code, systematize food products as shown in Figure 11:

[28] see: Danish Food Information (2012).

Figure 11: Classes of product characteristics as stated by LanguaL™

A.	PRODUCT TYPE [A0361]
B.	FOOD SOURCE [B1564]
C.	PART OF PLANT OR ANIMAL [C0116]
E.	PHYSICAL STATE, SHAPE OR FORM [E0113]
F.	EXTENT OF HEAT TREATMENT [F0011]
G.	COOKING METHOD [G0002]
H.	TREATMENT APPLIED [H0111]
J.	PRESERVATION METHOD [J0107]
K.	PACKING MEDIUM [K0020]
M.	CONTAINER OR WRAPPING [M0100]
N.	FOOD CONTACT SURFACE [N0010]
P.	CONSUMER GROUP/DIETARY USE/LABEL CLAIM [P0032]
R.	GEOGRAPHIC PLACES AND REGIONS [R0010]
Z.	ADJUNCT CHARACTERISTICS OF FOOD [Z0005]

Source 5: based on Danish Food Information (2012)

This list of general criteria can be used to describe the products systematically, so that insights on product specific process plans can be gained. By transferring these general criteria and their specific sub-classes into a morphological box, exhaustive and mutually exclusive classes can be obtained, as demanded for example by Bailey (1994). This tool has been developed initially to systematically develop ideas on improvements for existing products, where each combination of potential attributes along different criteria creates a new product (Andler 2011). However, in this context, by filling the morphological box with all potentially possible attributes of food products as captured by LanguaL™, each product may be identified by a combination of one attribute from each criterion.

Based on these general classes of product characteristics, LanguaL™ allows for a stepwise concretization of the products up to the actual attribute of a specific product. However, the first class, namely product type can be specified in LanguaL™ on the basis of different classification approaches. For instance, by the European Union alone five different standards for classifying food products are included, each with a different purpose, while internationally, four more standards are included. On the one hand, thereby LanguaL™ integrates many different standards, which increases the applicability of the system, while on the other hand, the user has to firstly decide on which of the standards to use. For the purpose of this illustration, the standard based on the European Commission Regulation (EC) No 178/2006 was selected, since it is firstly widely applied throughout the European Union, secondly because (EC) No

178/2006 is one of the basic binding regulations governing European food supply chains (Abad et al. 2009; Banterle & Stranieri 2008). However, based on the application context, the selection can be changed.

Following thus this classification of product types, a total of 42 specific product types result. In class B, FOOD SOURCE, six sub-classes exist, whereof the first sub-class, ALGAE, BACTERIA, OR FUNGUS [B1215] already consists of approximately 80 attributes. As all other classes also include sub-classes, which in turn contain a variety of attributes, the question arises whether this amount of information is required for the purpose of illustration. For the sake of brevity and transparency, in the following, only those attributes will be taken, which can be found at most on the second layer of sub-classes. This reduction of complexity affects of course the level of specificity of information content. However, the degree of specification depends on contextual requirements (Engelhardt 2005; Hahn & Pichhardt 2008) and does not affect the general rules for the development and functioning of the scoring model.

The codes displayed for every criterion and attribute are fixed by LanguaL™. Thereby, any product can be unambiguously identified and differentiated from other food products. The resulting code when combining the respective attribute for each criterion could be used to compare the susceptibility to disruptions across food chains for the same product. However, it should be noted that while moving from one process to the next, the code might change due to applied activities. Thereby, the question arises, whether processes and products can in fact be seen as two separable aspects of process plans. However, whereas the process activities focus on the transformation or transport of products (i.e. the task), the description of the product itself is focused on the input or output of a process (i.e. the object). Therewith, they address different dimensions of process plans and should therefore according to Kromrey (2009) be regarded individually.

The following figure illustrates the methodology of the morphological box for food product characteristics.

Figure 12: Morphological box for product characteristics based on LanguaL™

CRITERION	ATTRIBUTES					
A. PRODUCT TYPE [A0361]	FRUIT FRESH OR FROZEN; NUTS [A1221]	VEGETABLES FRESH OR FROZEN [A1227]	PULSES, DRY [A1236]	OILSEEDS AND OILFRUITS [A1237]	CEREALS [A1240]	...
B. FOOD SOURCE [B1564]	ALGAE, BACTERIA OR FUNGUS USED AS FOOD SOURCE [B1215]	ANIMAL USED AS FOOD SOURCE [B1297]	CHEMICAL FOOD SOURCE [B1041]	FOOD SOURCE NOT KNOWN [B0001]	LIQUID AS FOOD SOURCE [B2974]	...
C. PART OF PLANT OR ANIMAL [C0116]	EXTRACT, CONCENTRATE OR ISOLATE OF PLANT OR ANIMAL [C0228]	PART OF ALGAE OR FUNGUS [C0247]	PART OF ANIMAL [C0164]	PART OF PLANT [C0174]	PART OF PLANT OR ANIMAL NOT APPLICABLE [C0005]	...
E. PHYSICAL STATE, SHAPE OR FORM [E0113]	LIQUID [E0130]	NOT KNOWN [E0001]	MULTIPLE [E0108]	SEMILIQUID [E0103]	SEMISOLID [E0144]	...
F. EXTENT OF HEAT TREATMENT [F0011]	EXTENT OF HEAT TREATMENT NOT KNOWN [F0001]		HEAT-TREATED [F0022]	HEAT-TREATED, MULTIPLE COMPONENTS, DIFFERENT DEGREES OF TREATMENT [F0023]		NOT HEAT-TREATED [F0003]
G. COOKING METHOD [G0002]	BY DRY HEAT [G0004]	BY MICROWAVE [G0011]	BY MOIST HEAT [G0012]	WITH FAT OR OIL [G0024]	NOT APPLICABLE [G0003]	...
H. TREATMENT APPLIED [H0111]	COMPONENT REMOVED [H0238]	COMPONENT SUBSTITUTED [H0103]	FOOD MODIFIED [H0141]	INGREDIENT ADDED [H0225]	NO TREATMENT APPLIED [H0003]	...
J. PRESERVATION METHOD [J0107]	NO METHOD USED [J0003]	METHOD NOT KNOWN [J0001]	BY ADDING SPICES OR EXTRACTS [J0153]	BY CHEMICALS [J0109]	BY CHILLING OR FREEZING [J0142]	...
K. PACKING MEDIUM [K0020]	NO MEDIUM USED [K0003]	EDIBLE MEDIUM [K0011]	GAS OTHER THAN AIR [K0014]	WITH AEROSOL PROPELLANT [K0015]	MEDIUM NOT KNOWN [K0001]	...
M. CONTAINER OR WRAPPING [M0100]	BY FORM [M0195]	BY MATERIAL [M0202]	NOT KNOWN [M0001]	OTHER [M0004]	NONE USED [M0003]	...
N. FOOD CONTACT SURFACE [N0010]	FROM HUMAN-MADE MATERIAL [N0051]	FROM NATURAL MATERIAL [N0050]		NOT KNOWN [N0001]	OTHER [N0004]	NONE PRESENT [N0003]
P. CONSUMER GROUP/DIETARY USE/ LABEL CLAIM [P0032]	CONSUMER GROUP [P0136]	CONSUMER GROUP NOT APPLICABLE [P0003]	CONSUMER GROUP NOT KNOWN [P0001]	DIETARY CLAIM OR USE [P0023]	FOOD ALLERGEN LABELLING [P0213]	LABEL OR LABELING CLAIM [P0160]
R. GEOGRAPHIC PLACES AND REGIONS [R0010]	CLIMATIC ZONE [R0193]	CONTINENTS, REGIONS AND COUNTRIES [R0509]	FISHING AREAS [R0124]	GEOPOLITICAL DESIGNATION [R0365]	GEOGRAPHIC PLACE OR REGION NOT KNOWN [R0001]	
Z. ADJUNCT CHARACTERISTICS OF FOOD [Z0005]	NOT KNOWN [Z0001]	OF MEAT, POULTRY OR FISH [Z0049]	OF PLANTS [Z0268]	BIOTECHNOLOGIC-ALLY DERIVED FOOD [Z0151]	FOOD CONTENT RANGE [Z0176]	...

Source 6: Own illustration based on Danish Food Information (2012)

Based on this morphological box, each product is characterized by selecting one attribute on each line. As can be seen, the enumeration of possible attributes is not complete for every row due to the already mentioned number of varieties. Furthermore, in some cases as for example for the last two criteria, the classification still remains on an aggregated level where little can be learned about the specific product, with a more expressive distinction on the next lower levels. Nevertheless, the methodology provided by LanguaL™ allows for a comprehensive and systematic description of products, including a codification which helps to unambiguously classify products. Additionally, where the level of description needs still further specification, the respective sub-classes may be used to further specify the product. Since the classification has already been used to classify 35.000 food products (Danish Food Information 2012), the approach seems thus to provide a satisfactory level of specification.

In other cases in turn, less specification might be required, if attributes are deemed to be less relevant for the specification of process plans. Alternatively, the attributes might also change during the different process steps. For example, the criterion packing medium can be changing during the stages of the supply chain with effects on the deduction of appropriate indicators. Indeed, especially the criteria F to M can change during the stages of the process, as these treatments cause a change in the product. However, it is also possible that these processing steps are ignored and only the resulting product is observed in later stages of the supply chain. Therefore, in order to correctly describe the product, also the specific process step has to be taken into account.

For the specification of the process plans, as well as of the concrete attributes of the product, an equally systematic approach is required for the description of process activities. As in the case of product classification, classes should be based on relevant characteristics of supply chain processes, should allow for a distinction of different activities (i.e. mutually exclusive), as well as different degrees of specification (i.e. exhaustive). Again, several approaches could be selected.

One option could be for example to base the classification on the SCOR model provided by the Supply Chain Council (Supply Chain Council 2010). This approach allows for the classification of processes on different system layers, which all find their correspondence on the next higher or lower level. The advantage of this approach is that it is generic, implying that it can be used for all types of supply chains. Another advantage is its wide spread acceptance and use from researchers and practitioners alike (e.g. Bolstorff, Rosenbaum & Poluha 2007; Berschet 2009; Halsband & Stölzle 2005). However, its general applicability is also a disadvantage, as it does not provide specific information on processes in food supply chains, whereby the identification of process-specific disruptions is inhibited.

Another option would be to base the classification of process activities on quality management standards dedicated to food supply chains, such as the International Food Standard (IFS) or the Cool Chain Quality Indicator (CCQI). As they deal with entire food supply chains and intend to cover all ranges of process steps, they might provide a suitable starting point for deducing general classes of process activities. However, both are more concerned with the structure of companies and the supply chain (see: International Food Standard 2012; Germanischer Lloyd 2009). Thus, whereas infrastructure and equipment are dealt with in detail, the actual process activities are disregarded to a great extent.

Another possibility would be to take official regulations as a basis for deducing classes of activities. These regulations also govern the entire supply chain and therefore need to specify how food products have to be handled along the supply chain. However, after a review of corresponding regulations, such as EC 178/2002 on Traceability of Foodstuffs (European Commission 2002), EC 852/2004 on the Hygiene of Foodstuffs (European Commission 2004), or the Current Good Manufacturing Practice in Manufacturing, Packing, or Holding Human Food (US Food and Drug Administration 1986), no adequate approach could be found which allows for a classification of activities along the food supply chain. Rather, as in the case of quality management standards, the focus lies on facilities and equipment and less on the process itself.[29]

Finally, a content-wise analysis of guidelines on food safety from farm to fork might result in the identification of generic classes. However, for such an approach to be successful, different food segments have to be covered, as they pose different requirements regarding handling and processing. Furthermore, the guidelines should be well established, tested and adapted on a global scale, to increase reliability and easiness of use. To assess whether all basic elements of supply chains have been covered, the activities named were assigned to the generic classes of the SCOR model, namely Source, Make, Deliver, and Return (Supply Chain Council 2010).

The basic document for global food chains is the Codex Alimentarius issued by the World Health Organization (WHO) and the Food and Agriculture Organization of the United Nations (FAO). It has been established in 1962 to guide global food policy making (Trienekens & Zuurbier 2008). Currently, it consists of 185 member countries, covering about 99% of the world population (Codex Alimentarius Commission 2013). During the years, the Codex Alimentarius Commission has published and updated about 212 standards, as well as several thematic compilations.[30] Of those, seven publications focus on a code of practice for different groups of food products. After an initial analysis, these documents were deemed to be a suitable starting point for collecting generic process activities in different types of food supply chains, as they cover the entire food supply chain and are similarly structured, but differ in activities depending on the food groups.

The following figure illustrates the general classes of activities encountered in the different Codex Alimentarius guidelines:

29 The focus on the structure of food supply chains instead of processes seems to be counterintuitive, considering that food quality can be negatively affected during handling and transit along the entire supply chain, not only while being kept in one premise or transport mode. The integration of a process perspective in current food quality regulations and standards could thus be helpful to improve the maintenance of optimal conditions along food supply chains.

30 See http://www.codexalimentarius.org/standards/en/.

Figure 13: Morphological box of process activities based on Codex Alimentarius

CRITERION	ATTRIBUTES							
1. SOURCE	RECEIVING & INSPECTING	RECEIVING & INSPECTING & SORTING	COLLECTING & INSPECTING	GATHERING & INSPECTING	RECEIVING & ANTE-MORTEM INSPECTING	NOT APPLICABLE		
2. STORE RAW MATERIAL	COLD STORING	PRE-COOLING	AMBIENT STORING	DRY STORING	FROZEN STORING	NOT APPLICABLE		
3. MAKE	FISHING & INSPECTING & PACKING	HARVESTING & INSPECTING & PACKING	HUNTING & PARTLY PROCESSING & PACKING	MILKING & INSPECTING & PACKING	SLAUGHTERING & POST-MORTEM INSPECTING & PACKING	EXTRACTING & INSPECTING & PACKING	PROCESSING & PACKING & LABELING	NOT APPLICABLE
4. STORE PRODUCTS	COLD STORING	AMBIENT STORING	DRY STORING	FROZEN STORING	NOT APPLICABLE			
5. DELIVER	LOADING, TRANSPORTING, UNLOADING	LOADING, SEPARATING, TRANSPORTING, UNLOADING	PRE-COOLING, LOADING, TRANSPORTING, UNLOADING	TRANSPORTING, UNLOADING	NOT APPLICABLE			
6. RETURN	DESTROYING	USING FOR OTHER PURPOSES THAN HUMAN CONSUMPTION	RETURNING TO SALEABLE STOCK	REPROCESSING	NOT APPLICABLE			

Source 7: Own illustration; numbers are used for description only

The classification of process activities based on the Codex Alimentarius follows the assumption that the guidelines are exhaustive and mutually exclusive, which is the requirement posed on classifications (see: Bailey 1994). As the commission created one basic text, which is applicable in case none of the specific guidelines is addressed or the specific guideline does not specify a certain activity (Codex Alimentarius Commission 2009), this assumption seems to be reasonable.

The reason for taking several activities into one field is that according to the Codex Alimentarius, these activities always have to be done for certain products. For example, for hunting, the Codex states explicitly that wild game has to be partly processed immediately after being killed, before it is transferred to a game depot. The reason for specifying these different steps instead of just referring to hunting is that it reduces the risk of omitting important aspects during the deduction of indicators, to assure that the identity of the object under study is maintained (Kromrey 2009). In contrast to the SCOR Model, the classification above includes storage of raw material and of products as separate steps. This was deemed necessary as storage conditions of ingredients and final food products may have significant effects on the quality of the product (Brecht et al. 2003; Smith & Sparks 2004; Georgiadis, Vlachos & Iakovou 2005) and should therefore be explicitly considered during deduction of indicators. Nevertheless, the activities named only provide a guideline for the deduction of indicators and can be further specified by e.g. referring to the company-specific process flow diagram, which is also mandatory in the Codex. Furthermore, to increase unambiguity of specifying process activities, each field should receive a unique code, as in the case of product characteristics.

Based on these two morphological boxes, it is now possible to describe specific products and specific process activities in a systematic and detailed way. The question is thus, how to combine these two to actual process plans, and how to derive indicators thereof, so that disruptions can actually be identified and measured. These questions will be addressed in the next section.

2.4.2 Specification of the Concept and Deduction of Indicators

Hence, whereas types of activities can now be broadly differentiated, some areas still need further specification. For instance, combining the process categories just leads to a chain of process activities in *one* process step of the supply chain, but does not follow an end-to-end perspective of supply chains. While this might be sufficient to evaluate disruptions on the company level, it does not help to identify weak points on the supply chain level. Therefore, a further differentiation of the processes is required.

Due to the large number of processing activities and their potential combinations, differentiating processing further does not seem to yield the desired limited number of combinations. Rather, specification might be achieved by adding another dimension of disruptions, which have already been discussed in 2.3.1. By adding another dimension to the process dimension, each disruption might be further specified and more process activities differentiated. Since the functional and structural dimension might be similar for different process steps of supply chains (e.g. in terms of objectives such as profit maximization or infrastructure such as cooling facilities), the institutional dimension seems to be appropriate for specifying process steps and linking them vertically to allow for an analysis of disruptions along the food supply chain.

According to Remer (1989), vertical differentiation refers to the division of a system into organizational steps. Thereby, different possibilities for dividing the overall task exist. The overall task of a supply chain encompasses all activities associated with transforming and transporting the product from raw material stage through to the end user (Handfield & Nichols 2008, cited in Seuring 2009). As the same product can go through different processing stages depending on its final purpose, the institutions executing the process should also be differentiated based on the final product, to increase consistency. This approach differs for instance from the approach of the SCOR Model, which uses a company-based differentiation of processes (i.e. supplier, own company, customer) (Supply Chain Council 2010). Thereby, disruptions could only be analyzed from a company point of view and not across supply chains.

Starting from the final product, each company in the supply chain could receive a code indicating its position in the supply chain. To further increase information content, the major task of each company could be indicated in a common way. In general, companies in a supply chain are in general involved in the conversion, logistics, and/or retail of products (Craighead et al. 2007). In line with this differentiation, process activities could be attributed to being executed by a manufacturer (M), a logistics company (L), or a retailer (R). Furthermore, in case that several companies are on the same process level, as for instance several producers of ingredients, the number could be further subdivided. The rank order should thereby be determined objectively, for example by the relative share of the ingredient in the final product.

With the help of this codification, supply chain steps can be unambiguously identified and combined to represent the entire food supply chain. The morphological boxes derived in 2.4.1 can thus be filled for every step to identify weak points more easily and to compare them along and in between supply chains.

In the next step, the process plans may be concretized based on the specific product characteristics and the specific process activities. To this purpose, both morphological boxes contain a range of criteria, which can be used to describe the process plans and to develop indicators for the identification of disruptions. These can now be combined for each actual case, to concretize the objects of operational planning, hence the content of transformation and transportation processes. Thereby, only the actual combination of attributes for a specific supply chain under study is considered, as is exemplified in Table 3.

Table 3: Example for the concretization of process plans as combination of attributes

PROCESS ELEMENTS	RECEIVING & INSPECTING & SORTING [1.2]	COLD STORING [2.1]	PROCESSING & PACKING & LABELING [3.7]	FROZEN STORING [4.4]	PRE-COOLING, LOADING, TRANSPORTING, UNLOADING [5.3]	NOT APPLICABLE [6.5]
A. FRUIT FRESH OR FROZEN [A1221]	A1221 | 1.2	...	...	...	...	...
B. PLANT USED AS FOOD SOURCE [B1347]	...	B1347 | 2.1				
C. PART OF PLANT [C0174]	...		C0174 | 3.7			
E. SOLID [E0151]	...			E0151 | 4.7		
...	...	...	...	...	...	... | 6.5

The illustration above is a combination of attributes of the morphological box for a specific food product and attributes of the morphological box for process activities. As an example, a fruit product was chosen which is subject to a manufacturing process.

Even though the process plans have now been specified, they are not directly observable and need therefore suitable indicators, to become ascertainable (Bortz & Döring 1995). The derived indicators have to be formulated as precise as possible, so that the empirical phenomena which shall be covered can be unambiguously identified (Kromrey 2009). Therewith it becomes not only transparent how results were obtained, but also the temporal-spatial and interpersonal applicability of the model and comparability of the results is enhanced. Furthermore, the indicators need to cover all relevant elements of process plans, to identify disruptions and to provide a realistic representation of the phenomenon. In this context, Kromrey (2009) stresses that the individual elements need to delineate the semantic field for which indicators shall be derived.

At this point, the semantic decomposition of disruptions from section 2.3.3 can be utilized for a systematic and encompassing deduction of indicators. Following this methodology, indicators should cover the material and immaterial process plans in their quantitative, qualitative, spatial, and temporal dimensions. Thus, based on the terminology of Remer (2004), which has been further developed in section 2.3.3, the following methodology for deducing indicators for disruptions is proposed:

Table 4: Framework for a systematic deduction of indicators for disruptions

	MATERIAL				IMMATERIAL			
	Quality	Quantity	Time	Space	Quality	Quantity	Time	Space
A | 1	$I_{A\|1}1$	$I_{A\|1}2$	...	...	...	...	...	$I_{A\|1}8$
B | 1	$I_{B\|1}1$	...	...	...	...	...	...	...
...	...	...	...	...	...	...	...	...
Z | 1	$I_{Z\|1}1$	...	...	...	...	...	...	...

A | 1 – Z | 1 = Process Plan for Product Characteristic A-Z and Process Activity Source

For every field of the matrix, process plans could now be specified. Nevertheless, in practice process plans do not necessarily cover every flow, every product characteristic and every activity to the same extent. This has already been observed by van de Ven & Ferry (1980) who admit that the distinction between product and information flow in practice frequently becomes "*blurred*" (p. 302). Instead, they are focused on the most important aspects, because dynamic changes, complexity of planning and environmental factors otherwise lead to obsolete planning (Shen, Wang & Hao 2006; Ahmed & Sahinidis 1998; Moon, Kim & Hur 2002). In consequence, some of the fields of the matrix might be left unspecified or process plans may span multiple fields, if formulated on a more aggregated level.

However, also in between those indicators developed, there might by differences regarding their importance. Therefore, the indicators should be weighted based on the relevancy of the dimension which shall be covered by the indicator. For instance, during processing, the quantity of provided inputs (i.e. quantitative vertical dimension) could be more critical than the parallelity of processing several semi-finished products (i.e. temporal horizontal dimension). A pair-wise comparison allows for prioritizing indicators which belong to the same field of the process plan.

With the prioritization of indicators, this approach follows the principles of the Analytic Hierarchy Process (AHP) developed by Saaty to structure and analyze complex decision making situations (e.g. Saaty 1982). According to this approach, the relative importance of each criterion is determined by pair-wise comparison between all elements which are on the same level. Their importance can be interpreted as their contribution to the achievement of the overall goal (Götze 2006). However, whereas Saaty suggests the use of a nine-point scale for the weighting of alternatives, the choice of scale may depend on the context of application and shall therefore not be taken here. The illustration below demonstrates the logic for a simplified case, where indicators are either more important (= 1), less important (= 0), or equally important (= 0.5).

Table 5: Exemplified rating of process steps based on pair-wise comparison

<table>
<tr><th></th><th>A|1</th><th>A|2</th><th>A|3</th><th>...</th><th>A|6</th><th>Σ</th></tr>
<tr><td>A|1</td><td>A|1=A|1</td><td>A|1 >A|2</td><td>A|1>A|3</td><td>...</td><td>A|1<A|6</td><td>0.5+1+1+...+0 = ...</td></tr>
<tr><td>A|2</td><td>A|2<A|1</td><td>A|2=A|2</td><td>A|2=A|3</td><td>...</td><td>A|2<A|6</td><td>0+0.5+0.5+... + 0 = ...</td></tr>
<tr><td>A|3</td><td>A|3 <A|1</td><td>A|3 =A|2</td><td>A|3=A|3</td><td>...</td><td>A|3 <A|6</td><td>0+0.5+0.5+...+0 = ...</td></tr>
<tr><td>...</td><td>...</td><td>...</td><td>...</td><td>...</td><td>...</td><td>...</td></tr>
<tr><td>A|6</td><td>A|6>A|1</td><td>A|6>A|2</td><td>A|6>A|3</td><td>...</td><td>A|6=A|6</td><td>1+1+1+...+0.5 = 3.5</td></tr>
</table>

A = Product Characteristic A; 1-6 = Process Activity 1-6
=: equal importance (0.5) ; >: higher importance (1); <: lower importance (0)

Apart from quantifying indicators regarding their relevancy, the question arises how to assess them regarding the extent to which process plans have been achieved, respectively to the extent to which disruptions occurred. The extent of compliance or deviation depends thereby also on the underlying measurement scale of the indicator, and may differ regarding measurement quality (Kromrey 2009; Bortz & Döring 1995). Thus, there is firstly a need for a general rule for how to operationalize indicators, as well as a rule for how to transform and aggregate these measures. These rules will be developed in the next section.

2.4.3 *Operationalization of Indicators*

Before being able to determine the value of each indicator, they have to be operationalized so that they can be measured (Diekmann 2002). According to Kromrey (2009), operationalization means a guideline for action for an empirical utilization of terms. This implies a reasoned and documented deduction of indicators, as well as of measures to be used for making indicators accessible for empirical evaluation. Where several measures have to be derived, they can again be weighted in pair-wise comparison, to assess their relative contribution in representing the indicator. They should thereby be selected in such a way that they cover the indicator exhaustively, while being mutually exclusive to avoid double counting and representation bias (Kromrey 2009). If the indicator is for example strawberry fruit quality, than measures could be firmness, shear force, (Paull 1999) and colour. Whereas colour might not be that important to describe fruit quality during commercial handling between supply chain partners, its relative importance might increase upon storage at retail, since consumers may evaluate the colour more easily than e.g. shear force. Thus, prioritization of measures might vary during different supply chain steps and cannot be assumed to be equal for every measure derived.

Once the values of the measures are obtained, the question arises, how to interpret the values and how to transform them into one consistent measurement model, where values based on different measuring units can be compared. Thus, firstly, for a measurement-internal interpretation, not only the actual values have to be known, but also the targeted ones, to obtain a benchmark. However, the targeted value may not be univocally defined, but may rather be a range in which the actual outcome should fall. To avoid a normative definition of thresholds for the scoring model, the range should rather be based on general principles of statistical evaluation. Furthermore, the proceeding should be based on already established techniques, to avoid redundant work, increase reliability and foster easiness of use of the tool. Sources for this information could be for instance quality control cards, in which processes are monitored and controlled with the help of target values and boundary values (Dietrich 2005). Since the method of quality control cards combines the use and interpretation of statistical techniques with the implementation in manufacturing processes, is based on international ISO standards and considers different types of data sources (Dietrich 2005), its methodology could be integrated into the framework.

The purpose of this scoring model is to unambiguously identify and measure disruptions. As disruptions are defined as significant negative deviations, deviations from optimal performance would have to be evaluated regarding whether they are significant or not. However, the measures derived may require different procedures to develop some kinds of thresholds for significance, due to for instance the nature of values, as well as the nature of distribution. According to Dietrich (2005), the first differentiation of measures can be done regarding the nature of measures, which describe an indicator for the process plans. They can be differentiated into being either quantitative or qualitative measures. Quantitative measures can be further differentiated into being either discrete measures, or continuous measures. Therewith, both kinds of measures cannot be illustrated on the same kind of scale, since discrete measures do not allow for an interpretation of points in between integral numbers, whereas continuous measures do allow this interpretation (Dietrich 2005; Kromrey 2009). The same applies also to qualitative measures, which are either on an ordinal scale or on a nominal scale. Reliable measurement and interpretation of values gets more difficult with less quantifiable values, whereby also the usability of statistical methods is reduced (Kromrey 2009). Thus, if possible, quantitative measures should be selected for identifying disruptions in a reliable and reproducible way.

Depending on the nature of the measure, different statistical distributions in the basic population can be assumed, which are important to determine for instance mean values of process performance (Dietrich 2005). Thus, the kind of distribution in the basic population may vary with the kind of measure chosen. The mean value of a measure in turn describes the average realization of process plans aggregated over all observations of this measure (Bortz 1995). Even though this value also only describes the *realized* outcomes and not the *planned* outcomes, it may serve as an orientation point for the identification of significant deviations. Based on the statistical distribution, each quantitative measure may be analyzed in the same way across companies and supply chains and interpreted regarding standard deviations of observations, as well as regarding kurtosis and skewness of distribution (Janssen 2012). This information could then be used to guide interpretation of process performance in a certain case. For the chosen measures, companies and supply chains can now be analyzed in the same way, provided that measures are valid for respective products and activities.

However, regarding a comparison of variations *between* different measures of the same supply chain, still some challenges exist. *Firstly*, a rule of interpretation is missing, as the data obtained needs to be analyzed regarding its conformance with the process plans. Therefore, the data needs to be analyzed in comparison to its reference point and the distance to it also requires identical interpretation across companies. This reference point could be either the mean or median value, if evaluations should be based on past experience. Otherwise, the reference point is determined in advance, for example by standards, experiments, or operative targets. *Secondly*, as already pointed out above, the measures are on different scales and cannot be interpreted all to the same extent. Consequently, some statistical operations are only reserved for those measures, which are either continuous or discrete, with qualitative measures being least interpretable (Kromrey 2009). *Thirdly*, the units of measurement differ, as one measure might be based on degree Celsius, whereas another is based on e.g. kilograms. Thus, also in between quantitative measures, comparison across measures is not possible, whereby correlations cannot be analyzed, nor measures be aggregated for complexity reduction. Therefore, the values of measures need to be transformed to be interpretable on one scale, to allow comparisons and categorization of values.

In general, it is possible to transform one scale into another one, if transformation does not lead true statements to become wrong and vice versa (Kromrey 2009). However, transforming nominal measures into measures with rank order is normally not feasible, as their qualitative content can only be interpreted regarding equality or inequality (Diekmann 2002). Therefore, these measures are normally undesirable if one wishes to interpret data in more dimensions than only regarding equality or inequality. The integration of such qualitative measures may on the one hand allow for a more complete picture of the process plans, but on the other hand reduces the interpretability of data. Therefore, wherever possible, qualitative measures without rank order should be translated into qualitative measures with rank order, or replaced by other measures, if the objective is to compare disruptions. However, if the objective is to analyze a specific disruption in detail, such qualitative measures can be maintained. In any case, the trade-off between precision and universality as discussed by Chmielewicz (1979) should be considered during the development of measures.

The other three types of measures can at least be interpreted on an ordinal scale, hence the values can be compared regarding their relative position (e.g. regarding utility) and their median values (Diekmann 2002). Therewith, at least indicators could be compared for different shipments or different process steps, to identify where the process plans were achieved best and where worst. However, for the unambiguous determination of performance, measures should be either discrete or continuous. Whereas it is not possible to transform a scale of a lower measurement level into a higher one, it is always possible to transform a higher measurement level into a lower one (Kromrey 2009). Thereby, the continuous measures could be attributed to classes, which reduces on the one hand their information content regarding the actual value, but at the same time increases the comparability across values and measurements.

Therewith, mean values across measures could be compared and variances calculated (Bortz 1995), which would allow for the definition of identical thresholds for the identification of significant deviations.

However, since the range of potential categories of measures with rank order depends on the context (Kromrey 2009), the operationalization has to be effected in such a way, that the entire range of alternatives is allocated on a scale, which incorporates both ends of the possible range (Eisenführ 2010). Once all alternatives have been allocated, they can be grouped to classes on a numerical rating scale, e.g. a Likert scale, whereby the number of classes depends on the context and is still a point of debate in the literature (Greving 2009). Thereby, classes have to fulfil again the requirement of exhaustiveness and exclusiveness. Furthermore, they have to be of equal size, to avoid bias in interpretation (Kromrey 2009). By the end of this operation, all values obtained from the measures can now be compared and put into relation on a single scale.

By comparing the classes or points attained in prior satisfactory supply chain processes to a specific case under study, it is then possible to assess whether the current performance lies within the standard range of process performance. If it does not fall into this range, a deviation from the process plans has occurred. Depending on the extent of deviation and the limits of acceptance defined, disruptions can be identified and measured regarding their severity. Thereby, each class not belonging to the range of acceptance should receive a proportional value, which indicates its distance to the desired class. The alternatives for determining thresholds are illustrated in the form of a decision tree to cover all possible procedures in a flexible and context-specific model (Götze 2006) in Figure 17.

Figure 14: Decision tree to transform measures for the identification of disruptions

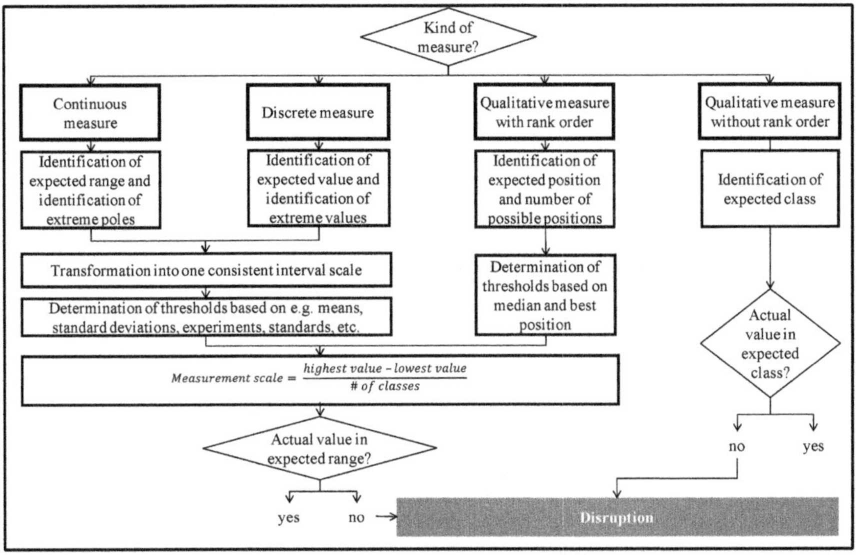

In a final step, the values can be weighted and aggregated to identify and evaluate disruptions. In order to obtain for every part of the process plan a weighted disruption score after data collection, the indicators need to be aggregated based on an aggregation rule. A general rule is provided for instance by Multi Attribute Utility Theory (MAUT), where alternative choices are evaluated and compared based on weighted selection criteria. Normally, these criteria are independent from one another, wherefore each alternative is evaluated regarding its weighted fill rate of every criterion and aggregated for all criteria (Götze 2006). Furthermore, as the scoring model focuses on disruptions and not on actual process performance, the results are normalized to one:

$$(1) \qquad D_{A1} = \sum_{k=1}^{K} \frac{w_k \times n_k}{100}$$

D_{A1} = disruption score process plan A | 1; w_k = weighting factor criterion k; n_k = utility fill rate criterion k

The same methodology can be used to aggregate the disruption scores for subsequent process steps, as well as supply chain steps. Since both, measures and indicators have been constructed in such a way as to be independent from others, multiplying weighted measures with one another would lead to a falsification of results. The compliance of one value with its thresholds could thus lead to the conclusion that no disruption occurred, even though another value has been out of range. However, process plans cover a wide range of aspects, where a lack in fulfilling one aspect cannot necessarily be compensated by over-fulfilling another one. Therefore, the weighted values of measures are added for each indicator, and subsequently for each field of the product/process matrix. Therewith, for each aspect of the process plan, the presence of disruptions is identified by a disruption score larger than zero, while the extent of disruption as well as its relevance can be assessed based on the share of the disruption score of the maximum score of deviation. The individual components of the scoring model are illustrated for an example in Figure 15.

Figure 15: Exemplified course of action in the scoring model for disruptions

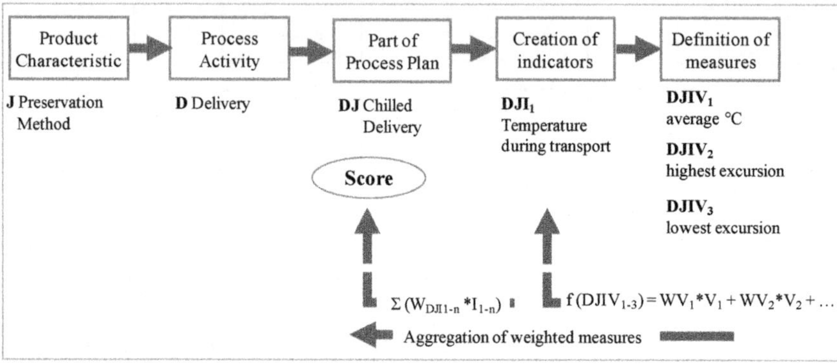

Source 8: Own illustration, methodology based on Hülsmann & Grapp (2006)

An amendment to this approach would be to consider uncertainty in decision making, by assessing the relative importance of each criterion in different scenarios (e.g. Götze 2006). Furthermore, if the same indicators are used at several steps of the process, e.g. temperature variation, outstanding values can be monitored and disruptions predicted, if rules exist for how to cumulate values across process steps. Such rules can be provided for instance by mathematical models of effects of temperature deviations (Özilgen 2011), pressure (Hendrickx et al. 1998), or relative humidity (Sacilik, Keskin & Elicin 2006) on food quality. Therewith, the values of the measure in following process steps can be simulated for different scenarios and a dynamic adaptation of interpretation rules of single measures or of entire indicators created. These dynamically adapted interpretation rules can then serve as a decision support for individuals receiving the food products next in the process. However, before trying to analyze causal relations in empirical investigations, the question arises, which causal relations have been identified already. Therefore, the next section shall provide an overview on empirical research on causes of disruptions, to avoid redundancies and gain starting points for own empirical research.

2.5 Deficits in Existing Causal Explanations of Disruptions

2.5.1 Scarcity of Explanations of Disruptions in General

In order to show the relevancy of research on causes of supply chain disruptions in general, and more specifically in food supply chains, the purpose of section 2.5 is to illustrate the status-quo of research encountered in the literature review. Furthermore, starting points for the identification of causes of disruptions shall be determined.

For the literature review on causal relations, this thesis follows the suggestions made by Kornmeier (2007). He stipulates that the literature considered for a first overview on the phenomenon under study should at least either include empirical observations on the phenomenon in question, or should build on a theory-based argumentation, including the deduction of hypotheses. Therefore, only those publications will be considered here, which build on empirical observations, or which provide theory-based hypotheses on causes of disruptions in supply chains.

As indicated earlier, research on disruptions in supply chains is still rather fragmented. Systematic analyses of causes of disruptions are therefore scarce, and anecdotal evidence prevails. Following Popper (1973), the conclusion of observations in one case on the basic population is invalid, wherefore no general causal relations can be derived from this anecdotal evidence. Nevertheless, as Chmielewicz (1979) argues, these observations of single cases are suitable for the discovery of potential general causal relations and may serve as a starting point for the creation of hypotheses. The question is therefore, how to decide on the inclusion or exclusion of publications in the identification of possible causes of supply chain disruptions.

Kornmeier (2007) differentiates research contributions based on their science theoretic quality into *narrative*, *empirical*, *vague theoretical connection*, *eclectically-used theory*, and *theory-driven empirical* publications. Furthermore, a fifth class was created, since many publications dealt with the development of simulations or formal models to assess potential impacts of disruptions. These publications were also excluded from further analysis, since the data is generally based on rigorously defined assumptions that do not directly measure real-world phenomena (Axelrod 2007), which is especially true for such complex phenomena as disruptions. Therefore, all publications were assigned to one of these classes based on a content-analysis, and only those publications further considered, which had either an empirical focus, or were theory-driven empirical publications.[31] All in all, 24 publications matched the quality criteria and can be found in Table 6.

[31] The assignment was not unambiguously possible in all cases. If a publication could not be unambiguously assigned to one of the classes excluded, this ambiguousness was neglected since in either case, the publication is not further regarded. However, where an assignment to either the excluded or included classes was not clear, it was opted to assess the publication on the next exclusion criterion and to decide thereafter. An overview on the allocation of publications can be found in the explanation volume.

Table 6: Remaining publications and brief description of content

	Source	Topic
Empirically-Driven Approach	Gang Yu et al. 2003	Crew planning at continental airlines
	Blackhurst et al. 2005	Research issues for managing disruptions
	Holl, Pardo & Rama 2010	Sophistication of manufacturing and choice of suppliers
	Levy 1997	Lean production in an international context
	McKinnon 2006	Effect of disruptions on the British economy
	Bamber & Lansbury 1988	**Effect of managerial strategy on disruptions**
	Hendricks & Singhal 2008	Effect of supply chain disruptions on shareholder value
	MacPherson 2008	Impact of Bio terrorism law on border delays
	Manuj & Mentzer 2008	Classification of risks and proposal of mitigation framework
	Elkins et al. 2005	Best practices of supply chain risk management
	Closs D. & McGarrell 2004	Enhancing security in supply chains
	Gorton, Dumitrashko & White 2006	**Disruptions in Moldovan dairy supply chains**
	Jüttner 2005	**Issues in supply chain risk management**
	Hendricks & Singhal 2003	Effect of glitches on shareholder wealth
	Oke & Gopalakrishnan 2009	**Risk categorization and mitigation strategies**
	Zsidisin & Wagner 2010	Supply side risks of disruptions and frequency of occurrence
	Kleindorfer & Saad 2005	Framework for risk assessment to avoid disruption
	Norrman & Jansson 2004	Proactive risk management & classification of risks
	Craighead et al. 2007	**Design of supply networks to mitigate disruption risks**
Theory-Driven Empirical Approach	Desai 2011	Reaction of companies on disruptions scrutiny
	Wagner & Bode 2006	**Relationship between vulnerability and risk**
	Wu et al. 2006	Impact of IT on supply chain performance
	Wagner & Bode 2008	Dimensions of risk and performance
	Nair & Vidal 2011	Network design effects on robustness

Apart from the quality assessment based on the research on the science theoretic quality of the publication, the remaining publications were assessed regarding their contribution to generate starting points for the identification of causes of disruptions. Regarding the quantity of publications on supply chain disruptions, it can be observed that the majority of contributions focuses on how disruptions might be mitigated (e.g. Christopher & Lee 2004; Chopra & Sodhi 2004; Kleindorfer & Saad 2005; Tang 2006; Tang & Tomlin 2008), or how the resilience of supply chains after disruptions might be increased (e.g. Christopher & Rutherford 2004; Sheffi 2005; Sheffi & Rice 2005; Zsidisin & Wagner 2010). In consequence, they were excluded of further analyses as the research focus does not match the requirements of this thesis.

However, regarding the quality of papers, few papers provide theoretically grounded and empirically tested causal analyses. Rather, they provide conceptual frameworks for the assessment of risks (e.g. Gaonkar & Viswanadham 2004; Sarathy 2006; Smith et al. 2007; Manuj & Mentzer 2008), or deliver suggestions for practitioners on how to reduce the vulnerability of supply chains (e.g. Yossi Sheffi 2001; Smith, Jennings & Castro 2005; Rice Jr 2011). Those publications which dealt with causes of disruptions are marked in bold in Table 6. Finally, six publications remained for a more thorough analysis.

One of the first publications on disruptions in production and distribution systems based on empirical data dates back to 1988, when Bamber & Lansbury (1988) presented the results of a long term observation of the performance of two identical technologically advanced distribution centres (DCs) for dry food. Whereas one of them performed well and increased its productivity steadily, the other one experienced considerable performance inferiorities and frequent disruptions of supply. The causes for these disruptions were traced back to enduring conflicts between the workers and the management of the DC, which led to labour strikes, boycotts and acts of sabotage. They conclude that managerial strategies, work organization and patterns of industrial organization may have a larger impact on organizational behaviour and productivity, than the type of technology applied. Hence, in this case a disruption occurred because of intentional deviations by the employees. Therewith, disruptions were at least accepted by the employees, though not necessarily expected by the management. Thereby, this case highlights that discrepancies between objectives of the management and objectives of employees are not necessarily the same and may provoke the occurrence of disruptions.

This view is supported by Albino, Garavelli & Okogbaa (1998), who investigate the vulnerability of a production system in a multi-supplier network and conclude that the performance of the system is dependent on the system's characteristics. The focus of analysis is thereby on delays in the throughput time and backorders, influenced by the number of product types and mean size of product mix per container. In a case study, they come to the conclusion that vulnerability to disruptions can be reduced by reconsidering the design and management of the production system, for example by introducing buffers or investing in new facilities. Hence, the design of the quantitative and spatial process flows could influence the probability of disruptions.

The decision on facility locations is also a central theme in Holl, Pardo & Rama (2010), who investigate the role of supplier location for the avoidance of disruptions in just-in-time (JIT) production in the Spanish automotive industry. They find out that in general, the risks of disruptions tend to increase with the travel distance between supply chain partners. However, they also point out that stable subcontracting relationships seem to allow for more geographic dispersion of companies. Thus, apart from physical distances, the relationship between companies seems to play a role in causes of supply chain disruptions.

However, stable relationships with suppliers or customers might also increase the exposure of companies to disruptions, if it comes to dependencies. Based on a case study of a US retailer, Oke & Gopalakrishnan (2009) report on the potential of disruptions due to shut downs of key suppliers from China. According to them, apart from supplier dependence, also dependence on customers might lead to disruptions, if demand is volatile and unpredictable. Furthermore, they state that seasonality of production can lead to disruptions, if supply cannot be adequately planned. Hence, volume uncertainty seems to influence how the kind of relationship affects the occurrence of disruptions.

Similar results of several focus group discussions are presented by Jüttner (2005), who highlights the importance of the relationships in the supply chain as a source of disruptions, which in turn are positively related to the complexity of the network and the degree of geographic spread of a supply chain. Hence, apart from physical distance of companies in the supply chain, the number of companies and relationships seems to influence disruptions as well as the degree of interdependencies. Taken together, these factors could be grouped to the quality of relationship between companies in the supply chain.

The importance of the quality of relationship is also highlighted by Gorton, Dumitrashko & White (2006), who investigated the performance development of the Moldovan milk sector after privatization of formerly state-owned farms. In this case, the privatization and split up of formerly land and milk production led to the fragmentation of the supply chain and resulted in considerable performance losses for the entire sector. From a case study, they report on how a dairy processor tackled the problem of frequent disruptions due to contamination and lacking cold chain equipment with its suppliers. In order to assure a steady supply and certain quality, this company was forced to establish long-term contracts with suppliers on the one hand, and to invest in quality monitoring equipment at its suppliers on the other hand. Therewith, the company achieved a reduction of disruptions and improvement of its market position. Hence, the quality of relationship was increased by transaction specific investments and more long-term relationships with transaction partners, whereby the probability of disruptions was reduced.

In a cross-sector empirical research, Craighead et al. (2007) find also evidence for the important role of the supply chain design in the occurrence and severity of supply chain disruptions. Based on their findings from industries such as the automobile and pharmaceutical industry, as well as from retailers and logistics service providers, they propose that the geographical density of nodes in a supply chain, the complexity of the supply chain, and the node criticality seem to be positively related to the severity of supply chain disruptions.

Apart from these empirical publications, only four publications were identified, which developed theory-based hypotheses on supply chain disruptions, and tested them empirically afterwards. Of those, only one was concerned with the identification of *causes* for the exposure of supply chains to disruptions.

Based on a literature review on supply chain management risks and disruptions, as well as Normal Accident Theory[32], Wagner & Bode (2006) derive hypotheses on the influence of supply chain design factors on the impact of supply chain disruptions. In a large scale and cross-industry survey in German companies, they find evidence for their assumptions on the relationship between inter-company dependence and types of sourcing on the impact of demand, supply and catastrophic disruptions. Specifically, the study comes to the conclusion that demand-side risk (as the effect of a disruption) is amplified by strong customer dependence and strong supplier dependence, whereas supply-side risk is enhanced by supplier dependence, single sourcing and global sourcing. Additionally, a highly significant effect was found for the reliance on global sourcing in the presence of catastrophic disruptions. Interestingly, single sourcing was found to be less detrimental to supply-side risk than general dependence on few suppliers. The authors argue that this might be due to the closer relationship, which enforces long-term commitment, mutual trust, open communication and joint activities. Thus, it seems as if the kind of exchange relationship a company develops with its exchange partners may determine the severity of disruptions for the company.

In summary, these empirical contributions suggest that the design of relationships between supply chain partners affects the probability and severity of supply chain disruptions, even though the literature basis is still thin. However, either the theoretical and empirical foundations are insufficient, or the research did not ask for causes of disruptions. Hence, what has not been addressed in the literature up to date is a theory-based and empirically tested possible relationship between the design of relationships in supply chains and the *occurrence* of disruptions.

In consequence, generally valid, theory-based, and empirically tested causal explanations of why disruptions occur, are lacking, or still in development. Nevertheless, from the scarce evidence available, there seems to be agreement that the way in which supply chain partners design their relationships specifically with each other, and how they deal with factors emerging from their general business environment influences the probability of disruptions. Furthermore, these results show that also for food supply chains, little research has been conducted to identify organizational causes of disruptions. However, especially in these supply chains, disruptions are of high relevance, as will be shown in the following.

---

32 E.g. Perrow (1999), Perrow (2006), Shrivastava, Sonpar & Pazzaglia (2009).

2.5.2 Multitude of Challenges in Food Supply Chains

As already stated earlier, disruptions in food supply chains are increasingly gaining attention from researchers, practitioners, but also official authorities and the society in general. However, whereas food scandals rise awareness of challenges in food supply chains, actual data on food supply chain disruptions remains scarce, as actors in food supply chains are normally highly protective of their data (e.g. Gustavsson et al. 2011; Parfitt, Barthel & Macnaughton 2010; Bechini et al. 2008). A recent review of the literature on food supply chain disruptions can be found in Hülsmann & Brenner (2011), who address mainly the questions of where the disruptions occur in the food supply chain, what kind of disruptions seem to prevail, and how their occurrence and effects could be mitigated. In this study, empirical analyses of challenges in food supply chains have been gathered and summarized, to identify major problems. Based on this meta-analysis, the study comes to the conclusion that disruptions may lead to food waste of about 30-50% between the farm and the consumer (Hülsmann & Brenner 2011). It seems therefore that the field of disruptions in food supply chains is firstly, still lacking further research, and secondly, solutions to reduce these significant losses along the food supply chain.

This meta-analysis shall serve three purposes in this thesis: firstly, it affirms the relevancy to explain the occurrence of disruptions in the context of food supply chains. Secondly, it provides an overview on food supply chain specific challenges and of the sector in general. And thirdly, it enables the identification of starting points for the analysis of causes of disruptions, by revealing relevant areas of disruptions in food supply chains. The following paragraphs therefore are to large extent excerpts of this study and subsume the findings on characteristics of food supply chains, as well as potential causes of disruptions.

The internationalization of trade has substantially affected the complexity of supply chains (Böing & Schwarz 2005). Logistic service providers (LSP) face increasingly complicated business processes, coupled with more sensitive customers as well as fast changing demand behaviour (Hasselmann 2008). The reasons making international logistics so challenging are manifold. They include among others:

- frequent transport mode changes
- longer distances to overcome
- disruptions due to border crossings
- larger order sizes
- different laws and regulations (Waters 2009)

Consequences are time-consuming logistic operations, increased risks regarding quality and conformity of transport and commodity, as well as more irregularities (Waters 2009). Especially for fresh food products such as fruit and vegetables (produce), transport obstacles play a significant role, as the shelf life is restricted and directly related to the maintenance of exact temperature ranges (Frith 1991). In order to avoid shrinkage and economic losses, it can be stated that it is imperative to maintain optimal conditions in terms of temperature, humidity and handling from harvest to the home of the consumer (Nunes et al. 2009).

The reason why temperature plays an important role is that storage life varies significantly between different types of horticultural products and can be considerably reduced by storing the product under wrong temperatures (Paull 1999).While temperature control is required to reduce metabolic processes of produce, relative humidity (RH) should be kept at elevated rates as the moisture contained in fruit and vegetables evaporates if stored at regular ambient humidity levels, resulting in moisture loss and increased wilting (Zhang 1997). The specific characteristics of produce have not only implications for storage, but also for all other activities associated with handling the product in supply chains.

For instance, pre-cooling is crucial to prolong the potential shelf life of the produce and to reduce field heat prior to loading (Frith 1991). Correct packaging is necessary to avoid mechanical damages which can account for elevated loss rates (Nunes et al. 2009). Furthermore, packaging can help to protect the produce from ambient temperature and humidity losses (Manalili, Dorado & van Otterdijk 2011). During transport, the constant maintenance of optimal temperature conditions has to be achieved to provide produce and other fresh products in best quality (Brecht et al. 2003). Thereby, not only the duration of transport is crucial, but also the frequency and extent of temperature deviations encountered in transit (Nunes, Emond & Brecht 2006). Thus, the susceptibility to disruptions seems to be especially high as during transportation and transformation processes, special conditions have to be met, which are not determined by the supply chain partners, but by the products shipped. The question is thus, whether the determinants of causes of disruptions identified in the general supply chain literature are firstly, the same for food supply chains, and secondly, can be further specified. The following paragraphs are the summary of findings from the literature as reported by Hülsmann & Brenner (2011). In this study, the results have thereby been divided based on the analyzed process flow into monetary flow, information flow, and product flow and regarding the institutional perspective into company level, relationship level, and environmental level:[33]

At the level of **monetary flow**, relatively few observations on causes of supply chain disruptions have been made. On the company level, no obstacles were reported, which is supposedly attributed to the lack of information and the difficulty to generalize findings of company specific financial concerns.

At the level of interaction of companies, it has been stated that the certification according to private quality management standards is a costly process (e.g. Smith & Sparks 2004). This is especially a concern for poor farmers, as they might be excluded from the export industry of fruit and vegetables. In South Africa for example, 10% of all apple producers faced liquida-

[33] The following paragraphs have been published in a previous version in Hülsmann & Brenner (2011, pp. 21–24).

tion of their businesses in 2000 (Hardmann, Darroch & Ortmann 2002). While by reducing the supplier base, the quality management is supposedly enhanced, companies might need to find other ways to cut costs, such as to hire unskilled staff or to postpone investments in equipment. At the same time, farmers and exporters are in an unfavourable position, as they cannot control the handling of their products up to the delivery. Even if they fully comply with the demands of their customers at the company level, they do not have the means to assure the same level of accuracy by the numerous handling companies (Vermeulen et al. 2006). Consequently, the lack of control and transparency leads to inferior assurance of property rights.

Regarding the level of external impacts, it has been reported that the economic situation of companies can be affected by legal and environmental changes. Especially the increasing importance of food safety regulations can impact on the business environment and can result in further investments, changes in daily practices and the structure of trade. Lister (1992) even reports that due to changes in national law, economic shifts between companies can occur. This is a source of uncertainty for companies and requires the permanent observation of the market forces.

Regarding the **information flow** at the company level, the inefficient use or applicability of temperature monitoring equipment poses difficulties for the seamless traceability of products (e.g. Bechini et al. 2008). Furthermore, the data obtained from the monitoring process is not meaningful in itself, but requires correct interpretation in the context of the circumstances to allow for an assertion on the quality (Wild 2005). This makes the quality control prone to subjective valuations, as objective and generally accepted maturity standards are missing.

Most problems concerned with the flow of information were found on the level of interaction among the companies (e.g. Alfaro & Rábade; van der Vorst et al. 1998; Manthou, Matopoulos & Vlachopoulou 2005). The general impression is provided that the implementation of inter-company information and communication systems has not been developed to the required extent, yet. This is partly due to resistance of managers to the implementation, ignorance of the acquaintance with the technology and due to the heterogeneity of the perishable trade sector. The lack of an adequate information infrastructure leads to a deficient information and communication, while the demand for information by customers and authorities keeps rising. An exemplified consequence is reported by Chandra & Fisher (1994), who found out that the operating costs can be reduced by 3% to 20% only by improving coordination.[34]

Further obstacles are added from the external perspective, where problems were related mainly to complex and inharmonious legislation (e.g. Long 2004; MacMaoláin 2007). The lack of harmonized regulations leads to redundancies in documents and more pressure on every link of the cold chain. One study asserts for example that for a pilot project, four pallets

[34] Note by the author: this example is a computational study of supply chains in general. As can be seen, it serves for illustration of potential improvements, and does not refer to causes of disruptions.

of fruit were used, which required 40 documents during transport (Polderdijk et al. 2006). Thereby, the inefficiencies of the information flow are aggravated and the compliance with regulatory demands endangered.

At the level of the **product flow**, a huge number of handling-related problems have been observed at every single step of the cold chain (e.g. Nunes, Emond & Brecht 2006; Nunes et al. 2009). Especially the management and equipment in cold chains show a range of inferiorities, which are avoidable. Lacking, delayed or wrong cooling are persistent not only at interfaces[35], but also on the company level, which indicates missing appreciation and knowledge on how to correctly handle the produce.

Furthermore, at the inter-company level, major concerns were related to the human aspect in cold chain logistics (e.g. Fearne & Hughes 2005; Kader 2005). The lack of skills in terms of handling or management was reported frequently as the origin of cold chain ruptures. These human causes have a direct impact on the quality of the produce, especially losses due to poor temperature management and mechanical damage can be attributed.

From the external perspective, as has been the case at the level of the monetary flow, regulatory and environmental changes were reported to affect the flow of the produce. An additional challenge, which is special to the trade of fruit and vegetables and which has been mentioned frequently, is the seasonality of the produce availability (e.g. Georgiadis, Vlachos & Iakovou 2005; Vega 2008). Thereby, more pressure is put on the logistic process, creating bottlenecks in peak seasons and idle capacities in off-seasons.

In general, it is not possible to determine the influence of specific causes on the overall performance of cold chains. As has been shown, there is a wide range of obstacles, which affect the fruit quality negatively. To assess the significance of every single problem for the remaining shelf life and for every commodity is not feasible, yet. However, the overall result is that estimated losses from farm to fork amount to 30% to 50% of fruit and vegetables produced (e.g. Kader 2005, Vega 2008).

Regarding the findings of the literature research, it can be stated that the majority of studies revealed obstacles in the information and material flow, whereby the relationship between supply chain agents was the typically affected management perspective. Thus, it can be said that most problems seem to arise when the produce is handed over to the next agent and that the inter-company management of interfaces causes major ruptures. This is especially problematic, since the supply chain for agricultural products is still very fragmented. If the major

[35] The term interface design is frequently used in the disciplines of computer science and engineering (e.g. Hennessy & Patterson 1998; Lopez Jaquero et al. 2009; Vicente 2002; Puerta 2009). The term interface is also used in the context of ruptures (see: Koyanagi et al. 2004), and additionally, has already found its way into the supply chain management literature (see: Peck & Jüttner 2000).

weaknesses do not occur on the level of the single company, strategies to improve the performance might not yield the expected results, if only taken by one actor.[36]

The observations summarised in the study cited above indicate firstly, that supply chain disruptions play a significant role in food supply chains. Secondly, there seem to be a multitude of possible causes of disruptions, being either external to the system, internal to the system, or internal to the single organisation. Since the consideration of causes on the external level would significantly increase the complexity of analysis and reduce the manageability of causes for organizations, the following sections will focus on those potential causes within the scope of supply chain organizations. This focus of attention is further stressed by the observation that most challenges seem to exist at interfaces between companies, as apparently these are the areas where most supply chain disruptions occur. Referring back to the determinants of disruptions encountered in the general supply chain related research in section 2.5.1, the design of relationships also seem to be a determinant of disruptions in food supply chains. In consequence, the design of relationships and their potential impacts on disruptions in food supply chains will be put into focus in this thesis.

However, even though potential determinants of disruptions have been highlighted in this section, causes of disruptions still remain on a rather abstract level. Furthermore, as the results of the meta-analysis are based partly on case studies and many publications included lack theoretical foundation, a more thorough analysis of causes of disruptions is required. Therefore, in section 2.5.3, the research focus will be further refined, to allow subsequently identification of a suitable theoretical basis and the following deduction of hypotheses.

2.5.3 Weak Points in Food Supply Chains

Considering the multi-causal nature of disruptions as illustrated in section 2.2.3, and the lack of comprehensive empirical data on disruptions in food supply chains as pointed out above, the question is how to identify causes of disruptions in food supply chains. To this purpose, the study by Hülsmann & Brenner (2011) provides again a starting point, as in the appendix of the study, causes of disruptions encountered in the literature are provided not on an aggregated level, but how they were encountered. This list cites the causes encountered during the literature review, which can therefore be analyzed in detail.

As has already been argued for the classification of disruptions, the causes of disruptions listed in this study shall be categorized based on a content analysis into different groups of causes. However, as the focus of this research lies on causes which emerge from inside the supply chain, those causes from the larger environment will not be considered. Therefore, a classification framework is required, which decomposes supply chains conceptually in a comprehensive and systematic way, to allow for an identification of groups of causes for supply chain disruptions. Such a classification can be done for instance with the matrix framework

---

[36] The previous paragraphs have been published in a previous version in Hülsmann & Brenner (2011, pp. 21–24).

for supply chain optimization provided by Bolstorff, Rosenbaum & Poluha (2007). First, they decompose a supply chain into the *elements* institution,[37] process, people/tasks, and technology to indicate the focus of analysis. Second, they decompose the *activities* or managerial tasks into objectives of the supply chain strategy, structuring of the supply chain, and planning, controlling, and measuring of the supply chain. Supply chain disruptions can thereby be categorized depending on *where* the disruption is observed, and depending on *what* causes the disruption.

Objectives of the supply chain strategy are concerned with the question, whether an overall strategy exists at all, whether this strategy has been adequately linked across company borders along the supply chain, and whether tasks and work requirements are adequately connected to planning, purchasing, production, supply- and return processes (Bolstorff, Rosenbaum & Poluha 2007). Regarding the structuring of the supply chain, the performance is determined by the questions, whether the supply chain structure is efficient and effective on the institutional, the process-related, the personnel, and the technological level. And finally, regarding planning, controlling and measuring of supply chain elements, the framework is concerned with whether the desired performance is adequately determined by sub-goals and rules for action to be adhered to during execution for compliance with the objectives (Bolstorff, Rosenbaum & Poluha 2007). This procedure does not demand for completeness, but shall only provide a broad overview on starting points for a systematic and more profound analysis. Even though the number of publications addressing a certain field of the matrix does not necessarily reflect the importance of the dimension, the overall amount of publications considered may serve as an indicator for major weak points of food supply chains deemed relevant in the literature. The following table shows the results of the qualitative classification of the determinants of disruptions by the publications, which have been included by Hülsmann & Brenner (2011).

[37] Even though Bolstorff, Rosenbaum & Poluha (2007) use the German term "Organisation", they refer to an organized social system Remer (2005) and therewith to the institutional aspect of "Organisation". Even though they follow thereby the understanding of the term as prevalent in the Anglo-Saxon organization literature Hill, Fehlbaum & Ulrich (1994), for reason of unambiguity the term institution is selected in the translation of the framework. For a discussion of different understandings of "Organisation", see e.g. Hülsmann (2002).

Table 7: Qualitative allocation of causes of food supply chain disruptions

		Managerial Task			
		Objectives	Structuring	Planning, Controlling & Measuring	Σ
Supply Chain Element	Institution		supply chain complexity(1); heterogeneity of actors(2); fragmented supply base(3); complex links between production and consumption(4); fragmented supply chains in emerging countries(5); inadequate infrastructure; complexity of interaction of chain members(6); big scale differences of actors(7)38	lack of administration of transactions (Trienekens & Zuurbier 2008)	**8**
	Process		long transport distances(1); transport mode changes; interfaces(2); superfluous stages(3); long distribution routes(4); small order sizes, frequent deliveries, interfaces, frequent transitions(5); distance to market(6); transport mode changes(7); inadequate transportation systems(8)39	necessity of cost reduction, fluctuations in demand (1); maintenance of optimal temperature not attained(2); poor coordination(3); variety in production, export and losses(4); premature loading(5); lack of cooling at reception and issue(6); time pressure(7); defects caused in transit(8); poor control of environment(9); coordination not easy(10); temperature deviations during loading and unloading(11); delays(12); difficulties of controlling temperature(13); inadequate temperature(14); delays(15); inadequate control(16); fluctuations in supply performance; uncertainties(17); loosely controlled storage(18); lack of administration of transactions, inadequate food control, lack of preventive action and education; weak sanction mechanisms(19)40	**27**

38 (1) Bourlakis & Weightman 2004; (2) Canavari et al. 2010; (3) Dolan & Humphrey 2000; (4) Lundqvist, de Fraiture & Molden 2008; (5) Mowat & Collins 2000; (6) Vega 2008; (7) Zhang 1997.

39 (1) Bentrup 1969; (2) Bogataj, Bogataj & Vodopivec 2005; (3) Drewry Shipping Consultants 1990; (4) Imsirovic 2009; (5) Littek 2005; (6) Lundqvist, de Fraiture & Molden 2008; (7) Siebel 2000; (8) Vega 2008.

40 (1) Böing & Schwarz 2005; (2) Brecht et al. 2003; (3) Chandra & Fisher 1994; (4) Drewry Shipping Consultants 1990; (5) Freight Best Practice 2006; (6) Hasselmann 2008; (7) Jedermann et al. 2006; (8) Lange & Nienhoff 2007; (9) Laurin et al. 2006; (10) Long 2004; (11) Meier 1979; (12) Nunes et al. 1995a; (13) Nunes, Emond & Brecht 2006; (14) Nunes et al. 2009; (15) Nunes et al. 1995b; (16) Rodriguez-Bermejo et al. 2007; (17) van Aramyan et al. 2007; (18) Aidoo 1993; (19) Trienekens & Zuurbier 2008.

		Managerial Task			
		Objectives	Structuring	Planning, Controlling & Measuring	Σ
Supply Chain Element	Persons / Tasks			lack of managerial skills; mechanical damage[(1)]; resistance of managers[(2)]; sanitary violations, pesticide violations and unregistered processes[(3)]; lack of skilled staff; fluctuation of staff [(4)]; mechanical damage[(5)]; ignorant handlers[(6)]; theft, untrustworthy and poorly paid staff[(7)]; untrained and ignorant staff[(8)]; wrong loading and storage[(9)]; mechanical damage[(10)]; lack of education, unskilled staff and misunderstandings[(11)]; cultural differences[(12)]; lack of skilled staff[(13)]; mishandling[(14)][41]	**14**
	Technology	Agreements for tracking and tracing difficult to reach (Canavari et al. 2010)	lack of standardization of traceability systems[(1)]; heterogeneous ICT[(2)]; ineffective transport/storage technologies [(3)]; absence of refrigerated facilities[(4)][42]	dispersed information; lack of association with a given product[(1)]; decentralized data storage[(2)]; lack of temperature control[(3)]; lack of data sharing[(4)]; problem of recording temperature[(5)]; heterogeneous use of internet[(6)]; lack of information on product's needs[(7)]; unspecified data definitions[(8)]; erroneous controllers[(9)][43]	**14**
Σ		**1**	**19**	**43**	**63**

Source 9: Own illustration; content from Hülsmann & Brenner (2011)

From the literature review encountered in Hülsmann & Brenner (2011), a total of 63 statements were identified, which dealt with causes of disruptions internal to the food supply chain. Of those, only one statement dealt with causes for disruptions on the level of objectives of the supply chain strategy. This statement has been made by Canavari et al. (2010), who note that agreements on tracking and tracing are difficult to reach along the entire supply chain and that without such an agreement, the information flow remains inefficient. Therefore, the *objectives* regarding the institutional, process-related, personnel and technological elements of food supply chains do not seem to be a major cause for disruptions and will consequently be excluded in the following.

On the *level of structuring* of supply chain elements, in total 19 statements were found. Regarding the institutional element, Zhang (1997) for instance criticizes the large scale differences between actors in the supply chain, while Dolan & Humphrey (2000) complain about

41 (1) Aidoo 1993; (2) Alfaro & Rabade 2009; (3) Bundesamt für Verbraucherschutz und Lebensmittelsicherheit 2007; (4) Fearne & Hughes 2000; (5) Holt, Schoorl & Muirhead; (6) Kader 2005; (7) Long 2004; (8) Meier 1979; (9) Mercantila Publishers 1989; (10) Nunes et al. 2009; (11) Raspor 2008; (12) Schieck 2008; (13) Trienekens & Zuurbier 2008; (14) Vega 2008.

42 (1) Abad et al. 2009; (2) Coronado Mondragon, Coronado Mondragon & Coronado Mondragon 2009; (3) Lundqvist, de Fraiture & Molden 2008; (4) Nunes, Emond & Brecht 2006.

43 (1) Banterle & Stranieri 2008; (2) Bechini et al. 2008; (3) Frith 1991; (4) Kader 2005; (5) Küppers 2002b; (6) Manthou, Matopoulos & Vlachopoulou 2005; (7) Nunes, Emond & Brecht 2006; (8) van der Vorst et al. 1998; (9) Wild 2005.

the fragmentation of supply chains. These authors see in the size or number of agents a major reason for disruptions. Regarding the process-related structuring, the necessity to supply small order quantities is identified by Littek (2005) as a reason for food supply chain disruptions, whereas Lundqvist, de Fraiture & Molden (2008) note that the distance to markets is a cause for disruptions. On the technological level, Nunes, Emond & Brecht (2006) complain about the absence of cooling facilities, while Coronado Mondragon, Coronado Mondragon & Coronado Mondragon (2009) add use of non-efficient ICT. Thus, whereas already more causes are named on the level of structuring, especially for the process element of supply chains, the majority of reasons are identified on the last level of managerial tasks.

The level, to which most of the publications refer when addressing causes for food supply chain disruptions, is the level of planning, controlling, and measuring supply chain activities. Regarding the institutional element, Trienekens & Zuurbier (2008) name the differences in standardization of processing and distribution activities across European food supply chains. However, as there is just one publication referring to this level, it seems to be negligible for further analysis. More publications already address the technological element, where e.g. Küppers (2002b) speak of problems in recording temperature, van der Vorst, Beulens & van Beek (2005) note the lack of specifying data definitions, and Wild (2005) observes frequent temperature ruptures due to erroneous controllers. Hence, regarding the technological element of supply chains, there seem to be major problems in controlling and measuring activities.

Nevertheless, even though the technological element seems to play a role in the occurrence of disruptions, it is still named fewer times (i.e. 9 times) than the personnel/tasks (i.e. 14 times) and the process element (i.e. 19 times). Thus, whereas e.g. erroneous controllers fulfil the definition of unexpected events which might lead to disruptions, they seem to occur less frequent than errors committed by individuals, hence, deviations due to ignorance or failure "*to enact his or her intention successfully*" (Hofmann & Frese 2011, p. 3). Therefore, these two will be regarded in more detail.

On the *level of the personnel and tasks*, optimization potential can be identified according to Bolstorff, Rosenbaum & Poluha (2007) by asking, whether the executing personnel is in possession of required knowledge and abilities to attain the objectives of the task at hand and knows the rules and regulations to comply with. This does not always seem to be the case in food supply chains, as e.g. Fearne & Hughes (2000) and Trienekens & Zuurbier (2008) recognize a lack of skilled staff, whereas Kader (2005) notices a lack of knowledge on how to maintain quality, which is supported by Meier (1979) who speaks of ignorant staff. Furthermore, Vega (2008) reports mishandling, while others report excessive use of pesticides (Bundesamt für Verbraucherschutz und Lebensmittelsicherheit 2007) or wrong storage (Mercantila Publishers 1989). And finally, personnel should be rewarded in an adequate way for attaining their goals and performance feedback should be provided. Again, in food supply chains, Trienekens & Zuurbier (2008) report weak sanction mechanisms, whereas Long (2004) observes that personnel is frequently not paid adequately. With a lack of incentives, in the form of e.g. performance-based premiums or a higher compensation in general, motivation is likely to be low, whereby the level of attention for the execution of tasks might be reduced. As a consequence, more errors might result. Therefore, it can be assumed that inferior sanction and reward mechanisms also contribute to the probability of disruptions. All in all, 14 statements could be attributed to this level of the supply chain.

On the *process level*, the identification of optimization potential is concerned e.g. with questions regarding, whether sub-goals for the planning, purchasing, production, supply, and return processes have been determined, whether the performance of these processes is adequately controlled and measured, and whether interfaces between process steps are planned, controlled, and measured (Bolstorff, Rosenbaum & Poluha 2007). Considering the observations made in food supply chains, this seems to be frequently not the case. Trienekens & Zuurbier (2008) for example report a lack of administration of transactions, inadequate control of food quality, and a lack of preventive action. Hasselmann (2008) notes a lack of cooling at the reception and issue of food, Freight Best Practice (2006) the widely used practice to load vehicles too early, and Nunes, Emond & Brecht (2006) that containers with perishables are left during hours on hot aprons. Furthermore, Chandra & Fisher (1994) highlights the importance of inferior coordination of the processes, which is supported by Drewry Shipping Consultants (1990), who state that temperature deviations are especially occurring at the interfaces in food supply chains. Thus, it seems as if processes are not adequately planned, controlled, and monitored at interfaces between supply chain partners. All in all, 19 statements were found which referred to causes of disruptions in the planning, control and measurement of the supply chain processes.

Subsuming the results of this categorization, it seems as if most frequently, disruptions are not caused by technical failures or wrong supply chain strategies, but rather by lacking process coordination and human error during execution of operational activities. Thereby, failures in the managerial tasks of planning, control and measuring seem to be a major reason, why food supply chains experience disruptions. According to Reason (1990) human errors occur when decisions do not lead to the expected results. If they happen on a regular basis in the same or similar context, then they are systematic errors (Badke-Schaub, Hofinger & Lauche 2008). Due to the reported frequency of disruptions in food supply chains in the same or similar contexts, it can hence be assumed that these errors occur systematically. In such cases, either the position has not been filled suitably, or the individual lacks instructions on how to perform its tasks, or the surrounding conditions do not allow for optimal decision making of the individual. In any case, the instruments employed by the organization to achieve its goals have not worked as expected, which is according to Hill, Fehlbaum & Ulrich (1994) the classical organizational problem. However, this content analysis also bears some constraints as some important causes of disruptions might not have been identified in prior research, which would consequently also be omitted here. Furthermore, the attribution of reported issues to the classes bears the risk of lacking inter-subjective or inter-coder reliability (Kromrey 2009).

Therefore, in order to validate the conclusions drawn from this content analysis, an exploratory survey with 20 cold chain experts was conducted on most important causes of disruptions in food supply chains.[44] Based on the results of the meta-analysis, managers of companies providing services in cold chain management were asked to name the biggest challenges for seamless **process** flows in cold chains. Thereby, 70% considered the information flow to be more problematic than the product flow, whereby especially communication (90% confirmation) and the information flow between companies (95% confirmation) was identified as the main impediment of seamless processes. Therewith, the cold chain experts affirm the conclusion of the content analysis that the coordination of processes at the interface between supply chain partners seems to affect the susceptibility to disruptions.

According to Frese, Graumann & Theuvsen (2012), coordination efforts at interfaces can be reduced by regulating communication between affected units, and by employing structuring measures to define coordination requirements. By deciding on coordination measures, the inter-organizational structure is addressed and how it is designed to optimally achieve the coordination of sub-tasks of the system (Hill, Fehlbaum & Ulrich 1994). At the same time, Frese, Graumann & Theuvsen (2012) see restrictions to the management of interfaces by regulating communication, since conflicting goals of departments may impede coordination in conformance with overall goals. Especially at interfaces between companies such conflicts are probably more pronounced than between departments of a single company. Therewith, the regulation of communication and structuring of coordination may depend on the similarity or divergence between the goals of supply chain partners. Considering that whether supply chains are more or less susceptible to disruptions seems to depend *firstly*, on the quality of relationship between supply chain partners, *secondly*, on the planning, monitoring and control of processes and humans or tasks and *thirdly*, on the communication and coordination at interfaces, the question results:

> **How does the organizational design of interfaces in supply chains affect the vulnerability to disruptions?**

Before this question can be answered, it has to be translated into hypotheses and subsequently operationalized (Kromrey 2009). Therefore, the theoretic framework for translating this question into hypotheses will be developed in section 3.

2.6 Interim Conclusion

The purpose of section 2 is according to the descriptive research aims firstly, the identification of the problem, and secondly the provision of a terminological and taxonomical framework for the description and classification of disruptions, to allow for the deduction of hypotheses and their empirical testing.

---

[44] The survey and its results can be found in the explanation volume.

Based on a literature review, in **section 2.2.1**, the first task was to describe the use of the term disruption in general and in different contexts, to enhance the comprehension and the differentiation of the term. As could be shown, this term is intertwined with the term "rupture", which is also important in the contexts of food supply chains, since it refers to a break in the cold chain and which shall be understood as a sub-category of supply chain disruptions.

The literature review on disruptions in the supply chain literature yielded a variety of definitions of differing qualities, and no common understanding of the term (see **section 2.2.2**). Substantial differences in the phenomena described by this term imperil the transferability of research results. Furthermore, no generally applicable suggestions for action can be deduced, if phenomena are not similar. Even more, a lack of unified definition of disruptions bears the risk that the counter measures based on suggestions derived from another case may not work or even harm in another case. Therefore, based on an analysis of the fundamental aspects of the definitions encountered, a disruption was defined as "*an unexpected, temporal event which leads to a negative deviation from the planned outcome of a supply chain process.*"

From the literature review, it became apparent that not only the definitions of disruptions were differing, but also that the understanding of a disruption has several dimensions. These dimensions might lend themselves to different approaches to explain disruptions and might result in different variables for the identification, classification, and evaluation of disruptions. Considering these dimensions and the definition of disruptions, in **section 2.3.1**, the a disruption was described as the inability to realize logically interconnected activities in the material or information flow as planned, due to humans, machines, information-related causes, or a combination of them (**process perspective**). From a **structural perspective**, it can be described as occurring inside a company or node, between adjacent nodes (i.e. inter-organisational), in the entire network (i.e. intra-supply chain), or the larger environment (i.e. extra-supply chain). From an **institutional perspective**, a disruption could be described as the violation of one or more components of the legal, regulatory, and bureaucratic rule base. Finally, the **functional perspective** understands a disruption of the supply chain as a deviation from the cost-optimal output, or the non-realisation of an expected competitive advantage. For the identification of suitable theories for explaining disruptions, this implies that an adequate theoretic basis for the development of hypotheses on causes of disruptions needs to be able to provide explanations within its structural, processual and institutional dimensions.

In order to differentiate between types of disruptions, which might differ from each other regarding causes, organizational location of occurrence, and mitigation methods, a typology of disruptions is required. In **section 2.3.2**, typologies encountered in the literature review were illustrated, and potential shortcomings highlighted. Inconsistencies in the definition of classes may result in the non-uniform classification of disruptions by different researchers, wherefore the transferability of research results is again imperilled (see above). Furthermore, some classes of disruptions might not be considered which would leave them unconsidered during analysis and development of counter measures. Consequently, in **section 2.3.3**, a descriptive classification framework was developed, based on the terminology for describing management systems proposed by Remer (2004). This framework allows for a classification of disruptions based on a semantic decomposition of operational planning.

This descriptive framework has been integrated in **section 2.4**, which aimed for the identification, measurement and analysis of disruptions in empirical investigations in food supply chains. In order to describe process plans systematically and exhaustively, a general yet concrete classification of product characteristics and process activities was depicted in **section 2.4.1**. By basing the classifications on standards accepted and implemented in food supply chains, namely LanguaL™ and Codex Alimentarius, usability of the scoring model is enhanced. In **section 2.4.2** a general guideline for the deduction of indicators based on section 2.3.3 and prioritization has been developed. Prioritization shall reduce the efforts and complexity of implementation, whereas the guideline for the deduction of indicators shall increase the completeness of the scoring model. Finally, the transformation of indicators into measures has been dealt with in **section 2.4.3**. Hereby, statistical methods, data from experiments or standard ranges can be used to define thresholds for specific values, whereby different natures of values are considered for the selection of methods. To allow for the analysis of results across measures and across indicators, a decision tree shows how to develop consistent scales depending on the kind of measures chosen. The scoring model forms therewith the basis for statistical analyses of empirical data on disruptions, as well as for causal analyses.

After having developed a model to identify and measure the negative effects of disruptions, in **section 2.5**, the literature was assessed regarding potential causes of disruptions. Apart from anecdotal evidence on causes of disruptions (e.g. Albino, Garavelli & Okogbaa 1998; Bamber & Lansbury 1988; Holl, Pardo & Rama 2010), and empirical studies on the effects of disruptions (Wagner & Bode 2006), no theoretically developed and empirically tested hypotheses on causes of supply chain disruptions seem to exist (see **section 2.5.1**). Without generally applicable causal explanations, no counter measures can be developed effectively, so that impact and frequency of disruptions could not be reduced. Consequently, a considerable research gap exists regarding theory-based causal explanations for the occurrence of disruptions in supply chains.

In order to identify specific areas of potential causes of disruptions, and to assess the suitability of theories for explaining these causes for disruptions, the review in **section 2.5.2** focused on food supply chains. Findings suggest that not only the product flow is prone to disruptions, but also the flow of information. Furthermore, disruptions seem to be frequently due to inferior inter-organizational management of the processes. Thus, a suitable theory needs to address and explain inter-organizational management and should allow for explanations of inefficiencies of inter-organizational management. **Section 2.5.3** specified the focus of research further to the design of interfaces. To this purpose, a content analysis of publications on disruptions in food supply chains was conducted to reveal – from a supply chain management perspective – that major problems seem to exist at the process and human error level of supply chains. These results were validated and enriched by an exploratory survey with 20 cold chain experts who stressed the lack of adequate coordination between companies. Thus, interfaces between supply chain partners were found to be especially susceptible to disruptions, which results in the concretization of the research question.

In summary, section 2 provided the descriptive foundations of this thesis by *firstly*, analyzing disruptions regarding semantic meaning and dimensions of reality incorporated, whereby the phenomenon was also distinguished from similar phenomena. *Secondly*, two frameworks were provided to use in the analysis of disruptions, one conceptual framework for the logical decomposition of disruptions, and one empirical framework, for the measurement of disruptions. *Thirdly*, the status-quo of research on causes of disruptions has been depicted for concretizing and specifying the research question of this thesis. Based on these descriptive research results, the theoretic foundation and subsequent deduction of hypotheses on causes of disruptions can now be pursued and are the research objectives of section 3.

3 Interface Design as Driver of Susceptibility to Disruptions

3.1 Introduction to the Section

The objective of section 3 is to specify potential causal relations between the organizational design of interfaces and the occurrence of disruptions. According to Chmielewicz (1979), the science-theoretic objective is to develop cause and effects statements up to theories, which are true as well as informative. To this purpose, the terms used for constructing statements have to be defined in such a way that they can by tested empirically. Since the terms developed in section 2 are limited to the investigation of disruptions, the existing system of terms has to be completed by a system of terms for the potential causes to be analyzed, before statements can be derived. Furthermore, the organizational design as object of investigation should be allocated in existing knowledge, as for instance theories and methods, which allow for a specification and support the deduction of hypotheses (Kromrey 2009). Therewith, section 3 includes the conceptualization of organizational design, the identification of a theoretic framework for the connection of both constructs, as well as the deduction of a system of hypotheses in preparation of the empirical analysis.

In order to derive hypotheses, the adoption of a theoretic reference frame is useful, to support the systems of hypotheses and integrate causal assumptions in the status-quo of research (Kromrey 2009). According to (Popper 1973, p. 75) these theoretic reference frames build "*bridges over swampy ground*". Therefore, section 3.2 is concerned with the assessment of existing "*bridges*" regarding their suitability as a reference frame for this investigation.

In section 3.2.1, several theories will be depicted and assessed regarding their ability to explain the occurrence of disruptions from an organizational design perspective. Therefore, the methodological procedure will be explained and the selection of theories depicted. Based on several quality criteria, each of these theories will be assessed regarding its applicability and ability to explain causal relations between the organizational design and disruptions. Based on the findings, the choice of theoretic reference framework will be narrowed down to the theoretic streams of new institutional economics.

Subsequently, the three major streams will be briefly depicted in section 3.2.2, before transaction cost theory as selected framework will be depicted in more detail. Thereby, its main components, terms and assumptions will be depicted to gain a deeper understanding regarding its explanatory power of why organizational interfaces are designed in a certain way and how this may affect the susceptibility to disruptions. Therewith, a reference framework for the design of interfaces is provided, which also gives starting points for the explanation of disruptions. However, as already noticed by Hill, Fehlbaum & Ulrich (1994), the design of organizational structures to define tasks and regulate behaviour is on a higher system level than actual task execution and behaviour of system members. Therefore, to link the interface design to the susceptibility of disruptions, an additional theoretic reference framework is required, which explains the behaviour of system members.

The selection of this reference framework is subject to section 3.2.3. As transaction cost theory as one reference framework has already been selected, the choice of a theory for the explanation of behaviour on the process level is determined by commensurability of assumptions, understanding of terms, and main components between the two theories. Therefore, descriptive decision theory is chosen as additional framework and will be described in this section.

In section 3.3, the interface structure as object of investigation will be concretized. Even though there exists a multitude of investigations on organizational design, they differ partly substantially in the use of terms and terminological systems. Furthermore, these terminological systems have not been applied to the structure of interfaces between companies. In consequence, based on the terminology presented in the management system by Remer (2004), the description of organizational structures will be adapted to the description of interface structures, to remain in a consistent framework and enhance the systematic description of interfaces.

Therefore, the purpose of section 3.3.1 is to provide a terminological foundation to describe organizational structures. On the one hand, the understanding of organizational structure and design in general, and of interface structure and design in particular has to be derived and brought into context, to identify relevant aspects for the purpose of this thesis. Based on this overview on concepts and definitions, in the following sections the terminology for the organizational structure is transferred and adapted to interfaces.

To facilitate the analysis and reduce its complexity, the description and specification of the two main components will be divided between section 3.3.2 and section 3.3.3. The already existing terminological system will be adapted and applied to interfaces, to allow for consistency between company-internal organizational structures and inter-organizational structures. Therewith, the development of redundant and non-transferrable terminological systems shall be avoided, to increase the assertiveness of terms requested by Chmielewicz (1979). Based on the developed methodology for describing and decomposing organizational structures, hypotheses can be derived on causal relations between shapes of organization and the occurrence of disruptions.

One of the main objectives of research is to offer explanations and prognoses based on theoretical statements (Chmielewicz 1979). Therefore, section 3.4 aims at the provision of such theoretical statements. As Schnell, Hill & Esser (2011) note, the majority of theories and terms used in social sciences is formulated in a relative unspecific way and need specification before empirical analyses can take place. Consequently, in section 3.4.1, first of all, the construct of interface structure will be concretized by narrowing down the scope of analysis to the components of special relevance in this context.

Next, in section 3.4.2, the connection between interface structure and susceptibility to disruptions will be developed. Therefore, hypotheses will be derived based on the assumptions of decision theory on behaviour of individuals in socio-technical systems. Thereby, disruptions as result of human error will be explained and hypotheses on causal relations between interface structure and disruptions developed.

The question, how the kind of partnership in a transaction may facilitate or prevent disruptions is addressed in section 3.4.3. Therewith, observations by previous research in other supply chain contexts or case studies will be taken into account and integrated to test these assumptions for their applicability and general validity.

According to Bortz & Döring (1995), theories in social sciences have a relative low degree of formalization, which reduces the transparency of assumed causal relations. However, they continue that by transforming these cause-and-effect relationships into formal models, such as e.g. path models or structural models, transparency can be increased and comprehensiveness enhanced. Therefore, the hitherto separated analyses of causal relations will be consolidated and transformed into one model of hypotheses in section 3.5.

To this purpose, in section 3.5.1, the hypotheses developed in section 3.4.2 and 3.4.3 will be connected, to finally establish causal relations between interface design and the susceptibility to disruptions. Therewith, not only the actual structure of interfaces and its effects are taken into account, but also the potential reasons for why a specific structure has been selected by supply chain partners.

In preparation of the model of hypotheses, section 3.5.2 presents the methodology applied and how the hitherto developed theoretical relations between the constructs can be integrated into such a model. Requirements will be depicted and their implications for the empirical design highlighted. Based on the already existing system of hypotheses, additional hypotheses are developed to complete the model.

Finally, in section 3.5.3, a structural equation model is developed, which includes all constructs and the causal relations between them. As the theoretic considerations also have implications for the design of the structural equation model (e.g. Backhaus et al. 2011; Diamantopoulos & Siguaw 2006; Bagozzi & Yi 2012) and the subsequent empirical analysis, these considerations will be discussed also in this section. In the end of section 3.5, the complete structural equation model on hypothesized causal relations between determinants of interface design, interface design and probability of disruptions will be presented.

As in section 2, this section closes in section 3.6 with an overview on outcomes of each section, to summarize the results.

3.2 Starting Points for Theoretical Explanations of Disruptions

3.2.1 Methodology and Overview on Theoretical Frameworks

A fundamental aim of this thesis is to analyse possible effects of design options of interfaces between actors on the susceptibility to disruptions. Therefore, a theoretic framework for design options has to be developed. In order to develop such a framework, an adequate theory, which provides starting points for the explanation of disruptions, has to be identified. However, after a cursory inspection of the literature, a disruption can be considered from different perspectives, which are not necessarily all identical regarding their explanatory background. Additionally, the resulting understandings of disruptions might tend to favour different theoretical approaches for the identification and explanation of potential causes of disruptions. Thus, an overview on theories and theoretic approaches will be given and their potential to serve as a theoretical framework for this thesis assessed.

A theoretic approach is hereby regarded as a preliminary step of a theory. According to authors such as Chmielewicz (1979), Hill, Fehlbaum & Ulrich (1994), Bea & Haas (2001) and Wolf (2008), the process of theory-building consists of basically the following steps: development of a terminological framework, the description, as well as the explanation of relationships between variables, and the prognosis and provision of recommendations for action. The reason why theoretic approaches are also included in the overview is that they might also inhibit explanatory power for the occurrence of disruptions. Nevertheless, in order to inhibit such explanatory power, they need at least to have passed the step of explaining relationships between variables (Schulenburg 2008).

For brevity, the terms theory and theoretic approaches are thus used interchangeably. However, since this thesis is concerned with organizational aspects of disruptions, technical, psychological, or other theoretical explanations[45] will not be considered in the following. Only if in the field of organizational theories no satisfactory explanation for the occurrence of disruptions can be found,[46] the search shall be extended.

However, already in the field of traditional organizational theories, many different approaches and streams exist. According to Scherer (2006), organization theory is concerned with many different problem areas related to organizations, for instance relationships between members of organizations and organizations themselves, relationships between structures and processes of organizations, or relations between different organizations. Depending on which relationships shall be investigated, different theories can therefore serve as a theoretical basis

---

45 Those could be for instance ecological interface design approaches (e.g. Rasmussen & Vicente 1989; Vicente & Rasmussen 1992; Vicente 2002), human error research (e.g. Reason 1997; Reason 1990; Dhillon 2007), fluid dynamics (e.g. Chen & Yao 1992; Batchelor 1999; Mobley 2000) or information theory (e.g. Shannon & Weaver 1976; Krippendorff 1986; Cover 1991).

46 Popper (1973) states that theories are the net which we throw out to explain real world phenomena and that research aims for the narrowing of meshes in the net (p. 31). In consequence, those theories are considered more closely, which already seem to incorporate meshes able to explain the phenomenon in question.

(Scherer 2006). Therefore, the explanatory power of theoretic approaches shall be assessed following a set of criteria derived from the understanding and dimensions of disruptions.

As a starting point, Schulenburg (2008, pp. 129–130) provides an overview on organizational theories, which were extracted out of a literature review of eighteen international textbooks and edited volumes on organizational theory. The theoretic approaches encountered in these books were listed according to the frequency of their citation to assess their degree of prevalence. For the consideration as theoretical framework of this thesis, the focus will be put on those organizational theories, which were described in at least one half of the publications. The assumption behind this decision is that theoretic approaches, which are recognized by more publications on organizational theories, are more mature as they are recognized by more authors. Consequently, it is assumed that their explanatory power is larger, their contributions and limitations better known, and that their applicability for empirical research better tested.[47] Therefore, a total of nine theories remain for further investigation. Of those, two approaches were identified to be more suitable to explain individual behaviour and human error,[48] wherefore they will be explained in more detail in section 3.2.3. The remaining organizational theories as presented by Schulenburg (2008) are:

- Scientific Management
- Bureaucracy Approach
- Systems Theory
- Contingency Approach
- Evolutionary Theory Approach
- New Institutionalism
- New Institutional Economics

Apart from the degree of maturity, several other quality criteria are required to assess the explanatory power of these theories in the context of this research. The first criterion is, as in the case of quality criteria for definitions, the usefulness of a theory to analyze the research question. In order to be considered for a deeper investigation, the theoretic approaches have therefore to be able to *explain the occurrence of disruptions* in supply chains, *based on* differences in the *organizational design*. In analogy to the dimensions of disruptions and with reference to the explanation there, the theory should therefore be able to provide explanations for disruptions *on the institutional, structural, and processual dimension*. Furthermore, for being eligible as theoretic foundation of this thesis, they have to be compatible to the *ontological*

47 At the same time, this approach might exclude theories with higher explanatory power for the phenomenon under study. Additionally, the number of publications citing a certain theory may have been a criterion for excluding or including theories in further publications, which might result in self fulfilling prophecies. However, as noted for example by Diekmann (2002), there is a trade-off between the increase in research quality and the efforts spent. Considering that in total nine theories will be scrutinized, the risk of ommitting crucial theoretic contributions seems to be relatively low.

48 Those theories are decision theory and the behavioural science approaches.

position of this thesis, hence the *critical rationalism*. Additionally, while the objective of innovation of statements can be neglected for the choice of a theoretic background, the criteria *information content* and *proximity to truth* as demanded by Popper (1973) and Chmielewicz (1979) for all statements in experiential science, can also be applied here. Therefore, the theories stated above will now be briefly depicted and their suitability assessed.

The **scientific management** approach seeks to identify the most efficient integration of humans and machines in the production system (Wolf 2008). For this purpose, operations are seen as transparent and controllable systems, with strong segmentation of horizontal and vertical labour. According to Taylor 1977, the segmentation of labour shall prevent errors stemming from the execution of diverse activities by one employee. Furthermore, if employees execute both, operational and managerial tasks, they could obscure their actual work performance. The underlying idea of man is grounded on the homo economicus, which is additionally unwilling to work, and has limited cognitive capacities (Wolf 2008, p. 91). Additionally, Taylor (1977) stresses the conflict of interests between managers and employees of companies, whose interests are rarely identical. Based on the scientific management approach, and following the definition of disruptions developed in 2.2.2, disruptions could occur when humans and machines are not adequately integrated so that planned and actual work performance deviate from each other. This would imply that operations would be organized in such a way, that worse outcomes could not be attributed to specific employees (i.e. lack of transparency), or that operations could not be measured or evaluated (i.e. lack of control), so that the tendency of employees to avoid work could not be curtailed. Another possibility would be a lack of segmentation of labour, which delegates tasks to employees, who lack the cognitive abilities to effect the tasks as required.

The role of management is also stressed in the **bureaucracy approach** by Weber & Winckelmann (1976). According to them, authority means the chance to receive obedience from a determined group of people for specific orders (Weber & Winckelmann 1976, p. 122). As a basis for authority, not only motivational and rational reasons are required, but also the belief in legitimacy. The bureaucratic model represents organizations therefore as rule-based operations, in which authority is legitimated by legal, impersonal and objective order. These rules are general in nature, relatively abstract, stable, exhausting and learnable (Weber 2005). Strict separations of competences and work tasks, as well as a strictly defined flow of information inside the organization form the basis of the bureaucratic organization (Wolf 2008, pp. 66–72). However, Weber & Winckelmann (1976) stress the description of an ideal type of organization. Furthermore, the bureaucracy approach mainly deals with how managers are elected and omits the consideration of the impacts on the performance. Therefore, this approach seems to lack the potential to explain disruptions caused by organizational design.

One theory, which lends itself to be used for the structural dimension is **systems theory**. Originally developed in the context of biological systems, it has been adapted and applied to economic settings. Von Bertalanffy (1972, p. 51) defines a system as "*a complex of interact-*

ing components together with the relationships among them that permit the identification of a boundary-maintaining entity or process". These components inhibit a hierarchical structure, whereby elements, sub-systems and the system as a whole possess certain characteristics and maintain certain kinds of relationships, which make the system distinguishable from other systems. At the same time, a continuous exchange of resources and knowledge with the systems environment, especially with stock- and stakeholders, takes place (Wolf 2008, pp. 157–165). A disruption from this perspective could be described as the lack of exchange of material or immaterial resources between the system and the environment, or between sub-systems, or elements. However, concrete causes for such a lack of exchange could not be identified, which contradicts the usefulness and information content requirements of this thesis. Therefore systems theory seems to have limited power to explain disruptions and is eliminated from further analysis.

According to Staehle (1999), the abstraction of system theory has resulted in a demand for more concrete suggestions for how to design organizations in practice. This has been prompted by the development of **contingency theory** (Staehle 1999, p. 48). With focus on empirical research, its purpose is to determine, which organizational structure is best suited for a certain organization, depending on the situation of the organization (Kieser & Walgenbach 2007, pp. 43–46). The assumption is thereby that there is no one best solution for all kinds of organizations, but that depending on factors like the environmental circumstances, the technology used, or the market of the company, different organizational structures might lead to optimal performance (Woodward 1975). In this context, organizational structure has been operationalized as the degrees of e.g. specialization, formalization, standardization, centralization, configuration, and flexibility (Pugh & Hickson 1979). According to contingency theory, a disruption could be described as a lack of "fit" of the organizational structure, and the characteristics of the organization and the environmental situation. However, since this lack depends on many contingent variables as described above, a more specific explanation of why disruptions occur is not possible. Furthermore, the falsification of hypotheses is not possible, as a lack of support could always be attributed to a circumstance of the situation, which has not been regarded. Therewith, contingency theory does not meet the requirements of the ontological position of this thesis and is therefore excluded.

A promising approach seems to be **evolutionary theory**. From this point of view, organizations are seen as self-changing, self-evolving and self-organizing systems, which are not completely controllable (Malik & Probst 1982). It includes the possibility of misbehaviour of the human being in its assumptions, thus does not follow the ideal of the homo economicus. Additionally, it differentiates between the genotype (the set of design dimensions) of an organization and its phenotype (the set of functions a system performs) (Foster & Hölzl 2004), considering therewith that organizations might be designed differently, depending on their functions. Furthermore, it assumes a limited set of possibilities, which are available to adapt the organization to the environmental constraints and highlights the importance of complexity, leading to sub-optimal development of the organization. This sub-optimal development is further fostered by the reluctance of managers to try new options, if approaches from the past were relatively successful, and are well embedded in the organization (Wolf 2008, pp. 370–381). However, as Wolf (2008) remarks, especially von Hayek (1983) stresses the trial-and-error nature of organizational development. From this perspective, a disruption could occur due to human misbehaviour, the mismatch between the system and its functions to be performed, and the path-dependent wrong adaptation of the organization to environmental changes. However, the importance of contingent factors again contradicts the ontological position of this thesis. Furthermore, the development by trial-and-error contradicts the research purpose, namely to identify how supply chain partners may design their interfaces in an optimal way. Finally, the translation of biological assumptions to organizations results in relatively abstract assumptions, wherefore the information content and proximity to truth are considered to be limited. Therefore, evolutionary theory is also excluded as theoretical foundation of this thesis.

The **new institutionalism** regards organizations as being formed by culture, norms, rules and regulations posed by other institutions on the organization. From this point of view, interests and ways of action of companies are predefined institutionally (Walgenbach & Meyer 2008). The perception of agents as rationally and autonomously deciding actors is hereby refused and is replaced by agents, which are reacting based on institutionalized rules and expectations. As organizations evolve and act in expectation-rich environments, where many stakeholders try to pursue their own interests, the structure of organizations trying to comply with these institutionalized expectations involves many externally induced elements (Scott 1987). In consequence, since the expectations are in general contradictory, the structure of organizations might include incompatible and conflicting elements (Kieser & Ebers 2006, pp. 356–359). For the role of the individual, these assumptions imply that on the one hand, it seeks to comply with the external expectations and that on the other hand, these expectations might by contradictory. Its decisions and actions in such situations are consequently dependent on the degree of institutionalization of different expectations, as well as the degree of internalization (Zucker 1977). From the new institutionalism perspective, disruptions might therefore be caused when organizations adopt conflicting institutional requirements. Depending on what is understood to be the objective of a process, the existence of a disruption could thus be depending on the point of view. However, this social constructivism perspective conflicts with the critical rationalism as stipulated by Popper (1973) and thus with the ontological position of this thesis. Therefore, new institutionalism will be discarded as explanatory theory for the purpose of this thesis.

New institutional economics approaches, as transaction costs theory, the principal-agent approach, or the property rights approach, could be starting points for an explanation of disruptions. By assuming imperfect markets and inefficiencies in the production of goods, these approaches differentiate themselves from the perfect market assumption of neoclassical theory.

A fundamental difference is that these approaches suppose that transfers of products and property rights between organizations generate transaction costs (Richter & Furubotn 2003). Furthermore, the human being is assumed to possess only bounded rationality and to follow its own plans, hence, being opportunistic (Kieser & Ebers 2006, p. 51). The resulting behaviour of a) a partner organization and/or b) the people involved in the execution of tasks is also dependent on whether non-compliant behaviour can be observed and penalized (Williamson 1979). By assuming imperfect markets and transaction costs, these approaches help to understand, why for complex and rare transactions, an organization-internal solution is favoured, whereas for standardized and frequent transactions, a market solution might be favourable. Wherever market transactions occur, the market, understood as a transaction regulating institution, shall secure the cost optimality of transactions and help to limit opportunistic behaviour (Held & Nutzinger 2006). Consequently, a disruption could occur on the one hand, because of the opportunistic behaviour of the partner company. This would be an explanation of disruptions at the process level. On the other hand, this opportunistic behaviour is only possible, if it cannot be controlled and penalized. Lack of transparency and means of repercussion in turn are due to inadequately designed institutions, which would be an explanation of disruptions from the institutional perspective. And finally, if there is no possibility to establish effective institutions to govern principal-agent relationships, companies should opt for hierarchical execution of tasks, implying a change in the supply chain structure to avoid disruptions.

The theoretic approaches illustrated above show many different starting points for an explanation of disruptions. According to Bortz & Döring (1995), the result of the regeneration of relevant theories for the context of research should be a tabular synopsis of central assumptions of the theories regarding the research question. Therefore,

Table 8 shows, how disruptions can be explained according to the assumptions of the considered theories.

Table 8: Potential causes of disruptions according to different theories

Theory	Institutional	Structural	Process-related
Scientific Management	--	Lack of horizontal and vertical segmentation of labour	--
Bureaucracy Approach	--	--	--
Systems Theory	--	--	Lack of exchange of resources
Contingency Theory	--	Lack of "fit" between the organizational structure and the environment	--
Evolutionary Theory	Institutionalized habits resulting in path-dependencies in decision making	Mismatch between organizational design and function	Human misbehaviour and bounded rationality
Neo Institutionalism	Amount and intensity of institutionalized expectations	Incompatibility of structural elements based on institutionalized expectations	Diverging and/or lacking internalization of institutionalized expectations
New Institutional Economics	Inadequately institutionalized rules	Wrong choice between hierarchical and outsourced execution	Non-compliant behaviour by partners and/or staff

The explanations of potential causes of disruptions provided by different theories as illustrated above do not claim for completeness. Rather, they may serve as starting points for analyzing disruptions from different perspectives, and to highlight different explanations in different contexts. Analyzing each theory in detail for explanations of disruptions would exceed the scope of this thesis and would result in a multitude of hypotheses and incommensurability. However, it becomes apparent that some theories seem to be more suitable than others to explain the susceptibility to disruptions in supply chains. Nevertheless, apart from the usefulness, they also have to comply with the other quality criteria, hence information content, proximity to truth and the ontological research position. Since evolutionary theory and neo intuitionalism were both excluded because of lacking conformance with these requirements, new institutional economics remains for further analysis. Thereby, it does not only provide explanations for disruptions for all three perspectives, but is also directly focussing on relationships between transaction partners, and provides detailed and concrete assumptions on how supply chain partners design their transactions. Therewith, it also matches the requirements regarding information content and proximity to truth, as well as the ontological position of this thesis. In consequence, in the following, the main streams of new institutional economics will be depicted in more detail, to select the theoretic foundation of this thesis.

3.2.2 Transaction Cost Theory as Overarching Framework

New Institutional Economics

The theoretic lines of new institutional economics began to emerge as an attempt to explain how institutions govern economic transactions. The driving questions were thereby: "*Which institutions inhibit for which kind of coordination problems in economic exchanges the relatively lowest costs and the highest efficiency? How do coordination problems, costs, and efficiency of exchange relationships affect the design and change of institutions?*" (Ebers & Gotsch 2006, p. 247). Since then, not one theory of new institutional economics has emerged, but rather three major lines of theoretic argumentation, namely property rights theory, transaction cost theory, and agency theory (Picot, Dietl & Furubotn 2008, p. 46; Wolf 2008, p 328; Ebers & Gotsch 2006). However, according to Wolf (2008, pp. 330–331), all three theoretic lines have some common basic characteristics. He summarizes these basic commonalities as:

- Institutions represent substitutes for imperfect markets.
- New institutional economics focus only on the economic efficiency of institutions, while other aspects like social efficiency are majorly ignored.
- As a consequence, the attempt is to use cost and utility measurements as the basis of analysis. Different institutional designs are therefore compared regarding marginal cost and utility differences.
- New institutional economics combines elements of microeconomics, business organisation theory, and jurisprudence in its attempt to provide an overarching explanation approach.

Furthermore, Wolf (2008, p. 332) identifies ten joint assumptions, namely:

- *Firstly*, the underlying cause of economic problems can be found in the scarcity of resources.[49]
- *Secondly*, individuals are free in their choices and form the basis of economic development (methodological individualism).
- *Thirdly*, actors intent to maximize their individual utility of economic activities.
- *Fourthly*, actors inhibit stable and consistent preferences, resulting in a stable utility function.
- *Fifthly*, there exists an imbalance regarding the distribution of information, knowledge, and skills, which shall be optimized by institutions in such a way that the overall profit is maximized. Economic actors intent to solve scarcity problems resulting from imbalances by specialization and exchange.
- *Sixthly*, during such exchange processes, friction losses occur, which worsen the problem of scarce resources.

---

49 According to Chmielewicz (1979), resource scarcity is one of the two basic problems that mark the object of research of economic sciences and that delineate it from other sciences. The other problem economic sciences intent to solve is profit maximization.

- *Seventhly*, due to exchanges and specialization, numerous interdependencies emerge, which have to be managed. These coordinative activities stand in the focus of the organizational problem.
- *Eighthly*, since the economic actors strive for utility maximization, exchange processes have to be governed by rules, which allow for the determination, purchase, sale, and execution of rights over goods.
- *Ninthly*, every analysis of economic activities has to start at the level of institutions, which are understood as a rule-based, relatively stable set of individual actors.
- *Tenthly*, said analysis has to take into consideration the prevalent information infrastructure, since the existence of information asymmetries is in institutional economics at the core of coordination problems (Wolf 2008).

Now that the major commonalities of the three theoretic lines have been depicted, the question arises, in which aspects they differ from one another. Significant differences can be found for instance in the characterization of individuals, institutions, as well as the focus of attention.[50]

Focus of Attention

Property rights theory for instance focuses on the reduction of not only economic costs of exchange, but also of social welfare costs (i.e. externalities) with the intention to increase overall utility of resource allocation and division of work (e.g. Furubotn & Pejovich 1972; Alchian & Demsetz 1972; Picot 1981). In transaction cost theory and agency theory in turn, social welfare costs are not explicitly considered. Rather, agency theory intents to reduce agency costs, which are the costs the principal faces for controlling the work done by the agent (e.g. Jensen & Meckling 1976; Fama 1980; Eisenhardt 1989). The focus of attention of transaction cost theory in turn lies on the comparison of alternative institutional arrangements (such as market vs. company) regarding production and transaction costs, including costs that occur after the transaction took place (e.g. Williamson 1979; Williamson 1981; Williamson 1991). Thus, whereas property rights theory is more concerned with macroeconomic costs, and agency theory focuses on control costs for transactions between different hierarchical levels, transaction cost theory intents to optimize the *sum* of costs occurred *during and after* transactions on mainly the same hierarchical level.

Institutions

As stated above, the major focus of new institutional economics is the efficient design of institutions to govern exchange relationships. However, every line of theory has a different focus regarding the type of institutions and exchange relationships to be explained and optimized. Here, property rights theory does not further specify different kinds of exchange relationships, apart from market or team production (Alchian & Demsetz 1972). Furthermore, the

[50] For a discussion of commonalities and differences of new institutional economics, see e.g. Picot, Dietl & Furubotn (2008, pp. 247–308); Wolf (2008, pp. 327–369); Ebers & Gotsch (2006).

role of official authorities, laws and state involvement as trade governing institutions is stressed (Furubotn & Pejovich 1972; Picot & Schneider 1988). In agency theory in turn, the major kind of institutions regarded are contracts, which structure and fix duties and compensations between a principal and an agent (Fama 1980; Eisenhardt 1989). According to Williamson (1979, p. 235), in transaction cost theory, institutions are frameworks "*within which the integrity of a transaction is decided. Markets and hierarchies are two of the main alternatives.*" Thus, in this context institutions may take many forms, depending on the kind of transactions possible.

Individuals

In property rights theory, the individual basically seeks to maximize its utility under constraints. However, as can be seen in major contributions to the theory, apart from utility maximization behaviour, little else is said about characteristics of the individual (e.g. Alchian 1965; Picot 1981; Hart & Moore 1990). As de Alessi (1987, p. 25) puts it: "*The ability of individuals to satisfy their wants is limited by the quantity of resources available, their allocation, their productivity, and the system of property rights.*" Similarly, Furubotn & Pejovich (1972, p. 1138) explicitly states that: "*significantly, each decision maker is assumed to be motivated by self-interest and to move efficiently toward the most preferred operating position open*" and adds "*the behavio*[u; A/N]*r of the firm (or other organization) is not interpreted in terms of the 'satisficing' hypothesis that has been advanced by some authors [...]*".

In contrast, agency theory and transaction cost theory make further assumptions regarding the characteristics of the individual. Two common points are the assumption of opportunistic behaviour, and of bounded rationality[51] of the individual (e.g. Williamson 1979; Teece 1984; Eisenhardt 1989). According to Williamson (2010, p. 678), bounded rationality is when human actors "*are neither hyperrational nor irrational but are attempting effectively to cope with complex contracts that are incomplete.*" Apart from these characteristics, agency theory further considers risk aversion of individuals, which can vary from person to person (Eisenhardt 1989). Thus, regarding the description of the individual, agency theory draws a more detailed picture than transaction cost theory, and both regard the individual more specifically than property rights theory.

Comparing the three lines of theory, it becomes apparent that property rights theory is more applied in a macroeconomic context, where the individual plays a less important role. As Wolf (2008, p. 340) puts it, the consideration of utility maximization as only assumption on the behaviour of individuals, leads to model Platonism, which would contradict the requirement of falsifyability as stipulated by Popper (1973). Since for the coordination and communication at interfaces, the individual plays an important role in this thesis, a more detailed view on its characteristics is required. Furthermore, in property rights theory, the purpose is to

51 For a discussion of the assumption of rationality and its implications for the existence of institutions see e.g. North (1993).

reduce the sum of transaction, as well as social costs of exchanges (Picot, Dietl & Furubotn 2008, p. 142), which is not at the focus of interest here. Additionally, the focus on optimizing a given utility function under a given organizational structure (Furubotn & Pejovich 1972) reduces considerably the complexity of regarded phenomena and therewith seems to reduce the information content and proximity to realistic assumptions on such complex phenomena as disruptions. Therefore, property rights theory is discarded as theoretic foundation of this thesis.

Regarding falsifyability of hypotheses on individual behaviour, agency theory has a slight advantage compared to transaction cost theory, since one further assumption (i.e. risk aversion) is made. Nevertheless, agency theory mainly regards hierarchical relationships, which exists for example between employer and employee or between a manufacturing company and a logistics service provider hired by the company. Even though these relationships also play a role in supply chains, the focus may be too narrow for the purpose of this thesis, since the major interest lies on interfaces between companies, where in general horizontal relationships are the focus of analysis (Frese, Graumann & Theuvsen 2012). Furthermore, agency theory argues that agency costs emerge due to quality characteristics of the service to be performed, which are not observable for the principal (Picot, Dietl & Furubotn 2008, p. 142). However, thereby deviations from process plans are explained to be by purpose, which is not the major focus in the context of disruptions due to unexpected events. Therefore agency theory will not be used as theoretical foundation for this research.

Compared to the other two lines of new institutional economics, transaction cost theory has been widely applied in empirical research, as well as in various different contexts.[52] Fields of application are for example the explanation of outsourcing activities, the choice of internationalization strategies, and forms of organizational cooperation (Wolf 2008, pp. 351–352). Additionally, transaction cost theory has been already used in the context of supply chain management, and even in food supply chain management to explain the governance structures of transactions between supply chain partners (e.g. Hobbs 1996; Loader 1997; Banterle & Stranieri 2008). Therefore, the assumptions of transaction cost theory seem to be provide a thorough basis to explain how the organizational design of interfaces between companies affects the occurrence of supply chain disruptions.

According to Williamson (1981, p. 552), a transaction occurs when "*a good or service is transferred across a technologically separable interface. One stage of activity terminates and another begins. With a well-working interface, as with a well-working machine, this transition occurs smoothly. In mechanical systems, we look for frictions [...]. The economic counterpart of friction is transaction cost: do the parties to the exchange operate harmoniously, or are there frequent misunderstandings and conflicts that lead to delays, breakdowns, and other malfunctions?*" Three points are especially noticeable about this observation. Firstly, the reference to mechanics, which has in 2.2.1 been identified as probable source of the term "cold chain rupture" and where ruptures are an important topic. Secondly, the notion of interfaces, which is also the primary focus in this thesis. And thirdly, the transfer of the concept of frictions in mechanics to transaction costs in economics. In sum, these observations further support the choice of transaction cost theory as a theoretic basis for this thesis, since the focus of attention is similar.

Transaction Cost Theory

The origin of transaction cost theory can be traced back to Coase (1937), who noticed that under the assumptions of perfect markets, where production factors are allocated at zero costs by the market mechanisms, no firms would be required. He argues that if the market's price mechanism is not used, the reason must lie in some kind of costs associated with the use of this mechanism, which results in favourable production costs of company-internal prodcution. These costs are related for instance to the identification of the market price (i.e. search costs), or the negotiation and finalization of contracts for transactions.

Williamson (1979, p. 234) summarizes the basic assumptions which find consensus as follows: "*(1) opportunism is a central concept in the study of transaction costs; (2) opportunism is especially important for economic activity that involves transaction-specific investments in human and physical capital; (3) the efficient processing of information is an important and related concept; and (4) the assessment of transaction costs is a comparative institutional undertaking.*" He understands opportunism thereby as "*a variety of self-interest seeking but extends simple self-interest seeking to include self-interest seeking with guile. It is not necessary that all agents be regarded as opportunistic in identical degree. It suffices that those who are less opportunistic than others are difficult to ascertain ex ante and that, even among the less opportunistic, most have their price*" (p. 234). With the notion of efficient information processing and the difficulty to ascertain ex ante whether an agent behaves opportunistically, he refers to the costs mentioned by Coase (1937) which precede a transaction. For the characterization of transactions, Williamson (1979, p. 239) suggests therefore to assess a transaction regarding "*(1) uncertainty, (2) the frequency with which transactions recur, and (3) the degree to which durable transaction-specific investments are incurred*". He further specifies different frequencies into being either once, occasional, and recurrent, whereas investments are specified as being non-specific, mixed, or idiosyncratic.

Uncertainty

According to Williamson (1981) the monitoring costs of a transaction are especially high, when significant transaction-related uncertainty exists, the transaction occurs for the first time, and/or requires considerable investments in physical as well as human assets. Uncertainty

---

[52] For an overview on empirical investigations based on transaction cost theory, see e.g. Shelanski & Klein (1995) and David & Han (2004).

firstly can refer to the unknown outcome of a transaction regarding product performance or costs of production (Williamson 1971), hence referring to production uncertainty. This is frequently the case for complex or innovative products, where not every production stage and its costs can be determined in advance. Uncertainty secondly can be understood as uncertainty regarding the behaviour of the partner (Williamson 1990), hence as behaviour uncertainty. The degree of uncertainty may thereby vary for different groups of partners, especially if international transactions are considered, which may vary not only regarding the governance structure of transactions, but also regarding polity, judiciary, bureaucracy, and cultural institutions (Williamson 2008). However, how this will affect a transaction is dependent on contingent variables and details of the contract and may not be determined in advance. Consequently, Williamson (1990) highlights the importance of establishing a monitoring and control system to govern transaction relationships.

Frequency

The establishment of such monitoring and control systems induces additional costs associated with the specific transaction. One can thereby broadly differentiate transaction costs into ex-ante costs, which involve all costs incurred before closing a contract, such as search costs and initiation costs, and ex-post costs for all costs incurred after contract closing, such as control costs and insurance costs (Wolf 2005). So, apart from the costs for investments in transaction-related assets, further investments in the institutional conditions of the transaction might be necessary. Therefore, transactions which occur more frequently reduce the costs of preparing, monitoring and control of every single transaction, since the once established system can be reused, and ex-ante costs reduced. Furthermore, frequency of transactions also encourages the building of a common language at interfaces and mutual trust, which reduces the probability of opportunistic behaviour (Williamson 1979). Therewith, behavioural uncertainty can be reduced as well as errors due to cultural barriers or misunderstandings.

Specificity

A transaction is called idiosyncratic, when the specific identity of both parties is crucial for the costs of the transaction. According to Williamson (1981), asset specificity plays a crucial role for the level of transaction costs and may occur in the form of site specificity, physical asset specificity, as well as human asset specificity.

Transactions which are based on investments into lasting, transaction-specific goods result in the dependence on the partner and increase the trade-off risk associated with a defection of the partner on the agreed-upon contract (Williamson 1990). In such a case, both parties are locked-into the transaction, since alternatives would lead to the incurrence of high change costs (Williamson 1979; Williamson 1981). Williamson (1990) differentiates costs into fixed and variable parts, as well as completely contract-specific and unspecific parts.

Which kind of governance and control of production and transaction activities *inside* one organization is favourable depends in turn basically on the specificity of human assets. Williamson (1981) suggests that the specificity of human assets, and therewith the dependency on these specific employees can be measured along two dimensions, namely the degree to which human assets are firm-specific and the difficulty of metering productivity. If both dimensions are low, than governance can also be low, and can be organized as an "*internal spot market*" (Williamson 1981, p. 564). If human asset specificity is low, but metering is difficult, employees can be easily replaced, but their individual contribution to the overall outcome cannot be measured, which impedes performance-based compensation. This is what Williamson (1981, p. 565) terms "*primitive team*". As "*obligational market*", he terms the situation where firm-specific learning is high, in either idiosyncratic technological experience or idiosyncratic organizational experience, and where the output can be metered easily. In such an organization, governance structures should be focused on rewarding employees for their specific performance and on discouraging employees from quitting. Finally, in a "*relational team*" (Williamson 1981, p. 565), human asset specificity is high, but metering is difficult. Firms will try to instil its social values and goals in its employees, while providing generous compensations to discourage job change.

This is also consistent with the kind of contracts, transaction cost theory focuses on, which are namely relational contracts (i.e. incomplete contracts) in contrast to property rights theory, which attempts to deal with complete contracts (Wolf 2008, p. 342). Thus, depending on the frequency, as well as the uncertainty and specificity of a transaction, different kinds of organization of transactions might be advantageous, ranging between spot-market transactions via bilateral contractual safeguards to company-internal production (Williamson 2002).

As can be seen, transaction cost theory offers a number of starting points for the purpose of this thesis. First of all, it allows for a differentiation and explanation of different kinds of organizational designs of interfaces based on different governance structures established by the partners. Secondly, transaction cost theory regards transactions from different perspectives, involving macro-level explanations as well as micro-level explanations for frictions and performance losses during transactions (Wolf 2008, pp 352–353). Therewith, the deduction of hypotheses is not limited to one level, but may be enriched by considering different levels.

Nevertheless, transaction cost theory also has some disadvantages. According to Wolf (2008), it assumes equal yields for all kinds of alternative organizational designs of transactions, as only costs are changing and lead to differences in performance. However, in the context of this thesis, this assumption seems to be negligible since here, all other things remaining equal, the susceptibility of supply chains to disruptions shall be investigated, which can be interpreted as costs, such as higher costs for insurance, quality control, or sourcing.

Another aspect, which seems to be more relevant for the purpose of this thesis, is that transaction cost theory is on the one hand able to explain disruptions caused by the actions of humans by assuming bounded rationality and opportunistic behaviour. However, on the other hand, the prevalence of bounded rationality and opportunism is not *explained*, but only *assumed*. This would imply that every human being would increase the susceptibility of supply chains to disruptions to the same extent, as no other determinants of human behaviour would explain different degrees of rationality and opportunism. This one-sided and simplistic picture of the individual does not seem to sufficiently reflect the influences of individuals in food supply chains (see e.g. section 2.5.3) and has been already criticized in the literature (see e.g. Heide & John 1992). Even Williamson (1979) acknowledges that human beings might be opportunistic to a different extent, but does not explain, how these differences can be reasoned. Furthermore, as for example stressed by Staehle (1999, p. 518), a goal-effective design of managerial processes requires the description and explanation of human behaviour in organizations, wherefore the integration of insights of social sciences into business management becomes an essential requirement.

Since the human being, its behaviour and decisions play a significant role in explaining disruptions, it seems therefore necessary to amend the theoretical framework of this thesis with a theory being able to explain the decision making of individuals.[53]

3.2.3 Theoretic Foundations for Explaining Human Behaviour

As has been shown in section 2.5.3, a comparatively high number of observations on food supply chain disruptions identified employees as a cause for inferior performance. However, no further distinction was possible to assess whether human error was caused by misbehaviour of the individual, or by misspecification of the tasks. According to Frese, Graumann & Theuvsen (2012), the structure of the interface determines thereby how interaction between individuals of different units shall take place. Hence, in order to identify whether the interface structure affects the susceptibility of supply chains to disruptions, the influence of structuring tasks in the operative processes on the decision making by employees needs to be elaborated in more detail. To this purpose,

Figure 16 provides a generic model to describe the process of individual decision making.[54]

[53] According to Chmielewicz (1979), economic theory and decision theory are two not identical, but overlapping scientific fields, which compose the basis for economic technology.

[54] These factors do not ask for completeness, but illustrate the range of aspects to consider. For a similar understanding see e.g. March & Simon (1958 pp. 139-140), Hill, Fehlbaum & Ulrich (1994 p. 58), or Newell & Simon (1976 p. 411).

Figure 16: Schematic framework of decision making and execution of tasks

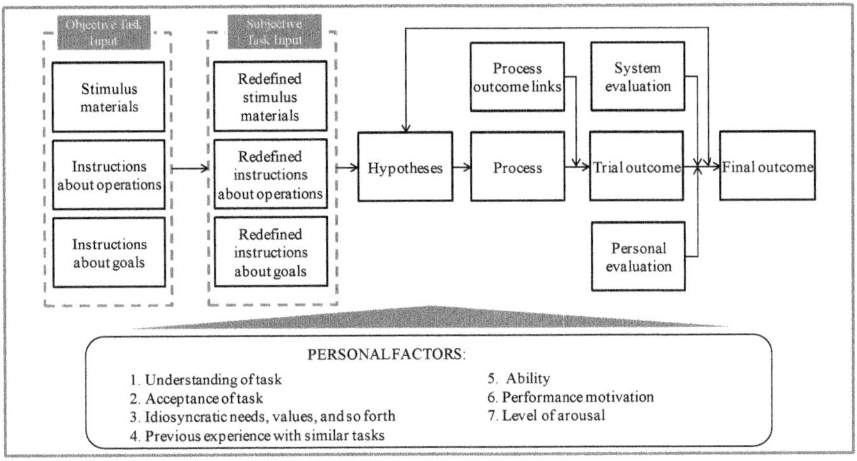

Source 10: own illustration; based on Hackman (1970)

According to Hackman (1970), the above illustrated framework is not intended to be a formal model of the mental task processing of individuals, but rather shall serve as a descriptive guideline for better understanding factors that are relevant in task performance. The box to the left represents the coded task which is given to an individual. In order to translate the included information in a form which the individual is able to process, the task is re-coded by the individual. The way in which the redefinition takes place is thereby dependent on some individual factors, which are illustrated in the box below. However, it should be noted that there are also some interdependencies between the presentation of the task and personal factors. If for instance an order document is written in Chinese, the ability of the individual to perform the task might not be relevant in the first place, but its ability to read in Chinese.

The interdependence between personal factors and the redefinition process is also highlighted by Hackman (1970), who states that in case the individual does not understand the task properly, the role of previous experiences with similar tasks will likely play a more important role in the redefinition of the task. After redefinition, the individual makes some hypotheses on how to execute the tasks in such a way that the desired outcomes are achieved, before it starts with the execution (i.e. the process). Its performance may thereby depend on its level of arousal, which can be at least partly influenced by the way the task is presented (Luthans 2005). Finally, either the final outcome is directly realized and is evaluated by the individual as well as by the surrounding system, or a trial outcome can be first evaluated to correct the process if necessary. By the end of this chain of activities, either the objective has been achieved, or an error has occurred during task re-specification or execution. Thereby, an error can be understood according to Reason (1990, p. 5) as follows:

Error is a generic term to encompass all those occasions in which a planned sequence of mental or physical activities fails to achieve its intended outcome, and when these failures cannot be attributed to the intervention of some chance agency

Thus, considering that at interfaces several individuals interact with each other, which might have different backgrounds and personal skills, the question arises firstly, how to explain their decision making in general so that causal relations between the instructions and resulting errors can be systematically derived. Secondly, the question arises how to present the tasks to achieve an optimal inter-subjective redefinition by individuals belonging to different companies and which interact in a specific transaction. Therefore, firstly a theoretic background for individual decision making is required, before secondly the way of presenting instructions can be reasoned based on the consideration of transaction specific criteria. In this context however, apart from assessing the quality criteria as stipulated in section 3.2.1, an additional requirement is that the theory is consistent with the assumptions from transaction cost theory, to avoid incommensurability.

To describe and explain the behaviour of individuals in a working environment, a range of theories from sociology, psychology, but also economic theories exist, as will be shown in the following. Stemming from sociology, **interaction theory** for instance assumes that during interactions, both agents influence each other reciprocally regarding their expectations and actions (Homans & Merton 1961; Gruner & Homans 1978). The structure of interactions only changes with the durability of interaction and may become asymmetrically based on e.g. differences in qualifications (Macharzina 1977). Individuals could thus commit errors, because the structure of interaction has changed while the requirements posed by the organization remain the same or because their qualifications do not longer match the interaction context. However, the rich context and reciprocal influence make an empirical testing difficult (Wolf 2008, p. 228). Furthermore, the unit of analysis is the interaction of individuals, not the single individual. Therewith, decision making could only be explained with reference to the interaction partner, but not based on the instructions received. In consequence, this theory does not seem to fit the requirements named in section 3.2.1.

In psychology, the study of human errors has received a lot of attention (e.g. Reason 1990; Rasmussen & Vicente 1989; Reason 2000; Thomas & Petersen 2003; Thomeczek & Ollenschläger 2006). Based on limited cognitive capacities, pattern recognition and framing, individuals only take a limited amount of information into account during their decision making. Different levels of action regulation can thereby be identified, ranging from conscious to unconscious attention to the activity at hand, whereby the level of attention depends on the task at hand (Hofmann & Frese 2011). Especially routines, but also exceptional events foster the lack of adapting their decision making behaviour, which may lead to failure and catastrophes. In supply chains, where individuals in the processes frequently effect routine actions, a slight change of situation might thus not be considered due to pre-selecting information or apparently obvious solutions. However, before considering theoretic approaches to explain decision making of individuals from other disciplines, theoretic approaches from economic theory shall be investigated first. Thereby, those focussing on rational behaviour can be already excluded due to the conflict in assumptions with transaction cost theory.

In the behavioural sciences, several approaches are grouped which put the human behaviour in the process into focus (Staehle 1999, p. 37). To be named here are for example the human relations approach, and the motivation theoretic approaches (Schulte-Zurhausen 2010, pp. 13–18). In the **human relations approach**, the so-called Hawthorne experiments showed that the performance of workers in the production process is based on their satisfaction concerning their work environment (Roethlisberger & Dickson 1961). This work environment is thereby majorly determined by group dynamics, individual needs, and other social aspects. Organizational conflicts and weak points are hereby understood as being caused by lacking or inadequate social relations (Mayo 1977). Thus, from this perspective, a disruption would be explained by a lack of social appreciation or a bad working climate, which would lead to dissatisfaction of the human being and consequential insufficient execution of tasks in the process. **Motivation-based approaches** follow this idea by focusing on the needs of humans and their consequential behaviour in organizations. Important factors are a match between the tasks to be done and the abilities of the worker, as well as an adequate compensation (e.g. time and money) for their work (e.g. Schreyögg 1999, pp. 213–226; Schulte-Zurhausen 2010, pp. 13–18). An important aspect is thereby, according to the ideas of Maslow 1978 or Herzberg, Mausner & Snyderman (1959) that the reward matches the needs of the individual, so that adequate incentives are set for the individual to execute the tasks at hand. For the occurrence of disruptions, this would imply that either the activities do not match the abilities of the employees, or that employees do not perceive the set incentives to be adequate for performing the tasks. Even though in both cases, some of the causes of disruptions named for food supply chains are considered (see section 2.5.3), the focus on a general inability or dissatisfaction seems to limit the scope of analysis, considering that the majority of disruptions occur at interfaces, which seem to pose additional challenges not adequately explained. Hence, the theoretic basis should be able to explain errors by some more mechanisms influencing the decision making process.

One branch of theory specifically focusing on decision making in organizations is **decision-theory** (e.g. Wolf 2008, pp. 123–155; Scherm & Pietsch 2007, pp. 23–34). The purpose of descriptive decision theory is to explain regularities in decision making processes occurring in the real world, without assuming rational behaviour (Wolf 2005). In contrast to normative decision theory, which attempts to derive how an individual *should* decide, descriptive decision theory[55] bases its assumptions on **bounded rationality** of actors (Staehle 1999, p. 520).

It understands organizations as a set of managerial decisions, which have to be taken under consideration of a variety of alternatives in complex situations. The decision maker is thereby characterized as being rationally-bounded, since his cognitive capacities to process and evaluate information are limited. This limitation restricts the decision making even more, the more complex a situation is. Additionally, the assumption of optimal solutions seeking individuals is repealed and replaced by individuals trying to find solutions, which are satisfying a certain requirements level (March & Simon 1958; Simon 1959). This may also lead to the situation that for repetitive decisions in similar contexts, the same decisions are taken, which were satisfying in the past, but which are not necessarily optimal in the current situation.

Its origin can be traced back to the works of Herbert A. Simon, who attempted to refine the simplistic assumptions of normative decision theory (Wolf 2008, p. 235).[56] He argues that the assumption of classical theory of rational actors have to be replaced, if one considers situations, which involve decision making under **uncertainty, goal conflict**, and **imperfect competition** of companies, e.g. due to interdependencies (Simon 1959; Simon 1979). Furthermore, he assumes that with increasing **complexity** of the situation, the ability of the individual to take all relevant information into account will be reduced, as **cognitive capacities** are **limited** (Simon 1978b; Simon 1978a).

Additionally, decision theory refutes the assumption of maximizing behaviour of individuals. In consideration of complex situations with information in abundance, it places a cost on **information seeking**, wherefore individuals stop the search for more information as soon as a satisfying solution becomes visible. Thus, instead of maximizing, individuals are regarded as being **satisficing** (Simon 1979). If the performance resulting from a decision does not yield the level of aspiration, new information seeking processes are induced, while at the same time, the **aspiration level** begins to **adjust** (Simon 1959). Hence, whereas cognitive capacities are regarded as being limited, there are **learning processes** involved in the decision making of individuals (Simon 1978b).

From this perspective, disruptions could occur due to wrong decisions, taken because of a lack of cognitive capacity, a more complex situation, a low aspiration level of the decision maker, or the interpretation of a situation according to an inadequate contextual pattern. Considering the hitherto lacking ability to explain theoretically why errors are committed by individuals, decision theory seems to be a suitable amendment. Furthermore, its basic assumptions do not contradict those of transaction cost theory, hence regarding bounded rationality, imperfect competition, goal conflict and uncertainty. Even more, Williamson (2002, p. 173) explicitly connects the two approaches, in order to "*describe the human actor in more realistic terms*".

With the identification of theoretic foundations, it is now possible to derive hypotheses on the link between organizational design and disruptions. However, before deriving hypotheses, the

---

55 Since the following paragraphs only deal with descriptive decision theory, the term decision theory is used for brevity.

56 Other advancements are e.g. the Garbage Can Model (see e.g. Cohen, March & Olsen 1972; Kingdon 1995), or cognitive dissonance theory (see e.g. Festinger 1962; Aronson 1969).

interface structure needs further specification, to identify different elements, which can be used as starting points for the development of hypotheses. Therefore, in the following, interfaces will be defined and decomposed, to allow for a deduction and operationalization of hypotheses.

3.3 Description of Interfaces in Supply Chains

3.3.1 General Framework for the Description of Organizational Structures

The basic assumption developed in section 2.5.3 is that in food supply chains, many disruptions occur because the execution of tasks does not yield the expected outcome, which in turn is caused by inappropriate organizational structures. From the point of view of organizational theory, organizational structures are the instruments to cause a desired behaviour of employees with the objective to achieve organizational goals (Hill, Fehlbaum & Ulrich 1994; Staehle 1999; Frese, Graumann & Theuvsen 2012). March & Simon 1958 for instance notice that external and unforeseen events may require the individual to react even though it is executing its tasks, which leads to an allocation problem of cognitive and/or physical resources. The organizational design has thereby the function to structure the surrounding conditions in such a way that the preconditions for optimal decision making to achieve the organizational goals are given (Gross 1953). This point of view is also highlighted by Normal Accident Theory (NAT), which assumes that the configuration of a system may foster the emergence of errors, as well as the combination of their effects, which may lead up to catastrophes (Perrow 2006). In order to analyze potential effects of organizational configurations however, organizational structure has to be decomposed in its basic components, to analyze their potential effects on human behaviour.

The understanding of organizational structure as well as its components is thereby rather fragmented in the literature. Aiken, Bacharach & French (1980, p. 634) for instance state that "*organizational structures refer to those objective properties of organizations per se that cannot be reduced to or deduced from properties of the organization's members*". This implies that organizations exist independently from their members, which for instance is also the regulatory understanding of organizations. However, while this understanding focuses on the institutional perspective, many others have a more instrumental understanding of organizational structure.

March & Simon (1958) for instance understand organizational structure as the division of members of an organization into several hierarchical levels, whereas Hage, Aiken & Marrett (1971) further specify the division by stating that organizational structure includes vertical and horizontal differentiation of power and programs. Hereby, the purpose of organizational structure is put into focus, thus the intentional design of organizations to achieve organizational goals (Hill, Fehlbaum & Ulrich 1994).

Mintzberg (1980, p. 324) in turn focuses on the one hand only on the division of labour, but on the other hand includes the coordination of divided work by stating "*organization structur-*

ing focuses on the division of labo[u]*r of an organizational mission into a number of distinct tasks, and then the coordination of all of these tasks to accomplish that mission in a unified way*". A similar understanding can be also found in Stoner, Freeman & Gilbert 1996 and Hall (2002). As the definitions indicate, organizational structure has a crucial task to fulfil before organizations can start pursuing their goals. At the same time, this task is challenging, as a balance has to be found between dividing work and connecting it again in such a way that the goals can be optimally achieved. Thereby, according to the understanding by Mintzberg (1980), the more the work is split into distinct tasks, the more tasks have to be coordinated to accomplish the mission.

However, the understandings of elements of organizational structure are not similar in every case, but differ partly considerably. As Mintzberg (1980), Oliveira (2012) postulates that basic elements of organizational structure are differentiation and integration, whereas Hage, Aiken & Marrett (1971) name complexity, centralization and formalization as elements. Therewith partly identical elements are addressed, yet with different terms. For example, complexity of occupations (i.e. "*their sheer number*" Hage, Aiken & Marrett 1971, p. 863) is what Oliveira (2012) refers to as differentiation, thus the division of labour into distinct positions, for instance by departmentalization and the creation of different management layers. Here, even though different terms are used, the basic idea is the same. As already stressed in section 2, using different terms for the same research object imperils the comprehensiveness of research results and may also reduce the transferability of research results (Kromrey 2009).

Integration in turn is understood by Oliveira (2012, p. 11) as being responsible for "*uniting efforts or for maintaining interactions among parts toward accomplishment of organizational objectives or structural functions*". This is what is also understood by Mintzberg (1980) as coordination. However, in the concept of Hage, Aiken & Marrett (1971), coordination is *influenced* by complexity, centralization and formalization, thus it is on a different layer of analysis. Therewith, using these understandings in empirical research would result in substantially different research designs and results, wherefore caution must be taken when choosing the concept to be used.

A recent exemplary overview on elements of organizational structure found in the literature has been conducted by Cordes-Berszinn (2013), who identified more than 30 partly substantially diverging conceptualizations of variables of organizational structure. This diversity highlights the importance of using one overarching framework of variables, to assure at least internal consistency and a holistic description of organizational structures. Furthermore, as the focus of research lies on interfaces, this framework has to be generic in the sense that it can be expanded and adapted to interfaces. In order to assess the applicability of such frameworks, first of all, the understanding of interfaces needs further refinement.

The question how interfaces are designed refers thereby to the instrumental understanding of organization, which can be understood as e.g. "*the entirety of measures taken to achieve purposes and aims, with which a social system is structured, and with which activities of the peo-*

ple pertaining to this system, the use of input factors, and the processing of information is structured" (Hill, Fehlbaum & Ulrich 1994, p. 17). Hence, organizational design is the *action* taken, whereas organizational structure is the *outcome* of this action. Following this understanding of organization, Remer (1989) highlights the difference between organization and planning, which is also important in the context of this thesis. According to him, the main difference between organizational structure and process planning is that the planned events are still a floating, undifferentiated sequence, which has to be decomposed (i.e. structured) with respect to its mediums (i.e. people or tangible means) into different roles. The importance of this distinction is also highlighted by Aiken, Bacharach & French (1980, p. 634) who state that "*the failure to distinguish between structures and processes and the consequent treatment of the latter as properties of the organization per se has resulted ,methodologically, in* [...] *highly misleading empirical results*". Hence, based on the understanding of organizational structure by Remer (1989) and Remer (2005), Cordes-Berszinn (2013, p. 112) defined organizational structure as follows:

Organisational structure is a system of regulations aiming to steer the behaviour of the members of an organisation

This understanding of organizational structure is thereby broader than for instance the one by Perrow (1967), who understands it as the form of interaction between individuals involved in a process of changing materials. However, even though interaction is a major point for the analysis of interfaces, the broader definition of organizational structure seems to be more appropriate here, to avoid a reduction of the focus on interactions, before interfaces have been described in their entirety.

According to Röder (2001), realizing complex tasks in labour-divided processes results in interdependencies and relationships between the different groups involved in the process. By dividing processes in functional fields, interfaces are generated between these fields (Brockhoff 1989). In order to achieve the overall goal, the fulfilment of these sub-divided tasks has to be coordinated across these interfaces (Röder 2001). Thereby, interfaces are part of the organizational structure, across which processes have to be coordinated.

Following this understanding, according to Beckmann & Specht (1996, p. 406), interfaces can be defined as follows:

Interfaces are transition and connection points, between relatively autonomous organizational entities, which access joint resources, and/or handle connected processes based on division of labour[57]

That organizational entities are only relatively autonomous implies that they do not necessarily belong to the same company, but that also supply chain partners, who are dependent on

[57] For similar understandings, see e.g. Lawrence & Lorsch (1967); Brown (1983); Brockhoff (1989); Röder (2001); Weinkauf et al. (2005).

suppliers and customers, can be considered. At the same time, this definition can also encompass different departments or locations of the same company. This is also stressed by Brown (1983, p. 1), who states that these entities (or social units) "*may be groups, departments, or whole organizations, and their contact may be recurrent and well-established or fleeting and episodic*". Thus, interfaces do not only exist in companies, but also on the supply chain level, and interactions may have different patterns of frequency. However, in the following, only interfaces between companies, hence inter-organizational structures, will be regarded.

Nevertheless, as for instance Riechey (2008) notes, conflicts at interfaces may be more profound between different organizations than within departments of the same organization, as a higher hierarchical entity, which might resolve the conflict, is lacking. This is also supported by e.g. Brown (1983), who states that at interfaces conflicts emerge as parties with diverging and common interests, as well as compatible and incompatible behaviour come together. Frese, Graumann & Theuvsen (2012) explain such conflicts with interdependent decision areas, whereby interdependencies either emerge due to sequential links of the planning of realization processes by entities, or due to overlapping decision areas. Considering that at interfaces, realization processes between entities are linked by exchanges, and that each entity also has to plan parallel exchange processes for optimal capacity and resource utilization, both causes of conflicts seem to exist.

Additionally, with the lack of a common hierarchical entity at interfaces, also the ability to control the output of employees is reduced. As Kieser & Walgenbach (2007) observe, with more autonomy in the execution of complex tasks, the identification and unambiguous attribution of errors to the responsible person becomes more difficult. However, another explanation for increased susceptibility of interfaces to disruptions is that the instruments to guide and control employees are inadequate, as shared norms and rules are lacking (Kieser & Walgenbach 2007). Nevertheless, also inter-organizational interfaces incorporate an organizational structure (Trist 1977), even though they are considered as given (Frese, Graumann & Theuvsen 2012). This view is illustrated in Figure 17.

Figure 17: Understanding of interfaces in supply chains

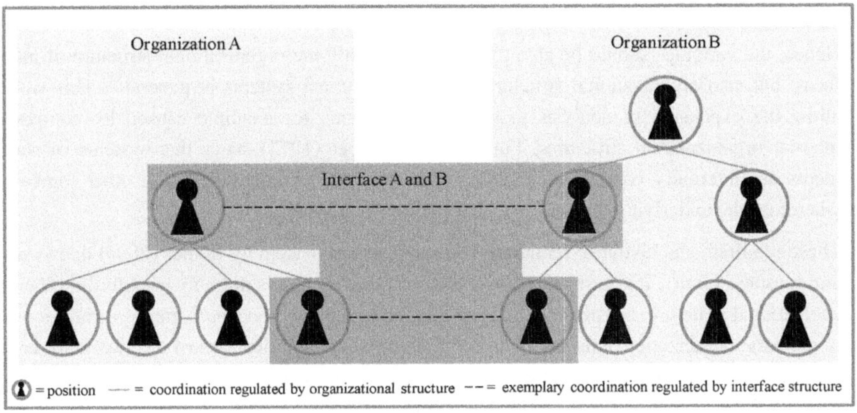

As can be seen, Figure 17 shows two organizations with different structures and one common interface. Since positions in organization A and B do not share one common superior, the focus is on horizontal coordination instead of horizontal and vertical coordination. According to this understanding the organizational structure of the interface between supply chain partners determines how connected processes between organizations are realized. Since the people and machines involved in these processes belong to different companies, this structure has thereby to be agreed upon by relatively autonomous organizational entities (see definition above). According to Ansoff & Brandenburg (1971), the purposeful selection of options of organizational structure in consideration of the organization's strategy, as well as environmental conditions impacting the organization, can be understood as the process of organizational design. With reference to this understanding, and with regard to the terminology used in this thesis, organizational design is defined as follows:

Organizational design is the purposive selection of an organizational structure under consideration of strategic and environmental conditions

Thus, organizational design results in the targeted organizational structure, or at least in the structure, which is as similar to the desired structure as the organization can get.[58] The design of interfaces is here therefore understood as how the structure of the interface has been chosen by the supply chain partners in a certain transaction context. Based on these explanations, the structure of interfaces can now be decomposed into its general elements based on a terminological system describing organizational structures. By transferring the terminology from or-

58 Of course the realized organizational design may vary over time. In reality, intended structure and realized structure are likely to differ to some degree from one another (see e.g. Remer 2005). A similar understanding of organizational design can be found e.g. in Ben-Ner, Kong & Lluis (2011).

ganizational structure to the structure of interfaces, the general validity of statements is enhanced (e.g. Chmielewicz 1979; Wolf 2008).

Hence, the variables should be able to describe not only the organizational structure of interfaces, but also organizational structures of socio-technical systems in general[59]. This would allow the expansion of analysis to explain disruptions for example caused by company-internal organizational structures. Furthermore, Popper (1973) states that systems of statements are internally consistent, implying that they do not contradict each other logically, wherefore the underlying terminology also has to be consistent.

These requirements favour to remain in the management system by Remer (2004) due to several reasons. *Firstly*, it is general, since the descriptive system is not only used to describe organizational structure, but also planning, potential, and policy. *Secondly*, many variables used to describe organizational structures in the literature are specifications of the two main components of organizational structures (Remer 1989), namely differentiation and programming, which will be further described in the following paragraphs. *Thirdly*, it is specific, as the elements can all be divided into smaller entities of interest and filled with content depending on the focus of interest, as has been done for the classification of disruptions in section 2.3.3. Therefore, the organizational structure of interfaces shall also be described following the terminology by Remer.

Consequently, the first step is to de-compose the element organization into organizational sub-elements, which are then described regarding *objects*, *directions*, and *dimensions,* as well as the characteristics *type*, *degree*, *form*, *standardization*, and *formalization*. The systematic approach for the de-composition and description of organizational structure can be found in Figure 18.

59 Companies can be basically understood as combinations of mechanical and human resources and therewith as socio-technical systems Hülsmann (2002).

Figure 18: Systematic description and decomposition of organizational structures

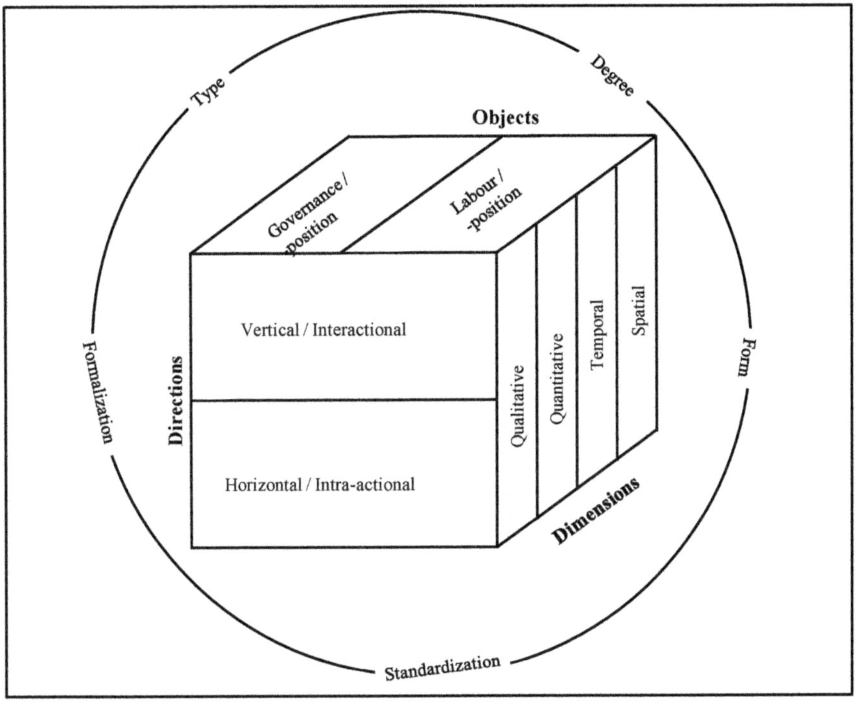

Source 11: Own illustration, based on Remer (1989)[60]

Organization can thereby be understood as "*a system of roles, which is constituted by purpose-oriented (instrumental) expectations*" (Remer 1989, p. 2)[61]. How the system of roles is structured, i.e. how each role is defined in the context of other roles and the overall system, depends on decisions regarding the organizational *differentiation*. Remer (1989) considers this variable as the primary variable, since without defining roles, no organization in the understanding above exists. The secondary variable is *programming*, which refers to the formulation of purpose-oriented expectations posed on a role. In the following, the variables differentiation and programming shall therefore be systematically described and applied to the context of interfaces, or, more specifically, to interfaces in (food) supply chains.

60 The original publication is in German, wherefore the vocabulary had to be firstly translated into English. A suggestion for translation of Remer's model can be found in Cordes-Berszinn 2013. However, whereas the original differentiates objects of programming into *instances* and *positions*, Cordes-Berszinn introduces the terms, *governance positions* and *labour position,* which will also be used here.

61 For similar definitions see e.g. Grochla (1978, p. 12); Frese (1992, p. 2); Hill, Fehlbaum & Ulrich (1994, p. 56).

3.3.2 Differentiation of Organizational Structures at Interfaces in Supply Chains

The aim of this section is to adapt Remer's systematic description of organizational structures to the description of interfaces in (food) supply chains. Therefore, each of the two variables will be described regarding objects, directions, dimensions, type, degree, form, standardization and formalization. Furthermore, these descriptions will be set in the context of interfaces in supply chains and some examples provided for the application in food supply chains.

As stated above, *differentiation* refers to the definition of roles in a system (Remer 1989; Remer 2005). More specifically, organizational differentiation has been defined by Cordes-Berszinn (2013, p. 133) based on Remer (1989) as follows:

Organisational differentiation is the quantitative, qualitative, temporal and spatial horizontal as well as vertical decomposition of labour and governance into positions and instances (governance positions).

Organisational differentiation allows thereby the creation of capacities by allocating resources to certain tasks, wherefore the purpose of this sub-element is to create capacities (Remer 1989). *Objects* of differentiation in social systems are *labour positions* and *governance positions*, which refer in the first case to the division of labour and in the second case to the division of power (Remer 2005). These can be further specified regarding the *directions* of differentiation. As has already been mentioned during the decomposition of operational planning, differentiation can be split into *vertical differentiation* and *horizontal differentiation*. The four resulting variables, namely *vertical differentiation of labour*, *horizontal differentiation of labour*, *vertical differentiation of governance*, and *horizontal differentiation of governance* can be further specified regarding the same dimensions as already used in section 2.3.3, hence *quality*, *quantity*, *time*, and *space*. In order to avoid redundancies and to depict the essence of the terminological system, in the following, examples for the application at interfaces in food supply chains will be primarily given for differentiation either of governance, or of labour.

The *vertical differentiation of governance* refers to the gradation of authority to issue orders (Remer 1989). It divides positions in a system according to making commands or receiving commands (Remer & Hucke 2007). As organizations generally do not design interface-specific vertical chains of command, as joined hierarchies are lacking, each position involved in the process receives or issues commands to other positions within its organization, but normally not across the interface to positions at the other organization. However, regarding *vertical differentiation of labour*, several levels of labour positions can be involved, which are responsible for different tasks necessary to execute the shared processes. Upson, Ketchen & Ireland (2007) for instance note that in the case of strategic supply chain management, strategic, operational, and technological integration takes place between supply chain partners. Therefore, it seems to be likely that at least for longstanding partnerships, processes across interfaces span more positions from different levels of each organization, such as operations, strategic management, and IT. However, also in the case of less stable partnerships, the exchange of products (i.e. material flow) and the exchange of information (i.e. information flow) do not necessarily take place on the same hierarchical level. In consequence, interfaces may differ regarding the number of levels, on which tasks concerned with the shared process are executed.

Horizontal differentiation of governance reflects the division of authority on the same level, e.g. between managerial and technical units (Remer 2005). Whereas division of labour has been frequently regarded as a measure to increase efficiency,[62] division of authority is a less analyzed aspect (Remer 1989). In the context of interfaces in supply chains, the partners would have to decide, how many units or positions would coordinate the process, and what kind of functional positions to involve. For instance, the increased use of private quality management standards in food supply chains (e.g. Beulens et al. 2005; Fulponi 2006; Banterle & Stranieri 2008), may lead to an additional involvement of the quality management department in the exchange processes, where previously maybe only the logistics department was involved. Therefore, interfaces can be also characterized by the number of different positions or units from the same hierarchical level involved in shared processes.

The dimension *quality* would further decompose labour and governance regarding the content of each hierarchical level or unit (Remer 1989). *Qualitative horizontal labour differentiation* could for example differentiate logistics personnel based on expert knowledge for specific product groups. Especially in food supply chains this seems to be useful, since product requirements during handling and transport may differ widely (Frith 1991). Depending on the kind of process, the interface could thus involve different positions of the same unit.

The *quantity* refers to the amount of authority or work at each level or unit (Remer 2005). In supply chains, labour could be separated vertically depending on the setup of amount of work (e.g. a truck driver can only drive one truck at a time, whereas one expeditor can control several trucks at a time). Horizontally, labour could be for instance divided between the supplier and a sub-contractor based on idle work capacities. Hence, both partners have to agree on how much of the shared process is executed by each of them.

In a *temporal* sense, horizontal differentiation of governance could be according to Remer 1989 temporally separated into authority projects. Vertical differentiation of labour delimits a position regarding the point in time or period of time (Remer 2005), for which its tasks are separated from higher or lower hierarchical levels. In food supply chains, where transit times are crucial (Bourlakis & Weightman 2004), supply chain partners could for instance agree to execute shared processes in shift work.

Spatially, vertical differentiation of governance divides the authority depending on levels, such as global authority versus local authority (Remer 1989). Regarding the design of interfaces, organizations could agree for instance on which decisions can be taken at every hand-

---

[62] This aspect has been intensively regarded in e.g. REFA (n.d.) studies, or in the example of pin production by Smith (1791).

over of products for example at the distribution centre, and which decisions would be taken during meetings of both parties at the head office. Horizontal spatial labour differentiation refers to the work places of positions (Remer 2005). Whereas interfaces in cold chains require organizational and technical links to assure, supervise and document the maintenance of the cold chain upon handover (Küppers 2002a), other positions involved in the shared processes might not be required to be physically close to one another. Hence, for those positions involved in the material flow of products at the interface, horizontal spatial differentiation seems to be limited, whereas for those positions involved in the immaterial flow, more design options exist.

As already mentioned above, vertical and horizontal differentiation of governance is further specified by the characteristics *type*, *degree*, *form*, *formalization*, and *standardization* (Remer & Hucke 2007). However, whereas type, degree, and form further describe and specify the organizational structure, formalization and standardization take a kind of intermediate form, as they do not describe organizational structure itself, but its general validity (Remer 2005).

Regarding *type* of differentiation, it can be oriented more towards the *requirements* of the planned governance programme, or more towards the existing *potential* of the governance system (Remer 1989). For supply chain partners, the horizontal and vertical governance structure can thus either be differentiated based on the requirements of the planned transaction, or based on the available tools and methods for issuing commands (e.g. by automatic order release), and for controlling their execution (e.g. by shipment tracing).

The *degree* of vertical and horizontal differentiation refers to the question, how intensive (i.e. segmented) and how extensive (i.e. fragmented) for example the labour structure of the system is differentiated. *Segmentation* regulates hereby the (dis-)similarity of work units or management levels,[63] whereby *fragmentation* defines how many units or levels of the same kind exist (Remer & Hucke 2007). Each of the two can be either high or low, but are not completely separable from one another, as there exist trade-offs between them (Remer 1989). Supply chain partners could for instance decide that there is only one unit (i.e. low fragmentation) issuing all kinds of commands for the execution of shared supply chain processes (i.e. low segmentation). However, this configuration would result in a huge complexity and amount of tasks, which could possibly not be handled appropriately. Additionally, (Remer 1989) stresses that the configuration of the degree of differentiation may depend on the situation. Furthermore, he adds that a high degree of differentiation in one criterion (e.g. vertical authority grading) can be partly compensated by a low degree in another criterion (e.g. horizontal authority distribution).

The *form* of differentiation refers to whether the system of roles is a manifestation of a fixed perception of the system and its purpose (i.e. inward-oriented or system-oriented), or whether

---

63 Similarly, Frese & Beecken (1995, p. 135) define segmentation as "*horizontal de-composition [...] by creating coequal parts*".

the system has been designed in response to environmental conditions and constraints (i.e. outward-oriented or environment-oriented) (Remer & Hucke 2007). For instance, is the differentiation of governance of an interface an expression of the purpose of the interface (e.g. cost-efficient transactions)? Or is it the expression of environmental constraints (e.g. compliance with regulatory requirements)?

An organizational structure is *standardized*, if and in so far it is fixed in the long-run (Remer 2004). The degree of standardization incorporates thereby two aspects, firstly, the *temporal durability* of fixation, and secondly, the *validity without exception*.[64] For vertical and horizontal governance differentiation, standardization refers to the temporal duration of rules. However, as in the case of other characteristics described above, not all aspects have to be standardized to the same extent (Remer & Hucke 2007). In the case of interfaces, supply chain partners may fix for example the structure of the chain of command (i.e. vertical governance differentiation) for all transactions ever to be done (i.e. durability and without exceptions), whereas the number of involved units (i.e. horizontal governance differentiation) can vary for sub-sequent transactions or depending on the products transferred (i.e. durability and invariability). If for instance perishable food products are transferred, it may be important to always involve apart from the logistics department also the quality management department, whereas this may not be necessary if the same partners transfer e.g. dry solids. In this case, the interface structure would be of high temporal durability, but situationally variable.

Finally, the differentiation of governance can be formalized, receiving validity for a group of roles (i.e. socio-spatial *infinity* of validity) and being more or less compulsory (i.e. socio-spatial *rigidity* of validity) (Remer 2005, pp. 123–124). Therewith, *formalization* helps in making random rules to universally valid rules (Remer & Hucke 2007). In fact, in supply chains, formalization is frequently regarded as a crucial aspect of successful collaboration (Min et al. 2005). This is especially important for instance in international food supply chains, where partners of different cultural backgrounds with different habits and social rules have to agree upon the design and execution of transactions. As such, they might perceive risks differently and follow different implicit models of relationships (Canavari et al. 2010). Thereby, the formalization of rules by e.g. explicit and extensive contractual agreements refers to the binding nature of the agreed-upon governance structures, and the fixation of penalties helps to assure that both partners will not deviate from the contract.

Considering these different aspects for structuring organizational differentiation of governance and labour, it can be observed that they all provide continua of possible designs.[65] If one combines then different manifestations of each characteristic with each other, an abundant array of combinations of governance differentiation arises (Remer 1989; Remer 2004; Remer

[64] Cordes-Berszinn (2013, p. 137) translates this element into "rigidity of validity". For a better differentiation from socio-spatial rigidity, in the following, the term "invariability" will be used.

[65] This is also true for other approaches which differentiate between elements of organizational structure, see e.g. Oliveira (2012) and Aiken, Bacharach & French (1980).

2005; Remer & Hucke 2007). Even if only the end points of the continua would be regarded, numerous options would be possible.

This could be done for instance, if only completely standardized governance differentiation options would be compared to singular governance differentiation options. However, as observed for example by Hülsmann, Grapp & Li (2008), a balance between flexibility and stability is required to be able to react to changing environmental circumstances. Nevertheless, only by indicating once the entire sphere of possible configurations of organizational structure, it becomes possible to allow for managerial decisions (Remer 2004). These can be furthermore supported by regarding the second element of organizational structure, namely programming, which will be introduced and adapted to interfaces in the following.

3.3.3 Programming of Organizational Structures in Supply Chains

According to Remer (2004), organizational programming has to be differentiated from program planning, since the latter refers to the creation of plans, whereas the former refers to the transfer of plans into role expectations (i.e. instructions). Hence, whereas operational planning refers to the content of work (i.e. *what* has to be done), programming refers to the way of working (i.e. *how* something has to be done). In accordance with Cordes-Berszinn (2013, p 141), organizational programming can be defined as follows:

Organisational programming is the assignment of quantitative, qualitative, temporal and spatial instructions on intra- as well [as; A/N] interactional activities to positions and instances

Thus, whereas the differentiation is required to create capacities, programming of roles has the purpose to control. Furthermore, as in the case of differentiation, programming can be specified into *objects*, *directions*, and *dimensions*, and characterized by *type*, *degree*, and *form*. The validity of this configuration is again determined by the characteristics *standardization*, and *formalization* (Remer 2005). Items to be instructed are following Remer (1989) *governance positions* and *labour positions*, which can be instructed in two directions, firstly, regarding their content (i.e. *intra-actional* programming), and secondly, regarding their relations with other roles (i.e. *interactional* programming). The difference between governance positions and labour positions can be seen analogously to governance and labour. While the labour position refers to functional tasks such as accounting, the governance position refers to governance tasks such as delegating work. As both items can be described and configured in the same way, in the following, governance positions and labour positions shall be used interchangeably. How these items can generally be instructed and described will be shown in the following paragraphs.

Remer (1989) differentiates the programming of governance positions and labour positions regarding their task program (i.e. *intra-actional programming*) and their cooperation program (i.e. *interactional programming*), which is identical to the differentiation of programming of positions. Thereby, *intra-actional programming* of governance positions answers the question, how a leadership role shall execute its regulating function, thus, which methods to use for governing (Remer 1989). In analogy, labour positions are programmed regarding which activities they are expected to complete to produce the envisaged outcome. In contrast, *interactional programming* refers to the specifications of interaction, hence how a position is instructed to cooperate with other positions.[66]

In the context of supply chain interfaces, supply chain partners could for instance determine that employees have to be monitored by their superiors more closely than normally, if the service provided is new to the partner, or if products or processes are highly sensitive towards disturbances. Defining how and when to control employees is part of the interactional programming of governance positions. Furthermore, the partners might agree on regular meetings or information exchange between managers of both partners on managerial practices. In the food and retail sector, this might include for instance quarterly meetings, where customer demand, new items development, in-store display support, cost-benefit analyses of inventory holding versus direct shipping etc., can be discussed (Min et al. 2005). Another example for such reciprocal, continuous and structured exchange of knowledge and information are communities of practice, which emerge in long-term exchange relations of several partners (van Baalen, Bloemhof-Ruwaard & van Heck 2005). As can be seen, there is a multitude of options of how supply chain partners can program positions at interfaces. To structure these options further, intra-actional and interactional programming can be additionally described along the four already known dimensions *quality*, *quantity*, *time*, and *space*.

Qualitative intra-actional programming of governance positions determines e.g. which methods to use (Remer 1989). For instance, partners in supply chains could agree to set targets for employees, e.g. by using a defined set of Key Performance Indicators (KPI), instead of giving detailed instructions on how to perform a task. However, the use of different KPIs has been identified as an issue in collaborative supply chain performance improvement, since the use of diverging KPIs may result in conflicts between supply chain objectives (Cai et al. 2009). Therefore, not only the type of methods has to be agreed, but might need further specification or interpretation in a specific context.

Qualitative interactional programming of labour instructs positions for the continuously emerging cooperative requirements (Remer 1989). Therewith, it is not only determined that an exchange takes place, but also the nature of exchange. In a supply chain context, partners can among others specify the channels of communication, for instance to use the internet instead of paper-based communication, to reduce excessive paperwork and increase visibility along the chain (Bourlakis & Weightman 2004). The qualitative interactional programming may be especially important at interfaces in international food supply chains due to the heterogeneity of cultures and practices (Waters 2009).

---

[66] According to Cordes-Berszinn (2013) organization literature mainly refers to coordination or integration.

Quantitative intra-actional programming of governance positions refers to the amount of governance executed (Remer 1989). As such, for example the frequency of controlling the achievement of targets could be fixed, as well as the determination of fault tolerance in the compliance with instructions. Said fault tolerance may differ substantially in food supply chains, considering for example that 2.5 degrees deviation from the optimal temperature reduces shelf-life of bananas by approximately two days, whereas such a deviation can cause in avocados a shelf-life loss of 17 days (Paull 1999). Consequently, the monitoring and evaluation of careful product handling by employees might need adaptation, if it is based for example on compliance with shipping temperatures.

Quantitative interactional programming of labour positions defines the extent of interaction of positions (i.e. cooperation) which has been defined by instructions (Remer 1989). This aspect is frequently regarded in supply chain management literature, since it involves for example decisions on the extent of information sharing between supply chain partners, which is frequently seen as a performance driver (e.g. Steckel, Gupta & Banerji 2004; Seuring 2004; van Baalen, Bloemhof-Ruwaard & van Heck 2005; Bechini et al. 2008). Hence, depending on the depth of partnership, supply chain partners may agree differently on the quantity of interactional programming.

As examples for *temporal intra-actional programming*, Remer (1989) suggests the determination of points in time for the execution of labour tasks, or the determination of duration of certain tasks. As temperature deviations occur frequently at interfaces, for example during loading of a container or due to early disconnection of reefers prior to being loaded on a vessel (Drewry Shipping Consultants 1990), supply chain partners could fix the duration of loading operations or the time of plugging off the reefer before loading.

From the *interactional* perspective, governance positions have to decide on when to cooperate (Remer 1989). Partners in food supply chains for instance agree on allowing facility inspections by the partner in random intervals (Hobbs, Fearne & Spriggs 2002). In general, it can be assumed that the time of cooperation is primarily fixed in a broad sense by the duration of contract. However, this does not cover the frequency or number of cooperative exchanges within duration of the contract. Therefore, the frequency of interaction might differ depending on the duration of partnership and depending on other characteristics of the partnership, for example the frequency of transactions.

The *spatial intra-actional programming* of governance positions refers to the question of where the governance tasks have to be effected (Remer 1989). Especially in supply chains, where employees are transporting goods from and to different locations, managers might not be required to be in a physical office to issue orders, if employees are somewhere else. However, for the design of the interface, the question might be more important, where governance positions have to issue their tasks, for instance depending on the criticality of process steps. If for instance certain assembly steps are very sensitive, a supplier might demand a subcontractor to supervise these production steps more closely than the rest of the process.

The *interactional spatial programming* in turn defines the places of cooperation or the spatial pre-conditions for cooperation (Remer 1989). Supply chain partners may for instance decide to cooperate only in certain regions of the world. Another important question is also the division of authority between them. In international trade, this is frequently determined by agreeing on International Commercial Terms (Incoterms), which stipulate where the financial risk for the cargo is shifting from one partner to the next (Weick 2012). As an example, South African fruit and vegetable exports to Europe are frequently based on Free on Board (FOB) terms, which mean that the buyer takes over responsibility for the product upon loading on the vessel (Ortmann 2005). In this case, the border of authority over decisions on the handling of the product would end for the seller upon loading, where the authority would be transferred to the buyer (as far as the authority of the shipper is not concerned).

The *type* of interactional and intra-actional programming of governance and labour positions can be either oriented towards the conditions of programming, or towards the intentions (Remer 1989). *Intentional programming* would be based on certain rules or regulations, which would be applied irrespective of the case at hand (Remer 2004). For example, the EU regulation (EC) No 852/2004 on the hygiene of foodstuffs prescribes food business operators to implement procedures following HACCP[67] principles (European Commission 2004). *Conditional programming* would rather determine the aspects, which have to be considered in the situation-specific decision making (Remer 2004). For example, governance positions in food supply chains would have to consider the product-specific requirements in terms of temperature and relative humidity in their decision making on transport modes to be used.

The *degree* of interactional and intra-actional programming of governance and labour positions can be again either high or low. Thereby, the degree of programming is constituted by firstly, the level of detail of instructions, and secondly, by the preciseness of instructions (Remer 1989). The level of detail is high, if the entire pattern of behaviour is covered by instructions (Remer 2005). For example, the level of detail would be high, if positions involved in shared processes are not only instructed regarding loading and unloading of products, but also regarding checks to be conducted on the products, the documents to be exchanged, and the procedures for registering the shipment in the data management system. Preciseness of instructions in turn is high, if a position has no more freedom of choice on its work technique, rhythm, or workload (Remer 2005). Examples here are instructions for positions at assembly lines or in JIT production systems, where the customer pulls material through the production system (Wilhelm, Som & Carroll 1992).

The *form* of programming can be inward-oriented or outward-oriented (Remer 2004). However, in contrast to the form of differentiation, the form of programming does not refer to environmental and system perspective, but rather to the position-orientation and organization-orientation. It is *position-oriented*, if each entity is programmed based on expectations associated with this position (Remer 1989). For example, the position "Quality Manager" is expected to be an expert on quality management in its business unit (Saraph, Benson & Schroeder 1989). It is *organization-oriented*, if the programming is based on fixed expectations of the structural organizational context, such as joint problems, interdependencies, etc. (Remer 1989). Examples are production teams, which work across conventional organizational boundaries relative autonomously to achieve a joint outcome (Cohen & Bailey 1997).

By *standardization*, the instructions of governance positions receive their long-term enduring character (Remer 2004). The degree of standardization is again composed by its *temporal durability* and its *validity without exceptions* (Remer & Hucke 2007). Supply chain partners may decide to instruct the relevant governance positions only for the duration of one transaction (e.g. for the delivery of one container of apples), or they might instruct the governance positions in such a way that it is valid for all future transactions (e.g. for the steady supply with apples). Furthermore, they might instruct all governance positions to act in all situations in the same way, or might provide standard operating procedures, which only apply if nothing else has been negotiated (i.e. invariability).

Finally, *formalization* refers to the *range of addressees (socio-spatial validity)* and *rigidity* of programming of governance positions (Remer 1989). For instance, governance positions in more creative work areas (e.g. Product Development) do not receive instructions, whereas governance positions e.g. in Accounting receive instructions (i.e. low range of addressees). Furthermore, deviations from the instructions can be either tolerated or penalized, if for example deviations from instructions imperil the participation in the system (Remer 2005). For example, retailers in European countries nowadays often require their suppliers to implement Efficient Consumer Response (ECR) or Category Management (CR) programmes to increase food quality and to cut costs. Those suppliers not able to comply with these requirements are replaced (i.e. high rigidity) (Fearne & Hughes 2000).

The resulting variety of how organizational structure can be described is illustrated in Figure 19. Therein, elements, objects, directions and dimensions form together the sub-object of organizational structure or operational planning (marked in grey), which can then be characterized along different general categories (outlined in grey).

[67] HACCP is the abbreviation for Hazard Analysis and Critical Control Point. For further reading, see e.g. Mortimore & Wallace (2000).

Figure 19: Combinatorial options to describe organizational structures

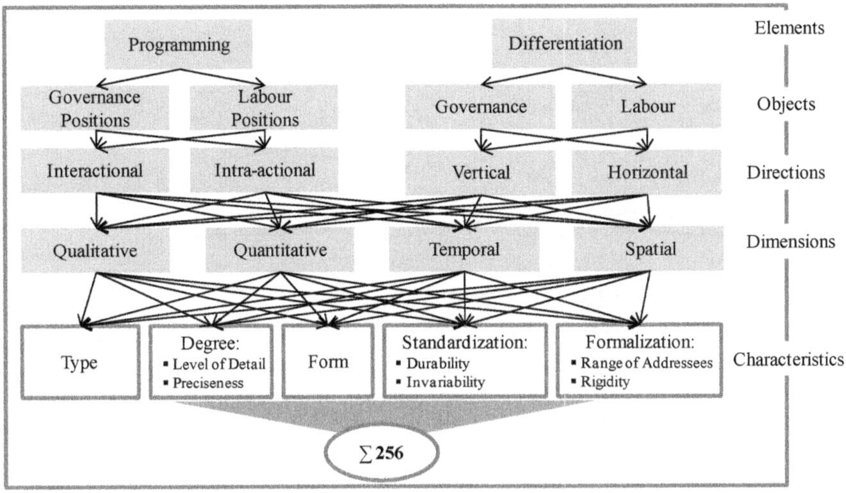

Source 12: Own illustration based on Remer (1989); arrows do not indicate causal relations

As can be seen, the approach offers a considerable variety of design options and descriptive specifications of elements of organizational structure. Even though the terminological framework by Remer (1989) has a broad applicability across organizational designs and even across organizational boundaries, it also bears some disadvantages, which have to be mentioned.

Firstly, the measurement of organizational structures is difficult to realize. Especially in social science, the operationalization of research objects represents a challenge, due to the intention to analyze abstract constructs, which cannot be directly observed in reality (Kromrey 2009). This problem has also been acknowledged by Remer (1989), who therefore illustrates some potential indicators of organizational structure. *Secondly*, the complexity of combinatorial options might not allow for a complete empirical examination and validation of hypotheses. As the options in Figure 19 only cover the construct of organizational structure, for the analysis of hypotheses, these design options would have to be linked to disruptions, which in turn have also been decomposed based on this terminological system. Considering all possibilities, in which organizational structures and deviations of operational planning can be described and modified, a total of 4.096 combinations would result. This is illustrated in Figure 20.

Figure 20: Combinatorial options of organizational structures and operational planning

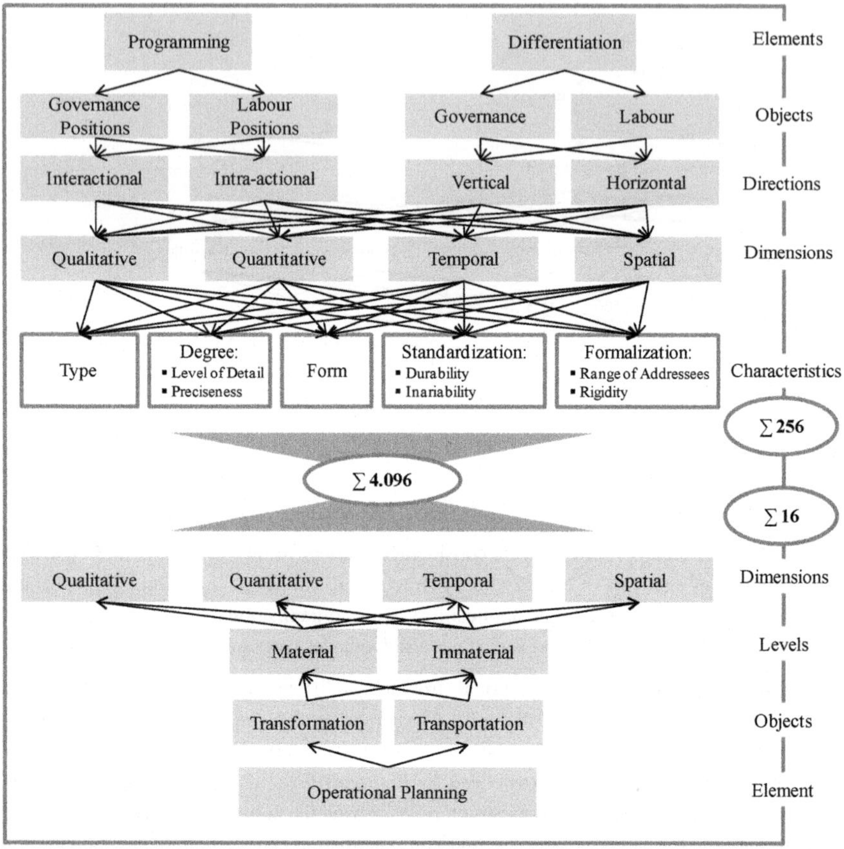

Source 13: Own illustration based on Remer (1989); arrows do not indicate causal relations[68]

In this context, Remer (1989) states that normally not all basic elements for the description and analysis of organizational structures will be used, but that they are reduced to those deemed important in the specific situation. As Kromrey (2009) asserts, the depth of theoretical decomposition of research objects depends on the research question and Schulte-Zurhausen (1999) suggests the reduction of complexity based on prioritizing sub-objects of investigation. Consequently, the framework by Remer (1989) will be condensed following the purpose of this thesis.

[68] Theoretically, even more combinatorial possibilities would exist, if the omission of steps in the sequence of combination would be considered.

3.4 Design of Interactions as Drivers for Supply Chain Vulnerability

3.4.1 Concretization of Interface Structure

As has been shown in section 3.3.3, describing the organizational structure of interfaces based on the methodology provided by Remer results in 256 possibilities to modify the interfaces (see Figure 20). According to Kromrey (2009), the determination of the research design can be deduced from the research purpose. Consequently, in order to reduce this complexity without neglecting aspects of high importance, relevant aspects will be prioritized based on the research purpose.

The research object of this thesis is the reveal causal relations between on the one hand, organizational structures of interfaces, and on the other hand, disruptions in food supply chains. Thus, for prioritizing aspects of organizational structure, the interface management literature may serve as a starting point, whereas for disruptions in food supply chains, one may refer to the literature on disruptions in (food) supply chains. Furthermore, the purpose is to deduce and empirically test hypotheses on causal relations between the structure of the interface and the occurrence of disruptions. Therefore, following the ontological foundation of this thesis by Popper (1973) also the feasibility of deducing falsifiable hypotheses needs to be considered. Hence, the following paragraphs will reason the exclusion of aspects based on the relevant literature.

According to Remer (1989), differentiation is the primary variable to describe organizational structures, as without it, no role-like structuring of a system would exist. However, he also states that even though programming can be sometimes neglected, especially in larger social systems, roles have to be instructed regarding the expectations of other system members. Furthermore, if an event occurs that requires a reaction to avoid the occurrence of a disruption, adequate programming of positions may reduce the amount of coordinative efforts. This is also supported by March & Simon (1958, p. 163), who state that "*the organization has available a repertory of programs, so that once the event has been classified the appropriate program can be executed without further ado*". Therefore, *programming* seems to be especially important in this context and is considered as a focal aspect of interface design.

Regarding the organizational design of interfaces, Schulte-Zurhausen (2004) stresses the importance of process-oriented organizational structures. He specifies that "*companies can only react flexibly and quickly, if decision processes do not have to pass numerous hierarchical levels*" (Schulte-Zurhausen 2004, p. 24). This is also observed by Trist (1977), who argues that relations at the inter-organizational level are organized less tightly, so that individuals are more often on their own. Similarly, Röder (2001) states that the number of hierarchical levels at interfaces is reduced, while the positions, in absence of higher hierarchical levels, coordinate activities horizontally between them. Therefore, the objects *differentiation of governance* and *programming of governance positions* seem to be of less relevance and will be excluded in the following.

As the literature on interface management indicates, one of the main characteristics of interfaces is the challenge to co-ordinate activities horizontally between different companies (Brown 1983; Brockhoff & Hauschildt 1993). Furthermore, interface management has been acknowledged to be more crucial for the success of companies than the isolated optimization of single business areas (Reiß & Corsten 1995). Thus, company-internal optimization seems to be less important than the optimization of how to interact on a horizontal level. Consequently, *vertical differentiation of labour* and *intra-actional programming of positions* will not be regarded in the following, as both focus on company-internal aspects.

The remaining objects are horizontal differentiation of labour and interactional programming of positions. According to Remer (1989, p. 20), horizontal differentiation of labour represents "*the embodiment of labour organizational differentiation*". It serves thereby the capacity effect by decomposing the overall task. At the same time, it is a constituent part of the definition of organizational interfaces as illustrated in section 3.3.1. By focussing on the interface between companies, which jointly handle connected processes, the horizontal differentiation of labour is already determined by the transition point. This implies for instance that qualitative horizontal differentiation of labour, or "specialization" as Remer (1989) terms it alternatively, is determined by the agreement to decompose the shared process into different parts done by different companies. This is also supported by Frese, Graumann & Theuvsen (2012) who state that the competence structure at interfaces can be considered as given. Furthermore, the purpose of this thesis is not to determine how companies should select their specialization in the process, hence to move the interface along the process, but to analyze the effect of the existing interface on the probability of disruptions. Also the quantitative (i.e. division of amount of work), the temporal (i.e. division of phases of work), and the spatial (i.e. the location of work) horizontal differentiation of labour, the main conditions are set by the type of process, the companies involved and other contextual parameters (e.g. geographic location). The possibility to modify these conditions for already existing supply chains thus seems to be relatively low. Furthermore, Remer (1989, p. 11) states that "*in certain limits, the two variables differentiation and programming can take over the function of the other one respectively*". Therefore, the analysis of potential impacts of *horizontal differentiation of labour* is considered to be of less importance for the purpose of this thesis.

The dimensions for describing interactional programming of positions seem all to be at least theoretically important, since no evidence helps to prioritize dimensions. Furthermore, Remer (1989) stresses that in general all dimensions will be used to define a position, though to different extents. Therewith, these dimensions specify the content of programming wherefore their general manifestations can only be differentiated into being more or less defined. Their effective direction seems to be therefore similar to the effect of programming in general and will thus be subsumed under programming. The relevancy of this focus of attention has also been stressed by e.g. Harland (1996), who acknowledges the importance of analyzing dyadic relationships between positions in supply chains to gain insights into supply chain behaviour.

Furthermore, as Kieser & Walgenbach (2007) notice, coordination tasks require different qualifications than execution tasks, which increases the demands posed on individuals considerably, if they are required to do both kinds of tasks. This argument could help to explain, why disruptions seem to occur more frequently at interfaces. Consequently, the following deduction of hypotheses will focus on the *interactional programming of positions* at inter-organizational interfaces.

Regarding the abstract characteristics type and degree, as well as the concrete characteristic form of organizational structure, Remer (1989) asserts that the *type* of differentiation and programming is prone to perception errors, as indicators can mostly not be generated on the instrumental level, but on the level of actions or physical structure (e.g. office layout). Additionally, March & Simon (1958) acknowledges that concerning the *form* of differentiation and programming, contingent decisions regarding focus points have to be taken. Therewith, both characteristics do not seem to allow for the deduction of "strong" hypotheses in the sense of falsification and are therefore not considered explicitly in the following.[69]

As Remer (2005) states, the above-mentioned characteristics describe the substance of organizational structure, whereas the characteristics *standardization* and *formalization* concern its general validity. For the context of interfaces, the general validity is important, as otherwise it would not be possible to assess whether these structures were also applied in a certain transaction. Without their determination, the applicability of the previously defined organizational structure is imperilled, as it is not clear, for whom and for which work units the structure is defined. Consequently, once the organizational structure in its elements, objects, directions, dimensions and degrees has been defined, it has to be determined, how far it is standardized and how far it is formalized. However, not for every aspect of organizational structure, the standardization and formalization has to be the same. Indeed, Remer (2005) stresses that for instance maximizing standardization regarding its temporal durability as well as its exceptionlessness would endanger the ability of the system to adapt to changing requirements. He suggests therefore varying the degree of standardization for different objects. Hence, standardization as well as formalization may therefore take different forms in the same transaction, but for different activities and will therefore be considered. Thus, this thesis will focus on the analysis of how interactions between supply chain partners at interfaces are programmed regarding degree, standardization and formalization.

According to Remer (1989), interactional programming of positions comprises the instructions for a position on how and with whom to be in contact. The degree of programming in turn describes the extensity and intensity of instructions (Remer 2004). Such contacts comprise the mere *forwarding* of objects or information, as well as the *exchange* of information between positions (Remer 2005). Interactional programming is therefore necessary, as posi-

---

69 The exclusion does not imply that they are non-existent. Rather, the assumption is that for the specific situation, there exist "typical" shapes. Thus, for the rest of the analysis, type and form will be ceteris paribus held constant.

tions linked by workflow stand in exchange relationships and have to form a communication network to fulfil the tasks of the work process (Kosiol 1962). If positions are not instructed with rules for how to cooperate, they are offered a high degree of autonomy of decision making for how to design the communication and exchange processes with other positions, or whether to communicate and exchange at all. However, according to Luthans (2005, p. 335) "*horizontal communication is required to make coordinated, cross-functional effort in achieving organizational goals*". Thus, apart from fulfilling their tasks determined by their intra-actional program, individuals also have to make sure that the process is continued in such a way that overarching goals are achieved.

By standardizing interactional instructions, positions receive stable and durable rules for joint activities (Remer 2004). According to van de Ven & Ferry (1980), coordination of work flows across organizational boundaries can be achieved by e.g. standardizing language, establishing rules for coordination, policies, procedures, and monitoring the effectiveness by periodic memos, reports, and computerized information systems. Hence, standardization of interactional programming seems to be an instrument which can also be applied in an inter-organizational context, to achieve a certain degree of stability.

Formalization of interactional programming refers to the extent to which instructions on co-operative activities have to be followed by the entire system and include penalties for non-compliance (Remer 2004)). It provides the individuals working in a system with certainty regarding the expectations they have to consider in their decision making (Remer 2005). Thereby, uncertainty for the individual is reduced and the level of aspiration is easier to attain, as all relevant information is available. Consequently, a certain level of formalization may foster the avoidance of errors. Therewith, all three remaining characteristics seem to be of high relevance for inter-organizational programming and seem to provide starting points for the explanation of varying performance at interfaces in supply chains. The resulting range of combinatorial possibilities to describe and modify organizational structures of interfaces[70] is illustrated in Figure 21.

[70] For the sake of brevity, in the following it will be referred to interface structure.

Figure 21: Remaining combinatorial options to describe structures of interfaces

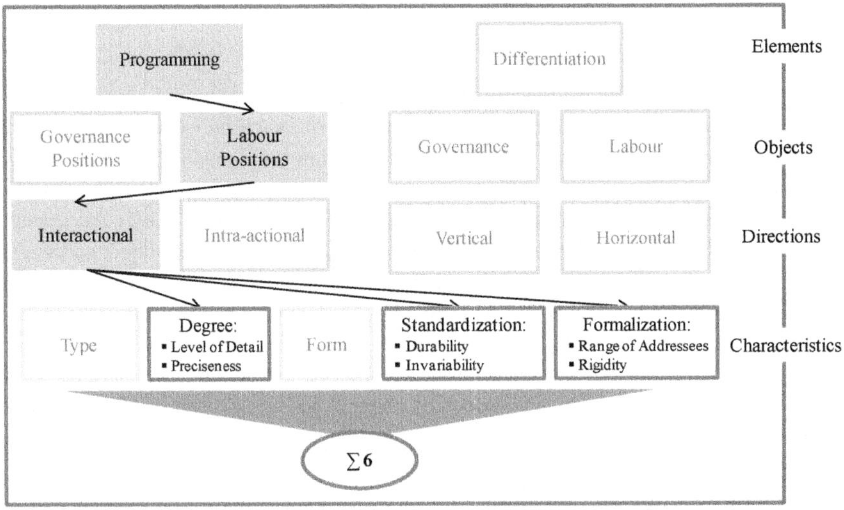

Source 14: Own illustration based on Remer (1989); arrows do not indicate causal relations

As can be seen, the amount and complexity of possible combination for the description of interface structures is considerably reduced. The question is now, how these aspects of interface structure can be causally related to the occurrence of disruptions. However, due to the process character of disruptions, first of all, the question has to be answered, which part of the disruption has to be causally explained.

As has already been noted in section 3.3.3, the framework by Remer offers many starting points for the description of interface structure and deviations from operational planning, yet does not allow for a causal connection of these two parts of the management system, as it is a descriptive framework. Nevertheless, it helps to classify deviations from operational planning based on empirical data on disruptions and helps therefore to differentiate between different kinds of disruptions and to assess the relevancy of specific types of disruptions. However, it only helps to classify the observable part of the disruption, namely the deviation from operational planning. The first part, namely the error, is not reflected by the description. Nevertheless, since the occurrence of an error marks the point where a potential disruption becomes a latent disruption (see section 2.2.3), the connection between errors and resulting deviations will be regarded in the following as a black box. The research question can therewith be further concretized to:

> **How does the interactional programming of positions at interfaces affect the susceptibility of supply chains to disruptions?**

In the following, the objective is to deduce hypotheses on the assumed causal relations between configuration of interactional programming and errors.

3.4.2 Impacts of the Interface Structure on Operational Performance

The purpose of this section is to focus in more detail on potential effects of interactional programming of positions at interfaces on the susceptibility of food supply chains to disruptions. Thereby, different manifestations of degree, standardization and formalization and their components shall be juxtaposed to illustrate different design options and potential consequences for the achievement of operational plans. According to Bortz & Döring (1995), the formulation of so-called unspecific hypotheses without indication of direction of effect and size of effect is common to exploratory research, where no previous findings can be used as a basis. As previous research in this field is still scarce, the development of directed hypotheses cannot be reasoned based on prior findings, wherefore unspecific hypotheses will be developed. Thereby, the null-hypothesis is the counterstatement to the hypothesis to be analyzed, as the truth can only be approached by falsification of wrong hypotheses (Popper 1973). For a better differentiation, these unspecific hypotheses will be called propositions, to distinguish them from hypotheses deduced after empirical validation.

Impacts of Degree of Interactional Programming on Operational Performance

Consistent with Remer's distinction of physical forwarding and information exchange, in supply chains, the physical flow of goods is accompanied by a physical flow of information, which comprises basically shipping documents and other logistics-related information (Ruiz-Garcia, Steinberger & Rothmund 2010). Apart from this physical flow, supply chain partners have to exchange information regarding the handover of shipments and property rights. Considering that a key aspect of supply chains is the temporal-spatial change of availability of products, and the numbers of transaction effected by both companies, these handovers take place in a dynamic transaction environment. Furthermore, at interfaces, employees normally have more autonomy due to the lack of control by a joint superior governance position (see section 3.3.1). Additionally, diverging interests, and different norms and culture in each company stamp the individuals (Kieser & Walgenbach 2007) and make coordination more exigent than within one company. Thus, the complexity of coordination and thereby of decision making for each employee increases, if the transaction partners do not specify how exchange processes at the interface shall be executed.

Following the assumptions of decision theory, individuals have limited cognitive capacities and tend to make decisions based on pattern recognition instead of consideration of all available information, if the information becomes too complex. Non-availability of instructions on how to execute a task can have according to Hackman (1970) two consequences for the performance of the individual. Either, its effectiveness increases as the decision freedom is encouraging to take over responsibility and matches its abilities. Or, the lack of instructions is threatening and the individual will seek an escape from executing the task. In such a case, the individual might do the work in the process it is supposed to do (i.e. its intra-actional program), and go on to the next task without interacting with the next individual in the process to avoid a situation which it feels unable to handle. This could explain for instance an observation by Nunes, Emond & Brecht (2006), who report that containers with perishables are standing during hours on a hot apron before being transferred to the airplane. A third option would be that the individual will try the same methods of interaction which it applied successfully in other transactions (i.e. pattern recognition). However, whether this approach is successful depends on many factors, ranging from interface structures of the companies involved, cultural backgrounds (Luthans 2005), as well as cognitive capacities of the interaction partner (Remer 1982).

The opposed case would be an unlimited interactional programming of positions, which would tell the individual precisely and in detail, how it should interact with other individuals at interfaces. As Hackman (1970) asserts, very detailed instructions should lead to more uniform performance across individuals, as they leave less room for interpretation. This is also supported by Remer (1982), who states that instructions issued by the formal organization may lead to a reduction of the psychologically burdening complexity. However, he also sees limits to the usefulness of extensive instructions by acknowledging that in complex and dynamic environments, they may lead to "*dysfunctional consequences*" (Remer 1982, p. 266). In such a case, individuals might be confronted with conflicting goals, if the instructions do not fit other parameters of the transaction. Satisficing behaviour could then favour complying with the precise instructions for interaction, instead of interpreting them in such a way that the process plans are met. Consequently, the individuals would do what they were instructed to do, leading in this case to unintended deviations from the process plans.

Additionally, the time required to fix such agreements between supply chain partners may outweigh the benefits. Furthermore, transaction cost theory and Remer (1989) acknowledge that agreements can never be exhaustive. From the perspective of the individual, a high degree of interactional programming can reduce job satisfaction and performance, if the individual cannot participate in the decision making, but has only an execution function (Luthans 2005). Thus, a relationship between the degree of interactional programming and the probability of errors and consequential deviations from operational planning can be assumed and leads to the following proposition:

Proposition 1 If the degree of interactional programming changes, then the achievement of operational planning does not change

The extensity of interactional programming of positions refers to the *level of detail*, with which every cooperative task of positions are determined (Remer 2004). This can be for instance the elaborated illustration of how agreement conflicts have to be solved (Remer 1989). In a food supply chain, this could be the detailed description of transfer proceedings for a shipment between agents.

By enhancing the level of detail of information, the amount of information, which is understood as the number of facts/figures with their meaningful connection (Hoffmann 1980), is increased. According to decision theory in turn, with information in abundance, the individual places a cost on information seeking and stops its search once a level considered to be satisfactory is reached (Simon 1979). It might thus tend to execute the tasks at hand "as usual" instead of considering carefully the instructions for the transfer of the specific batch. This would be a typical case of automatic unconscious action as named in psychology (e.g. Hofmann & Frese 2011). Nevertheless, without information on what the individual is expected to do, the complexity of the situation and uncertainty again increases, which may in turn lead to more errors.

Proposition 1.1 **If the level of detail of interactional programming changes, then the achievement of operational planning does not change**

Regarding the intensity of programming, this refers to the *preciseness* of instructions for the cooperation work of positions. An example by Remer (1989) is the exact explanation of agreement procedures for the cooperation of divisions. An example for interfaces in food supply chains could be the exact statement of type of documents (e.g. Bill of Lading, BOL) to be exchanged upon transferring a box of bananas. Therewith, supply chain partners could check more easily, whether all documents required are provided, which would reduce the probability of e.g. import refusals or delays at transition points.

Nevertheless, if the preciseness of interactional programming is very high, individuals do not have any flexibility to react to unforeseen obstacles. If for example the two parties agreed upon that any information exchange has to be made in writing (e.g. due to liability reasons), but there is an event which would require urgent reaction from the partner, such agreements might impede quick information exchange. Assuming satisficing behaviour, the individual would then solve the conflict by prioritization of goals, preferring the "learned" solution instead of seeking new solutions. In consequence, the coordination might be too slow to effectively solve the problem. In the opposite case, if the preciseness of instructions is very low, individuals may react more flexibly to unforeseen obstacles, but at the same time, there is more room for interpretation of instructions. Considering that for interaction, at least two individuals have to receive and interpret the instructions (Hackman 1970), the potential for misunderstandings rises. Since decision theory assumes that individuals are able to learn from past experiences, at interfaces in food supply chains, where individuals of different companies and even cultures interact (Canavari et al. 2010), interpretation of instructions may vary significantly, whereby the probability of errors rises. Thus, whereas the kind of effect of preciseness of instructions may vary depending on circumstances, in general, the preciseness of interactional programming seems to have an impact on the probability of disruptions.

With the same logic, potential effects of for example temporal interactional programming of positions can be reasoned. Remer (1989, p. 44) calls temporal programming the "*points in time of work cooperation*". These points in time are not necessarily absolute time specifications, but general ones, such as weekly recurring cooperation times or with reference to deadlines. One example for the latter case in supply chains is the so-called 24 hour rule by the US Customs and Border Protection. This rule demands for the submission of information on all cargo on a ship calling in US ports 24 hours prior to loading in a foreign port (Bichou et al. 2007). Without receiving these instructions, individuals might ignore the rule if shipments to the US are rare, which could consequently lead to disruptions at customs clearance. However, if in a special case there is an exception of this rule, individuals with satisficing behaviour may not pay attention to specific instructions, which could cause disruptions somewhere else in the supply chain. Proctor & van Zandt (2008) differentiate between the former and the latter kind of error by referring to the first as *error by omission*, and to the latter as *error of commission*.[71] In consequence, the following proposition can be deduced:

Proposition 1.2 **If the preciseness of interactional programming changes, then the achievement of operational planning does not change**

Thus, as depicted above, even though the general link between the degree of interactional programming of positions and the probability of deviations from operational planning seems to be existent, no general assumption can be made regarding whether a high degree or a low degree increases the probability of errors. Rather, the direction of effect may differ depending on the initial value of instructions, and depending on the decision making situation. Furthermore, as the degree of interactional programming is a combination of two elements, which in turn also may have different manifestations from low to high, a multitude of potential combinations result, as depicted in Figure 22.[72]

---

71 An error of omission is when "*the operator fails to perform a required action*". An error of commission in turn is when "*an action is performed, but is inappropriate*" Proctor & van Zandt (2008, p. 60).

72 The choice of low, middle, and high manifestations has been chosen for easiness of illustration, more correctly would be the indication of continua since both variables can in principle have continuous manifestations.

Figure 22: Potential effects of preciseness and level of detail on errors

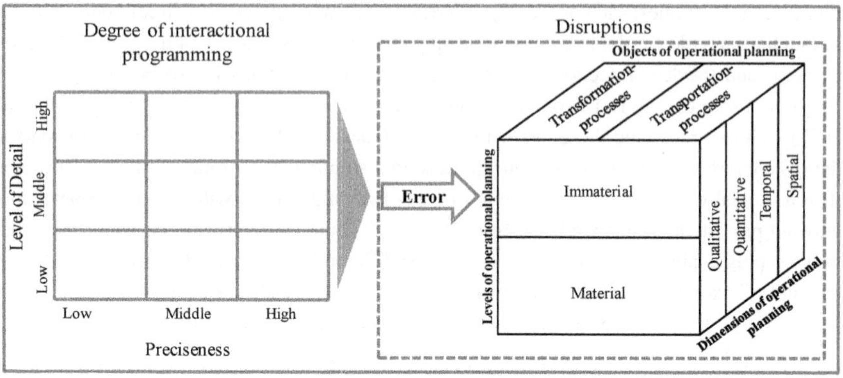

Impacts of Standardization of Interactional Programming on Operational Performance

An example by Remer (2004) for a highly standardized programming of positions is a construction plant, where the attempt is to keep the instructions of all roles constant in the long run, so that the personnel is able to adapt to the requirements to assure smooth operations. For the cooperative work of positions in food supply chains, a high level of standardization could imply that every position is instructed in the same way, no matter if the transaction occurs inbound or outbound, for deep frozen or chilled products, and is maintained for a long period of time. The advantages of standardization of activities have also been acknowledged in this context, where private quality management standards are increasingly implemented, to assure food quality and safety along the supply chain (Smith & Sparks 2004; Jaffee & Masakure 2005; Trienekens & Zuurbier 2008).

Thereby, individuals could on the one hand be supported in reaching via their decisions the previously defined aspiration level. This is also affirmed by van de Ven & Ferry (1980), who state that by repetitive following these rules, they are absorbed by the individuals and become an unconscious part of their work activities. On the other hand, a highly standardized interactional programming would in case of conflicting goals presumably lead to errors. In such cases, individuals potentially would not notice changing requirements as information seeking would be very limited and recognized stimuli would lead to automated responses (i.e. pattern recognition). If for example the coordination of forwarding some new and demanding products (e.g. hatching eggs) would be handled the same way as some staple and simple products (e.g. potatoes), the probability that errors occur increases, which leads to the following proposition:

Proposition 2 If the standardization of interactional programming changes, then the achievement of operational planning does not change

As has been reasoned above, decision theory assumes that individuals stop to seek more information once an apparently satisfying solution is found, which might lead to diverging outcomes from operational planning. However, decision theory further assumes that if the results based on satisfying decision making do not attain the level of aspiration, individuals will seek more information the next time and thus learn from errors in the past (Simon 1978b). Learning requires therefore that situations occur recurrently, which demands for *durable* instructions. At the same time, the level of attention might decrease with repetition, whereby new information will not be considered during decision making, as based on familiar facts, a decision is taken which yielded satisfactory results in the past. Durability of interactional programming in food supply chains is for instance limited by increasing automatic information exchange for tracking and tracing (Smith & Sparks 2004; Abad et al. 2009; Bechini et al. 2008). By applying new technologies, instructions for information exchange thus might have to be adapted on a regular basis, restricting therewith temporal stability.

Proposition 2.1 **If the durability of interactional programming changes, then the achievement of operational planning does not change**

A high *invariability* of interactional programming might reduce the complexity of the decision making situation to a great extent, if the instructions for the individual apply to all kinds of situations. However, due to the interaction with different transaction partners, fixing instructions without exceptions might not be feasible, if both parties have to agree upon them. Furthermore, depending on differences in products, operations, etc., invariable instructions might lead to conflicting goals, whereby the probability of errors would again be increased.

If instructions in turn are highly variable, the decision making situation becomes again more complex, as the individual has to choose which instructions to apply given the situation. At the same time, higher variability of instructions might be favourable for the product quality, as decisions on how to handle the product could be based on the status of the products received. An example for such a variable handling of products is the First-Expired-First-Out (FEFO) procedure used for perishable food products, which requires a technological basis on which such decisions can be taken (van der Vorst et al. 2007). Hence, on the one hand, the decision making situation would become more complex, as not every product is handled identically, but at the same time, more precise information would become available to guide the individual in its decision making. Therewith, it would be possible to reduce errors and deviations of desired product quality by enhancing variability of procedures. Based on these explanations, the following proposition can be deduced:

Proposition 2.2 **If the invariability of interactional programming changes, then the achievement of operational planning does not change**

As already indicated for the degree of programming, also durability and invariability cannot be completely separated from one another and their configuration depends on the situation and ranges on a continuum of potential manifestations (Remer 2005).

Figure 23: Potential effects of durability and invariability on errors

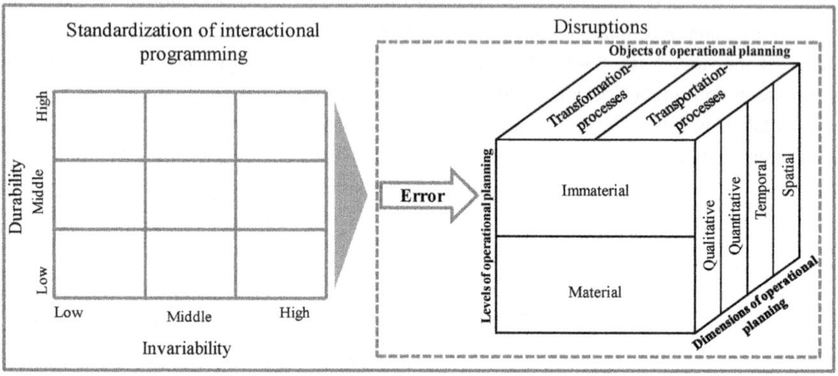

Impacts of Formalization of Interactional Programming on Operational Performance

For the inter-organizational context van de Ven & Ferry (1980, p. 303) define formalization as "*the degree to which rules, policies, and procedures govern the role behaviour and activities of organizations [...]*". Thereby, "*rules*" and "*policies*" already imply a notion of rigidity, wherefore here, the term "*procedures*" is favoured. While therewith complexity of decision making is reduced, at the same time, decisions might be legitimated, which were not optimal regarding the achievement of the desired outcome (Remer 1989). If for instance in a truck there is still space available for a batch of perishable food, which is already in a critical condition but could thereby arrive at its destination still fit for consumption, the instruction that every batch has to wait for the previously assigned truck would foster food quality disruptions. Formalization can therewith also provide incentives, which are only positive in certain situations.

Proposition 3 If the formalization of interactional programming changes, then the achievement of operational planning does not change

Formalization of rules refers firstly to the *range of addressees* of rules (Remer 2005). If every individual involved in a transaction has to obey to the same instructions regarding its cooperation with individuals from the other company, the range of addressees of interactional programming is high. With an increasing range of addressees, uncertainty regarding the behaviour of cooperation partners is reduced, which otherwise endangers rational decision making (Simon 1979). Every person would know that the other one is instructed in the same way and could therewith make decisions more easily. This is especially important in international supply chains, where communication may be difficult due to cultural and linguistic barriers (Waters 2009). Furthermore, the range of addressees may also be expanded to sub-contractors of transaction partners, if the physical transport is fully or partly outsourced. Prior research in food supply chains indicates the extension of the socio-spatial validity of procedures to sub-contractors, as these companies have to meet much higher requirements for outsourcing compared to other industries (van Hoek 1999). If in turn only one of the two parties at the interface has to obey to the instructions, misunderstandings might increase the probability of errors. At the same time, a high range of addressees may also hinder the appropriateness or preciseness of procedures, as not necessarily the interaction of all positions is identical.

Proposition 3.1 **If the range of addressees of interactional programming changes, then the achievement of operational planning does not change**

The second aspect of formalization is the *rigidity* of rules. Diverging behaviour from strictly formalized rules could thus endanger the participation in the system and hence lead to expulsion (Remer 2005). Following the logic of decision theory, the individual would attempt to obey its interactional instructions to a higher degree, if non-compliance is linked to penalties. In complex situations where the correct decision might not be clear from the beginning, the individual would thus seek more information, as the aspiration level or gains from making the right decision is higher. If in turn no penalties are linked to non-compliant behaviour, the individual might have a lower aspiration level, which would increase the probability of making decisions deviating from operational planning. However, individuals with satisficing behaviour could also use the rigidity of rules as an excuse for deviations from operational planning in the case of conflicting goals. These considerations lead to the following proposition:

Proposition 3.2 **If the rigidity of interactional programming changes, then the achievement of operational planning does not change**

In the case of formalization of interactional programming, decision theory suggests that a higher formalization leads to a lower probability of disruptions. However, not all instructions do necessarily require the same extent of formalization, as some instructions might be critical to the realization of the planned outcome (i.e. must-be instructions), while others might have lower priorities (i.e. should-be instructions). Nor do all interface designs necessarily require the same degree of rigidity and range of addressees. As in the case of degree and standardization of interactional programming, many combinatorial possibilities exist, as shown in Figure 24.

Figure 24: Potential effects of range of addressees and rigidity on errors

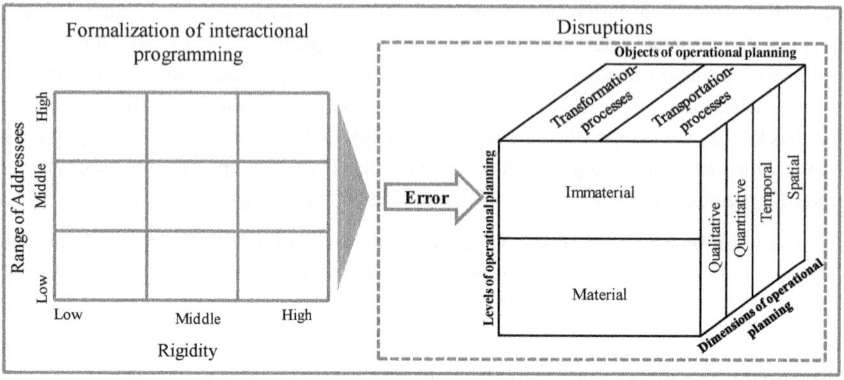

In conclusion of the options for programming cooperation work, it has been shown that firstly, selecting different manifestations of the characteristics may have different effects on the occurrence of errors. Secondly, every characteristic discussed above can affect the probability of errors, which also implies that the interface structure as result of a purposeful combination of characteristics of interactional programming in general may affect the probability of errors. Thirdly, the effect of manifestations of the elements may furthermore depend on the transaction parameters. Fourthly, for every characteristic, a variety of design options exist. The question is thus, how the *combination* of different manifestations affects the probability of errors. To answer this question would in principle require analyzing every possible combination for both elements of degree, standardization, and formalization of interactional programming respectively. The resulting variety, if only the manifestations low, middle, and high of the three characteristics and their respective two components are considered, is shown in Figure 25.

Figure 25: Effect of degree, standardization, and formalization on disruptions

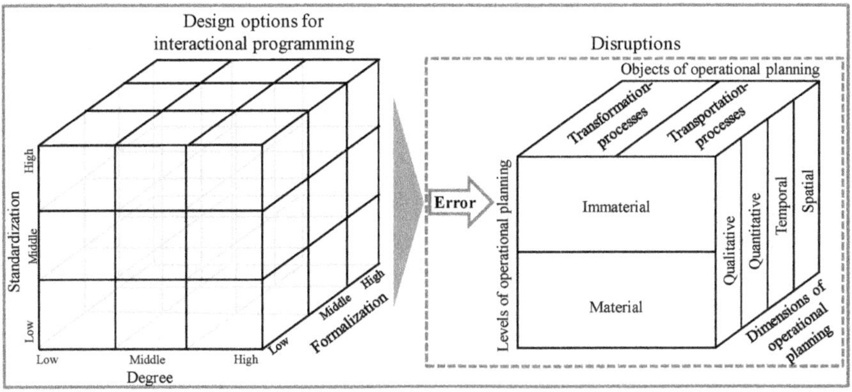

The illustration above shows how diverse interactional programming can be theoretically designed, even without consideration of *type* and *form* of interactional programming. By only considering three main classes of manifestations, the complexity is already substantially reduced, as transitions of manifestations can in principle be infinite. Nevertheless, in organizational literature, the level of abstraction is in general higher (Remer 2005), as otherwise comparison and analysis of different design options results in less pronounced results. Reflecting the explanations of how decisions by individuals may be influenced, it becomes apparent that these decisions and the attainment of desired outcomes might not only be dependent on the equipment with instructions, but may also depend for instance on product specifications, equipment, or whether supply chain partners are from the same region. According to March & Simon (1958), a large disparity between the aspiration level and the achievements is frequently due to a sudden shift in the organizational environment, for example caused by a recession. Therewith, the transaction environment requires further analysis regarding potential direct impacts on decision making and the susceptibility of supply chains to disruptions. This will be discussed in the following section.

3.4.3 Impact of the Transaction Type on Operational Performance

As has been illustrated in section 3.3.3, the variety of variables to describe interface structures is at least theoretically extremely large, which results in a complex array of potential combinations. However, with an increasing level of detailed separations, the ability to deduce general hypotheses on causal relations decreases (Chmielewicz 1979). The same holds true for the type of transaction, as there is at least theoretically an unlimited number of variables to be considered, which in combination yield a complex array of possible transaction types. Previous research regarding the impact of relationship management on performance in supply chains indicates that identifying relevant dimensions of relations is highly problematic (Wilding & Humphries 2006). At the same time, Williamson 1979 identified uncertainty, frequency and specificity of transactions to be critical dimensions, which also found considerable support in the literature.[73] Therefore, transactions will here be characterized by the most important attributes identified by transaction cost theory, namely *specificity*, *uncertainty*, and *frequency*.

From a theoretic point of view, typical constellations of transaction dimensions can be identified by considering two anti-poles of production, namely hierarchical production and market production. According to transaction cost theory, a market transaction is chosen, if uncertainty, specificity, and frequency are low (Williamson 1971). In such a case, market mechanisms are sufficient to control that the outcome of transactions meets the expectations. Hierarchical production in turn is chosen, if a market transaction would involve high uncertainty, high specificity, and high frequency (Williamson 1985). In such a case, the risks associated with the transaction would outweigh the costs of company-internal production. However, as company-internal transactions are not considered in this thesis, this would imply that only the low type of transaction would be prevalent. Furthermore, as high uncertainty and high specificity make transactions more complicated due to difficulties in planning and control as assumed by transaction cost theory, while higher frequency reduces these problems, different effect directions are assumed. Therefore, each variable will be regarded individually. Thereby, the decision making situation of the individual is specified in such a way that general causal hypotheses can be deduced. However, the decision making of individuals is normally not only dependent on these situational factors, but also on others, as for instance personal ones (see section 3.2.3). In order to be able to derive hypotheses nevertheless, all other factors are therefore assumed to remain constant. For example, the individuals making the decision are assumed to be the same in all cases, having therewith a fixed amount of cognitive capacities.

Impacts of Uncertainty of Transaction on Operational Performance

In principle, March & Simon (1958) distinguish three cases for decision making: *firstly*, the case of *certainty*, where the individual has complete and accurate knowledge on the consequences of each alternative. *Secondly*, in the case of *risk* the individual knows at least the probability distribution of consequences for each alternative. And *thirdly*, in the case of *uncertainty*, the decision maker cannot assign probabilities to the occurrence of a specific consequence of each alternative, as multiple possible consequences exist and their probability distribution is unknown.[74] In other words, the link between the decision and its consequence is weak or perturbed by other influencing factors so that the causal relationship between decision and consequence cannot be adequately determined and quantified. The decision maker would thus have two options, either taking a decision without being able to control his hypotheses (see Figure 16), or searching for more information to make better prognoses on the

73 E.g. Hobbs (1996); van der Vorst & Beulens (2002); Artz (1999); Ahmed & Sahinidis (1998); Loader (1997); Ben-Ner, Kong & Lluis (2011).

74 See also e.g. Götze (2006); Eisenführ & Weber (2010); Dreyer (1975).

probability distributions. However, how might uncertainty of transactions affect the decision making of individuals and therewith operational performance?

In transactions, where a high amount of uncertainty, e.g. regarding the behaviour of the partner or the fluctuations in transaction volumes exists, the assessment of decisions and their potential consequences requires more information processing abilities than if uncertainty is low. However, since a disruption is defined as an unexpected event, the case of purposeful deviations from operational planning will not be considered, as in such cases, at least one of the parties (i.e. the deviating party) knows that there will be a deviation from the process plan. Furthermore, as for instance Heide & John (1992) remark, transactions are normally embedded in social structures, where opportunism is rather the exception than the norm. In consequence, only uncertainty as a lack of information on production and transaction parameters will be considered.

In general, the probability of wrong decision making seems thus to be higher, when uncertainty is high, since the willingness to search for more information is according to decision theory restricted. The assumption of satisficing behaviour means that the individual will only search for more information as long as the marginal improvement possible by searching is higher than or equal to the marginal costs of information seeking (March & Simon 1958). However, under uncertainty, there exist numerous alternatives for decision making, but the consequences remain unclear. This implies that even if the decision maker searches for more information, the marginal improvement possible is low as the overall amount of information required which would allow to take decisions under risk (see above) is too large.

In order to reduce the complexity of its task to come to a decision, the individual has to reduce the level of detail with which it regards the problem and to focus on more abstract structures of the task, hence making decisions based on pattern recognition (Simon). Thus, in the face of uncertainty in a transaction, the individuals who should coordinate the transaction process are likely to apply methods which have been successful in the past without knowing whether it might be the appropriate action in the new situation and with this interaction partner.

If individuals are recurrently exposed to decision making situations, where their ability to handle the complexity is exceeded, they lose motivation, become exasperated and will not try to produce optimal decisions any more (Hill, Fehlbaum & Ulrich 1994). Additionally, as at interfaces their performance cannot be unambiguously evaluated due to lower supervision (see section 3.3.1), the incentives to invest in information seeking and production of optimal decisions is reduced. In consequence, the probability of errors is increased firstly, by limited cognitive capacities, and secondly, by lacking incentives.

At the same time, less predictability may also be favourable, to enhance attention paid to each shipment. Especially for non-staple foods, fluctuations in demand and shipping may be larger, due to seasonality of supply and consumer habits (Drewry Shipping Consultants 1990). In particular, perishability of products creates uncertainty for the buyer regarding availability and quality (Georgiadis, Vlachos & Iakovou 2005). In such situations, the aspiration level may be higher, as quality of products is more variable wherefore products require more thorough inspections and care during handling. In either way, it seems likely that uncertainty of transactions has an impact on the achievement of process plans, wherefore the following proposition is stipulated:

Proposition 4 If uncertainty of transaction changes, then the achievement of operational planning does not change

Similarly to the variables of interface structure, the variables characterizing the type of transaction may also take different manifestations on a range from low to high. In this case however, constructs are not the result of two variables, wherefore there is only one dimension to consider. Figure 26 illustrates the potential influence by uncertainty on the achievement of operational plans.

Figure 26: Effect of uncertainty of transaction on the achievement of operational planning

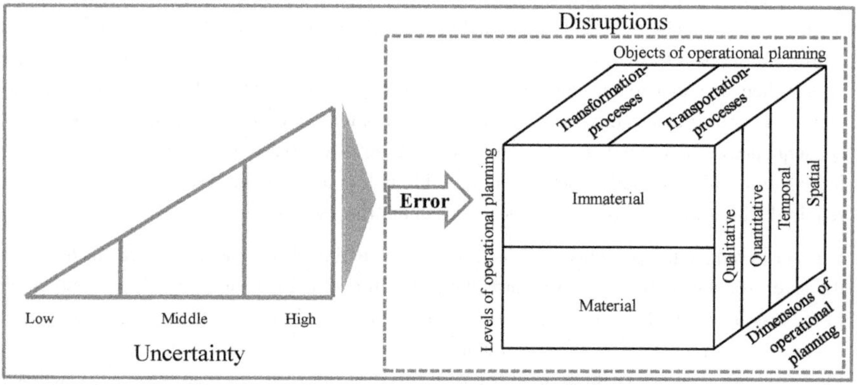

Impacts of Frequency of Transaction on Operational Performance

According to transaction cost theory, frequency is relevant in two aspects, namely regarding set up costs and reputation effects (Williamson 2008). The costs of preparing and executing a transaction decrease with increasing frequency of transaction (Williamson 1990), which Williamson (1979) differentiates into once, occasional, and recurrent. However, how might frequency of transactions affect the decision making of individuals and therewith operational performance?

Frequent transactions would thereby help individuals to learn from past decisions regarding their ability to achieve the aspiration level. An individual can hereby for instance integrate feedback on whether the information provided has been understood correctly by its interaction partner into the repeated provision of information. This is also supported by Kosiol (1971), who states that more intensive interactions are in general associated with less information losses caused by different levels of cognitive abilities. Even more, in established cooperation, the relationship can also be modified and changed, by incremental mutual adaptation processes (van de Ven & Ferry 1980).

Consequently, individuals could refine their decisions for how to execute future interactions with other individuals at the same interface. According to Hill, Fehlbaum & Ulrich (1994) combining and re-combining procedures which the individuals have already learned, their decision making is then narrowed down to selecting the optimal program (i.e. routinization of tasks) instead of developing new solutions starting from zero (i.e. problem solving). Therewith, uncertainty in individual decision making would be reduced by higher frequency through limiting the number of decision options. If transactions in turn are infrequent, execution of tasks becomes less routinized, as the retrieval of information on how to handle a specific exchange process may be perturbed by other information obtained in the meantime. Thereby, the probability of errors might become higher.

At the same time, individuals might pay more attention to a specific exchange if it is occurring less frequent, for instance due to seasonality of the product (see above). In such cases, the probability of errors of omission might be reduced as the level of arousal is higher. In either way, the following proposition can be deduced:

Proposition 5 If transaction frequency changes, then the achievement of operational planning does not change

Figure 27: Effect of frequency on the achievement of operational planning

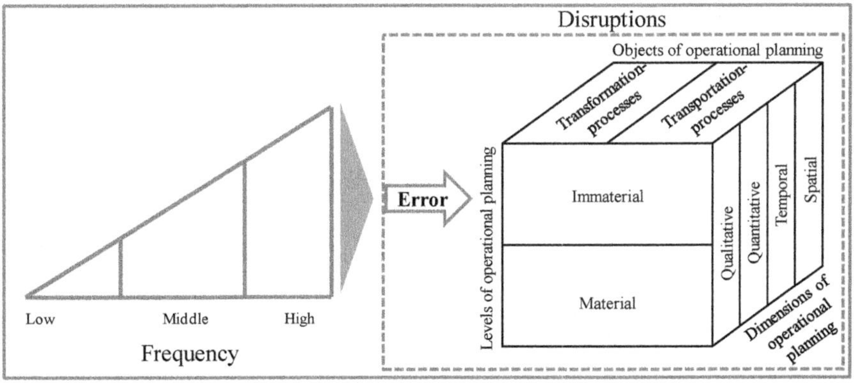

Impacts of Specificity of Transaction on Operational Performance

According to Williamson (1979), the more partner-specific assets are employed, the higher is the dependency on this partner. He sees therefore this variable also as the primary driver of different governance structures of transactions. Specificity refers thereby to the need to make transaction-specific investments, being it in e.g. humans, physical infrastructure, or brand name and is a sign of bilateral dependency (Williamson 2008) as a termination of the relationship would result in sunk costs (Heide & John 1992). Williamson (1979, p. 239) further explains "*items that are unspecialized among users pose few hazards, since buyers in these circumstances can easily turn to alternative sources, and suppliers can sell output intended for one order to other buyers without difficulty*". Hence, specificity of transactions can lead to higher sunk costs, as the second best option for investments taken generates either far less utility, or there is no second best option at all. However, what kind of effect can specificity of transactions inflict on the decision making of individuals and therewith on operational performance?

On the one hand, the presence of asset specificity and risk of sunk costs may encourage employees to more careful execution of their work and interaction programs, to avoid reprehensions or penalties. The risk of losing the transaction partner might also lead to a more thorough monitoring of employees by the company, rising awareness of risks associated with non-compliance. Hence, the aspiration level might be higher and spending more efforts on executing tasks correctly seems to be rational. Even more, such specific investments might also be targeting employees directly, by investments into training and qualification of the transaction partner (Subramani & Venkatraman 2003). In such cases, the probability of errors might be reduced by increasing the levels of aspiration and the ability of employees to deal with requirements.

On the other hand however, dealing with new requirements and using specialized equipment might also foster the occurrence of errors, especially in the learning phase. Employees might try to use learned procedures to deal with new challenges, due to erroneously recognizing patterns and applying learned solutions to new problems. Furthermore, such new stimuli might involve a higher amount of problem-solving tasks instead of routinized tasks, increasing the complexity of decision making. Therewith, specificity of transactions might also lead to more errors.

Proposition 6 If specificity changes, then the achievement of operational planning does not change

Figure 28: Effect of asset specificity on the achievement of operational planning

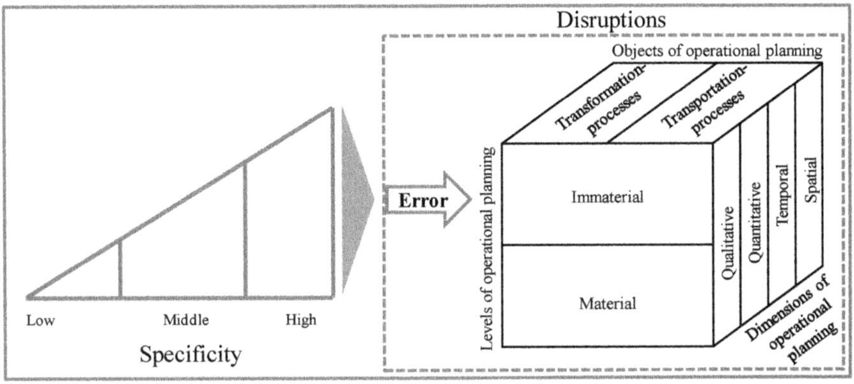

In summary, for each of the three characteristics of the transaction type considered, an effect on the probability of errors can theoretically be reasoned. Each of the variables may thereby take different manifestations, ranging on a continuum between low and high. Altogether, the transaction type can be configured along three axes, resulting in an unlimited number of configurations. A reduction of this complexity can again be achieved, by considering only low, middle, and high manifestations of the three dimensions.

Even though transaction cost theory does not focus on the effects of how types of transactions may affect the probability of errors in the exchange processes, such effects seem to be probable given the considerations above. Hence, whereas decisions on with whom and how to collaborate may be taken on higher hierarchical levels, these decisions may have an influence on the executing levels as well. Figure 29 subsumes the hitherto developed propositions on how operational plans may be influenced by transaction types and interface structures.

The illustrated complexity of the object of analysis is already one potential reason, why little empirical research has been found on causes of disruptions in supply chains (see section 2.5). Even more, with interface structure and transaction type, only two potential determinants of the occurrence of disruptions have been considered, whereby many other determinants might be left to explore. However, as the purpose of this thesis is to analyze the impact of the *interface design* on the susceptibility to disruptions, the effects of transaction type on interface structure still have to be considered, to explain the choice of a given interface structure by transaction partners. Thereby, the causal model will be completed for the subsequent empirical analysis. The completion and transformation of the causal model is subject to section 3.5.

Figure 29: Hypothesized effects of interface structure and transaction type on disruptions

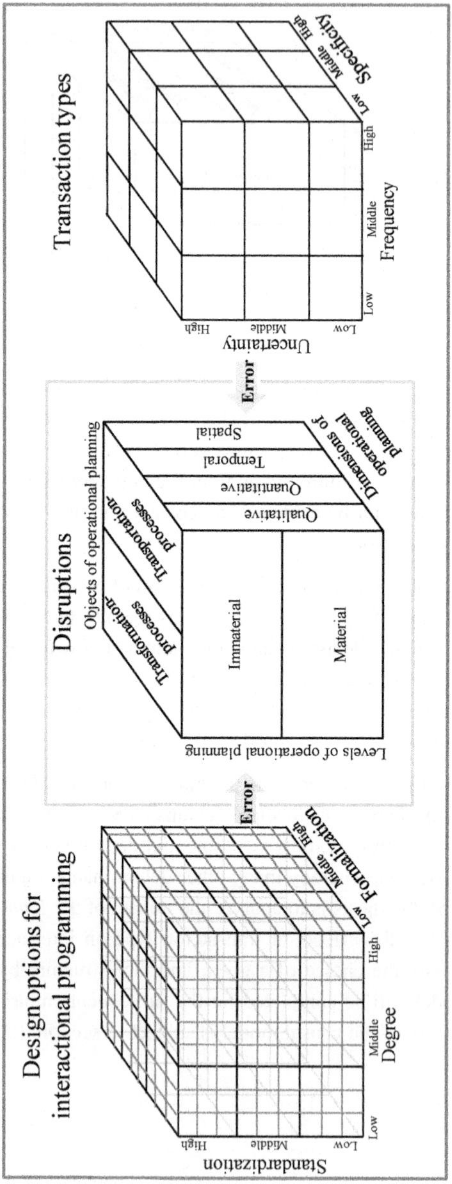

3.5 Consolidation of Causal Assumptions into one Causal Model

3.5.1 Impacts of Transaction Type on the Interface Design

As has been elaborated in section 3.3.1, the interface structure does not take its form by coincidence, but is configured under the considerations of constraints, what has been termed as interface design. In the case of interfaces, transaction cost theory assumes that the transaction environment has a considerable influence on how exchange processes are governed. Hence, apart from direct effects of the transaction type on the occurrence of disruptions, it is furthermore assumed that the transaction type inhibits direct effects on the interface structure. Therefore, in the following, the hitherto developed propositions on effects of interface structure and transaction type on the occurrence of disruptions will be complemented by interaction effects between the components of the transaction type and the components of the interface structure.

In order to assess potential effects of transaction characteristics on the structure of interactional programming, it is assumed that the contracting parties are autonomous at the outset. This implies that whereas transaction cost theory suggests different contractual forms between market and hierarchy (Williamson 1985), for the purpose of this thesis, only transactions between two legally independent supply chain partners will be considered. In the following, the potential effect of different values of characteristics of transactions on interactional programming will be analyzed.

Impacts of Uncertainty of Transactions on Interface Design

Uncertainty in the context of transaction cost theory refers on the one hand to the behaviour of the transaction partner, and whether he can and is willing to comply with the agreed-upon contract (Williamson 1990). On the other hand, it refers to the lack of information regarding production and transaction parameters (Williamson 1971).

Uncertainty in supply chains depends on many variables, such as volatility in supply, processing, or demand, and interdependence with other processes (e.g. Ben-Ner, Kong & Lluis 2011; Ho, Chi & Tai 2005; van de Ven & Ferry 1980). In line with these variables,van der Vorst & Beulens (2002) stress the susceptibility of food supply chains to uncertainty, due to the perishable nature of the end product, variable harvest and production yields, as well as the impact of weather conditions on consumer demand. According to the authors, such volatile conditions demand for more flexible contractual agreements, to allow for consideration of contingent factors. Simultaneously, the requirements posed on employees are also higher, as they need to be more flexible in decision making.

However, with regard to the ability of transaction partners to give clear instructions to their employees under high uncertainty, some restrictions become obvious. For such a situation, Williamson (1971, p. 120) states that "*in the face of a highly variable and uncertain environment, the attempt to program responses is apt to be inefficient.*" This has been confirmed empirically for firm internal uncertainty by Ben-Ner, Kong & Lluis (2011) who observed that high uncertainty in terms of non-routine tasks, complexity of tasks, and variability of tasks increases delegation of decision making to individuals. Fixing precise and detailed instructions for how to interact with other positions across companies could thereby also lead to the shortfall of objectives, if transaction-specific information is lacking upon agreeing on the transaction. Especially for long-term contracts, a high degree of programming is not always feasible, as future contingencies cannot be reasonably determined in advance, nor are the means for problem solving always clear before the situation materializes (Williamson 1981). In consequence, in transactions where uncertainty prevails, the probability of erroneous programming increases.

If uncertainty is low, then positions can be programmed to a higher extent, as more reliable information on the transaction is available. In such a situation, Williamson (1971, p. 120) states that "*coordination could proceed by contract*", as the conditions could be exhaustively described. However, whereas such controlled situations might be found in e.g. bureaucratic organizations and factory plants (Remer 1982), it seems unlikely that they exist in food supply chains, due to the already mentioned characteristics. Nevertheless, if certainty cannot be achieved, at least uncertainty could be low, wherefore more precise and detailed agreements could be possible.

In consideration of the argumentation above, it seems as there is a dilemma for companies facing uncertainty in transactions, with on the one hand the need for programming, but on the other hand the inability to do so correctly. This dilemma is one of the reasons, why vertical integration is favoured compared to market transactions under uncertainty (Hobbs 1996). The question arises, whether the same causal relations can be assumed for standardization and formalization of interactional programming. Considering that according to Remer (2005), both characteristics concern the *generalization* and *stabilization* of instructions, high standardization and formalization of programming seem to conflict with high uncertainty in transactions, which according to Williamson (1971) require *adaptive* coordination. Hence, the stabilizing function of standardization and formalization would under high uncertainty lead to mismatches between instructions, constraints, and the organizational goals, which represents according to Hill, Fehlbaum & Ulrich (1994) the classical organizational problem.

This is also consistent with findings in empirical studies, where in case that the instructions did not match the requirements of the situation, either the compliance with them led to inefficiencies, or the decision makers deviated consciously from the instructions (Gross 1953). In consequence, it can be assumed that transaction partners will consider the degree of uncertainty during the design of interfaces and adapt the inter-actional programming respectively, which can be hypothesized as:

Proposition 7 If uncertainty of transactions changes, then the degree of interactional programming does not change

Proposition 7.1 **If uncertainty of transactions changes, then the level of detail of interactional programming does not change**

Proposition 7.2 **If uncertainty of transactions changes, then preciseness of interactional programming does not change**

Proposition 8 **If uncertainty of transactions changes, then standardization of interactional programming does not change**

Proposition 8.1 **If uncertainty of transactions changes, then durability of interactional programming does not change**

Proposition 8.2 **If uncertainty of transactions changes, then invariability of interactional programming does not change**

Proposition 9 **If uncertainty of transactions changes, then formalization of interactional programming does not change**

Proposition 9.1 **If uncertainty of transactions changes, then the range of addressees of interactional programming does not change**

Proposition 9.2 **If uncertainty of transactions changes, then rigidity of interactional programming does not change**

In consequence of the discussion above, optimal interface design seems to be challenging, as companies would have to design the interface structure in an area of conflict between interface goals and transaction-related restrictions. However, as already Remer (2005) points out, the decisions on interface design do not have to be taken for all dimensions, directions, and objects identically. Rather, general guidelines considering different scenarios could be provided, but authority regarding whether to comply with these guidelines could be assigned to the decision maker. However, the costs associated with developing such general guidelines also depend on the frequency of transaction, wherefore this aspect will be regarded in the following.

Impacts of Frequency of Transactions on Interface Design

According to Williamson (1979, p. 239), only recurring transactions support a highly specialized interface structure. In consequence, the costs of programming would decrease, as initial set up costs can be distributed over more transactions.

Supply chain partners, who work together more often, would thus be able to formulate more detailed and precise interactional instructions, since once established cooperation procedures could be used repetitively at lower cost. Especially ex-ante transaction costs, such as search costs and negotiation costs are reduced in repeated transactions with the same partner (Williamson 1985). A higher durability and socio-spatial validity of interactional programming may then also justify investments into the infrastructure for interaction. For instance, the implementation of information exchange systems to increase traceability in food chains is often observed when supply chain agents are frequent transaction partners (Smith & Sparks 2004). These intentionally programmed instructions will be furthermore supported by behavioural expectations formed regarding reciprocal rights and obligations (van de Ven & Ferry 1980). However, over a longer period, repeated interaction reinforces cooperation (Lambert, Emmelhainz & Gardner 1996), whereby the relative importance of formalized programming of interactions is likely to decline in favour of informal coordination of interaction. Additionally, the advantage of long-term partnerships is dependent on the ability of both parties to adapt their agreements flexibly in face of changing conditions (Heide & John 1992). Hence, in recurrent transactions, standardized and formalized instructions of interactional programming are likely to be used less, whereas the degree of programming might be higher.

In transactions where the frequency is low with everything else being equal, the costs of preparing the transaction would then not justify the creation of highly specialized structures. If companies would adjust the instructions given to their employees for every transaction, the advantage of relative stability of interface structure would be lost. While employees working at interfaces normally already possess a comparatively higher degree of autonomy (Riechey 2008), this autonomy would be increased even more as controlling their work would require knowing exactly which instructions they follow for each transaction. In consequence, more standardized and formalized instructions are likely to be prevalent. Furthermore, as with a higher standardization of instructions, contextual parameters of the specific transaction cannot be considered, it is likely that the degree of programming will be lower, especially regarding preciseness of programming. Therefore, the following propositions can be deduced:

Proposition 10 **If frequency of transactions changes, then the degree of interactional programming does not change**

Proposition 10.1 **If frequency of transactions changes, then the level of detail of interactional programming does not change**

Proposition 10.2 **If frequency of transactions changes, then preciseness of interactional programming does not change**

Proposition 11 **If frequency of transactions changes, then standardization of interactional programming does not change**

Proposition 11.1 **If frequency of transactions changes, then durability of interactional programming does not change**

Proposition 11.2 **If frequency of transactions changes, then invariability of interactional programming does not change**

Proposition 12 **If frequency of transactions changes, then formalization of interactional programming does not change**

Proposition 12.1 **If frequency of transactions changes, then the range of addressees of interactional programming does not change**

Proposition 12.2 **If frequency of transactions changes, then rigidity of interactional programming does not change**

The assumptions above only consider the frequency of transaction, regardless of what is transferred between them. Nevertheless, the ability to program, standardize, and formalize interactions also depends on the variability of tasks associated with the transaction and therewith depends on the content of transaction. Hence, in the following, the specificity of transaction will be analyzed as the third parameter characterizing transactions.

Impacts of Specificity of Transactions on Interface Design

Transaction-specific investments imply that an adaptation of one company to the requirements of another company takes place. In consequence, specificity will in general be higher, the more dissimilar companies are and the more this transaction differs from the rest of transactions a company executes.

In food supply chains, product specificity might be for instance the difference between a staple, which can be stored for a long time (e.g. rice) (Sharp & Timme 1986), and an exotic, highly perishable product (e.g. fresh scallops) (Ashie et al. 1996). Whereas the dry good can be stored and used for other purposes without great efforts, the perishable product needs to be handled with great care and has to be sold as soon as possible, to avoid spoilage. Therefore, in the second case, more careful planning is required to make sure that the product can be used for its intended purpose. Dissimilarity in turn could be related to size (e.g. smallholder interacting with a multi-national retailer), culture, or interface structure and has been frequently regarded as a source of challenges in food supply chains (Fearne & Hughes 2000; Louw et al. 2007; Luning & Marcelis 2007).

As a consequence, for transactions with less routine and higher specificity, companies will be willing to prepare the transaction to a greater extent and to write more complete agreements (Williamson 2008). These may include more information regarding rights and responsibilities as well as special agreements regarding penalties or behaviour in certain situations. Therefore, whereas under specificity, the degree of programming and its formalization are assumed to be higher, standardization is assumed to be less, as fewer procedures can be adopted from other transactions.

If specificity is low, risks of sunk costs are reduced, wherefore the costs of preparing and controlling a transaction can be reduced. In such cases, governance of transaction is reduced to arm-length bargaining over price and quantity (Heide & John 1992). Standardized procedures result in lower costs of preparation and control of interactions, whereas fewer instructions are required. Formalization can be reduced as well, as routine transactions require less supervision of how employees handle the interaction. This leads to the deduction of the following propositions:

Proposition 13 **If specificity of transactions changes, then the degree of interactional programming does not change**

Proposition 13.1 **If specificity of transactions changes, then the level of detail of interactional programming does not change**

Proposition 13.2 **If specificity of transactions changes, then preciseness of interactional programming does not change**

Proposition 14 **If specificity of transactions changes, then standardization of interactional programming does not change**

Proposition 14.1 **If specificity of transactions changes, then durability of interactional programming does not change**

Proposition 14.2 **If specificity of transactions changes, then invariability of interactional programming does not change**

Proposition 15 **If specificity of transactions changes, then formalization of interactional programming does not change**

Proposition 15.1 **If specificity of transactions changes, then the range of addressees of interactional programming does not change**

Proposition 15.2 **If specificity of transactions changes, then rigidity of interactional programming does not change**

In the paragraphs above, potential impacts of uncertainty, frequency, and specificity of transactions on the interface structure have been depicted. As a matter of course, other determinants might also play an important role in the design of interfaces, such as technologies applied, socio-cultural background, or the industry regarded (Hill, Fehlbaum & Ulrich 1994). Given the objective to empirically investigate these propositions, and the already complex nature of the research object, first of all the hitherto developed propositions will be transformed into a causal framework, before new determinants will be included eventually. To this purpose, section 3.5.2 will outline methodological requirements, before the causal model can be derived.

3.5.2 Methodological Considerations for the Empirical Analysis

The purpose of scientific research does not only consist in developing new hypotheses, but also in the falsification of existing hypotheses to increase current scientific knowledge (Chmielewicz 1979). Therefore, hypotheses have to be formulated in such a way that they can fail in empirical research (Popper 1973). Consequently, social constructs, which cannot be observed directly, but to which hypotheses refer to, require adequate indicators to become ascertainable. However, the suitability of indicators depends on the choice of data collection method, as well as on the choice of analytical procedure (Diekmann 2002). Only if indicators can be observed with the selected data collection method, they can be used for hypotheses testing and falsification (Kromrey 2009). Therefore, in the following, first different methods for data collection and analysis will be discussed, before indicators are specified.

Typical empirical methods in social sciences can be generally attributed to content analyses, observations, and inquiries (Bortz & Döring 1995; Kromrey 2009). As the research interest in social sciences is frequently concerned with complex and abstract constructs which cannot be measured directly, procedures to obtain data normally consider more rich information, which has to be processed afterwards (Diekmann 2002). Even though the measurement of disruptions could be based on quantitative data e.g. temperature curves, manifestations of interface designs could not be assessed by direct measurements because of the level of abstraction and complexity. As for the data analysis already a statistical method which is able to handle such information was identified, there is no need to base the analysis only on directly quantifiable data. Hence, the typical methods of empirical social sciences seem to be more adequate and shall consequently be briefly depicted and assessed.

The **content analysis** is a research technique, which allows drawing conclusions that can be generalized beyond the data medium analyzed (Kromrey 2009). The information is stored in mediums such as documents, which shall provide insights on the issues of interest based on a systematic and objective analysis (Diekmann 2002). To the purpose of this thesis, content analysis could be for example used to identify the interface design agreed upon in contracts between transaction partners. However, a disadvantage would be that non-written agreements would not be considered and only the desired structure assessed, not the actual structure. Additionally, the amount of documents to be analyzed and the sensitivity of data mediums decrease the feasibility of content analysis considerably. This is supported by Kieser & Walgenbach (2007), who advise against content analysis for the identification of interface designs due to a lack of expressiveness. In consequence, this technique is discarded for this thesis.

Another typical technique in social sciences is **observation**. According to Laatz (1993), observation in a strict sense is the collection of experiences in a non-communicative process with the help of all possibilities of perception. In comparison to day-to-day observations however, scientific observation is more systematic, purpose oriented, and methodologically controlled (Laatz 1993). Object of research are social processes, which change constantly during observation (Kromrey 2009). In consequence, missed observations cannot be caught up on later. Furthermore, as the research focus is on structures and processes in international supply chains, this form of data gathering does not seem to be realizable *firstly*, because of potential lack of cooperation by companies and *secondly*, because of the amount of observations required. Due to the lack of inter-subjective and inter-temporal validity of observations, as well as its lack of feasibility in this research context, this procedure does not seem to be suitable and is therefore also discarded.

The third typical technique is the **survey method**. It is the technique mostly used in empirical social sciences and can be designed in many different ways, depending on the context (Bortz & Döring 1995; Remer 2005). In principle, one can distinguish oral interviews and paper-and-pencil interviews, whereby the types of questions may range between completely open questions and closed questions (Diekmann 2002). Open questions are used more frequently in exploring phenomena, whereas closed questions are used more often to explain phenomena. This form of empirical research is also favoured by Kieser & Walgenbach (2007) and Remer (2005) for the measurement of interface designs, as herewith the range of possible indicators is the largest and may therewith increase the exactness of measurements. As for the testing of the hypotheses derived above a large number of data sets is required and as food supply chains may include organizations in many different countries, this technique seems to be suitable for the purpose of this thesis.

However, apart from the method of data gathering, Bortz & Döring (1995) stress that empirical research requires substantial knowledge of different options to also analyze empirical data. Kromrey (2009) adds that these research steps cannot be considered separately from one another, but that they influence each other and therefore need joint consideration, as well as consideration of the research purpose.

The research purpose of this thesis lies in the testing of hypothesized causal relations between the interface design and the occurrence of disruptions in food supply chains. Empirical studies are developed to test assumptions on causal relations, differences, and changes in selected characteristics in specific populations (Bortz & Döring 1995). In general, for such purposes statistical procedures are used to analyze the data obtained (Kromrey 2009), which can involve univariate, bivariate, or multivariate phenomena (Diekmann 2002). According to Kieser & Walgenbach (2007), empirical analysis of relations between dimensions of a situation and dimensions of organizational structures is effected primarily by calculation of statistical relations, especially by correlation analysis. Thereby, theoretically predicted causal relations can be tested for their existence in practice, which helps to increase scientific knowledge (Schnell, Hill & Esser 2011). However, by analyzing empirical data with the help of statistical methods, also some limitations can be observed.

In order to make social phenomena accessible to statistical analyses, information content is reduced because variables and causal relations need to be quantified (Kieser & Walgenbach 2007). Therewith, important facets of the regarded construct might be lost, if it is not possible to translate them adequately in quantitative indicators. For instance, the perception of invariability and rigidity of the same instructions might differ between the employees of transaction partners, yet by quantifying and aggregating the variables, such information is lost. At the same time, it is lost in favour of higher generalization of the obtained results.[75] Nevertheless, it depends on the research question, whether such information loss can be justified or not.

The objective of this thesis is to identify general causal relations between interface design and the occurrence of disruptions. The focus lies thereby not on the explanation of why a specific

[75] For a discussion of the trade-off between preciseness and universality see e.g. Chmielewicz (1979) with reference to Popper (1973).

error occurred in a specific situation as such hypotheses could not be falsified and would therefore conflict with the ontological position of this thesis. Therefore, the loss of qualitative information seems to be justifiable if therewith empirical data on the hypothesized causal relations can be analyzed based on statistical methods.

As already pointed out above, a variety of statistical methods exists, which lend themselves to the analysis of causal relations in social sciences. The procedures range thereby from analyzing causal relations between two directly quantified variables, up to analyzing causal relations between constructs, which cannot be directly observed in practice and therefore require the construction of not only causal models, but also measurement models (see e.g. Bortz & Döring 1995; Albers et al. 2009; Backhaus 2011). For the investigation of the hypotheses developed here, the method of structural equation modelling (SEM) is selected due to several reasons, which are illustrated in the following.

SEMs can be understood as statistical procedures for testing and measuring functional, predictive, and causal hypotheses (Anderson & Gerbing 1988; Bagozzi & Yi 2012). The technique of SEM is an advancement of path analysis, which allows for the analysis of latent (i.e. unobservable) variables, and for the consideration of measurement errors (Bortz & Döring 1995). The resulting path coefficients indicate the strength of causal effects, if the causal model is correct. Therewith, the technique allows only for the exclusion of falsified causal models, but does not determine which of the remaining potential causal models is correct (Backhaus et al. 2011). This decision in turn is based on the previously logically and theoretically developed assumptions on causal relations. SEMs are to be preferred compared to e.g. influence diagrams, if the researcher is interested in the explanation of effects, not on their prognosis (Anderson & Vastag 2004).

The hypotheses to be investigated are hypotheses on relations between an environmental condition, an interface structure, and their effects on the probability of errors, resulting in disruptions. Thereby all three components are latent variables, which cannot be observed directly, wherefore the direct measurement of variables is not possible. Furthermore, the occurrence of errors and consequential disruptions might have more causes than those assessed here, wherefore measurement errors are likely. Furthermore, the research interest is here on the explanation of why disruptions occur, wherefore explanation is prioritized compared to prognosis. Therefore, SEMs seem to be a suitable technique for the purpose of this thesis.

In principle, a SEM comprises one structural model, and two measurement models (Backhaus et al. 2011). In the structural model, the assumed causal relations between exogenous and endogenous latent variables are stipulated (γ) (Anderson & Gerbing 1988). One of the measurement models measures the exogenous latent variable (ζ) with the help of adequate indicators (X) under consideration of measurement errors (δ), and the other one measures the endogenous latent variable η with the help of indicators (Y) including measurement errors (ε) (Backhaus et al. 2011). A simplified model shows Figure 30.

Figure 30: Structural equation model with one exogenous and one endogenous variable

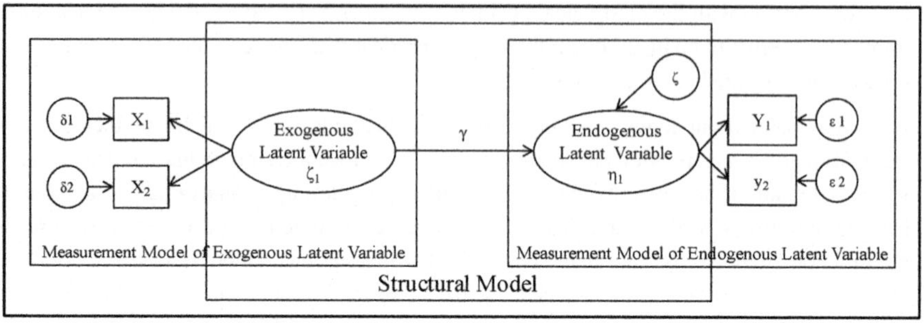

Source 15: Adapted from Backhaus et al. (2011 p. 341)

In summary, the SEM has the purpose to translate causal relations between abstract constructs into empirically observable, measurable indicators, which are connected by choosing adequate mathematical operations (Backhaus et al. 2011). However, before being able to derive indicators and measure the latent constructs, first of all, the assumed causal paths have to be identified, wherefore the propositions made in this thesis have to be combined in one structural model.

In conclusion of the above developed assumptions on the causal relations, the structural model includes three exogenous variables, which are influencing the interface structure, and which are also assumed to have a direct effect on the operational performance and its susceptibility to disruptions. Thereby, the interface structure can be regarded on two levels of analysis: firstly, on the more aggregated level, where interface structure is composed by degree, standardization, and formalization of interactional programming. As these elements are compositions of their sub-elements, this model will be termed *second order model* in the subsequent analysis and can be found in Figure 31.[76]

[76] This terminology is suggested for example by Vandenberg, Richardson & Eastman (1999) and Jarvis, MacKenzie & Podsakoff (2003).

Figure 31: Second order model linking transactions and interface design to performance

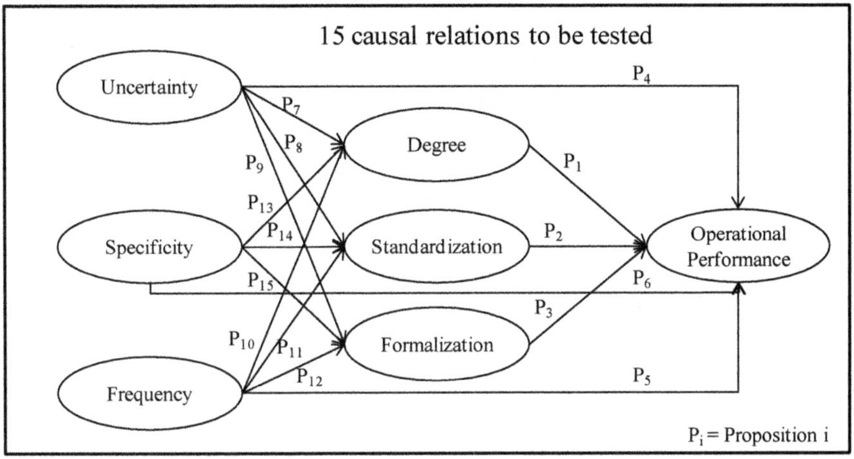

As can be seen, of the paths connecting the constructs have been marked with the proposition stipulating the assumed causal relation. In all, this structural model involves fifteen paths which have to be measured. However, as the three variables of interface structure have been further decomposed, this model can be further refined by splitting these elements into their respective sub-elements as shown in Figure 32. This model will be referred to as *first order model* in the following.

Figure 32: First order model linking transactions and interface design to performance

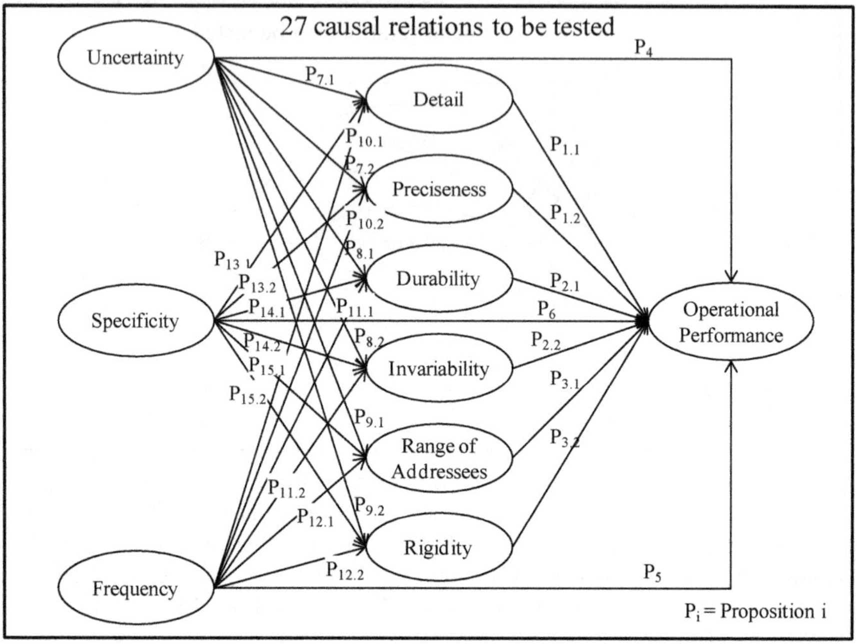

The amount of causal relations to be tested is substantially higher in the first order model compared to the second order model. Furthermore, the consideration of two levels of analysis also has implications for the measurement models, as will be shown in section 3.5.3. Regarding the question of suitable indicators, it is now possible to assert that *firstly*, values have to be retrievable with the survey-technique, and secondly, measurements have to be integrated in a SEM, taking the specification of constructs into account. Based on these considerations, in the next section, the SEM for the testing of how interface design affects the occurrence of disruptions will be developed.

3.5.3 Structural Equation Model on Impacts of Interface Design on Operational Performance

In the next step, the latent variables have to be operationalized, to allow for an empirical analysis of the hypothesized causal relations between these abstract constructs. Consequently, the measurement models have to be developed, which include empirical indicators for the latent constructs (Backhaus et al. 2011). Thereby, indicators can be distinguished regarding the assumed direction of causation between indicators and construct into reflective and formative indicators (Diamantopoulos & Siguaw 2006).

According to Christophersen & Grape (2009) *reflective* measurement models interpret latent variables as causes of observable indicators. If the latent construct changes, it is reflected in a change of all its indicators, wherefore they are interchangeable and measure the variable holistically. This connection is represented in Figure 30 by arrows, which go from the latent construct to the indicators. This type of model is therefore frequently used in explorative research, where large sets of variables are searched for common structures, which allow for a consolidation and aggregation of variables (Backhaus et al. 2011).

Formative measurement models in turn regard latent constructs as weighted combinations of its indicators, whereby these indicators impact on the construct. In Figure 30, this would be the case if the connection between indicators and latent construct would be the other way round because they constitute the latent variable. Accordingly, even though indicators may correlate with each other, they do not have to (Christophersen & Grape 2009). Therewith, they may represent different dimensions of the latent variable, which cannot be adequately covered by a set of equal indicators. However, this procedure requires more preparatory efforts to derive logical and theoretically consistent hypotheses and a complete set of indicators to measure all dimensions of a construct (Backhaus et al. 2011).

As Bagozzi & Yi (2012, p. 17) note "*the choice of whether to use reflective or formative indicators of latent variables is a controversial issue*" and Fornell & Bookstein (1982, p. 442) add that "*the selection of indicator mode may be difficult*". This has also been highlighted for the operationalization of inter- and intra-organizational coordination by Diamantopoulos & Siguaw (2006), who continue that despite this difficulty, the choice of operationalization mode of coordination has not been explicitly defended by prior research. Also research on organizational structures in general uses ambiguous approaches: many authors utilize reflective indicators for organizational structures, (e.g. Blain 1964; James & Jones 1980; Morrison 2002, Ramamoorthy & Flood 2004). However, this procedure does not necessarily have to be correct, as demonstrated by Diamantopoulos & Siguaw (2006). For a research design where formative indicators would have been required, they compared the results of a reflective and a formative model and showed that the former led to much less distinctive results. Therefore, they come to the conclusion that "*it is thus possible that the true effects of coordination as both the 'glue' that ensures organizational effectiveness and as a determinant of performance outcomes may have been underestimated as a result of a Type I error* [i.e. choosing reflective indicators, even though formative indicators would have been required, A/N]" (Diamantopoulos & Siguaw 2006, p. 273).

The choice is therefore of prime importance for the empirical research and needs to be addressed thoroughly. However, apart from these two options, also combined measurement models are possible, which include reflective operationalization of one latent variable, and formative operationalization of another one (Fornell & Bookstein 1982; Diamantopoulos & Siguaw 2006; Jarvis, MacKenzie & Podsakoff 2003). This kind of model can be used for example, if the observed variance in the endogenous reflectively measured variable shall be explained by the unobserved exogenous variables (Fornell & Bookstein 1982). In consequence, for each of the constructs, regarded in this thesis, the adequate type of indicators has to be chosen. As a support for the adequate choice, Jarvis, MacKenzie & Podsakoff (2003) provide a set of decision rules, which are illustrated in the following:

Figure 33: Decision rules for the selection of type of models

Question	Formative model	Reflective model
Direction of causality from construct to measure implied by the conceptual definition:	Direction of causality is from items to construct	Direction of causality is from construct to item
Are the indicators (a) defining characteristics or (b) manifestations of the construct?	Indicators are defining characteristics of the construct	Indicators are manifestations of the construct
Would changes in the indicators cause changes in the construct or not?	Yes	No
Would changes in the construct cause changes in the indicators?	No	Yes
Interchangeability of the indicators	Not necessarily	Yes
Should the indicators have the same or similar content?	Not necessarily	Yes
Do the indicators share a common theme?	Not necessarily	Yes
Would dropping one of the indicators alter the conceptual domain of the construct?	Yes	No
Is there co-variation among indicators?	Not necessarily	Yes
Should a change in one of the indicators be associated with changes in the other indicators?	Not necessarily	Yes
Does the nomological net of the construct indicators differ?	Yes	No
Are the indicators expected to have the same antecedents and consequences?	Not necessarily	Yes

Source 16: Own illustration, adapted from Jarvis, MacKenzie & Podsakoff (2003)[77]

Apart from this decision support, in the case of transaction type, the literature on empirical tests of transaction cost theory suggests that uncertainty and specificity should be operationalized with reflective indicators, e.g. (Heide & John 1988; Walker & Weber 1987; John & Weitz 1989; Coughlan & Narasimhan 1992; Foss & Laursen 2005; Ho, Chi & Tai 2005). This seems to be intuitive, considering that e.g. uncertainty may arise from a large field of factors, which need not be present in every case. For instance, for a manufacturer of staples such as pasta, seasonality of demand may be no source of uncertainty, whereas for a manufacturer of ice cream, it may play a significant role. Therewith, the operationalization of uncertainty as a formative measurement model would bear the risk of misspecification, omission of important causes and inclusion of negligible ones. Therefore, uncertainty will be operationalized based on a reflective measurement model.

The same can be argued for specificity of employed assets: whereas the concrete asset may be different for each company, the fact that investments have been made reflect the presence of

77 Further lists of criteria have been offered by e.g. Bollen & Lennox (1991) or Diamantopoulos & Winklhofer (2001), but the list chosen above is considered to be more comprehensive Podsakoff et al. (2003).

specificity. Therefore, specificity will also be operationalized based on a reflective measurement model.

Frequency of transactions in turn can be observed, hence quantified and measured directly, wherefore no latent construct including a set of indicators needs to be defined. Instead, frequency is a manifest variable, wherefore no measurement error has to be assumed, which is caused by operationalization bias (Kromrey 2009). In sum, the three elements characterizing the type of transaction have either already been operationalized or can be measured directly, which may reduce the preliminary efforts of the empirical analysis.

However, unfortunately this does not apply to the operationalization of the interface structure, or of disruptions. Based on the understanding of interface structure developed in this thesis and guided by Remer, the three latent constructs degree, standardization, and formalization are *constituted by their sub-elements*. Therefore, changes in these sub-elements would *result in a change* in the second order construct. Thereby, both sub-elements *do not necessarily correlate highly* with one another, as they are concerned with different aspects of the overall construct.[78] Hence, changes of e.g. level of detail of programming do not require changes in preciseness of programming, but both would *cause a change* of the degree of programming. Even though in empirical research this distinction is not always considered, they are both necessary to determine the degree of programming (Remer 1989). Therewith, these first order latent variables can be seen as the cause of the second order variables, rather than the other way round, and are thereby formative indicators for the second order constructs (Jarvis, MacKenzie & Podsakoff 2003).

The last level of organizational design as specified by Remer comprises the sub-elements of degree, standardization, and formalization. Their operationalization in turn can be attributed to the right column of Figure 33, due to the following reasons. *Firstly*, their indicators would not change the causal implications, as e.g. preciseness of programming may require different indicators depending on the application context, yet by replacing one indicator with another the nature of preciseness is not changed. Thus, indicators are interchangeable, non-constitutive, and do not alter the concept of the construct. *Secondly*, if the preciseness of interactional programming is changed, this change should be reflected by the indicators, as the overall degree of preciseness is either higher or lower. Therefore, the six first order constructs will be measured by reflective indicators.

For the operationalization of disruptions, first the question has to be answered how specific the measurement model shall be developed. Whereas in previous empirical research, disruptions were measured by abnormal fluctuations of shareholder value (Hendricks & Singhal 2008), this does not seem to adequately measure the construct as developed in this thesis. This is further stressed by the fact that the same authors used this kind of measurement once for "glitches" (Hendricks & Singhal 2003), and once for disruptions, whereby disruptions be-

---

78 See sections 3.3.2 and 3.3.3.

come an arbitrary term. Additionally, by measuring disruptions with financial indicators, the question emerges, whether indeed disruptions are measured, or performance in general. Furthermore, such indicators would imply that disruptions need to have a negative impact on shareholder value. However, as stressed in section 2.2.3, disruptions are primarily a deviation of actual operational performance from operational plans, which is not necessarily that detrimental that it impacts on company value as well. Therefore, the deduction of indicators should start from the comparison of operational plans and actual operational performance, which is consequently an ex-post evaluation of disruptions. Hence, because disruptions precede the observations, causal relations go from the construct to indicators, which have therefore a reflective character.

Thus, the final structural equation model includes both, formative as well as reflective indicators. This does not imply necessarily a contradiction, as the model incorporates first-order and second-order constructs, for which the directions of causation between indicators and latent construct do not have to be the same (Podsakoff et al. 2003). Nor does it imply that with further specification and definition, this complexity could be reduced, as interface structure is a multidimensional construct, which requires by definition formative indicators.[79] Nevertheless, the different directions of causality and specifications of measurement models have to be carefully considered during the analysis of the data. Based on the methodological considerations of this section, the structural model is composed by first order and second order models. As the specification of the reflective measurement models is still up to their actual operationalization and pre-tests, these measurement models will not be further included in the resulting causal model shown in Figure 36. Based on this model, in section 4 the empirical analysis of how interface design affects the susceptibility of supply chains to disruptions will be further prepared, executed and analyzed.

79 According to Law, Wong & Mobley (1998) a multidimensional construct consists of a number of interrelated attributes or dimensions, which can be conceptualized under an overall abstraction because it is theoretically meaningful and parsimonious.

Figure 34: Structural equation model for the impact of interface design on disruptions

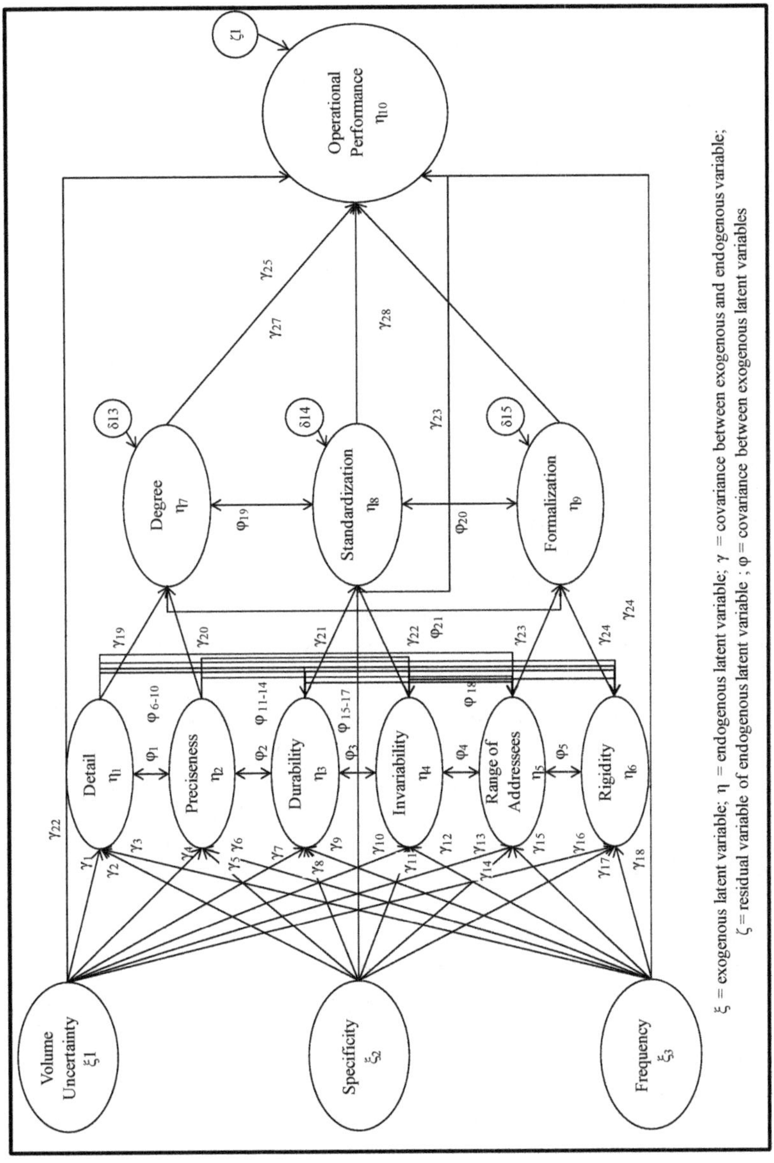

Source 17: Own illustration; reflective measurement models hidden

3.6 Interim Conclusion

Following the research aims as depicted in section 1.3 of this thesis, the purpose of section 3 was mainly the pursuance of analytic aims, hence the exploration of causal relationships between the variables, deduction of hypotheses and construction of the structural model.[80] The exploration of causal relationships and the deduction of hypotheses require thereby a theoretical foundation, to avoid eclectic assumptions (Popper 1980). Hence, before being able to investigate causal relations and to derive propositions, a suitable theoretical basis had to be selected, which is able to explain the phenomenon under study.

The illustration of major organizational theories in **section 3.2** followed the consideration of these requirements. In **section 3.2.1**, seven theoretic approaches were scrutinized for their explanatory power of disruptions. Based on the need to explain decisions on the design of inter-organizational relationships, new institutional economics was chosen as a theoretic basis, as it focuses on interactions of organizations and provides explanations for disruptions from an institutional, structural and process perspective. This choice was further refined in **section 3.2.2** to take transaction cost theory as theoretic framework for the deduction of hypotheses on interface design. However, with the choice of transaction cost theory, the occurrence of disruptions might be explained from a bird's eyes view, but would omit the role of the human being involved in exchange processes. As already observed by Chmielewicz (1979), economic theories and decision theory are to a great extent overlapping, because in economic systems as in all systems, decisions have to be taken based on respective objective functions. Nevertheless, he also points out that the facts and circumstances of decisions differ depending on the unit regarded. Therefore, in **section 3.2.3**, descriptive decision theory was selected as theoretic foundation for explaining human errors.

In order to investigate how interface design impacts on the susceptibility of supply chains to disruptions, the interface design decisions had to be linked to individual decision making. Thereby, the organizational structure of interfaces was identified as instrument, which organizations use to stir a desired behaviour in their employees (Hill, Fehlbaum & Ulrich 1994). These structures in turn represent conditions under which the individual takes its decisions, which either lead to desired results or to errors (see section 3.2.3). In the context of interfaces however, not all instruments might be employed to the same extent as within organizations. Therefore, the description of interfaces and identification of relevant elements of organizational structure was pursued in **section 3.3**, where interfaces were described and conceptualized to allow for a systematic deduction of hypotheses linking interface structure and disruptions afterwards. Based on a description of interfaces, **section 3.3.1** identified relevant dimensions of interfaces for the purpose of this thesis. This revealed that in comparison to company-internal structures, the role of vertical relations is reduced, due to the lack of a common authority. After this broad overview, the terminological framework by Remer was selected as a

80 See e.g. Chmielewicz (1979); Hill, Fehlbaum & Ulrich (1994); Bea & Haas (2001).

systematic basis to describe organizational structures, which were elaborated in the following sections. In **section 3.3.2** the primary variable of organizational structures, namely "differentiation" was described and decomposed. This resulted in 128 possibilities to configure organizational structures, which were exemplified in the context of interfaces in food supply chains to illustrate their relevance and resulting design options. In **section 3.3.3** the secondary variable, namely "programming" was described and decomposed in the same way. Again, the decomposition resulted in 128 possibilities to configure organizational structures at interfaces, which in combination with the primary variable created 256 possibilities to be considered in the design of interfaces.

Therefore, in **section 3.4.1** the research focus was narrowed down to the identification of interactional programming as being the most relevant object of organizational structure in this context. Furthermore, the characteristics degree, standardization, and formalization as well as their respective sub-elements were included for further analyses, resulting in the consideration of six possibilities to design interface structures. In **section 3.4.2** potential effects of interactional programming on individual decision making based on decision theory were proposed. This resulted in an unlimited range of potential configurations of interactional programming, which might have different effects on the potential for errors. This was followed in **section 3.4.3** by the deduction of propositions on causal relations between transaction types and operational performance amplifying the number of propositions to twelve, with again a nearly unlimited range of potential configurations.

In **section 3.5**, the hitherto separated streams of argumentation were combined content-wise and conceptually, to align and prepare them for the empirical analysis. Therefore, in **section 3.5.1** the causal assumptions on how the transaction type influences the interface structure shed light on the interface design process, which might also be important to assess the optimality of interface structures in a given transaction environment. After completion of the set of propositions to be tested, the methodology on which the empirical analysis will be based had to be selected and depicted. To this purpose, in **section 3.5.2** the survey technique was chosen as data collection method and structural equation modelling as method for data processing and testing of causal propositions Finally, in **section 3.5.3** the previously identified, conceptualized, and theoretically connected constructs were transformed into a structural equation model with reflective first order measurement models and second order formative models, which will be analyzed empirically in section 4.

4 Empirical Analysis of Disruptions in Cold Chains

4.1 Introduction to the Section

According to Diekmann (2002), empirical research comprises broadly five main phases: *firstly*, the formulation and specification of the research problem, *secondly*, the planning and preparation of data collection, *thirdly*, the collection of data itself, *fourthly*, the analysis of data and finally the report of findings. As the first phase has already been executed in the previous sections, section 4 focuses on the phases two to four. How they are distributed among the sub-section will be depicted in the following paragraphs.

The preparation and execution of the research process comprises a series of interconnected decisions, which are not entirely separable from one another (Kromrey 2009). The planning and preparation phase for instance comprises the operationalization of constructs, the definition of data collection method, and the determination of the target population, before pre-tests are carried out (Diekmann 2002). The *planning phase* is depicted in section 4.2, where the empirical analysis is tailored to meet the demands of this research. As the operationalization and selection of data collection method may differ with differing target populations, section 4.2.1 defines first of all the target population before a data collection method is selected. This is followed by the operationalization of transaction types (section 4.2.2) and interface structure and disruptions (section 4.2.3) as the three components of the causal model.

In these operationalizations, the requirements of the research method and target population are taken into account. However, to assure that measures are inter-subjectively comprehensive and unambiguous, especially in social sciences, extensive pre-testing of indicators and data collection methods is required (e.g. Bortz & Döring 1995; Diekmann 2002; Schnell, Hill & Esser 2011). This testing belongs to the *preparation phase* and is also part of the empirical component of this thesis, which is described in section 4.3. To this purpose, section 4.3.1 depicts the execution and results of the pre-tests of the indicators, whereas section 4.3.2 describes the survey and its pre-tests. The last sub-section of 4.3 finally comprises the *execution of the main survey*, which is the third phase of empirical research described by Diekmann (2002).

The first part of the fourth phase, namely the *construction of an analyzable data file* is conducted in section 4.4. In contrast to the natural sciences, social sciences are confronted with a lack of directly observable and measurable research objects, wherefore indirect measures have to be scrutinized extensively to assure their adequacy (Kromrey 2009). Therefore, section 4.4.1 starts with the illustration of evaluation criteria, which will be applied to the sample to assure the quality of measurement. The application or error control measures and data cleaning measures will then be applied to the entire data set, before the display of research findings starts with some descriptive statistics, which is generally done to inform about the characteristics of the sample and to provide a first overview on the data (Schnell, Hill & Esser 2011). In consequence, in section 4.4.2, the data set is cleaned first, followed by the display and comparison of information on respondents and the two cases. Thereby, initial quality corrections are executed to avoid biases in the evaluation of indicators, as well as in the statistical results. With the application of the quality criteria for the measurement models, the fourth phase is turning to its second part, which is the statistical data analysis (Diekmann 2002). This sub-phase starts with the construction of measures and analysis of indicators, and finishes with the analysis of causal relations. However, as many propositions have to be analyzed in two samples, section 4.4.3 focuses as the previous section on the illustration of results, which will be analyzed in the next section.

Therefore, section 4.5 is concerned with the last step of the fourth research phase, namely the analysis of the data itself (Diekmann 2002). To this purpose, section 4.5 focuses on the analysis of disruptions. Therefore, it illustrates the general findings on sub-samples and their commonalities and differences regarding disruptions, to provide insights on a phenomenon where empirical findings are scarce.[81] Based on these insights and the results of statistical analyses conducted in section 4.4.3, section 4.5.2 analyzes the effects of the interface design on the occurrence of disruptions. These findings are juxtaposed and compared in section 4.5.3 to the effects of the interface design on optimal process performance, to identify commonalities and differences between the interface designs in both cases and their impacts. Therewith, all remaining phases of empirical research have been completed, wherefore section 4.6 briefly summarizes the section and its main findings.

4.2 Tailoring of the Empirical Analysis

4.2.1 Description of the Target Population and Research Design

Before one can start with the empirical investigation, it is first of all necessary to determine the target population, which shall be represented by the sample (Diekmann 2002). The target population is thereby determined to a large extent by the research question, as well as data collection and data analysis methods (Kromrey 2009). However, the determination of the target population by means of statistical key figures poses a challenge in the context of this research due to a number of reasons.

Firstly, whereas for this research, statistics *across economic sectors* from primary production, via logistics services, manufacturing, and trade would be required, statistics by national or supra-national bodies differentiate companies mainly *sector-wise*, hence into primary, secondary, and tertiary sector (see for example statistic databases by Eurostat, World Trade Organization, OECD). Thereby, the possibility to characterize the target population becomes improbable, as key information is lacking.

---

[81] See section 2.5.1.

Secondly, whereas production companies still might be characterized sufficiently by the products produced, it becomes more difficult for logistics companies which provide the same services for a wide array of products, of which only a fragment belongs to the target group. To this purpose, the Federal Statistical Office Germany has been contacted, to inquire about availability of statistics on companies working in cold chain logistics or food logistics. However, this inquiry yielded no results, as again, the classification of companies is based on horizontal differentiation of the value chain, instead of vertical differentiation. Therefore, companies in this field are currently covered by several distinctive classifications, such as freight transport or warehousing,[82] wherefore unambiguous identification of the target population is not possible. Thereby, the generalization of findings is constrained, stressing the exploratory nature of the empirical investigation. At the same time, it highlights that reliable data on supply chains is still scarce and that more research is required in this field.

Considering that the target population cannot be identified unambiguously, the determinateness of derived findings is reduced, as the population for which the statement is valid cannot be specified to the same extent. Therewith, the information content of research would be reduced, which is according to Popper (1973) the most important objective of research. The question is thus, whether it is possible to increase the information content in another way to increase its relevance. As Chmielewicz (1979) observes, apart from the determinateness of statements, information content is also fostered by increasing universality of statements, hence their scope of application.[83] Therefore, it should be considered whether the empirical analysis should not be expanded in scope, to increase information content and therewith falsifyability of statements.

The expansion of scope of analysis seems to be feasible and useful due to a number of reasons. *Firstly*, considering the specificity of regarded supply chains, the sample size might be an issue, as it might be difficult to obtain sufficient participants for quantitative analyses of data. Therefore, expanding the scope of analysis also increases the number of potential participants and therewith the probability of satisfying basic requirements for statistical analyses. *Secondly*, the specialized equipment to be used for transport and storage of perishables, such as refrigerated trucks, reefer containers and temperature monitoring equipment increase the likelihood that LSP try to maximize the capacity utilization by offering services for other temperature-sensitive products as well. For instance, especially the airline industry increases its product portfolio, by offering services to high-value - low-volume cargoes, such a temperature sensitive pharmaceuticals (Transport Intelligence 2011). Therefore, a complete distinction of companies handling perishables from companies handling other temperature-sensitive products does not seem to be possible per se. *Thirdly*, the main focus of this research lies on disruptions and its causes. However, one of the main reasons for choosing the food sector as example for the analysis was the considerable impact deviations from process plans have on prod-

82 See: Statistisches Bundesamt (2008).
83 See also section 1.2.

uct quality, mainly due to the required cooling, which also implies considerable hazards and economic losses.[84] Therefore, an expansion to other temperature-sensitive products does not seem to alter the phenomenon under study, but may increase the universality of results. Furthermore, this proceeding is frequently observed in empirical research, because the definition of the target population is in general a compromise between the interesting objects and the available resources (Schnell, Hill & Esser 2011). Hence, based on the practical constraints and science-theoretic requirements, the empirical research will be expanded to increase the information content of derived findings.

Another challenge occurs regarding the approach of potential participants. Especially for rare target populations, selecting participants based on an existing list is not always possible (Diekmann 2002). As has been noted above, in supply chain research, the definition of accurate sampling frames is difficult, as the companies belong generally to different industry groups. If it is not possible to start from an already existing list of the target population, potential participants have to be identified in another way. Lumsden (2007) suggests notifying potential participants in publications most appropriate for the targeted audience, which may include e-mails, newsprints, flyers, advertisements on radio, and television, and person-specific correspondence. Lang (2007) in turn compiled a list of companies from different industry databases. Such databases are for example maintained by industrial organizations and provide a suitable starting point for contacting potential participants.

Many food producers and retailers are members of industry-specific organizations, such as the Fresh Produce Exporter's Forum (FPEF)[85], the World Farmers' Organisation (WFO)[86], the British Retail Consortium (BRC)[87], or the Dutch Food Retail Association (CBL)[88]. LSPs however offer a service for a specific supply chain segment, rather than for a specific product category. In consequence, associations representing LSPs also mainly focus on the kind of service, such as the International Air Transport Association (IATA)[89], the European Cold Storage and Logistics Association (ECSLA)[90], the Cool Chain Association (CCA), or Transfrigoroute International (TI)[91]. Members of these associations therefore normally do not only focus on food supply chains, but also handle other temperature-sensitive commodities, such as pharmaceuticals or flowers, as has already been suggested above.

Especially pharmaceuticals share some important features with food products. *Firstly*, they are also highly regulated (Backhaus 1983; Majone 2000; Wiktorowicz 2003) and partly covered by the same regulations as food products (Marucheck et al. 2011). This feature also dis-

---

84 See sections 1, 2.5.2, and 2.5.3.
85 http://www.fpef.co.za/.
86 http://www.wfo-oma.org/.
87 http://www.brc.org.uk/.
88 http://www.cbl.nl/.
89 http://www.iata.org/.
90 http://www.ecsla.eu/.
91 http://www.transfrigoroute.eu/.

tinguishes these two commodities from other temperature-sensitive products, such as flowers (Plaggenhoef 2007). Considering that regulatory requirements may also play a role in the definition of indicators for disruptions and that they may have a substantial effect on the organization of supply chains, [92] expanding the focus to cold chains in general might thus lead to biased results. *Secondly*, temperature ruptures can have significant impacts on the quality and fitness for use of pharmaceuticals as well (Matthias et al. 2007; Bell et al. 2001), wherefore the evaluation of disruptions is likely to more similar to food products as of those products not posing hazards to humans. *Thirdly*, temperature ruptures are not the only type of disruptions occurring, as disruptions occur also frequently due to errors in the information flow, such as labelling and misbranding.[93] These kinds of disruptions are also frequently observed on food supply chains,[94] wherefore both product categories are considered to be similar regarding structures, types of disruptions, significance of disruptions and regulatory background. Thus, regulatory impacts on the design of cold chains seem to be comparable, as well as the diversity of potential disruptions experienced.[95] Therefore, in order to increase the area of application of insights, and the information content of the empirical analysis, the focus will be expanded to cover not only food supply chains, but also pharmaceutical supply chains, which in the following for simplicity reasons will be referred to as cold chains. Hence, the target population can be specified to consist of companies being involved in cold chain logistics for food and pharmaceuticals.

Apart from constraints posed by the research question and target population, further constraints emerge from the choice of data collection method (Bortz & Döring 1995). The survey technique chosen for this purpose[96] is thereby the standard method in empirical social sciences and can be further differentiated into interviews and questionnaires (Schnell, Hill & Esser 2011). The survey is also the favoured technique by Remer (1989) to measure organizational structures, as herewith the choice of potential indicators is larger. As positions are filled by employees (i.e. the position owner), obtaining information directly from these employees increases the coverage of the actually effective interactional programming (Remer 2005). Therefore, the target population can be further specified to consist of company representatives, which interact with representatives of other companies, hence with customers, and/or suppliers, and/or logistics service providers.

The type of interrogations can thereby range from completely open interrogations to completely standardized ones, where all questions are fixed and have a limited set of predefined possible answers (Diekmann 2002). Open questions and unstructured surveys are thereby

---

92 See section 2.4.1.

93 See e.g.: http://www.accessdata.fda.gov/scripts/importrefusals.

94 See e.g.: European Commission 2013.

95 In contrast to food products however, profit margins for pharmaceuticals are in general considerably higher (e.g. Scherer 1993; Berndt 2002; Giaccotto, Santerre & Vernon 2005), and potential monetary losses due to disruptions in the supply chain significantly higher Matthias et al. (2007). Such differences need to be taken into account during the analysis.

96 See section 3.5.2.

most frequently used in qualitative empirical research, whereas standardized surveys with closed questions are generally used in questionnaires and quantitative research (Kromrey 2009). As the aim of this thesis is to identify general causal relations and to test hypotheses, a standardized survey seems to be more suitable to increase comparability and quantification of the results. The question remaining is therefore, whether a standardized interview or a standardized questionnaire is more suitable.

In interviews, the role of the interviewer is of high importance, as his or her behaviour may influence the responses of the interviewee, especially in the case of sensitive questions (Bortz & Döring 1995; Turner et al. 1998). This consideration is deemed to be important in the case of this research, as interviewees will be questioned about cases, where exchange processes showed inferior performance. A face-to-face interview could therefore result in "socially desirable" response behaviour, whereby the reliability of results would be imperilled. Furthermore, the higher flexibility for respondents in questionnaire-based surveys to respond whenever and wherever they have the occasion also favours the use of written responses (Roberts 2007). Another advantage of written surveys is that the respondent can take time to thoroughly consider the question before answering (Diekmann 2002), which is considered as important due to the abstract nature of the research question. Respondents have thereby not only to recall a specific transaction, but also to interpret the questions for their specific context, due to the heterogeneous type of companies involved in end-to-end supply chains.

The type of questionnaire can be further differentiated regarding the mode of submission. Researchers today have several options available, ranging from traditional paper-and-pencil surveys to web-based surveys (Ma & McCord 2007). Web-based surveys are increasingly used in social sciences, as the number of internet users is continuously increasing and especially companies grant their employees access to the internet (Strassnig 2009). Further advantages are the relatively low temporal and monetary expenses, whereby the number of potential participants is increased (Mühlenfeld 2004). Additionally, the hitherto existing technology is able to assess the data quality rapidly, to tailor the survey for specific participants, and to increase confidentiality, whereby the reliability of results is increased (Jansen, Corley & Jansen 2007). Disadvantages in turn can be seen in the difficulty to determine the target population, the representativeness of the sample, and high volatility in response rates, which ranges in general between 10-50% (Leopold 2004), but which is by trend decreasing (Roberts 2007). However, these disadvantages seem to play a less important role in this case, due to the exploratory nature and the difficulties to characterize the target population as discussed above.

Furthermore, in order to reduce discrepancies between the target population and the sample, web-based surveys can be personalized by sending a unique survey access link to the targeted respondents (Lang 2007). Even though especially in agricultural supply chains, the levels of Internet usage still vary considerably between large companies and small and medium-sized enterprises (SMEs), this difference is rather concerned with whether companies use the Internet for supply chain integration or just as a communication tool (Manthou, Matopoulos &

Vlachopoulou 2005). Hence, for the purpose of contacting potential participants and conducting the online survey, no substantial bias seems to result from the choice of a web-based survey. Therefore, an online survey will be conducted, to increase user-friendliness, number of potential participants and geographic scope. Now that the type of empirical research has been defined, as well as the target population, the latent constructs can be operationalized, which will be done in the following sections.

4.2.2 Operationalization of Transaction Type and Process Performance

In order to test latent constructs, they have to be operationalized in such a way that measuring and testing causal assumptions becomes possible (Kromrey 2009). For the development of adequate indicators, which can be measured with the methodology chosen, some theoretical and practical considerations become necessary, which will be detailed in the following.

From the theoretical perspective, some quality criteria have to be considered, to assure the quality of the measurement and testing of causal assumptions. For the assessment of empirical investigations, Zetterberg (1973, p. 143) suggests the following quality criteria:

1. logical and/or empirical validity of operational instructions,
2. reliability (i.e. preciseness and objectiveness) of operational instructions,
3. consensus between the trend of the data and the trend stipulated by the scrutinized hypothesis which consists of a) the degree, to which the direction of the trend is confirmed and b) the probability that the trend of the data is a coincidence,
4. control of alternative hypotheses,
5. representativeness of the selection and of the size of the population,
6. the degree, to which the hypothesis under scrutiny is already a substantial part of existing theory.

Of the quality criteria described above, especially the first two points are important for the operationalization of the latent constructs into empirically testable relations. An indicator is valid, if it really measures the targeted phenomenon (Kromrey 2009). Therefore it is important that every aspect of the theoretical term is considered in the operationalizations (Schnell, Hill & Esser 2011). Comparing the measurement models, this implies that in formative measurement models, all dimensions of a construct have to be covered by different indicators, whereas in reflective measurement models, one dimension is covered by several content-wise identical indicators (Diamantopoulos & Siguaw 2006).

Reliability of the measurement refers to the degree, to which the measurement is influenced by perturbations or errors (Bortz & Döring 1995). A reliable measurement implies furthermore that measurements conducted at different points in time (i.e. inter-temporal reliability), by different persons (i.e. inter-subjective reliability) and with different instruments (i.e. inter-methodological reliability) result in the same observations (Kromrey 2009). Measurement errors in one observation can be reduced by utilizing several indicators per dimension of a construct (Schnell, Hill & Esser 2011). Thus, from a theoretical perspective, more indicators are desirable, which Marsh et al. (1998 p. 214) formulates as "more is never too much".

In contrast, from a practical perspective, an excessive number of indicators is undesirable because of the demands imposed on the data collection, and the increase in the number of parameters to be estimated when the construct is embedded within a broader structural model (Diamantopoulos & Siguaw 2006). Furthermore, the willingness to participate decreases with longer duration of the survey, which in turn is increased by the number of indicators. Already existing research on online surveys revealed that participation was denied more frequently if a survey took more than 15 minutes (Kuckartz et al. 2009). This observation was also supported in discussions with cold chain managers, wherefore the number of indicators needs to demonstrate the adequate balance between reliable measurement and acceptable time frame.

In the literature, a general consensus exist that normally at least three indicators should be used per construct, but that under certain conditions two might also be sufficient (Marsh et al. 1998). However, as for the majority of constructs no already existing and tested sets of indicators could be identified, those constructs were operationalized first with six indicators each, from which those with the best fit were to be selected after pre-testing the scales. In the following, the process of indicator development will be depicted.

Transaction cost theory has already been widely applied in empirical research, wherefore a variety of operationalizations of uncertainty, frequency and specificity exist.[97] Bortz & Döring (1995) suggest if possible the use or adaptation of already existing scales, to reduce the workload for empirical investigations. Additionally, by using existing scales which have been used already by other researchers, inter-temporal and inter-subjective reliability of measurement can be enhanced. In consequence, the literature on empirical applications of transaction cost theory has been investigated to identify suitable operationalizations. The encountered sets of indicators revealed that the constructs have been specified in distinct ways to suit the respective application background, mainly with a clear focus on applications in production. In order to increase the validity of indicators, different sets were gathered based on a snowball system. Only those operationalizations, which had been successfully tested in empirical research, were considered to assure their reliability.

Based on the identified sets, during a workshop, several cold chain experts were asked to assess the relevance of aspects represented by the indicators. To this purpose, the aspects addressed in the indicators were listed and the experts were asked to attribute values between 1 (very important) to 5 (not important at all) to each aspect. The scores were then aggregated for each set of indicators and the most relevant operationalizations identified. In order to assess the scales not only regarding their practical relevance, but also regarding their theoretical relevance, as a further criterion, the journal ranking of each publication was taken as an indi-

97 For an overview on empirical research using transaction cost theory see e.g. Shelanski & Klein (1995) and David & Han (2004).

cator for scientific quality. To this purpose, JOURQUAL rankings of journals were taken as a basis, since this ranking is based on the weighted additive combination of review requirements and paper quality assessed by more than 500 management research experts (Hennig-Thurau, Walsh & Schrader 2004). Even though this approach may also be biased by subjective evaluation by the experts, choice of included journals, or choice of criteria, the risk is reduced by the large sample size and high correlations of the resulting ranking with other journal rankings (Hennig-Thurau, Walsh & Schrader 2004). A summary of the results is shown in Table 9 where the operationalization selected is market in bold.

Table 9: Overview and ranking of operationalizations of uncertainty

Source	Type of Uncertainty	Indicators	Score	Journal Rating
Walker & Weber 1987	Volume Uncertainty	▪ **fluctuations in volume** ▪ **accuracy in volume forecasts**	**2,29**	**A+**
John & Weitz 1988	Environmental Uncertainty	▪ fluctuations in market share ▪ predictability of trends ▪ volatility of industry volume ▪ accuracy of forecasts	2,96	B
John & Weitz 1989	Environmental Uncertainty	▪ volatility of industry volume ▪ accuracy of forecasts ▪ predictability of trends	2,90	A+
Allen & Lueck 1992	Supply Uncertainty	▪ seasonality of product supply	2,71	B

For **uncertainty**, the indicators by Walker & Weber (1987) were considered most relevant by the cold chain experts. Furthermore, this paper has been published in a journal with A+ ranking. Hence, uncertainty was operationalized following Walker & Weber (1987) as:

Table 10: Initial measures of the construct "volume uncertainty"

ID	Indicator
Un1	*To what extent are significant fluctuations in the daily/monthly volume requirement expected?*
Un2	*To what extent are volume estimates considered to be uncertain?*

Source 18: Walker & Weber (1987)

Even though the scale consists only of two items, its successful empirical testing suggests that it is sufficiently reliable. As it has also been applied to a similar sample size as sought here, it seems thus suitable for the purpose of this thesis. In the original survey, responses were given on a five point Likert scale, which has also been maintained for this thesis. This operationalization was taken as a basis which was further refined by adaptations during additional pretests, to increase suitability for the application field. The same procedure has been conducted for specificity of transactions and the results can be found in Table 11.

Table 11: Overview and ranking of operationalizations of specificity

Source	Type of Specificity	Indicators	Score	Journal Rating
John & Weitz 1988	Asset Specificity	▪ investments in training and qualifying	1,29	B
Heide & John 1988	Partner Specificity	▪ dependency on the partner ▪ easiness to replace the partner	2,32	A+
Heide & John 1992	Asset Specificity	▪ **investments in training & qualifying** ▪ **investments in tooling & equipment** ▪ **adaptation to special norms & standards** ▪ **changes in production / distribution system**	**1,93**	**A+**
Patnayakuni, Rai & Seth 2006	Asset Specificity	▪ investments in tooling & equipment ▪ knowledge of each other's organizational cultu-re ▪ knowledge of each other's procedures	2,08	A

The reason why specificity was not operationalized as suggested by John & Weitz (1988) is that only one indicator was provided, which imperils reliability of measurement (Chin 1998). Furthermore, the closest other operationalization included also this indicator, but also several other indicators also deemed important by the industry experts and was additionally better ranked. In consequence, **specificity** was operationalized based on Heide & John (1992) as:

Table 12: Initial measures of the construct "asset specificity"

ID	Indicator
Spec1	*We have made significant investments in tooling and equipment dedicated to our relationship with this supplier*
Spec2	*This supplier has some unusual technological norms and standards, which have required adaptation on our part*
Spec3	*Training and qualifying this supplier has involved substantial commitments of time and money*
Spec4	*Our production system has been tailored to using the particular items bought from this supplier*
Spec5	*Our production system has been tailored to meet the requirements of dealing with this supplier*
Spec6	*Gearing up to deal with this supplier requires highly specialized tools and equipment*

Source 19: Heide & John (1992)

Here, responses were provided on a seven point Likert scale ranging from "*strongly agree*" to "*strongly disagree*" (Heide & John 1992). However, during the pre-tests, this scale was reduced to a five point scale to reduce the complexity of response and increasing consistency between the scales for different constructs.

The construct **frequency** in turn does not require indicators, as it is directly observable and can be quantified directly. The choice of an adequate scale however depends on the application background, wherefore the scale was developed with cold chain experts during the pretests of the questionnaire. The original operationalization of asset specificity as cited above also required in part and adaptation to the cold chain logistics context to increase its suitability.

The focus on a production environment in the indicators for specificity would result in lack of applicability and confusion of those participants, which are from the transport or retail segment of the cold chain. Therefore, during the pre-tests, the experts were inquired and the indicators based on their suggestions adapted.

For the construct **process performance**, no existing set of indicators was encountered that would also allow for a measurement of disruptions as defined in this thesis. Therefore, different incidences, which are considered as disruptions in the literature were collected, adapted to the understanding of disruptions of this thesis and presented to the cold chain experts.[98] The list and assessment by the cold chain experts can be found below:

Table 13: Overview and assessment of operationalizations of process performance

Source	Indicators	Agreement
Huber & Michael 2007	**temperature excursions**	**yes**
Craighead et al. 2007	considerable production delay	no
Albino, Garavelli & Okogbaa 1998	**qualitative damage of products**	**yes**
Subramaniam, Raheja & Rama Bhupal Reddy 2005	breakdown of equipment	no
Albino, Garavelli & Okogbaa 1998	**quantitative damage of products**	**yes**
Ratick, Meacham & Aoyama 2008	contamination of products	no
Craighead et al. 2007	**considerable shipping delay**	**yes**
Subramaniam, Raheja & Rama Bhupal Reddy 2005	malfunction of handling equipment	no
Subramaniam, Raheja & Rama Bhupal Reddy 2005	rejection of supplies or deliveries	no

In the workshop, they were asked, which of these incidences they would call a disruption. From the nine incidences presented, five were not understood as a disruption by all experts. Considering the relatively small pre-test sample, for assuring substantive validity of indicators (Anderson & Gerbing 1991), all indicators not being agreed on by all experts were excluded to avoid ambiguity, resulting in a proportion of substantive validity of 1.0 for the remaining ones.

These four incidences represented a disruption for all of the seven experts. Thereby, the consideration of cold chain specific indicators has been confirmed, as temperature excursions were unambiguously identified as representing disruptions. At the same time, it becomes apparent that indicators address different aspects of operational plans, namely the performance in terms of the product, and the performance in terms of logistics operations. This finding suggests that the methodological considerations on which the scoring model has been developed in section 2.4.2 should indeed be considered during the measurement of disruptions. In consequence, operational performance will be split into two separate constructs, namely "logistics performance" and "product performance". Therewith, unidimensionality of measure-

98 The questionnaire and the results can be found in the explanation volume.

ment can be increased, which is of prime importance for correct measurement of underlying constructs (Gerbing & Anderson 1988). Furthermore, the information content becomes larger, as therewith also commonalities and differences in performance and in causal relations between different product groups can be identified. Finally, it allows for a validation of the procedure presented by the scoring model.

Additionally, three of the four basic dimensions of disruptions as understood and developed in this thesis, namely qualitative, quantitative, and temporal deviations from the process plans were addressed by the literature and considered important by the experts. However, the fourth dimension was not addressed in the literature which can be attributed to differences in understanding and methodological foundation. Nevertheless, Bortz & Döring (1995) note that the creation of a set of indicators should be based on both, practical, but also theoretical precognitions. As previous empirical research on disruptions is scarce, no established operationalizations were encountered. Due to the specificity of the target population and the difficulty to attract sufficient participants, no extensive pretesting with a sample of the targeted population was possible, wherefore the set of indicators was amplified to assure that sufficient indicators remained after quality evaluation of the main survey. In consequence, four more indicators were developed and all were tested again during the pre-tests of the questionnaire with another group of cold chain experts.

The first additional indicators were suggested by the pre-testers during the workshop and concerned the *correctness* and *completeness of documents*. As the information flow has also been identified as an important dimension in this thesis,[99] they were also added as indicators for disruptions in logistics performance. The third indicator was based on theoretical considerations, namely to also cover the spatial dimension of disruptions in the survey. Optimal routing in logistics for instance has gained a lot of attention by researchers during the last years (e.g. Dethloff 2001; Hwang 2002; Kim, Lewis & White 2005) and is also considered to influence significantly performance in cold chains (Custódio & Oliveira 2006). Furthermore, rerouting a shipment of temperature-sensitive products implies that adequate infrastructure is required at another location than the planned one. However, this is not always the case, as for example the capacities or power suppliers of harbours differ partially substantially (van Dyk & Maspero 2007). As a result, the continuous electricity supply is imperilled. Additionally, different transit points can require different documentation, as regulatory requirements for food and pharmaceuticals still differ considerably between countries (MacMaoláin 2007; Majone 2000). Such changes to the planned transport route could thus lead to the need to adapt shipping documents and to delays if products are retained by customs clearance due to lacking or incorrect documentation. Therefore, *incorrect routing* was included as an indicator for disruptions in product performance. Finally, as has already been highlighted during the development of the scoring model, the packaging is an integral part of the product and should therefore also be considered for the assessment of disruptions. Furthermore, in cold chains for pharmaceuti-

99 See e.g. sections 2.3.3and 2.4.2.

cals, product quality might not be directly observed, but would have to be tested by laboratory tests, wherefore packaging solutions are used to indicate quality of e.g. vaccines (Jain et al. 2003). Therefore, as another indicator for disruptions in product performance, *packaging damage* was included for further tests. In consequence of the considerations above, the four additional indicators were: *incorrect routing, packaging damage, incomplete documents,* and *inaccurate documents*.

As disruptions are negative deviations, questions regarding their occurrence are quite delicate and may imperil the correct measurement (Bortz & Döring 1995; Diekmann 2002). As a consequence, participants in the survey could opt for giving socially desirable answers (Mühlenfeld 2004), or drop out of the survey. This circumstance has been considered during preparation of the survey in such a way that the items were formulated reversely. For example, instead of asking for the extent of temperature excursions, participants were asked for the extent of temperature maintenance. Furthermore, the choice of subjective evaluations has been reported in previous research to increase participation rates and was found to show high convergence with objective measurements (Droge, Vickery & Jacobs 2012 and the sources therein), wherefore this approach was favoured also in this context. The initial scale for disruptions in "logistics performance" and "product performance" are presented below:

Table 14: Initial measures of the construct "logistics performance"

ID	Indicator
LP1	*Punctuality (R)*
LP2	*Correctness of documents (R)*
LP3	*Completeness of documents (R)*
LP4	*Correctness of transport route (R)*

Table 15: Initial measures of the construct "product performance"

ID	Indicator
PP1	*Temperature maintenance (R)*
PP2	*Product quality maintenance (R)*
PP3	*Accuracy of product quantity (R)*
PP4	*Integrity of packaging (R)*

The resulting eight indicators of the two constructs were presented to the panel of cold chain experts and slightly adapted based on their suggestions, which will be depicted in section 4.3.1. Whereas the four constructs presented here were either already based on empirically validated scales or developed based on suggestions by the literature and the specific target group, the indicators for measuring the constructs of the organizational structure required a different approach, as will be illustrated in the following section.

4.2.3 *Operationalization of Organizational Structure*

To generate a suitable set of indicators for each of the constituent elements of interactional programming of positions, the organizational structure and logistics literatures were reviewed to identify previous operationalizations. Subsequently, indicators from several existing and tested scales were modified and complemented by further indicators. Throughout this process, care was taken to avoid complicated formulations, such as long sentences, multiple negatives, jargon or foreign wording (Schnell, Hill & Esser 2011). Furthermore, care was to be taken to allow for unambiguous interpretability (Bortz & Döring 1995), which was tested extensively in the following pre-tests. To avoid redundant illustrations, the sets of indicators will be presented after adaptation and refinement in section 4.3.1.[100]

In an initial step, literature on organization theory has been investigated regarding existing operationalizations of the constructs. The topic of organizational structure and interaction has thereby already gained a lot of attention in conceptual as well as empirical research.[101] However, as has already been noted by Remer 1989, the understanding of the variables partly differ substantially between one author and another, and also with reference to the terminological system of this thesis. This is already evidenced by the understanding of coordination as such, as illustrated for example by Cheng 1984. He observes that coordination is understood basically along three lines of though: firstly, it is confused with cooperation, which would imply that both parties have a common goal instead of some shared processes. Secondly, it is confounded with organizational effectiveness, and thirdly, it is applied as both, structure and process. These different understandings encountered by Cheng (1984) have already been observed for the understanding of disruptions as illustrated in section 2.3.1 and stress the importance of a critical reflection of existing operationalizations of organizational structure. Nevertheless, some contributions included starting points for the development of scales to operationalize the constructs as understood here.

The first question which has to be answered is which elements of exchange are subject to programming in interactions between supply chain partners. Thereby, several parts of exchange can be differentiated. In a conceptual framework of inter-organizational relationships, Levine & White (1961) base interactions on some kind of exchange between organizations, which is voluntary and has the purpose to pursuit organizational objectives.[102] In their context in the health sector, they differentiate these exchanges into referrals of patient cases, resources such as technical equipment or information related to cases or technical matters, written and verbal communication, as well as joint activities. This understanding is similar to the understanding of material and immaterial exchange processes in supply chains, as already described in sec-

[100] The list of all indicators can be found in the explanation volume.

[101] E.g. Lawrence & Lorsch (1967); Blau (1954b); Blain (1964); Blau (1954a); Blau et al. (1976); Aiken, Bacharach & French (1980); Smith & Blau (1962); van de Ven & Ferry (1980); Levine & White (1961); Hage, Aiken & Marrett (1971); Heide & John (1992); Heide & John (1988); Cadogan, Diamantopoulos & de Mortanges (1999); Cheng (1984); Podsakoff & MacKenzie (1994); Kerr & Jermier (1978).

[102] For a similar definition and differentiation of exchanges, see: van de Ven & Ferry (1980).

tion 2.3.3. However, there seem to be two types of information involved in exchange processes, namely information directly associated with the object of exchange (i.e. patient cases), and a more general exchange of information. In this context, Frese, Graumann & Theuvsen (2012) state that coordination efforts can be reduced by the exchange of decision-relevant information between entities at interfaces. The same difference can be made in supply chains, where on the one hand there is information directly associated with the product (i.e. shipping documents), and a more general information exchange to coordinate the shipment.[103] Furthermore, what Levine & White (1961) terms joint activities, could be understood as any additional kinds of interactions. Thus, three main parts of interaction will be differentiated, which can be subject to different designs of programming, namely:

- exchange of products and documents,
- information exchange, and
- general interaction.

The next point is to identify appropriate indicators for interactional programming as such. Whereas intra-actional programming is captured for example by *job descriptions* (Hage, Aiken & Marrett 1971) or *written work programs* (Podsakoff & MacKenzie 1994), interface-specific instructions might not be captured by such stable and long-term instructions and have to be separated from intra-actional programming for the purpose of this thesis. Remer (2005) suggests such indicators as *unification procedures in conflicts*, *lists of coordination tasks*, or *reciprocal information duties*. Hage, Aiken & Marrett (1971) in turn use *scheduled committee meetings* as an indicator for interactional programming, whereas Heide & John (1992) refer to *prespecified agreements for information exchange*. An extensively tested and validated indicator for interactional programming in an inter-organizational context has been developed by van de Ven & Ferry (1980), who refer to *rules, policies, and procedures for coordinating work activities*. This indicator is less specific than the other ones, which has the advantage that it can be applied to more contexts.

At the same time, more specific indicators would increase the information content regarding how interactional programming takes place.[104] However, as the set of participants in this survey is relatively heterogeneous, more precise indicators might put their applicability to the specific context of each participant at risk. However, as the indicator by van de Ven & Ferry (1980) has been developed explicitly for the inter-organizational context and not only for the inter-departmental context as for example the one by Hage, Aiken & Marrett (1971), and has been tested extensively in a longitudinal research program (van de Ven & Ferry 1980), it seems to be a suitable starting point for this thesis. Additionally, as no literature was encountered, in which empirical research attempted to cover end-to-end food *and* pharmaceutical supply chains, further specification and detailed analysis of more specific indicators is left for future investigations.

[103] See also section 3.4.2.

The importance of harmonized procedures across interfaces in supply chains has long been acknowledged in the literature (e.g. Houlihan 1987; Cooper & Ellram 1993; Ballou, Gilbert & Mukherjee 2000). Especially the use of relationship-specific standard operating procedures (SOP) is thereby seen as a facilitator of efficient task execution between suppliers and customers (Subramani 2004). As opposed to procedures, rules and policies already incorporate the notion of rigidity of formalization as understood by Remer.[105] This seems also be the case for the understanding of van de Ven & Ferry (1980) or Podsakoff & MacKenzie (1994), as they differentiate on the level of indicators between rules and policies on the one hand, and procedures on the other hand. As indicators should be as precise and short as possible (Cadogan, Diamantopoulos & de Mortanges 1999), the objects of interactional programming were consequently formulated as *procedures for exchange of products and documents*, *procedures for information exchange*, and *procedures for exchange processes*.

As the six first order latent constructs are all measured reflectively, item pools consisting of six items were developed for each of the constructs. Whereas the quantity of interactions has already been operationalized with measures such as *hours per day spend with coordinating activities with other organizations* (van de Ven & Ferry 1980), or *frequency of information exchange* (Heide & John 1992), indicators for the level of detail of interactional programming have not been encountered. This lack of operationalizations has already been noticed by Remer (2005), who affirms that the existence or non-existence of interactions has already been investigated, but not the degree of programming, not to mention preciseness or level of detail. However, based on the understanding of level of detail as breadth of programming and preciseness as depth of programming, indicators for the first one refer to the *extensity* of procedures for the entire range of activities related to exchange processes, whereas indicators for the latter refer to the *intensity* of procedures for a specific step in the exchange processes.[106] Furthermore, the three different exchange processes as depicted above were considered during the development of indicators, to cover the exchange processes in their full breadth.

According to Remer (2005), a high degree of standardization bears the risk of organizational inflexibility. Flexibility of inter-organizational agreements in turn has been operationalized by Heide & John (1992, p. 37) as:

- Flexibility in response to requests for changes is a characteristic of this relationship
- The parties expect to be able to make adjustments in the ongoing relationship to cope with changing circumstances
- When some unexpected situation arises, the parties would rather work out a new deal than hold each other to the original terms

In the context of this thesis however, a further differentiation is required, as on the one hand the temporal standardization shall be analyzed, and on the other hand the standardization

---

104 See discussion of universality and determinateness in section 4.2.1.

105 See also section 3.4.2.

without exceptions. Thus, whereas the validity without exceptions refers to the *flexibility to varying situations*, temporal validity refers to how *enduring* once defined procedures are regarding *past and future validity*. Such a differentiation seems to be complicated based on the indicators above, as flexibility is rather executed on a meta-level, where procedures can be changed upon agreement, and does not specify the flexibility *incorporated* in the procedures, to change the exchange processes in this specific interaction. However, these indicators could be used as a starting point for the following adaption to this research context.

As another support for lack of unambiguous understandings of organizational structure, other operationalizations of flexibility rather tab the understanding of rigidity used in this thesis. Podsakoff & MacKenzie (1994, p. 707) for instance developed and tested twice a scale for organizational inflexibility:

- In this organization, violations of rules and procedures are not tolerated
- In this organization anytime there is a policy in writing that fits some situation, everybody has to follow that policy very strictly
- In this organization, rules and policies are considered to be the law
- The policies and rules in this organization are followed to the letter
- In this organization, little flexibility is allowed in the interpretation of the policies and procedures
- This organization takes a relaxed approach to rules and policies (R)

This scale of organizational inflexibility is thereby identical to the understanding of rigidity by Remer (1989), which is expressed in formulations such as "*not tolerated*", "*very strictly*", etc. Even though the scale was developed for an organizational context, the formulations expressing the rigidity of procedures were integrated and adapted to the current context.

Finally, for the range of addressees, again no operationalization was encountered. As the range of addressees is regarded here in an inter-organizational context, the number of addressees who have to adhere to agreed procedures may not only encompass specific employees, but also departments, certain company locations, subsidiaries or even sub-contractors. Therefore, the range of addressees may span only *specific employees*, but also *everyone* involved in the transaction.

Based on the considerations above, indicators were developed and where possible, existing scales integrated. However, in order to be suitable for the purpose of this thesis, the formulations had to be adjusted to fit the cross-company context and to be better suited for the cold chain logistics context. For instance, the formulation "*in this organization*" (Podsakoff & MacKenzie 1994, p. 707) was eliminated and the subjects unified to maintain the use of procedures as basic unit of interactional programming. Subsequently, the indicators were pretested to assure the quality of measurement and their suitability for the research purpose

[106] see also: Cordes-Berszinn (2013).

(Anderson & Gerbing 1991). The execution and results of the pre-tests are described in the next section.

4.3 Execution of the Empirical Analysis

4.3.1 Description of the Pre-Tests

According to Anderson & Gerbing (1982), a proper specification of the measurement model is required before the structural model can be meaningfully analyzed. Therefore, indicators need to be carefully selected before estimation and testing of the model can take place (Chou & Bentler 1995). In consequence, the developed indicators for the constructs of the interface structure were tested based on the methodology suggested by Anderson & Gerbing (1991) to identify which of the indicators adequately tab the intended construct.

In general, the development of indicators to measure latent constructs includes extensive pre-testing with a large number of respondents (Podsakoff & MacKenzie 1994; Cadogan, Diamantopoulos & de Mortanges 1999; Greving 2009). However, this might not be feasible, if certain restrictions exist, for example regarding the accessibility or size of the target population (Anderson & Gerbing 1991). These restrictions also apply to this research, as the target population is highly specific, official contact lists are not available, and participants are not contacted as private persons. This might increase the reluctance to cooperate, as intrinsic motivation might be lower, and participation interferes with their regular work. Therefore, Anderson & Gerbing (1991) developed an alternative approach to assess the substantive validity of indicators, which is explained in the following.

Following Holden & Jackson (1979), substantive validity of indicators exist, if they are theoretically linked to the construct they should measure. To assess their validity, it has to be assessed whether the indicators developed based on theoretical considerations and related literature are inter-subjectively correctly attributed to the intended constructs. An operationalization is inter-subjectively reproducible, if constructs are defined unambiguously, are clearly distinguishable, and exhaustive, so that in principle every encoder may attribute the indicators without any problems (Bortz & Döring 1995). On this idea bases also the procedure suggested by Anderson & Gerbing (1991), which requires a smaller group of pre-testers, yet where the quality evaluation also leads to better results in subsequent confirmatory factor analyses. Thereby, pre-testers familiar with the research context are provided with a list of definitions of the constructs in everyday language, and the set of indicators developed based on theory and literature reviews. Then, the pre-testers are asked to attribute the indicators to the construct they deem to be most appropriate. Based on the results, the validity of indicators is calculated and the scales refined for the subsequent use.

For the purpose of this research, fifteen pre-testers were asked to attribute the developed indicators to the constructs, of which thirteen participated, which is in the range demanded by Hunt, Sparkman & Wilcox (1982). All pre-testers were familiar with organizational research in a logistics context, had a management or engineering background, and were either involved in logistics research or from the industry. Based on the comments and results of the first eight pre-testers, some of the indicators were refined before being submitted to further five pre-testers. The final choice of indicators to be included in the survey was then based on the so-called substantive validity coefficient, which can be calculated as follows:

$$(1) \qquad c_{sv} = \frac{n_c - n_o}{N}$$

c_{sv} = substantive validity coefficient
n_c = number of correct assignments
n_o = highest number of incorrect assignments
N = number of total assignments

Hence, the validity is not only based on the number of correct assignments, but also on the number of assignments to the construct, to which it was most frequently wrongly assigned, increasing therewith discriminant validity (Bagozzi & Yi 1988). To assess whether the value for c_{sv} is statistically significant, thus whether the indicator measures reliably the intended construct, a binomial test has to be conducted, which results in the acceptance or rejection of indicators (Anderson & Gerbing 1991). For illustration, Anderson & Gerbing (1991) chose a significance level of .05 level, whereas Müller-Martini (2008) for instance conducted the test at a significance level of .1. However, as the constructs of the interface structure are quite similar, since they all describe another aspect of interactional programming, a lack of discriminant validity might be more prevalent and therefore needs to be assessed more carefully to allow for unambiguous measurement of the constructs. Under these circumstances, a significance level of .05 is deemed more appropriate. According to Anderson & Gerbing (1991), the test assesses whether the probability that the indicator is attributed to the intended construct exceeds 50%. After collecting the results from the pre-tests, the correct and false attributions were documented and the values of the substantive validity coefficient calculated. The results of the tests can be found in Table 16.

Table 16: Indicator pre-test results

ID$_o$	N	n_c	n_o	p_{sa}	c_{sv}	Significance Level .05	ID$_o$	N	n_c	n_o	p_{sa}	c_{sv}	Significance Level .05
SD1	**13**	**11**	**2**	**.85**	**.69**	**TRUE**	**DP1**	**13**	**10**	**3**	**.77**	**.54**	**TRUE**
SD2	**13**	**10**	**3**	**.77**	**.54**	**TRUE**	**DP2**	**13**	**10**	**3**	**.77**	**.54**	**TRUE**
SD3	**13**	**12**	**1**	**.92**	**.85**	**TRUE**	**DP3**	**13**	**9**	**4**	**.69**	**.38**	**TRUE**
SD4	**13**	**13**	**0**	**1.0**	**1.0**	**TRUE**	DP4	13	2	11	.15	.69	FALSE
SD5	13	0	13	0.0	1.0	FALSE	DP5	13	1	12	.08	.85	FALSE
SD6	13	7	6	.54	.08	FALSE	**DP6**	**13**	**10**	**3**	**.77**	**.54**	**TRUE**
SE1	13	8	5	.62	.23	FALSE	**FA1**	**5**	**5**	**0**	**1.0**	**1.0**	**TRUE**
SE2	13	7	6	.54	.08	FALSE	**FA2**	**13**	**10**	**3**	**.77**	**.54**	**TRUE**
SE3	**13**	**9**	**4**	**.69**	**.38**	**TRUE**	FA3	13	5	8	.38	.23	FALSE
SE4	**13**	**12**	**1**	**.92**	**.85**	**TRUE**	FA4	13	7	6	.54	.08	FALSE
SE5	13	7	6	.54	.08	FALSE	**FA5**	**13**	**12**	**1**	**.92**	**.85**	**TRUE**
SE6	***13***	***8***	***5***	***.62***	***.23***	***FALSE***	FA6	13	8	5	.62	.23	FALSE
DD1	**13**	**9**	**4**	**.69**	**.38**	**TRUE**	**FR1**	**13**	**12**	**1**	**.92**	**.85**	**TRUE**
DD2	8	4	4	.50	0.0	FALSE	**FR2**	**13**	**12**	**1**	**.92**	**.85**	**TRUE**
DD3	***13***	***8***	***5***	***.62***	***.23***	***FALSE***	**FR3**	**13**	**10**	**3**	**.77**	**.54**	**TRUE**
DD4	13	7	6	.54	.08	FALSE	FR4	13	8	5	.62	.23	FALSE
DD5	**13**	**9**	**4**	**.69**	**.38**	**TRUE**	**FR5**	**13**	**13**	**0**	**1.0**	**1.0**	**TRUE**
DD6	13	7	6	.54	.08	FALSE	FR6	13	8	5	.62	.23	FALSE

ID[o]: Original ID of the indicator; p[sa]: Portion of correct assignments; c[sv]: Coefficient of validity; FALSE formatted *italic*: indicator re-formulated adapted **bold**: indicator selected for measuring the construct; SD: Standardization - Durability; SE: Standardization - Exceptionlessness; DD: Degree - Level of Detail; DP: Degree - Preciseness; FA: Formalization - Range of Addressees; FR: Formalization - Rigidity

All indicators showing to reliably tapping the construct at a .05 level of significance were selected to operationalize the respective latent construct. Two more indicators, which did not attain the required level of significance were maintained nevertheless due to the following reasons. *Firstly*, they just fell short of one more correct attribution; *secondly*, they were correctly attributed by all the pre-testers of the second round after slight adaptations of definitions, indicating that comprehensiveness increased considerably. *Thirdly*, even though constructs are frequently measured only by two reflective indicators (Marsh et al. 1998), the approach was favoured to have at least three indicators per construct and to exclude indicators after the main survey if necessary. This procedure has also been acknowledged by Anderson & Gerbing (1991) as being sometimes necessary in empirical research. The indicators highlighted in bold were hence included in the questionnaire which was then revised by industry experts.[107] In consequence, the constructs were operationalized as follows:

[107] For the description of the pre-tests of the questionnaire see section 4.3.2.

Table 17: Initial measures of the construct "level of detail"

ID	Indicator
Det1	*We have a wide range of procedures to consider for all aspects of the information exchange*
Det2	*There are procedures on the entire range of tasks concerned with the exchange of products and documents*
Det3	*We do not have procedures for every detail we need to exchange with each other (R)*

Table 18: Initial measures of the construct "preciseness"

ID	Indicator
Prec1	*There are few specific procedures on single steps of exchange processes (R)*
Prec2	*In important matters, procedures are very clear for checking products and documents*
Prec3	*There are exact procedures on how to exchange information*

Table 19: Initial measures of the construct "durability"

ID	Indicator
Dur1	*The procedures for exchanging information change frequently (R)*
Dur2	*The procedures for product and document exchange have already been in use for a long time*
Dur3	*The procedures to exchange information were developed a long time ago*
Dur4	*We expect the procedures for the exchange of products and documents to endure for a long time*

Table 20: Initial measures of the construct "invariability"

ID	Indicator
Invari1	*We agreed that under all circumstances, the procedures for exchanging the product and documents are the same*
Invari2	*The procedures consider various alternatives to one standard approach of information exchange*
Invari3	*Our exchange procedures do not vary a lot (R)*

Table 21: Initial measures of the construct "range of addressees"

ID	Indicator
RoA1	*The procedures consider various alternatives to one standard approach of information exchange*
RoA2	*Procedures for information exchange are available to guide everyone involved*
RoA3	*Procedures exist for everyone involved in the exchange processes*

Table 22: Initial measures of the construct "rigidity"

ID	Indicator
Rig1	*The agreement contains penalties if procedures for the exchange of products and documents are not followed*
Rig2	*Procedures for information exchange are considered to be the law*
Rig3	*Any time there is a procedure for exchange processes that procedure must be followed very strictly*
Rig4	*Violations of procedures for exchanging products and documents are normally tolerated (R)*

Source 20: own operationalization based on Podsakoff & MacKenzie (1994)

As can be seen for example in Table 19, some of the items were coded in reverse order (R). Thereby, the tendency of some respondents to give affirmative answers to every question shall be counteracted (Greving 2009). Furthermore, as suggested by Anderson & Gerbing (1991), the measurement scales were not included in the lists for pre-testing, as all items are measured on standard scales which therefore do not require additional evaluation by pre-testers, and which could lead to confusion during testing.

Each of the indicators was measured on a five point Likert scale ranging from 1 "*strongly agree*" to 5 "*strongly disagree*" as for example suggested by Diekmann (2002). The so-called Likert scale is the most frequently used scale in empirical social sciences (Schnell, Hill & Esser 2011). Its advantages are for instance the relative simplicity and practical usability (Diekmann 2002). Due to its wide-spread use, it might also enhance the easiness of respondents to answer the questions correctly, as they might be already familiar with these kinds of answers in surveys. The triangle problem of measurement requirements, which consists according to Chmielewicz (1979) of reliability of measurement, validity of measurement, and strength of measurement has therewith been solved in favour of valid and reliable measurements. Even though the choice of metric scales would result in more unambiguous measurement, their ability to cover interface structures is considered to be limited.[108] In the majority of the cases, the scale incorporates either five or seven points, whereby the five point scale is used most frequently (Greving 2009). In order to reduce the complexity of the questionnaire and to use consistent scales for all constructs measured by Likert scales, the five point scale was also chosen for these newly developed indicators. In addition, a sixth response option was provided, namely "*not applicable*", as suggested by pre-testers and the literature (e.g. Russell & Purcell 2009). This was deemed necessary, as not every question might have been relevant to all supply chain segments, or to both product groups.

Based on the choice of operationalizations of the transaction type and disruptions as suggested by cold chain experts, as well as the results of the pre-test, the actual questionnaire was designed and again tested with experts from academia and industry. This phase will be described in the next section.

108 See section 3.5.2.

4.3.2 Description of the Questionnaire

The choice of submitting the questionnaire as a web-based survey also has some implications for its design (Ma & McCord 2007) which will be discussed in the following. Thereby, important points will be depicted and their consideration in this research revealed.

Online surveys are web-based surveys, which allow for more flexible sequences of responding, depending on the answers provided by the participant (Jansen, Corley & Jansen 2007). Thereby, questionnaires can be better tailored to each participant, increasing the comfort of participants during completion of the survey. Furthermore, Mühlenfeld (2004) suggests the use of a central server, because the security of the data is enhanced, as the data is then saved on the server and therefore not affected in case of a local computer crash. Security is indeed a point which requires considerable attention in online surveys (Jansen, Corley & Jansen 2007) and should also be considered during the choice of an online survey tool.

For the purpose of this thesis, the online survey tool *Unipark* was chosen, as it has been developed for the needs of research institutes, offers comprehensive guidelines and question templates at low costs for students. Furthermore, the provider is certified by the German TÜV, is equipped with doubled electricity supplies (e.g. to avoid data losses in case of blackouts) and offers a 24 hours site security service.[109] Therefore, the risks of data losses or fraud were considered to be relatively low. The choice of a survey platform developed for the needs of academia was also considered to enhance the willingness of potential participants to take part in the survey, as it might increase confidence in authenticity of academic purpose (Lang 2007).

Even though the tool offers the possibility to attract potential participants via logos and links put on websites frequented by the target population, it also offers the possibility to invite potential participants manually. As the target population is highly specific, the active sampling method was chosen as opposed to the self-sampling method (Jansen, Corley & Jansen 2007). By choosing an active and selective sampling method, the representativeness for this specific population is increased (Beidernikl & Kerschbaumer 2007) and the risk of biased results reduced. Furthermore, by personalizing invitations and addressing each person by its name, prior research found positive effects on response rates (Lang 2007). Therefore, participants were sought actively, bearing the additional efforts necessary to boost the number of respondents.

In general, a questionnaire comprises three main parts, which are the cover page with the introduction to the survey, the body of main questions, and the finish page (Ma & McCord 2007). As suggested by Lumsden (2007), on the cover page, the topic, objectives, benefits and procedure were shortly summarized. Furthermore, she highlights that the organization responsible for the questionnaire should be clearly visible, wherefore the logo of the university was incorporated and shown on every page of the questionnaire. In order to increase the motivation to complete the questionnaire, potential participants were informed that they could request the summary of results at the end of the questionnaire, as has been suggested by Mühlenfeld (2004). Therewith, it was intended to reduce the risk of drop outs and increase careful completion of the survey. The assurance of privacy and security of data should also be mentioned, as these issues may be additional barriers to participation (Gurau 2007; Lumsden 2007). The objective of this introduction page was thereby to increase the interest of potential participants and their motivation to participate.

The structure of the main question part should be designed in such a way that at the beginning, relatively easy and uncritical questions are asked to reduce suspensions and provide an easy start (Bortz & Döring 1995; Mühlenfeld 2004). Therefore, the questionnaire started with statistical information required from the participant. Even though the potential participants were selected and checked beforehand, a second screening test was performed to reduce the risk of unqualified responses (Lumsden 2007). This could have been the case, if for instance the target person forwarded the access link to somebody else in the company, who might lack the experiences required. Therefore, respondents were asked for their years of experience in handling temperature-sensitive products, their departmental affiliation in the company, and for the time spent on planning, monitoring and optimizing cold chain operations with different stakeholders. The most important criterion for evaluating the quality of responses was thereby the third question, as it reflects to what extent the person is directly involved in cold chain operations and may adequately assess the extent of programming.

Next, some questions should be asked which are easy to answer and have the purpose to increase the interest by the respondents (Diekmann 2002; Kuckartz et al. 2009). These questions were concerned with the use of cold chain-dedicated equipment or managerial practices by the company in general. Therewith, similarities and differences between supply chain segments, but especially between product groups were tried to be captured regarding the degree of specialization. Furthermore, prior discussions with cold chain experts revealed a substantial interest in such information, wherefore it also serves the purpose to raise interest.

Then, the questionnaire should continue with the main body of questions (Ma & McCord 2007). In this case, this section comprised the main questions referring to the interface design and performance. As disruptions occur not in every transaction, respondents were asked to think of the most recent transaction where a disruption occurred and to answer the questions based on this case. By focussing on a specific case, the intention was to reduce the risk that respondents undeliberately mix characteristics of different transactions, which would result in biased results. At the same time, if respondents would only be asked to describe the most recent transaction, then the probability of obtaining biased results would be high, as *firstly*, respondents might tend to choose a very positive case, *secondly*, because the unambiguous separation between disruptions and regular performance would become difficult. However, as

---

[109] see: http://www.unipark.com/63-1-efs-survey.htm.

disruptions are defined as significant deviations,[110] the significance of deviations can only be evaluated by comparing them to regular performance. Therefore, respondents were asked to describe another case, where operations were realized as planned.

Hence, to avoid biased results and to be able to unambiguously identify disruptions in the first place, the questionnaire included the main questions twice, once for the description of a regular transaction, and once for describing a case where a disruption occurred.

The regular transaction was the first case to be described by the respondents, as research on questionnaire design showed that difficult questions should be asked at about one third of the questionnaire (Diekmann 2002; Lumsden 2007), whereas critical questions should appear at two thirds of the questionnaire to reduce drop outs (Bortz & Döring 1995; Mühlenfeld 2004). Thus, when the critical transaction was asked for, respondents were already familiar with the questions from the first case and were already at a point, where a drop out would have resulted in high sunk costs due to the loss of gratification (Bortz & Döring 1995). Furthermore, by describing a case with decent performance before describing a case where a disruption occurred, respondents were able to compare the second to the first case, resulting in less ambiguous responses.

Finally, for the end of a survey, Bortz & Döring (1995) suggests easy questions, as the concentration by respondents is decreasing. A suggestion by Lumsden (2007) is to offer respondents a possibility to provide feedback or to ask questions, which may also indicate problems encountered during completion to be considered for the analysis. Therefore, after the second case, respondents were asked for general remarks regarding the survey, further research to be conducted in the area, and their opinion about how to yield superior performance in cold chains. Additionally, they were asked whether they would like to receive a summary of the analyzed findings and whether they would be available for further questions. In both cases, they were asked to leave their e-mail address, as otherwise no identification of the participant was possible. On the final page, gratitude for participation was expressed as well as information on the further use of the data provided (Gurau 2007; Lumsden 2007).

Regarding the general design of the questionnaire, questions were distributed on several pages to increase clarity and reduce information overload for respondents (Mühlenfeld 2004; Lumsden 2007). Another important point for orientation and motivation is a completion bar (Mühlenfeld 2004; Ma & McCord 2007), which was integrated on the top right of each page. Pages were coloured only subtly, to further increase clarity of the questionnaire and to reduce respondents fatigue (Ma & McCord 2007). Apart from the feedback question, all questions were asked in a closed form to increase easiness to answer as well as objective interpretability of the results (Bortz & Döring 1995).

After compiling a questionnaire, previous research suggests that it should be extensively pretested, to assure its technological functionality (Lang 2007), content validity (Ma & McCord

---

[110] See section 2.2.3.

2007), and comprehensiveness (Lumsden 2007). Therefore, in a first round, the questionnaire was tested by other researchers to increase its comprehensiveness and content validity from a methodological point of view, but also regarding accurate wording in English. These researchers were experts in the field of organizational theory, questionnaire based research, and research in food supply chain management. Based on their comments, the questionnaire was adapted and a second round of pretesting conducted.

The second round of pre-tests was conducted with five practitioners. These were mainly experts of cold chain logistics, which did not belong to the target group, but being software or equipment providers, consultants, or not involved in logistics operations. With two of them, the questionnaire was tested during a telephone interview, whereby the comments were directly put into the comments boxes provided by the tool. Based on these comments, the questionnaire was again slightly adapted to increase comprehensiveness and tailoring to fit cold chain logistics.[111] After having received and incorporated feedback by all of the pre-testers, the questionnaire was subsequently ready for conducting the main survey, which will be presented in section 4.3.3.

4.3.3 Execution of the Main Survey

An important point to assure that the empirical investigation can be interpreted and generalized to the basic population successfully is the determination of optimal sample size (e.g. Diekmann 2002; Schnell, Hill & Esser 2011; Backhaus 2011). However, the optimal sample size can only be determined, if specific hypotheses have been formulated including effect sizes (Bortz & Döring 1995). Since this research cannot build on prior investigations, such specific hypotheses cannot be formulated reasonably, wherefore it is rather exploratory in nature (Kromrey 2009). Furthermore, due to the lack of statistical information on general characteristics of the target population, the determination of optimal sample size is restricted further. Additionally, John & Weitz (1988) even argue that representative samples and large sample sizes should be sacrificed to test the assumption by transaction cost theory and to obtain detailed information. This is also consistent with the identified research gap in section 1.2, which is positioned on a relatively low level of universality, but therefore on a relatively high level of preciseness.[112] Therefore, the determination of an optimal sample size can only rely on general requirements for the application of statistical analysis.

These include the need to test causal paths for significance, to assess whether the proposed relation is confirmed or can be falsified. This requires in general significance tests, which assume normal distribution of the values in the basic population (Janssen 2012). However, even if normal distribution cannot be assumed, many statistical measures exist which may assess the significance of paths between latent variables nevertheless (Cheung & Lau 2008). Furthermore, if the number of observations is sufficiently large, i.e. if $n > 30$, then the distribu-

---

111 The final questionnaire can be found in the explanation volume.

112 See Figure 3.

tion of t-values can be approximated with the standard normal distribution (Janssen 2012). Therefore, even though an optimal sample size cannot be determined, the basic objective is to obtain at least 30 participants, to assure the validity of findings.

As suggested by Lumsden (2007), several types of media were used to contact potential participants. *Firstly*, attendees of sector-specific conferences and exhibitions were considered to be an appropriate starting point, as they belong most probably to the target group, have a professional interest in the topic, and their company affiliation as well as their positions can be identified via business cards or name tags. Therefore, potential participants were sought at a major international logistics fair, where companies belonging to the cold chain logistics field were contacted at their booth. Where possible, appropriate candidates were invited directly, in other cases, company representatives established the contact with potential participants via mail or phone. To allow potential participants a thorough consideration of the request, a flyer was composed and distributed, which summarized the research purpose, as well as relevant information on the university and the researcher.[113]

Furthermore, direct contacts were considered to increase the probability of participation, as questions could be directly answered and the nature of the survey explained. Therefore, *secondly*, managers involved in the preparation, monitoring, and optimization of cold chain logistics for food and pharmaceuticals were contacted during several cold chain-specific conferences, and informed about the survey. To this purpose, flyers were again distributed indicating the scope of the project, the proceeding, benefits for participants, as well as additional information on the researcher and the university.

Furthermore, overall ten associations were contacted and asked for their collaboration. Of those, five were representing food producers or retailers[114], and five represented cold chain logistics service providers[115]. Of those, three supported this research project by sending the flyer to their member base, publishing the flyer in their newsletters, or providing contact details of their members and affiliates. As has been suggested by Jansen, Corley & Jansen (2007) these contact lists were further refined by visiting the websites of companies to assess whether they belonged to the target group or not. Furthermore, where several contacts were provided for one company, the profiles of each contact were compared and appropriate one's selected.

Additionally, calls for participation were published in cold chain logistics-related and fresh food-related forums on LinkedIn, a social network for professionals[116], and on a website for producers of agricultural products.[117] The objective thereby was to amplify the scope of po-

113 The design and content of the flyer followed the suggestions by Gurau (2007) on ethical principles of online surveys.
114 World Farmers' Organisation, PMA, Centraal Bureau Levensmiddelenhandel, Papaya and Mango Producers & Exporters Association, Fresh Produce Exporter's Forum.
115 IATA, CCA, GCCA, ECSLA, Transfrigoroute.
116 Cool Chain Association - Discussion Forum http://lnkd.in/PdK72w and Fresh Produce Industry Discussion Group http://lnkd.in/_utZWB.
117 http://www.poscosecha.com/es.

tential participants to include more geographic areas. Furthermore, managers were also encouraged to distribute the flyer to their professional network or to directly establish a contact, whereby more participants were obtained. Therewith, potential participants were intended to get contacted, which were not participating in professional networking events, associations, or discussion groups.

Overall, 590 e-mail addresses were obtained. This list of e-mail addresses was corrected for persons not belonging to the target group (e.g. academics, representatives from NGOs, or managers without logistics or supply chain focus), and for companies not belonging to the target sector (e.g. software providers, consultancy, equipment manufacturers). Finally, 348 e-mail addresses were identified as belonging to managers of the target group and included in the database. This number of potential participants was then further adapted during the online survey by deleting those who could not be reached, and by adding people asking to participate. Finally, the adjusted overall sample consisted of 338 potential participants.

As prior research indicates that response rates are highest at the beginning of the week and declining towards the weekend (Ma & McCord 2007), the invitation e-mails were send out on a Monday morning. Personalizing e-mails and contacting participants before the main survey has been shown in prior research to have a positive effect on response rate, as well as sending out multiple reminders (e.g. Schaefer & Don A. Dillman 1998; Cook, Heath & Thompson 2000; Sheehan 2001). Therefore, as for the majority of participants, first name and family name were available, these contacts were addressed personally and where appropriate, it was referred to previous encounters, to distinguish this survey from potential other inquiries.

The initial e-mail contained as the previous hand-outs a summary on the research topic, the proceeding, benefits for participants and additional information on data handling. Furthermore, each e-mail contained a personalized link to the survey, to better control the field of participants and to be able to send out specific reminders. The optimal number and frequency of reminders is still up for discussion, since Cook, Heath & Thompson (2000) for instance mention beneficial, but also declining benefits of reminders, if potential participants are contacted too often. Therefore, reminders were send every second week on Monday mornings, to boost the response rate. A final reminder was send two days before the survey was closed, to inform the remaining potential participants about the end of the survey. Overall, the survey was accessible for six weeks to allow participants to schedule their completion of the questionnaire with some extra time, as many participants were expected to be on holiday during this period. As has already been noticed by others, e.g. Lang (2007) and Ma & McCord (2007), response rates differed considerably during the period of the survey, as can be seen in Figure 35.

Figure 35: Total and completed response rates during the survey period

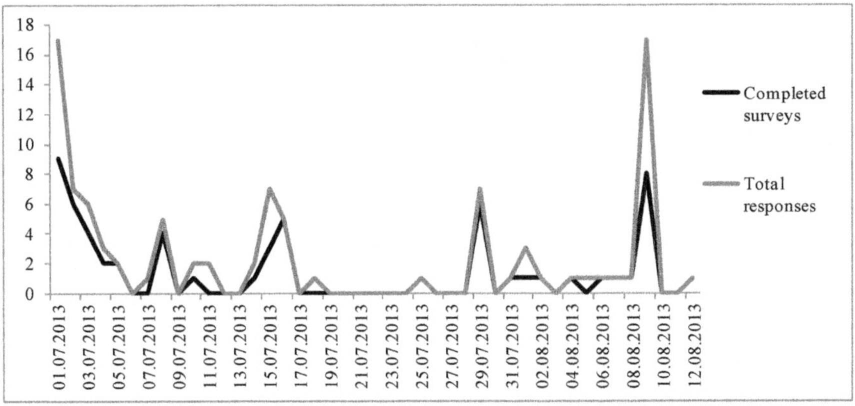

Overall, 96 participants started to complete the survey, and 60 participants completed it, yielding a response rate of 28.4% and a completion rate of 17.75%. Response rates in web-based surveys are in general rather moderate or poor (Fricker & Schonlau 2002) and were found to be continuously declining, with response rates below 28% rather common (Sheehan 2001).

Considering that the target group was highly specific, and participants were asked to complete the survey during their work time, this result seems to be quite satisfactory and is comparable to results in other industrial settings (Powell 1996; Diamantopoulos & Winklhofer 2001). The results of the survey will be depicted in the next section.

4.4 Description of the Findings from the Cold Chain Survey

4.4.1 Overview on Evaluation Criteria to be Applied to the Sample

According to Schnell, Hill & Esser (2011), already a small amount of units of investigation and a small amount of variables provide as much information that maintaining an overview without quantitative analysis is rather impossible. Considering that in total, more than 100 questions were included in the survey and 96 participants at least started the survey, the amount of information provided has to be structured in a systematic way. To this purpose, Diekmann 2002 proposes a step-wise approach to analyze the data, which will be followed here, and which will be explained and applied in the next paragraphs.[118]

The first step of data analysis is the *coding and transfer of data* from the information storage medium into a data file for the later analysis (Diekmann 2002). Codification of questions and answers helps thereby to structure large amounts of data and to avoid errors during data analysis (Schnell, Hill & Esser 2011). The variable names automatically generated by the

118 The complete plan and additional information can be found in Diekmann (2002 pp. 546-548).

software were re-coded for better interpretability and easiness of use during the following analysis.[119] As the answers by respondents were stored on the server provided by Unipark, the data was downloaded after the termination of the survey into an Excel database, containing an ID for every participant and all information provided by the respondent.[120]

The second step proposed by Diekmann (2002) is the *control and exclusion of defective data*. In this context, Diekmann (2002) and Schnell, Hill & Esser (2011) stress the importance of controlling *firstly* the data set for logical breaks, if for instance values occur which do not make sense. During this analysis, it turned out that the 6-point scales used were in part disarranged, as some scales included higher values or disarranged sequences of the items. This error has apparently been caused during the creation and optimization of the survey during the preparation phase, as rewording of items and deleting older versions of items led to new values attributed by the software to the respective item. However, since the values attributed were depicted in the codebook automatically generated by the software, affected scales could be easily identified and adapted.

Secondly, this task contained the deletion of all data sets, where not at least the eligibility criteria had been completed and all questions answered for at least the first case. However, apart from drop-outs, another issue in obtaining qualitatively useful answers are those sets of responses, where respondents simply "click through" the questionnaire (Mühlenfeld 2004, p. 85). In order to further increase the quality of the obtained information, every set of responses on successful and unsuccessful transactions was therefore checked regarding the involvement of the respondent, by testing for standard deviation of provided answers. In those cases, where all answers were identical, the probability of biased responses was deemed to be high and the cases were therefore excluded from further analysis.[121] This resulted in the deletion of one case of successful transactions, and two cases of unsuccessful transactions.

Thirdly, data sets, where respondents could not be attributed to the target group had to be excluded from the sample. However, none of the respondents failed to meet these criteria established in section 4.3.2. Additionally, as the vast majority of respondents left their e-mail addresses in order to obtain a summary of the findings, these were also checked to see whether these e-mail addresses indicated participants not belonging to the target group. In consequence, no evidence for responses by people from outside the target group could be found.

Fourthly, where respondents answered questions with "not applicable", a suitable method for coping with these values was required, as most data analysis procedures are not designed for dealing with missing values (Schafer & Graham 2002). However, before deciding on how to deal with these missing values, it had to be assessed, whether values are missing completely at random or in a systematic way, which would lead to biased results when data is replaced (Enders 2010). Therefore, Enders (2010) suggests conducting firstly a Missing Completely at

[119] The original codes and modified codes can be found in the explanation volume.
[120] The complete data set can be found in the explanation volume.

Random (MCAR) test to interpret the nature of missing values. Two of the advantages of this test are that it is firstly rather unaffected by non-normal distributions and secondly, that it is also rather unaffected by small sample sizes (Little 1988). Therefore, this test seems to be suitable as preparation for deciding on how to deal with missing data.

As has been noted by Schafer & Graham (2002), deleting data case-wise may result in biased results, as do other techniques such as mean replacement or single imputation methods. According to Enders (2010), one of the most applied mechanisms to handle and replace missing values is the so-called estimation-maximization (EM) algorithm, which is according to Longford (2008) more practical than for instance multiple imputation in settings with relatively few statistical procedures. Furthermore, its general nature and integration in many standard statistic tools allows its application to many different problems, which also explains its preferred use by many different researchers (Schafer & Graham 2002). Considering the relatively small sample size, the limited number of statistical procedures to be performed, the maturity of the method and its easiness of use, the EM algorithm will also be applied in this case.

The *re-coding of data and transformation of single variables into scales or indices* is part of the third step of data analysis. This step includes re-codification of reverse-coded items, grouping of variables into broader categories, and the evaluation of indicators for the subsequent inclusion into measurement models for latent variables (Diekmann 2002).[122] After the scales have been transformed appropriately, the data set was split into several categories for the subsequent analysis.

The first set comprised the information on respondents, companies, and introductory questions. This set will be used in the following for the general description of the field of respondents and the characteristics of the cold chains included in the survey. The second set of data comprises the answers to the first case, hence the example for a successful transaction, whereas the third set comprises the unsuccessful case. Therewith, the characteristics of the successful transaction can be compared with those of the transaction where a disruption occurred, to identify commonalities and differences with the help of descriptive and analytical statistical methods. However, before being able to analyze causal relations between latent variables, firstly, the quality of measurement models and structural models has to be evaluated and assured (Bortz & Döring 1995). Since these quality criteria are the same for both subsamples, the criteria will be depicted in the following paragraphs, before the results of their application will be illustrated.

The choice and interpretation of quality criteria for measuring latent variables is a much discussed topic in the literature, due to the large amount of different criteria and interchangeably used terms (Churchill, 1979). In order to assess the quality of the indicators, as well as of the latent constructs in the context of SEM, Götz, Liehr-Gobbers & Krafft (2010) propose five

121 The results of the involvement test can be found in the explanation volume.

122 The cleaned data set can be found in the explanation volume.

evaluation criteria: content validity, indicator reliability, construct reliability, convergent validity, and discriminant validity.[123] Therefore, in the following each of these points will be discussed and suitable quality criteria for each purpose derived.

The first evaluation criterion mentioned by Götz, Liehr-Gobbers & Krafft (2010) is the **content validity** of each indicator. It involves the logical analysis of indicators and whether they can be reasonably applied to measure what they are supposed to measure (Peter 1981). The evaluation of content validity has already been conducted during the pre-tests of the indicators, which resulted in the deletion of unsuitable indicators and the identification of valid ones. As all other scales used have already been empirically tested and validated also for this research, the content validity of indicators seems therefore to be given.

The next criterion is the **indicator reliability**, hence how well an indicator tabs the intended construct, and for which the factor loadings and error variances can serve as an indicator (Bagozzi & Yi 2012). This implies that for loadings of the latent constructs on an indicator of established scales, values larger than 0.7 are acceptable (Götz, Liehr-Gobbers & Krafft 2010). However, others authors qualify this threshold by naming values of 0.4 to 0.5 as sufficient (Backhaus 2011), while others specify that for new developed measurement models, values as low as 0.4 are acceptable (Hulland 1999). As the majority of measurement models applied in this research have been newly developed, this lower threshold seems thus to be applicable. In addition to high loadings on the intended constructs, indicators should also inhibit low cross-loadings on other constructs (Diamantopoulos & Siguaw 2006). Therefore, those indicators with loadings higher than 0.4 are further investigated regarding potential cross-loadings. However, some authors stress that indicator reliability is in general less relevant than the overall ability of the indicators to measure the intended construct adequately (Fritz 1995; Bagozzi & Yi 2012). Therefore, more attention should be paid to the next point, namely construct reliability.

Construct reliability refers thereby to how strongly associated indicators of the same construct are with one another and can be measured by Cronbach's Alpha coefficients higher than 0.6 (Götz, Liehr-Gobbers & Krafft 2010). Another important indicator for construct reliability, which draws on standardized loadings and measurement errors of each item, is the composite reliability which should take values of 0.7 and higher (Shook et al. 2004). Nevertheless, as Bagozzi & Yi (2012, p. 17) put it, such "*cut-off values*" for indicator and construct reliability should in the case of SEMs be applied more carefully and less restrictive, as the focus should lie on the hypotheses under scrutiny and therewith on the overall model rather than its parts.

Convergent validity refers to how well a construct is measured by its indicators and is represented by a strong correlation between measures and the respective construct (Duarte & Raposo 2010). It implies that each indicator loads with a significant t-value on its latent con-

---

123 For similar evaluation criteria see e.g. Fornell & Larcker (1981); Bagozzi & Yi (1988); Anderson & Gerbing (1988).

struct, hence, with values over 1.96 (Gefen & Straub 2005; Backhaus 2011). Convergent validity is generally assessed by the average variance extracted (AVE), which should take values greater than 0.50, as this indicates that a higher amount of variance is attributed to the construct instead to measurement error (Fornell & Larcker 1981). Both, Cronbach's Alpha and AVE are thereby criteria for construct reliability and convergent validity (Fritz 1995), and indicate how closely related these criteria are.

The importance of the AVE is also stressed by the next criterion, namely **discriminant validity**. In this context, Bollen & Lennox (1991) state that correlations between indicators of the same latent construct should be higher than between indicators of different latent constructs. However, they admit that no established thresholds exist for the extent of difference between correlations. According to Fornell & Larcker (1981), discriminant validity is satisfied if the AVE is larger than the squared correlations of the latent variable with any other latent variable in the model.

After evaluating the quality of the measurement models, Anderson & Gerbing (1982) stress that also the causal model has to be subject to a quality control. A logical indicator for the quality of the structural model has been claimed to be the determination coefficient R^2 of the endogenous variables (Götz, Liehr-Gobbers & Krafft 2010). However, as Backhaus (2011) states, there is no definite value of R^2 to assess the quality of the model, but that it rather depends on the research question which value seems to be appropriate. Given that disruptions can be highly contingent and prone to multiple complex causal reactions high values of R^2 are rather unexpected.

Even though all measurement models are reflective models in the first order, the latent second order constructs of degree, standardization and formalization of interactional programming also warrant some kind of quality evaluation. However, formative constructs partly require different quality criteria, as the underlying construction and measurement logic is different (Diamantopoulos & Siguaw 2006). Criteria named here by Götz, Liehr-Gobbers & Krafft (2010) are content validity, indicator reliability, and construct reliability. However, what has to be kept in mind is that these formative second order constructs are made up by reflective first order constructs, which has been categorized by Jarvis, MacKenzie & Podsakoff (2003) as type II second order models. The applicability of the general criteria for formative models has therefore to take into account the special considerations and limitations of the nature of measurements (Fritz 1995).

As in the case of reflective indicators, **content validity** of the formative constructs has been checked firstly by building on the relevant literature. Indicators of formative constructs should thereby not only be assessed based on empirical measures, but also and foremost based on theoretical considerations (Bollen & Lennox 1991). To assure that the construct is covered in its entire breadth by its composing indicators, the definition of the construct and the coverage by its indicators have to be carefully prepared (Diamantopoulos & Winklhofer 2001). Therefore, since the constructs have been defined and investigated in detail in the previous sections, and since the indicators of the first order constructs are subject to thorough empirical evaluation, content validity is deemed to be established.

Indicator reliability refers to the weight of every indicator on the formative construct, and should be compared between the indicators of the same construct to assess their relative importance (Götz, Liehr-Gobbers & Krafft 2010). Nevertheless, since indicators of formative constructs should not be deleted out of measurement theoretic assumptions (Hollnagel 2008) these values should be rather seen as information instead of a decision criterion. Another criterion mentioned by Götz, Liehr-Gobbers & Krafft (2010), is the variance inflation factor (VIF), which can be used to identify significant multicollinearity between indicators of the same formative construct. As a rule of thumb, VIF values larger than 10 indicate strong multicollinearity and may require corrective action (Kleinbaum et al. 2007). However, in case of second order models, Bagozzi & Yi (2012) note that high correlations between latent first order variables should prevail, to reason the aggregation into second order models. Nevertheless, since they do not specify what high correlations are in such a case, correlations will be calculated, to see whether constructs do not correlate at all.

Construct reliability can be assessed by the use of multiple-indicators multiple-cause (MIMC) models (Götz, Liehr-Gobbers & Krafft 2010), for instance by either including reflective indicators to measure the construct in a different way, or by including endogenous constructs, which are measured reflectively and which are caused by the formative constructs (Bagozzi & Yi 2012). As in this research, disruptions are operationalized with two reflectively measured constructs, this criterion is therefore considered as fulfilled.

Whereas the majority of criteria are specified with the help of some thresholds, others are left to the evaluation in the respective context. Therefore, where specific thresholds are missing, comparisons with similar research shall provide the basis for evaluating the quality of the models. Now that the quality criteria on the level of single values, response sets, indicators, constructs, and models have been specified, the next sections depict the execution of these steps on which the final step by Diekmann (2002) is based, namely the *statistical analysis of distributions and relations*. Thereby, sections 4.4.2 and 4.4.3 will illustrate the prepared data, before the data will be analyzed in section 4.5. For a better overview on the tasks for the data analysis, summarizes the proceeding to be followed in the next sections.

Figure 36: Proceeding to evaluate and analyze the data

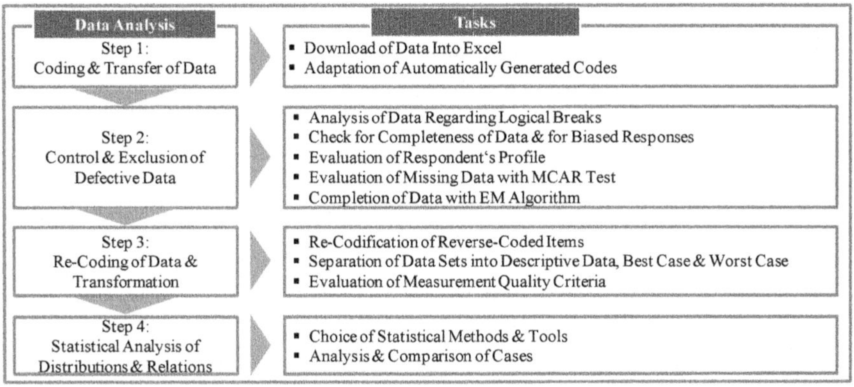

Source 21: Own illustration; proceeding based on Diekmann (2002)

As the choice of statistical methods partly depends on the results of previous process steps, methods and selection will be described before description of causal findings in section 4.4.3.

4.4.2 Illustration of the Sample and Sub-Groups

According to Schnell, Hill & Esser (2011), data analysis in social sciences always starts with the illustration of collected variables and some descriptive statistics of interest. Therefore, after application of the quality criteria, the demographic and professional profile of respondents will be depicted in the following, to gain insights on the range of participants and their dispersal among cold chain segments, product groups, and job profiles.

Based on the assessment of the overall data set and the established quality criteria, 35 data sets were excluded from further analysis due to a large amount of lacking data. The total drop-out rate was 37%, which does not seem to be high considering that participants were filling the questionnaire in during their work time, where interruptions by other tasks and inquiries seem to be likely and frequent. It seems noteworthy that 16 participants dropped out already on the welcome page and the first page, where respondents were asked about their experience in the sector and their affiliation. Here, one possible explanation is that these participants clicked on the link out of curiosity, but felt not addressed by the topic and sought target group. Another six dropped out when asked about technologies applied during transactions, and another four on the introductory page for the questions on the recent successful transaction. Hence, the majority of drop outs took place at the beginning of the questionnaire, before the questions of interest were asked.

Even more, none of the respondents dropped out at the beginning of the disruption case, and only one respondent dropped out afterwards, which indicates that there were little objections to answer questions on negative experiences. Nevertheless, during the analysis of standard deviations, two respondents had standard deviations of zero for the entire worst case, whereas one respondent had a standard deviation of zero for the best case, but was more involved in the second case.[124] Consequently, these three cases were excluded from the causal analysis.

Hence, to assess whether the data is missing completely at random, or involves systematic bias, with the remaining data sets, Little's MCAR test was performed using SPSS.[125] For both cases of transaction, all indicators were tested for systematically missing values, yielding a non-significant result in all cases.[126]

Figure 37: Number of indicators by percentage of missing values and MCAR test results

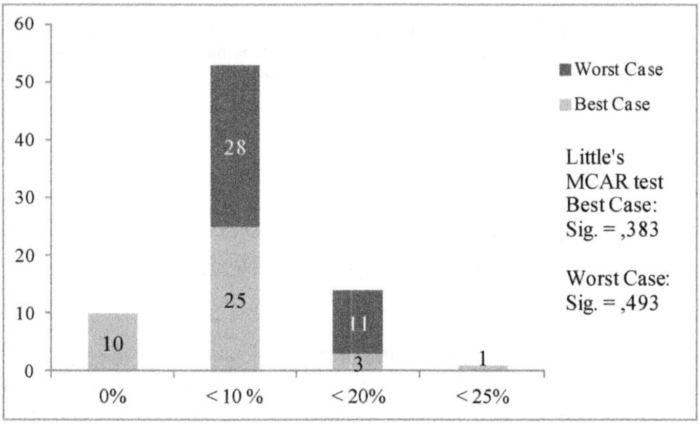

Based on these results, it is thus possible to replace missing data instead of deleting the entire data set. As in empirical research, the objectives innovation and information content are considered as being more important than proximity to truth (Chmielewicz 1979), elimination of data sets shall therefore be avoided. Hence, in the next step, the EM algorithm was applied.

The EM algorithm comprises two general steps. In the first step (expectation-step), the values for missing data are estimated based on observed values. In the second step (maximization-step) the model is then adapted to these new values and the process repeated until no further improvements are obtained (Dempster, Laird & Rubin 1977). The procedure has been conducted with SPSS, and missing values from the original sample replaced.[127] Therewith, a cleaned and completed data set has been obtained for the subsequent data analysis.

The remaining sample consists of 61 respondents, which will be illustrated in the following starting with the profile of respondents. In order to learn more about respondents, they were

---

124 The results of the involvement check can be found in the explanation volume.

125 SPSS is one of the most frequently used statistical software programs used in social sciences Diekmann (2002); Schnell, Hill & Esser (2011). For further information, see: http://www-01.ibm.com/software/analytics/spss/.

126 The results of Little's MCAR test can be found in the explanation volume.

127 The resulting data set can be found in the explanation volume.

asked to state their years of experience in handling temperature-sensitive products, as well as their departmental affiliation. The results can be found in the figure below:

Figure 38: Experience with temperature-sensitive products and departmental affiliation

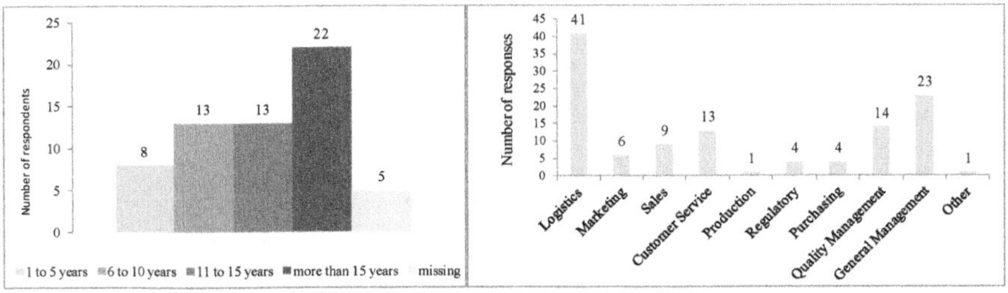

As can be seen above, 22 respondents have more than 15 years of experience in handling temperature-sensitive products. The remaining 39 respondents have on average 8 years of experience. The five respondents who did not indicate their years of experience were double checked to see whether they fit the target group. As all of them indicated to spend a considerable amount of time on cold chain planning, monitoring, and optimization, they were consequently not excluded from the sample. Regarding the four other groups, the ascending distribution seems noteworthy, suggesting that while all ranges have been covered, respondents in general tent to have a long standing record in handling temperature-sensitive products.

Regarding the departments to which respondents belong, the majority (67%) indicated that their job could be attributed to the logistics department, whereby more than half of them indicated also at least one other departmental affiliation, such as general management. The diversity of affiliations among other than the logistics department seems to suggest a broad range of responsibilities covered by respondents. However, as the departmental affiliation or years of experience do not necessarily indicate the cold chain logistics-related share of the current job profile, respondents were asked, how much of their work time they spend on planning, monitoring, and optimizing cold chain logistics together with customers, suppliers, logistics service providers, and within the company. The results are shown in Figure 39:

Figure 39: Time spent by respondents on optimizing cold chains with stakeholders

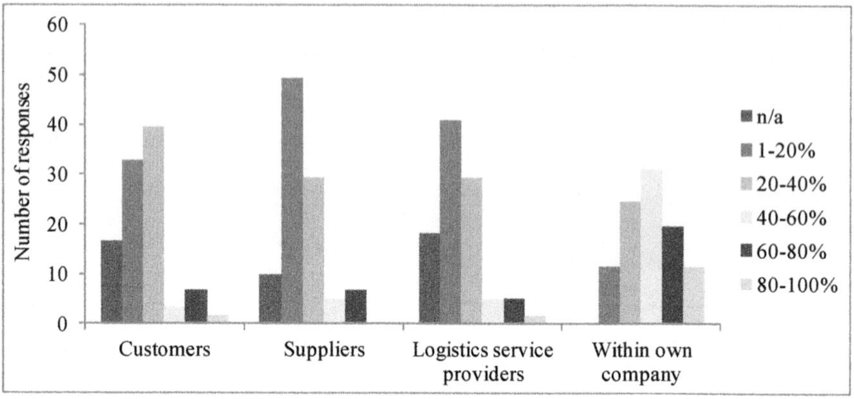

The graph above shows the average work time (in percent) spent by respondents on cold chain logistics activities with four major stakeholders, namely customers, suppliers, logistics service providers, and the own company. Thereby, not for every respondent necessarily every stakeholder group is of relevance, since for example logistics service providers are not necessarily involved. With customers, the largest share of respondents (approx. 40%) spends 20 to 40% of work time on cold chain logistics-related activities. With suppliers, the largest share of respondents (50%) spends less time on these activities, namely 1 to 20 %. This is similar though with a smaller share for logistics service providers, where the share of "not applicable" responses is also the highest for all groups. Very few respondents spend more than 40% of their time with one of the three external stakeholder groups, whereas the largest share of respondents spends 40 to 60% or more of their work time on cold chain logistics-related activities within the company. Every respondent spends at least with one of the stakeholder groups a considerable amount of time on planning, monitoring, and optimizing cold chain logistics. Therewith, all respondents are deemed to belong to the target population and to possess the knowledge required for completing the survey.

Apart from the profile of the individual, also the profile of companies is considered to provide insights on the composition of the sample. To this purpose, the next illustrations provide some more information on the company background of respondents.

Figure 40: Number of employees and country of residence

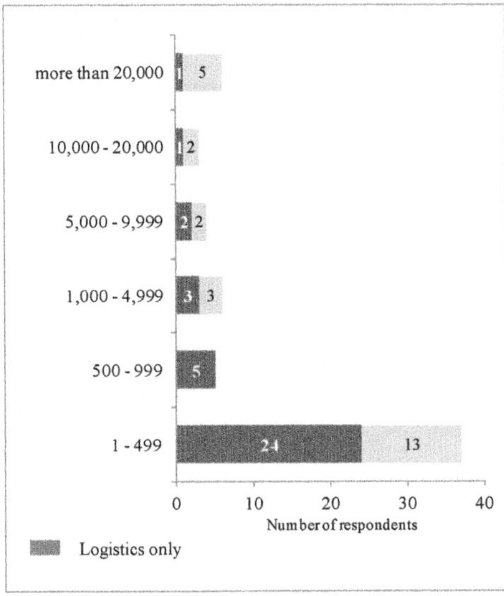

Country of Residence		
Country	**Frequency**	**Percent**
Austria	1	1,6
Belgium	3	4,9
Chile	1	1,6
Costa Rica	1	1,6
Denmark	1	1,6
Ecuador	1	1,6
France	2	3,3
Germany	18	29,5
India	1	1,6
Lebanon	1	1,6
Luxembourg	4	6,6
Netherlands	8	13,1
Norway	1	1,6
Slovenia	1	1,6
South Africa	2	3,3
Spain	1	1,6
Switzerland	5	8,2
United Arab Emirates	1	1,6
United Kingdom	1	1,6
United States	7	11,5
Total	**61**	**100,0**

The majority of respondents (about 60%) work in companies with less than 500 employees. Over the other categories, the distribution is relatively equal, ranging between 5% and 10% of respondents attributed to the respective category. The distribution of respondents regarding their country of residence also shows one focal point, namely Germany with nearly 30% of respondents. Overall, respondents came from twenty different countries, showing a concentration on Europe.

The huge amount of SMEs is in accordance with findings by other researchers, who observe that the cold chain logistics sector still is highly fragmented (Fritz & Schiefer 2009). Considering the large differences in company size, especially between companies specialized in logistics services and companies involved in production, wholesale, and/or retail, the harmonization of exchange processes in cold chain logistics seems to be even more challenging, as firms of different sizes frequently also incorporate different organizational structures (Hill, Fehlbaum & Ulrich 1994).

Figure 41: Cold chain segments and product categories covered

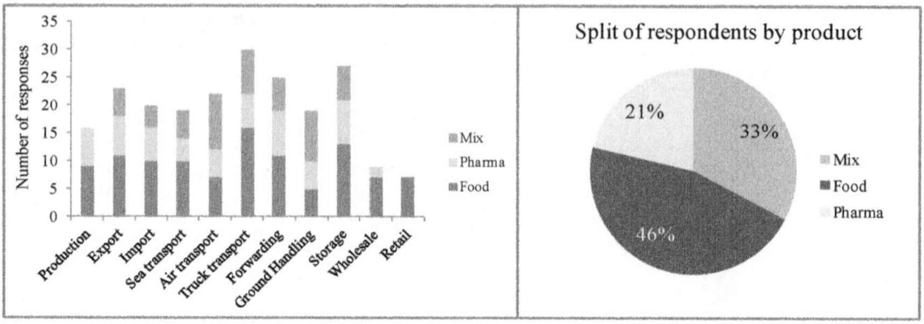

The distribution over different cold chain segments shows that overall, all major cold chain segments were covered by at least about 10% of respondents. Whereas respondents handling both types of products were present for all logistics segments, production, wholesale and retail were either exclusively focused on food products or on pharmaceuticals, with retail representatives entirely stemming from the food retail area. Overall, food handling companies were more represented than pharmaceutical handling companies or companies handling both. Hence, based on these findings, it seems unlikely that the sample incorporates normal distribution.

The application of many statistical procedures requires that the sample is normally distributed (Janssen 2012). Therefore, before starting to analyze the data with the help of statistical procedures, first of all it has to be clarified, whether the data is following a normal distribution or not. This assumption was tested for both cases individually, as well as jointly, since they represent opposite extreme examples, which are nevertheless measured on the same scale. However, in neither case, normal distribution can be assumed, which might have to be considered during the choice and application of the statistical methods presented hereafter.[128] However, as Janssen (2012) states, the majority of tests are relatively robust to breaches of normal distribution, which is furthermore in general approached by sample sizes larger than 30. Considering that for each case, at least a sample size of 59 is given interpretability of statistical tests thus does not seem to be notably reduced.

The lack of normal distribution can be explained by the focus of analysis on extreme poles of supply chain performances. The performance is consequently supposed to differ substantially between the two cases, as in the one case, the performance should be satisfactory, whereas in the second case, the performance should be significantly lower if indeed a disruption is described. Therefore, mean values for the performance indicators of both cases should be compared to see whether indeed two different cases of transactions have been described by the participants. Even though the case which does not refer to disruptions has been termed "best case" for easiness of use, respondents were asked to describe a transaction, where the logistics processes were realized as planned, thus a case without significant deviations in a positive or negative way. As the overall sample is sufficiently large to approach standard normal distribution, a dependent sample t-test was conducted to compare the means of all variables in both cases. Thereby, all performance indicators were found to differ significantly between the cases, confirming the intention of the survey design to obtain to opposite poles of process performance.[129]

Furthermore, since two product categories are considered, heterogeneity might also be due to substantial differences between these categories or other characteristics of the participants. Therefore, the sample has been decomposed into several sub-groups, to analyze commonalities and differences in performance not only between cases, but also between groups. Such a differentiation of descriptive statistics is frequently used to describe sub-groups in more detail, and may provide useful starting points for the following multivariate analysis (Schnell, Hill & Esser 2011). Table 23 illustrates the mean values for each performance indicator for the best case and the worst case, for transactions with food and with pharmaceuticals separately.[130]

---

[128] The results of the normal distribution check can be found in the explanation volume.

[129] The reuslts of the t-test for independent samples can be found in the explanation volume.

[130] To increase comprehensiveness, the indicators have been renamed to better identifiy their content.

Table 23: Comparison of performance indicator values per case and product category

Case	Product Group		PerfTem	PerfProQual	PerfPac	PerfPun	PerfAccPro	PerfAccDoc	PerfCom	PerfAdh
BestCase	Food	Mean	1,486	1,556	1,800	1,530	1,857	1,400	1,514	1,489
		N	35	35	35	35	35	35	35	35
		Std. Deviation	,5621	,5234	,6774	,5843	,8096	,5531	,6585	,5721
	Pharma	Mean	1,680	1,568	1,613	1,569	1,840	1,760	1,720	1,781
		N	25	25	25	25	25	25	25	25
		Std. Deviation	0,557	0,566	0,567	0,486	0,554	0,663	0,614	0,644
	Total	Mean	1,567	1,561	1,722	1,546	1,850	1,550	1,600	1,610
		N	60	60	60	60	60	60	60	60
		Std. Deviation	0,563	0,537	0,635	0,541	0,709	0,622	0,643	0,615
WorstCase	Food	Mean	3,213	3,248	2,748	2,417	**3,007**	2,465	2,495	2,474
		N	37	37	37	37	37	37	37	37
		Std. Deviation	1,320	1,187	1,233	1,213	1,397	1,235	1,281	1,204
	Pharma	Mean	3,577	3,044	2,554	2,023	**2,340**	2,066	2,013	2,141
		N	22	22	22	22	22	22	22	22
		Std. Deviation	1,045	1,118	0,948	0,968	0,939	0,987	0,857	0,925
	Total	Mean	3,349	3,172	2,676	2,270	2,758	2,316	2,315	2,350
		N	59	59	59	59	59	59	59	59
		Std. Deviation	1,228	1,157	1,131	1,135	1,280	1,156	1,157	1,112
Total	Food	Mean	2,373	2,425	2,287	1,986	2,448	1,947	2,018	1,995
		N	72	72	72	72	72	72	72	72
		Std. Deviation	1,338	1,253	1,104	1,053	1,280	1,099	1,133	1,067
	Pharma	Mean	2,568	2,259	2,054	1,782	2,074	1,903	1,857	1,949
		N	47	47	47	47	47	47	47	47
		Std. Deviation	1,255	1,137	0,896	0,776	0,792	0,835	0,744	0,800
	Total	Mean	2,450	2,360	2,195	1,905	2,300	1,930	1,955	1,977
		N	119	119	119	119	119	119	119	119
		Std. Deviation	1,304	1,207	1,029	0,955	1,124	0,999	0,997	0,967

Perf: Performance; Tem: Temperature; ProdQual: Product Quality; Pac: Packaging; Pun: Punctuality; AccPro: Accuracy of Product Quantity; AccDoc: Accuracy of Documents; Com: Completeness of Documents; Adh: Adherence to Preferred Transport Route; light grey: highest/lowest value; dark grey bold: differences larger than 0.5

As can be seen above, the first distinction has been conducted for the two product groups included in the analysis, to evaluate whether indeed they can be assumed to be relatively similar.[131] As Schnell, Hill & Esser (2011) mention, the analysis of sub-groups serves the transparent comparison of results between sub-samples, but may become confusing with increasing amount of information provided. As the purpose here is to identify major differences in the results per sub-group, differences above 0.5 are deemed noteworthy, as they represent a deviation of 10% on the five-point scales used. Considering that the best case and the worst case are regarded separately, these differences are probably even more pronounced, as good cases are expected to receive values in the lower range (i.e. 1 or 2), and bad cases in the higher range (i.e. 4 or 5). Those mean values of the food and pharmaceutical category showing a difference equal or higher as 0.5 are thus marked in bold, whereas for the total, the highest and the lowest mean values are marked in bold.

131 See section 4.2.1.

Regarding differences between product categories in the best case, on total, the "accuracy of product quantity" was rated worst, whereas "punctuality" received the lowest score and therewith the best score. Hence, participants were very satisfied with the punctuality of shipments, whereas they were comparatively unsatisfied with the quantity of products shipped. In the worst case, "accuracy of product quantity" for food products was considerably lower than for pharmaceuticals, indicating that the quantity of products planned and the actual quantity shipped differed far more for food shipments than for pharmaceuticals. As in the best case, "punctuality" received again the best score in total. The performance indicator with the highest and therewith the worst score was "temperature maintenance". Overall, the best mean value for food products has been attributed to the "accuracy of documents", with "accuracy of product quantity" receiving the worst score. For pharmaceuticals however, the best score has been attributed to the "punctuality", whereas "temperature maintenance" was rated worst. The difference between the best and the worst score is higher for pharmaceuticals than for food products.

Hence, while here already some differences in performance rating can be observed, differences might also be due to the *degree of specialization* by the companies involved, leading perhaps to different foci of attention and different supply chain structures. Therefore, Table 24 depicts the cases split by the products handled by participating companies into food, pharmaceuticals, and mixed.

Table 24: Comparison of performance indicator values per handling specializations

Handling Specialization			PerfTem	PerfProQual	PerfPac	PerfAccPro	PerfPun	PerfAccDoc	PerfCom	PerfAdh
BestCase	Food	Mean	1,481	1,519	1,741	1,519	1,704	**1,296**	1,370	1,400
		N	27	27	27	27	27	27	27	27
		Std. Deviation	0,509	0,509	0,526	0,580	0,775	0,465	0,565	0,571
	Pharma	Mean	1,769	1,622	1,692	1,633	1,923	1,692	1,692	1,683
		N	13	13	13	13	13	13	13	13
		Std. Deviation	0,439	0,477	0,630	0,461	0,494	0,751	0,630	0,748
	Mix	Mean	1,550	1,579	1,716	1,528	2,000	**1,800**	1,850	1,847
		N	20	20	20	20	20	20	20	20
		Std. Deviation	0,686	0,626	0,789	0,556	0,725	0,616	0,671	0,500
	Total	Mean	1,567	1,561	1,722	1,546	1,850	1,550	1,600	1,610
		N	60	60	60	60	60	60	60	60
		Std. Deviation	,563	,537	,635	,541	,709	,622	,643	,615
WorstCase	Food	Mean	**3,020**	3,134	**2,801**	2,443	2,749	**2,511**	**2,478**	**2,612**
		N	26	26	26	26	26	26	26	26
		Std. Deviation	1,375	1,308	1,200	1,239	1,290	1,267	1,204	1,167
	Pharma	Mean	3,488	3,024	**2,283**	1,944	2,751	**1,947**	**1,947**	**2,027**
		N	13	13	13	13	13	13	13	13
		Std. Deviation	1,042	1,156	1,017	,959	1,422	,960	,960	,918
	Mix	Mean	**3,685**	3,317	2,768	2,257	2,776	2,302	2,343	2,218
		N	20	20	20	20	20	20	20	20
		Std. Deviation	1,073	,975	1,103	1,105	1,238	1,113	1,212	1,126
	Total	Mean	3,349	3,172	2,676	2,270	2,758	2,316	2,315	2,350
		N	59	59	59	59	59	59	59	59
		Std. Deviation	1,228	1,157	1,131	1,135	1,280	1,156	1,157	1,112
Total	Food	Mean	2,236	2,311	2,261	1,972	2,216	1,892	1,914	1,994
		N	53	53	53	53	53	53	53	53
		Std. Deviation	1,281	1,272	1,057	1,060	1,174	1,121	1,081	1,091
	Pharma	Mean	2,629	2,323	1,988	1,788	2,337	1,820	1,820	1,855
		N	26	26	26	26	26	26	26	26
		Std. Deviation	1,175	1,123	,882	,754	1,125	,855	,806	,839
	Mix	Mean	2,617	2,448	2,242	1,893	2,388	2,051	2,097	2,033
		N	40	40	40	40	40	40	40	40
		Std. Deviation	1,400	1,195	1,086	0,939	1,076	0,924	0,998	0,880
	Total	Mean	2,450	2,360	2,195	1,905	2,300	1,930	1,955	1,977
		N	119	119	119	119	119	119	119	119
		Std. Deviation	1,304	1,207	1,029	0,955	1,124	0,999	0,997	0,967

Perf: Performance; Tem: Temperature; ProdQual: Product Quality; Pac: Packaging; Pun: Punctuality; AccPro: Accuracy of Product Quantity; AccDoc: Accuracy of Documents; Com: Completeness of Documents; Adh: Adherence to Preferred Transport Route; light grey: highest/lowest value; dark grey bold: differences larger than 0.5

In this categorization, the only considerable difference in the best case can be observed between the food handling respondents and those handling both product groups. Here, the food handling respondents rated "accuracy of documents" more than 0.5 points better than those respondents from the mixed category, showing a considerable better evaluation of performance in terms of accurate shipping documents. In total, the "accuracy of product quantity" was rated best, with "punctuality" again being rated worst. In the worst case scenario, several differences can be observed. Firstly, operational performance in terms of temperature maintenance was considerably better rate by food specialists than by mixed-handling specialists. The "integrity of packaging" in turn was better maintained in those transactions reported by pharmaceutical specialists than in those reported by food specialists. Another significant difference between these groups can be found for the "accuracy of documents", which is rated more than 0.53 points worse by the food category. This difference is even more pronounced between the two for the case of "completeness of documents". Finally, for the "adherence to the agreed transport route", the food category rates the performance again much worse than the pharmaceutical category. In total, "accuracy of product quantity" is rated best, whereas "temperature maintenance" is again rated worst. For the overall evaluation, the food category rates "accuracy of documents" best and "product quality" worst, whereas the pharmaceutical category rates the "accuracy of product quantity" best and "temperature maintenance" worst. The same rating can be found for the mixed category and the total result.

Finally, a third possibility would be that there are distinctions induced by the different supply chain segments regarded. The respondents can be broadly separated by the nature of value-added in the supply chain, into those companies generating profits by production or retail of food or pharmaceuticals, and those companies providing logistics services to these companies. Therefore, Table 25 distinguishes means, standard deviations and sample size by supply chain segment.

Table 25: Comparison of performance indicator values per supply chain segment

Supply Chain Segment			PerfTem	PerfProQual	PerfPac	PerfPun	PerfAccPro	PerfAccDoc	PerfCom	PerfAdh
BestCase	Logistics	Mean	1,463	1,528	1,764	1,878	1,531	1,537	1,585	1,606
		N	41	41	41	41	41	41	41	41
		Std. Deviation	,596	,558	,692	,678	,562	,596	,631	,544
	Production and Retail	Mean	1,789	1,632	1,632	1,789	1,579	1,579	1,632	1,621
		N	19	19	19	19	19	19	19	19
		Std. Deviation	,419	,496	,496	,787	,507	,692	,684	,762
	Total	Mean	1,567	1,561	1,722	1,850	1,546	1,550	1,600	1,610
		N	60	60	60	60	60	60	60	60
		Std. Deviation	,563	,537	,635	,709	,541	,622	,643	,615
WorstCase	Logistics	Mean	3,455	3,262	2,684	2,750	2,132	2,248	2,272	2,374
		N	40	40	40	40	40	40	40	40
		Std. Deviation	1,201	1,029	1,135	1,300	0,908	1,117	1,169	1,217
	Production and Retail	Mean	3,124	2,982	2,659	2,775	2,562	2,459	2,407	2,297
		N	19	19	19	19	19	19	19	19
		Std. Deviation	1,287	1,400	1,153	1,271	1,495	1,253	1,158	0,877
	Total	Mean	3,349	3,172	2,676	2,758	2,270	2,316	2,315	2,350
		N	59	59	59	59	59	59	59	59
		Std. Deviation	1,228	1,157	1,131	1,280	1,135	1,156	1,157	1,112
Total	Logistics	Mean	2,447	2,385	2,218	2,309	1,828	1,888	1,924	1,985
		N	81	81	81	81	81	81	81	81
		Std. Deviation	1,373	1,197	1,040	1,116	0,807	0,956	0,992	1,010
	Production and Retail	Mean	2,457	2,307	2,145	2,282	2,070	2,019	2,020	1,959
		N	38	38	38	38	38	38	38	38
		Std. Deviation	1,161	1,241	1,018	1,156	1,209	1,094	1,017	0,880
	Total	Mean	2,450	2,360	2,195	2,300	1,905	1,930	1,955	1,977
		N	119	119	119	119	119	119	119	119
		Std. Deviation	1,304	1,207	1,029	1,124	0,955	0,999	0,997	0,967

Perf: Perfomance; Tem: Temperature; ProdQual: Product Quality; Pac: Packaging; Pun: Punctuality; AccPro: Accuracy of Product Quantity; AccDoc: Accuracy of Documents; Com: Completeness of Documents; Adh: Adherence to Preferred Transport Route; light grey: highest/lowest value; dark grey bold: differences larger than 0.5

The best score in the best case obtains the "accuracy of product quantity", while participants were relatively unsatisfied with "punctuality" of shipments. In the worst case, again the quantity of products meets the expectations best, whereas considerable temperature excursions occurred in all supply chain segments regarded. In total, the logistics segment rates "accuracy of product quantity" best and "temperature maintenance" worst, whereas the production and retail segment differs with respect to the best score, which they attribute to the "adherence to the agreed transport route". Overall, operational performance is best in terms of accurate product quantity, whereas temperature excursions seem to be the major weak point across supply chain segments. However, little differences between segments become obvious compared to the other two categorizations.

As has been argued in section 3.4.2, the degree to which third parties are involved in the shipping process might also have an impact on the susceptibility of supply chains to disruptions. Therefore, as a control variable, respondents were asked to what extent third parties were involved in the shipping process for both cases. Table 26 shows the differences of means and t-statistics for this variable in both cases.

Table 26: Comparison of third party involvement in both cases

	Paired Differences					t	df	Sig. (2-tailed)
	Mean	Std. Deviation	Std. Error Mean	95% Confidence Interval of the Difference				
				Lower	Upper			
BestCase Resp - WorstCase Resp	-,481	2,035	,277	-1,037	,074	-1,739	53	,088

As can be seen, the difference between both cases regarding the involvement of third parties is not significant at the .05 confidence level, but at the .1 level (sig. .088). In the worst case, third parties were reported to be involved to a larger extent than in the optimal case. Variance in turn was equal for both cases, so that no significant difference in the distribution of third party involvement between both cases is supported.

Hence, from these descriptions of the sample, the performance, and differentiations of groups and cases, already many insights can be gained on cold chain logistics and aspects of operational performance especially susceptible to disruptions. Following the general sequence of empirical analyses as described for example by Schnell, Hill & Esser (2011) and Kromrey (2009), the hitherto presented results have been mainly concerned with the description and structuring of the data based on univariate or bivariate statistical processing. To analyze multiple relations however, the procedures of multivariate statistics have to be presented and applied (Kromrey 2009). Therefore, in section 4.4.3, the methods and their application to the SEM will be presented.

4.4.3 Illustration of the Causal Findings on Disruptions

For the use of SEM, Backhaus et al. (2011) assert that several steps have to be completed. These include among others the choice of estimation method, evaluation of the model, and modification of the model.

For estimating SEM, one can generally distinguish between covariance-based procedures, estimating the maximum likelihood such as LISREL, and variance-based procedures, called Partial Least Squares (PLS) (Temme, Kreis & Hildebrandt 2010; Blunch 2008). According to Anderson & Gerbing 1988, the major difference between both procedures is that traditional covariance-based procedures aim for the explanation of covariance between variables, whereas PLS focuses on the exact definition of component scores by assuming a lack of random error variance. Furthermore, maximum likelihood estimations with LISREL require multinormality of variables, whereas PLS does not make such assumptions (Fornell & Bookstein 1982). Consequently, Esposito Vinzi, Trinchera & Amato (2010) assert that PLS is especially useful in exploratory research, as it does not make any assumptions regarding distribution, measurement, or number of samples (Barroso, Carrión & Roldán 2010). Another advantage is that PLS can deal with formative and reflective indicators, even within the same structural equation model (Götz, Liehr-Gobbers & Krafft 2010). Given the exploratory nature of this research, that it involves formative and reflective constructs, and that the sample size is relatively small, PLS seems therefore to the appropriate choice of estimation method.

According to Götz, Liehr-Gobbers & Krafft (2010), software packages to evaluate structural equation models based on the PLS approach have become more readily available recently (e.g. PLS-Graph, PLS-GUI, smartPLS). The question is thus, which of these software tools to use for the purpose of this thesis. A recent assessment of different software packages has been conducted by Temme, Kreis & Hildebrandt (2010), who compared requirements, methodological options, and ease-of-use of six different software packages. Based on this assessment, the software package smartPLS is chosen, as it showed advantages in the estimation of interaction effects, easiness of data export, and showed no incorrect results in simulations involving missing data and multicollinearity. Especially estimation of interaction effects seems to be important, considering the complex structure of the model. Based on the PLS approach, next, the measurement models have to be evaluated regarding their adherence to the previously defined quality criteria. Table 27 provides an overview on the results for the first order model in the worst case scenario, based on the quality criteria established in section 4.4.1.

Table 27: Evaluation of measurement quality of reflective constructs

Construct	Indicator	Initial Loading	Corrected Loading > 0.4	AVE > 0.5	Composite Reliability > 0.7	Cronbach Alpha > 0.6
Asset Specificity	Spec1	.778	.783	.611	.886	.846
	Spec2	.852	.855			
	Spec3	.797	.783			
	Spec4	.810	.811			
	Spec5	.638	.663			
	Spec6	*-.034*				
Volume Uncertainty	Un1	.931	.933	.831	.908	.799
	Un2	.892	.890			
Level of Detail	Det1	.906	.921	.747	.855	.674
	Det2	.821	.803			
	Det3	.360				
Preciseness	*Prec1*	*-.376*		.775	.872	.757
	Prec2	.761	.779			
	Prec3	.966	.972			
Durability	*Dur1*	*.562*		.661	.851	.736
	Dur2	.783	.863			
	Dur3	.899	.919			
	Dur4	.621	.627			
Invariability	Vari1	.543	.547	.645	.770	.629
	Vari2	*.460*				
	Vari3	.953	.995			
Range of Addressees	*RoA1*	*.976*		.837	.911	.851
	RoA2	.111	.834			
	RoA3	-.182	.989			
Rigidity	Rig1	.619	.610	.507	.753	.537
	Rig2	.726	.721			
	Rig3	*.593*				
	Rig4	.728	.793			
Logistics Performance	LP1	.772	.822	.775	.932	.905
	LP2	.943	.932			
	LP3	.943	.922			
	LP4	.867	.840			
Product Performance	PP1	.712	.718	.575	.797	.650
	PP2	.925	.925			
	PP3	.603	.595			
	PP4	*.313*				

Overall, the majority of indicators were found to be appropriate fulfilling the quality criteria. Thereby, "frequency" has not been included in this overview, as it is operationalized as a manifest variable. Those indicators loading weakly on the intended construct were excluded in a one-at-a-time approach to evaluate simultaneously the resulting changes in construct reliability, which may also result in further deletions of indicators (Nitzl 2010). The resulting scales adequately comply with the quality criteria for the constructs. Only in one case the limit is not reached, namely regarding Cronbach's Alpha for rigidity of interactional programming, which indicates a relatively high perturbation by measurement error.[132] However, as Bagozzi (1981) observe, in empirical research with SEM, it is quite common that one or two quality criteria are violated in the entire set of criteria for convergence in measurement and differentiation in constructs. However, several scales had to be reduced to two indicators respectively, which may weaken the adequacy of measurement and should be considered during analysis (Chin 1998).

The final criterion to be assessed for the reflective measurement models is **discriminant validity** of the constructs. To this purpose, the correlation matrix of the latent constructs has been adapted, whereby the AVE has been placed on the diagonal line and correlations between the constructs replaced with their squared correlations. As can be seen in Table 28, the constructs all inhibit sufficient discriminant validity, as the AVE is substantially larger than any squared correlation with all other constructs.

Table 28: Discriminant validity of the reflective measurement models

	Spec	Dur	Freq	Det	LP	Prec	PP	RoA	Rig	Invari	Un
Asset Specificity	**0,611**	0	0	0	0	0	0	0	0	0	0
Durability	0,183	**0,661**	0	0	0	0	0	0	0	0	0
Frequency	0,176	0,008	**1**	0	0	0	0	0	0	0	0
Level of Detail	0,172	0,000	0,175	**0,747**	0	0	0	0	0	0	0
Logistics Performance	0,012	0,005	0,030	0,001	**0,775**	0	0	0	0	0	0
Preciseness	0,007	0,107	0,093	0,320	0,005	**0,775**	0	0	0	0	0
Product Performance	0,054	0,083	0,001	0,016	0,049	0,007	**0,575**	0	0	0	0
Range of Addressees	0,000	0,154	0,008	0,070	0,011	0,207	0,006	**0,837**	0	0	0
Rigidity	0,009	0,106	0,015	0,005	0,040	0,128	0,000	0,089	**0,507**	0	0
Invariability	0,047	0,070	0,063	0,009	0,004	0,081	0,007	0,104	0,027	**0,645**	0
Volume Uncertainty	0,054	0,000	0,100	0,027	0,002	0,013	0,027	0,017	0,003	0,000	**0,831**

Subsequently to the evaluation of the measurement models, the quality of the structural model needs assessment (Götz, Liehr-Gobbers & Krafft 2010). In this context, Bagozzi (1981) states that the first hints at model misspecification are negative error variances, correlations greater than one, and extremely large parameter estimates. Even though the matrix depicted above shows the squared correlations, it becomes immediately obvious that no correlations are greater than one. Also the other two anomalies were not detected in the results, which will be presented below.

132 See section 4.4.1.

As already mentioned, the R^2 can be used as an indicator for the quality of the structural model to explain and predict the endogenous constructs. As an orientation, Merschmann & Thonemann 2011 call an R^2 of 0.39 good, Ringle, Wende & Will (2010) call a R^2 of 0.239 as a moderate level for PLS path models, and Stan & Saporta (2010) call 0.27 a satisfactory result. In a supply chain management context, with seven latent variables including multiple interactions in several cause-and-effect chains, Subramani (2004) for instance reports values between 0.19 and 0.30, and Droge, Vickery & Jacobs (2012) in a similar context R^2 of 0.23. In other research, values of 0.17 are deemed to be high if purposefully only specific determinants are regarded in the analysis of multi-causal variables such as company success.[133] Given the complexity of the phenomenon under study, such values therefore seem to be quite satisfactory. Therefore, the explanatory and predictive ability of the structural model seems to sufficiently high for the majority of constructs. Figure 42 illustrates the determination coefficients for the endogenous variables of this structural model.

Figure 42: Determination of organizational structure and disruptions by the model

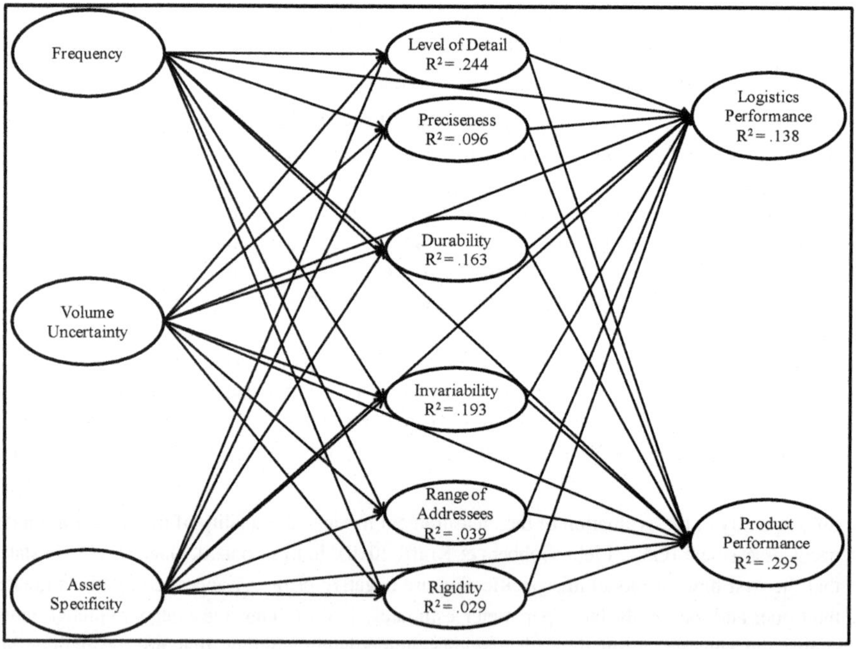

As can be seen, the largest predictive capacity in the model relates to the determination of "product performance", which is explained to nearly 30%. This seems to be a very high value, considering the complexity and diversity of the products under study. This is followed by the

133 For a discussion, see Nitzl (2010).

"level of detail", "durability", and "invariability", which are also explained to a satisfying extent, given the diversity of companies, variety in interfaces, and the multitude of influencing factors. The determinants explain approximately 14% of "logistics performance" and explain therewith logistics deviations only half as well as product deviations, but still to an adequate extent. Comparatively low values can be found for "range of addressees", "preciseness" and "rigidity", which seem to be nearly undetermined by the transaction type.

The final step is the evaluation of the overall model. However, for this assessment, rules of thumb are prevalent, which may not be suitable for specific data sets (Shook et al. 2004). An additional issue regarding the assessment of overall fit arises, as for PLS, conventional quality indicators are lacking (Götz & Liehr-Gobbers 2004; Esposito Vinzi, Trinchera & Amato 2010). Furthermore, Chin (1998) argues that such rigid Goodness of Fit (GoF) measures have frequently been criticized for ignoring side effects and that instead of focussing on measurement power, one should focus on the predictive power of the model by evaluating the strength of structural paths, which should ideally be above 0.2 or 0.3 to be considered meaningful. Furthermore, the significance of paths should be calculated to evaluate their reliability (Götz & Liehr-Gobbers 2004; Götz, Liehr-Gobbers & Krafft 2010).

According to Cheung & Lau (2008), the bootstrapping procedure is a suitable method in this context, as it can be applied if normal distribution assumptions are violated or distribution is unknown. Furthermore, it is frequently applied in PLS-based SEM research to calculate t-values and assess the significance of structural paths and factor loadings (Hair et al. 2012; Gefen & Straub 2005). In the bootstrapping procedure, the sample is regarded as a small representation of the basic population, from which in an iterative process with k repetitions samples are drawn, calculated and results recorded (Hayes 2009). Cheung & Lau (2008) suggests a minimum of k = 1.000, whereas Hayes (2009) suggests to take at least 5.000 samples, which is also advocated by others (e.g. Cordeiro, Machás & Neves 2010; Real, Roldán & Leal 2012). As the results become more accurate with a larger amount of bootstraps (Davidson & MacKinnon 2000), k = 5.000 will also be applied here. Considering these requirements, Table 29 shows the path coefficients, standard errors and t-statistics for the cleaned first order model as calculated with the PLS algorithm and subsequent bootstrap. To enhance comprehensiveness, significant relationships at the .05 and .01 level are marked in bol.[134]

[134] According to Schnell, Hill & Esser (2011), significance is normally tested at these two levels, wherefore the .1 level will be disregarded in the following.

Table 29: Statistical results on hypotheses of the first order model

	Original Sample	Standard Deviation	Standard Error	T Statistics
Asset Specificity -> Durability	**-0,4427****	**0,119**	**0,119**	**3,7213**
Asset Specificity -> Level of Detail	-0,3842	0,2001	0,2001	1,9199
Asset Specificity -> Logistics Performance	**0,2894***	**0,1383**	**0,1383**	**2,0927**
Asset Specificity -> Preciseness	0,1629	0,1556	0,1556	1,0465
Asset Specificity -> Product Performance	-0,0605	0,1411	0,1411	0,4288
Asset Specificity -> Range of Addressees	**0,3125***	**0,1311**	**0,1311**	**2,3839**
Asset Specificity -> Rigidity	-0,049	0,1379	0,1379	0,3556
Asset Specificity -> Invariability	-0,067	0,1676	0,1676	0,3998
Durability -> Logistics Performance	0,2784	0,1711	0,1711	1,6272
Durability -> Product Performance	**-0,2773***	**0,1245**	**0,1245**	**2,2277**
Frequency -> Durability	0,109	0,1201	0,1201	0,9075
Frequency -> Level of Detail	**0,4313****	**0,1609**	**0,1609**	**2,6808**
Frequency -> Logistics Performance	**0,296***	**0,1185**	**0,1185**	**2,4986**
Frequency -> Preciseness	0,2114	0,1203	0,1203	1,7572
Frequency -> Product Performance	**0,321***	**0,1226**	**0,1226**	**2,618**
Frequency -> Range of Addressees	0,0288	0,1227	0,1227	0,2343
Frequency -> Rigidity	0,1656	0,1139	0,1139	1,4535
Frequency -> Invariability	-0,1333	0,1703	0,1703	0,7827
Level of Detail -> Logistics Performance	-0,0546	0,1172	0,1172	0,4657
Level of Detail -> Product Performance	-0,0654	0,1008	0,1008	0,6491
Preciseness -> Logistics Performance	-0,0879	0,2013	0,2013	0,4365
Preciseness -> Product Performance	**-0,4867****	**0,1413**	**0,1413**	**3,4451**
Range of Addressees -> Logistics Performance	-0,0269	0,1919	0,1919	0,1401
Range of Addressees -> Product Performance	**0,4211***	**0,1701**	**0,1701**	**2,4753**
Rigidity -> Logistics Performance	-0,1179	0,159	0,159	0,7416
Rigidity -> Product Performance	0,1177	0,1225	0,1225	0,9611
Invariability -> Logistics Performance	-0,191	0,1528	0,1528	1,2497
Invariability -> Product Performance	-0,0586	0,1307	0,1307	0,4489
Volume Uncertainty -> Durability	0,044	0,1183	0,1183	0,3723
Volume Uncertainty -> Level of Detail	-0,0571	0,1212	0,1212	0,4714
Volume Uncertainty -> Logistics Performance	0,0029	0,123	0,123	0,0239
Volume Uncertainty -> Preciseness	-0,1306	0,1372	0,1372	0,9518
Volume Uncertainty -> Product Quality	0,0289	0,1065	0,1065	0,2717
Volume Uncertainty -> Range of Addressees	-0,2046	0,1094	0,1094	1,8709
Volume Uncertainty -> Rigidity	-0,1733	0,1074	0,1074	1,6125
Volume Uncertainty -> Invariability	0,1133	0,1698	0,1698	0,6674

N= 59; $*\alpha = 0.05$; $**\alpha = 0.01$;

The values above do not indicate any of the anomalies such as excessive standard errors as reported by Bagozzi (1981) wherefore misspecifications do not seem to exist. However, several path coefficients are quite small and therefore cannot be considered to be relevant for the causal explanation of the respective endogenous construct. On the other hand, other path coefficients are quite large, which indicates important causal relations and which is further supported by the reported t-statistics. The first-order model seems thus to provide useful insights on effects of interface design on performance in case of disruptions, which will be analyzed in section 4.5.2.

Furthermore, the model might also provide useful insights regarding design options of interface structures and how the components interact with each other across constructs in practice. Therefore, the first order construct is tested for correlations to assess the assumptions of the framework provided by Remer and to gain further insights on causal relations between the variables.

Table 30: Correlations of first order constructs of interface structure

		Detail	Durability	Preciseness	Range of Addressees	Rigidity	Invariability
Detail	Pearson Correlation	1	.076	.581**	.215	-.023	.217
Durability		.076	1	.386**	.362**	.295*	.258*
Preciseness		.581**	.386**	1	.461**	.352**	.275*
Range of Addressees		.215	.362**	.461**	1	.321*	.323*
Rigidity		-.023	.295*	.352**	.321*	1	.241
Invariability		.217	.258*	.275*	.323*	.241	1
N= 59; *α = 0.05;**α = 0.01;							

As illustrated, there are partly substantial correlations between the first order constructs. For instance, even though "preciseness" correlates strongest with the "level of detail" (.581***), it also correlates significantly with all other constructs. "Level of detail" in turn only correlates with "preciseness", whereas "range of addressees" correlates strongest with "preciseness", while the smallest significant correlation is attributed to "rigidity". Overall, every construct correlates at least strongly with one other construct. Furthermore, to exploit the model to the full extent, also the second order model with its formative indicators has to be evaluated. To this purpose, the reflective first order constructs have to be transformed into the formative second order constructs by applying the repeated indicator approach as suggested by Hair et al. (2014). After running the PLS algorithm for the first order model, the thereby obtained latent variable scores are used as manifest variables for the second order model, so that again the path coefficients and t-statistics can be calculated and relationships identified.

As already indicated in the previous section, formative constructs follow different rules for evaluation as reflective constructs and therefore require a stronger theoretically grounded evaluation as reflective ones (Diamantopoulos & Siguaw 2006). Table 31 shows the results of the applied quantitative evaluation criteria.

Table 31: Evaluation of the second order formative constructs

Construct	Indicators	Weight	Correlation < 0.9	VIF < 10
Degree of interactional programming	Level of Detail	.539	.581**	1,511
	Preciseness	.586		
Standardization of interactional programming	Durability	.842	.258*	1,071
	Invariability	.364		
Formalization of interactional programming	Range of Addressees	.679	.321	1,115
	Rigidity	.548		
N= 59; *α = 0.05;**α = 0.01;				

The quality criteria applied to the formative constructs indicate that the constructs are reliable, with each indicator having a substantial influence on the latent variable, low correlation and no hints at multicollinearity. The weights are thereby distributed relatively even in the case of the "degree" of interactional programming, whereas "formalization" shows a slight tendency towards "range of addressees", while "standardization" is more influenced by "durability" of instructions than by "invariability". As a final criterion, again the path coefficients and t statistics shall be assessed, to evaluate the overall explanatory power of the model as suggested by Chin (1998) and Götz & Liehr-Gobbers (2004). Since the constructs are compositions of the first order constructs, variations in the first order constructs could be evened out at the level of the second order constructs, since at a certain point, it is assumed that one dimension may only grow at the expense of the other.[135] In consequence, explanatory power might be reduced. At the same time, weak effects on the first order constructs might turn into significant effects of the second order constructs, if their dimensions reinforce each other. Therefore, the model was computed to produce latent variable scores, which were used as input for the second order formative constructs. The results of the PLS algorithm and bootstrap procedure are shown in Table 32.

135 See section 3.3.2 and 3.3.3.

Table 32: Statistical results on hypotheses of the second order model

	Original Sample	Standard Deviation	Standard Error	T Statistics
Asset Specificity -> Degree	0,0758	0,1245	0,1245	0,6089
Asset Specificity -> Formalization	-0,0971	0,1112	0,1112	0,8735
Asset Specificity -> Logistics Performance	0,1629	0,1241	0,1241	1,3131
Asset Specificity -> Product Performance	0,1951	0,1071	0,1071	1,8219
Asset Specificity -> Standardization	**-0,4402****	**0,1111**	**0,1111**	**3,9628**
Degree -> Logistics Performance	-0,1144	0,1385	0,1385	0,8258
Degree -> Product Performance	-0,0667	0,0887	0,0887	0,7511
Formalization -> Logistics Performance	**-0,2417***	**0,1187**	**0,1187**	**2,0368**
Formalization -> Product Performance	**0,218****	**0,0793**	**0,0793**	**2,7477**
Frequency -> Degree	**0,3369****	**0,1132**	**0,1132**	**2,9758**
Frequency -> Formalization	0,0366	0,107	0,107	0,3422
Frequency -> Logistics Performance	0,174	0,1138	0,1138	1,5295
Frequency -> Product Performance	0,0552	0,1094	0,1094	0,5047
Frequency -> Standardization	0,2267	0,123	0,123	1,8428
Standardization -> Logistics Performance	**0,2751***	**0,1187**	**0,1187**	**2,3175**
Standardization -> Product Performance	**-0,2769***	**0,108**	**0,108**	**2,5633**
Volume Uncertainty -> Degree	0,0309	0,0967	0,0967	0,3198
Volume Uncertainty -> Formalization	-0,0507	0,0827	0,0827	0,6126
Volume Uncertainty -> Logistics Performance	-0,12	0,1223	0,1223	0,9812
Volume Uncertainty -> Product Performance	-0,2129	0,1156	0,1156	1,8418
Volume Uncertainty -> Standardization	-0,0229	0,0939	0,0939	0,2443
	N= 59; *α = 0.05;**α = 0.01;			

Regarding the predictive power of the model, Figure 43 shows the R^2 for all five endogenous variables of the structural model with the second order formative constructs of organizational structure.

Figure 43: Predictive power of the second order structural model

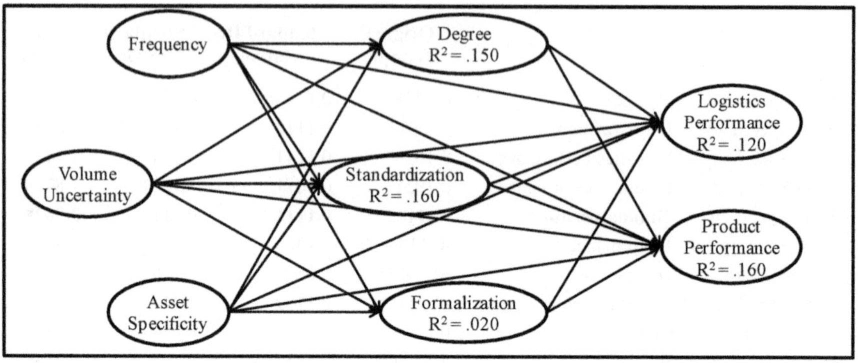

Overall, the predictive power of the model declined in comparison to the first order model. Whereas the predictive power of deviations in "logistics performance" remained relatively equal, the predictive power for deviations from "product performance" declined significantly. This is probably due to the opposite direction of effects of "level of detail" and "preciseness" on "product performance". In combination, they might ease-out effects, which is also supported by the lack of significance for the path between "degree" and "product performance". Furthermore, whereas degree and standardization of interactional programming still can be explained to an acceptable extent, formalization of interactional programming is not explained at all. The same picture emerges for the second order constructs as shown in Table 33.

Table 33: Correlations of second order constructs of interface structure

		Degree	Standardization	Formalization
Degree	Pearson Correlation	1	.326*	.369**
Standardization		.326*	1	.471*
Formalization		.369**	.471*	1
				N= 59; *α = 0.05;**α = 0.01;

Here, "formalization" is correlated strongly with both other constructs, while "standardization" and "degree" of interactional programming are only correlated slightly. The correlations might be explained by the nature of constructs, which describe several dimensions of the same object, namely programming interactions at interfaces. Furthermore, it indicates that there are typical combinations of design options for the characteristics of programming, which has also been pointed out by Remer 1989, 2004. However, all significant correlations are positive, which indicates that the limits, where one dimension can only be extended to the expense of another dimension are either not reached yet, or do not exist.

To further substantiate the overall quality of the model, the adapted model after the quality evaluation has been applied to a second set of data, namely the best case scenario. Even though both samples are not entirely independent from one another as the respondents were the same, substantial misfit could indicate inferior quality and inapplicability of the model to a more general context of supply chain performance assessment. However, the test of the model with the second sample did not reveal major quality issues, as again, the entire set of quality criteria for the first order model was only breached in two cases, which is quite normal in empirical research (Bagozzi 1981).[136] Hence, the developed scales to measure interface structures and operational performance in terms of logistics performance and product performance seem to be applicable also to changing contexts in cold chains. Apart from the rather cold chain-specific measurement model of "product performance", the other scales might also be applicable to other kinds of supply chains. Additionally, the adopted measurement scale for "asset specificity" shows that even with context-specific adaptations, the indicators measure the construct reliably, increasing therewith its applicability.

However, in the case of the second order model, the two variables of "standardization" show a high correlation (+.981**), while the two variables of "formalization" have a high VIF (26.612), indicating problems with multicollinearity.[137] Hence, the influence of each first order construct on the second order construct cannot be measured reliably, as indicators cannot be separated clearly from one another anymore (Diamantopoulos & Winkelhofer 2001). Apparently, in the best case scenario, the indicators measuring the different constructs were all answered nearly identically. On the one hand, this might indicate that both dimensions of these constructs are designed similarly and that such a balanced manifestation fosters optimal process operations. On the other hand, it might indicate some measurement problems, wherefore the comparative analysis of both cases will focus more on the first order models than on the second order models, to prevent misinterpretations.

Based on the results of the data analysis and of the evaluation of the SEM, the empirical findings can now be analyzed in detail and set into relation to the relative quality of the model. Therefore, the section 4.5 will analyze the findings and their implications for the hypothesized causal relations between transaction type, organizational structure, and the occurrence of disruptions.

136 For the test results see Appendix 4.
137 For the test results see Appendix 6.

4.5 Analysis of the Findings and Possible Implications

4.5.1 Comparison of Performance Scenarios and Sub-Groups

Comparison of the Best Case and the Worst Case Scenario

As has been outlined in section 4.1, this section is concerned with the final part of the fourth step of empirical research as outlined by Diekmann (2002), namely the analysis of the findings presented above. In section 2.2.3, disruptions have been defined as significant exceptional negative deviation(s) from supply chain process plans caused by one or more unexpected temporal events. To evaluate whether there is indeed a significant negative deviation from process plans, thus whether the understanding is consistent with the empirical findings, Figure 44 shows the two performance profiles of both cases as differences in mean scores of the eight indicators for cold chain performance.

Figure 44: Performance profiles of best case and worst case

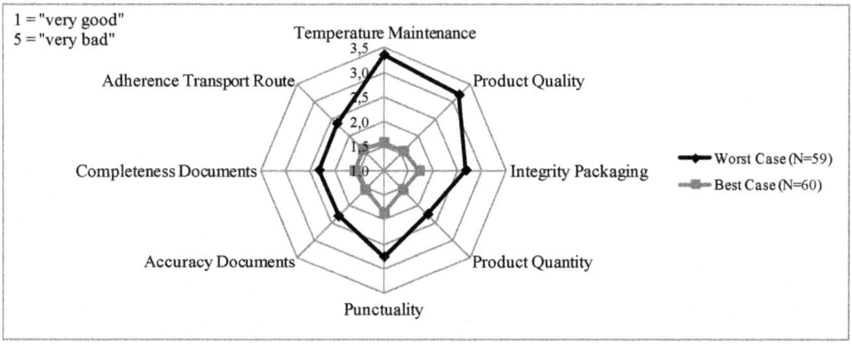

As can be seen, there is indeed a substantial difference in the performance profiles between both cases. Whereas performance is quite uniform around the score of 1.5 in the best case, differences are more pronounced in the worst case, with "temperature maintenance" showing the largest deviation from optimal performance. Overall, there is a considerable gap between the performance profile in the best and in the worst case. This difference is consistent with the definition of disruptions as negative deviations from optimal performance. Therefore, the worst case can be indeed considered to represent supply chain disruptions, enhancing therewith the validity of the developed understanding and measurements of disruptions.

The comparison of the two scenarios shows that overall the best case scenario was rated by the participants with values ranging between 1.55 for accuracy of product quantity and 1.85 for punctuality, with small standard deviations.[138] Considering that the scale ranged from 1 to 5, participants rated the performance very positively between "very good" and "good". This indicates that the scenario to be described has been understood correctly and that in successful

[138] The results for means, standard deviations, and standard errors can be found in the explanation volume.

transactions, apparenlty little deviations in process performance take place. In cases where operations can be executed as planned, the only drawback seems to be "punctuality" of shipments, but which is apparently tolerated as the overall performance is considered to be satisfactory nevertheless. The comparatively lower rating of "punctuality" can be interpreted in three ways: one interpretation could be that opposed to the other three indicators of "logistics performance", time can be measured more reliably, wherefore also slight deviations can be observed. Alternatively, the indicator might be deemed more important than the other three, wherefore respondents are more critical when it comes to adherence to time frames. Finally, shipments might indeed be not as punctual as the customer would prefer. Since delays were frequently reported as performance inhibitors, and since cold chains might be especially time sensitive because of shelf life restrictions,[139] a combination of higher importance of punctuality and difficulties to achieve this goal seems to be probable.

Regarding the worst case scenario however, the picture is somewhat different. Whereas the best rated performance indicator is again accuracy of product quantity, which was rated with 2.27 still better than the average of the scale, the worst rated was "temperature maintenance" with 3.35, closely followed by product quality with 3.17. The performance in the worst case scenario varies therefore substantially more across indicators, with a stronger impact on the product-related performance, which supports the operationalization of disruptions as two distinctive constructs. Furthermore, the scale is again not fully used, but this time, the distance to the nearest extreme point 5 (very bad) is also larger. This might on the one hand be explained by a reluctance of participants to rate transactions with own participation extremely negative. On the other hand, this observation supports the focus of this thesis on disruptions with high likelihood, and (relatively) low impact. The comparably good rating of "accuracy of product quantity" also explains why the indicator had to be excluded for the use in the SEM, as it did not load sufficiently high on the construct (see Table 27). This results in the conclusion that if disruptions occur, product quantity is affected least.

The heterogeneity of variance between the two cases has been evidenced by the results of the Levene's test reported in section 4.4.2, which shows significant differences between the two scenarios. As can be seen in Figure 44, in the worst case, the distance between the different performance indicators is larger, as well as the standard deviation for each indicator, which is approximately twice as large as in the best case scenario. This finding supports the understanding of disruptions developed in section 2.2.3, which refers to a continuum of shapes of disruptions, instead of absolute shapes. At the same time, it highlights the importance of the choice of indicators, to adequately cover the construct.

Another noticeable comparison of the two cases is the degree of third party involvement. This has been reported to be higher in the worst case as in the best case, but showed to be not significant at the .05 level. At the .1 level of confidence however, the difference was significant,

---

[139] See section 2.5.3.

which would imply that a higher degree of third party involvement would be associated with inferior performance. However, another explanation could be that respondents tend to assume less responsibility if asked to report on a recent disruption. To see whether respondents rate the involvement of third parties higher when being asked to report transactions with inferior performance, or whether a general causal relation can be assumed, the effect of third party involvement on logistics and product quality was assessed for both cases, using again the PLS algorithm. In both cases, the degree of third party involvement had a significant effect on product quality, as shown in Table 34.

Table 34: Effect of third party involvement on performance in both cases

	Original Sample	Standard Deviation	Standard Error	T Statistics
Best Case				
3rd Party Involvement -> Logistics Performance	0,1286	0,1117	0,1117	1,1505
3rd Party Involvement -> Product Performance	0,1893*	0,0938	0,0938	2,0179
Worst Case				
3rd Party Involvement -> Logistics Performance	0,1083	0,1554	0,1554	0,6968
3rd Party Involvement -> Product Performance	0,3468**	0,0851	0,0851	4,0755
				$*\alpha = 0.05; **\alpha = 0.01;$

As already indicated by the comparison of means in section 4.4.2, in the case of disruptions, third party involvement has a significant effect on performance, and more specifically, on product quality. This would imply that the higher the extent of third party involvement, the worse is product performance. However, it also has a significant effect, even though to a lesser extent, on product quality in the optimal case. This indicates that this causal relation exists apart from a potential desire by respondents to attribute responsibility to somebody else, if something goes considerably wrong. The extent of third party involvement might of course also depend on the kind of supply chain regarded, or the perspective of the respondent. Thereby, respondents from production and retail might experience more third party involvement as logistics service providers, if they do not execute part of the shipping process on their own, but outsource the shipping process to LSPs. However, also after controlling for a potential bias by eliminating all respondents involved in production, wholesale and retail from the sample, still a weak negative effect of third party involvement on product quality in the best case, and a strong negative effect in the worst case were observed.[140] Therewith, the extent of third party involvement is negatively impacting on product quality. However, the causal relation requires further research, as extent of third party involvement might refer to the *share* of shipping process conducted by a single third party, or the *number* of third parties involved, which would increase also the number of interfaces. Therewith, as there is initial evidence on

140 See Appendix 1.

which direction of effect might be prevalent, a specific hypothesis for future research requirements can be deduced:

hypothesis 1 The higher the extent of third party involvement in the shipping process, the lower is product performance.

Apart from the differences observed between the two scenarios, section 4.4.2 also indicated differences of performance in several sub-groups. These results will be analyzed next.

Comparison of Sub-Groups in the Case of Disruptions

Also regarding the overall profile of disruptions, especially between product handling groups, some differences became obvious. Figure 45 shows the resulting performance profiles in the case of disruptions in food and pharmaceutical supply chains.

Figure 45: Disruption profiles for food products and pharmaceuticals

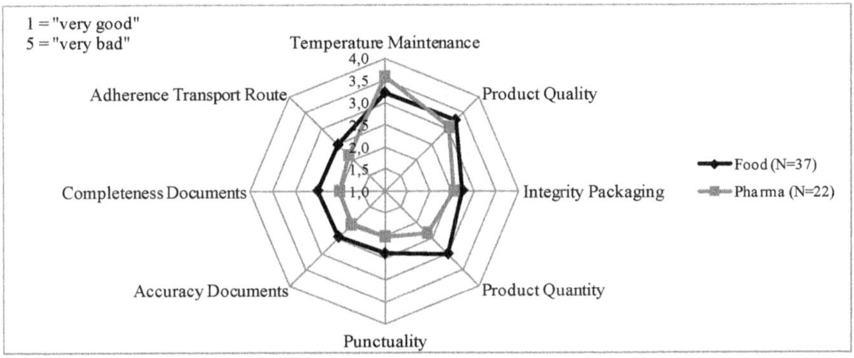

Whereas the disruption profiles are nearly identical regarding "product quality" and "integrity of packaging", "punctuality" has been rated considerably worse in food supply chains. This could be explained by better adherence to transportation schedules in pharmaceutical supply chains, for example because of a higher degree of automatization, or because of higher priorities given to pharmaceuticals as regulatory requirements are more strict than for food products (Marucheck et al. 2011). "Temperature maintenance" in turn has been rated worse in the case of pharmaceutical supply chains, which is indicated by higher values. On the one hand, this could be explained by an increased use of temperature monitoring equipment in pharmaceutical supply chains, which provides better evidence on cold chain ruptures. Indeed, respondents handling pharmaceuticals reported more frequently to use temperature monitoring devices in 75% to 100% of transactions as respondents handling food.[141]

On the other hand, the difference could be explained by differences in perceptions of significance of temperature deviations, as temperature deviations in pharmaceutical supply chains

[141] See Appendix 2.

may have significant detrimental impacts on the effectiveness of pharmaceuticals, and therewith on patient's life (Matthias et al. 2007). Furthermore, the more wide-spread use of active cooling technologies in food supply chains might be an advantage, as active cooling allows for greater flexibility and active temperature management (Siebel 2000). Thereby, counteractions can be taken more easily and fast upon observation of temperature excursions.

Additionally, it becomes obvious that in the pharmaceutical supply chain disruptions, disruptions are more limited to deviations from product plans, while in the food supply chain disruptions, the overall performance is lower. This could be explained by a larger interdependency between the product quality and the logistics quality, as for example delays also reduce shelf life,[142] and stresses the importance of considering both aspects in the evaluation of operational performance. The distinction between both product groups becomes slightly more pronounced when controlling for the type of handling company as shown in Figure 46.

Figure 46: Disruption profiles for product category handling groups

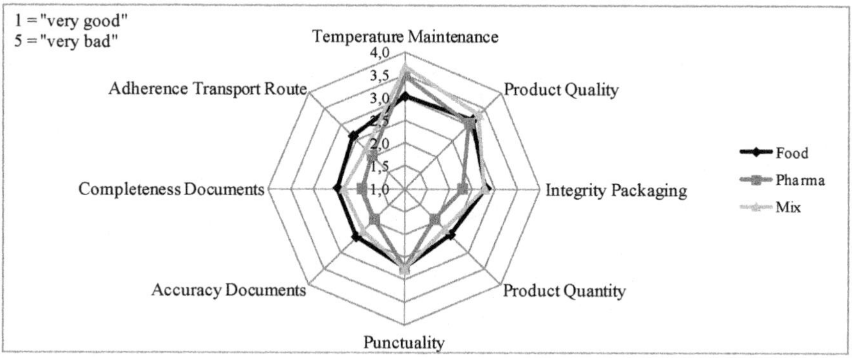

Especially regarding "integrity of packaging", there is a larger difference between the product groups. Furthermore, whereas before "punctuality" was different between the two groups, no significant differences can be observed if handling groups are taken into account. For the majority of indicators, the handling group for food and pharmaceuticals lies in between the other two groups, wherefore a differentiation into handling groups does not seem to yield additional insights, as the product categories provide a clearer picture. The same can be observed for different supply chain segments, which is highlighted in the disruption profile:

142 See section 2.5.2.

Figure 47: Disruption profiles in logistics and production and retail

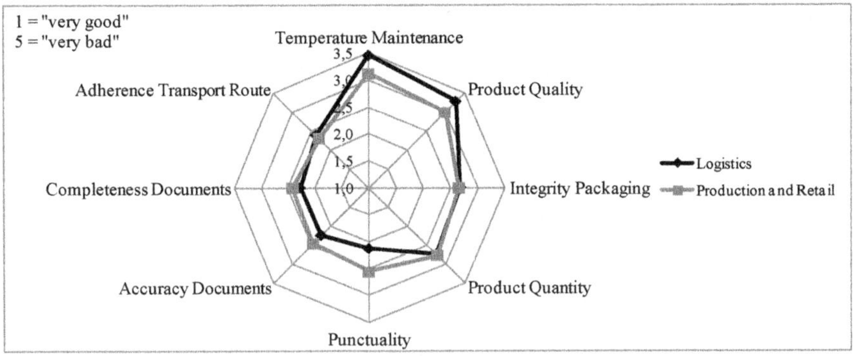

Whereas slight differences exist in “accuracy of product quantity” and “temperature maintenance”, overall the disruption profile is quite similar for the different segments. In consequence, the distinction of product groups seems to be the most important factor for explaining differences in the extent of supply chain disruptions.

Comparing all three profiles, it becomes apparent that there is a tendency of disruptions to affect to a larger extent the product performance than the logistics performance. On the one hand, this might be due to a better ability of supply chain agents to fulfil general logistical requirements in comparison to cold chain specific requirements. On the other hand, this could be explained by the relative ease of judging the product quality as the outcome of the process compared to judging the process itself. This would also explain why punctuality was rated worse than the other indicators of logistics quality, as it is easier to observe and to measure than the other indicators. However, based on the findings on disruptions and differences between logistics performance and product performance, the question results, how these differences can be explained. Therefore, section 4.5.2 focuses on the analysis of empirical findings on causal relations between transaction type, interface structure, and operational performance in the worst case, hence the case where a disruption occurred.

4.5.2 Effects of Interface Design on the Extent of Disruptions

In sections 3.4.3 and 3.5.1, it has been hypothesized that the interface structure as well as the achievement of operational planning depends on the characteristics of the transaction. Therefore, the type of transaction has been characterized by three variables, namely “asset specificity”, “frequency”, and “volume uncertainty”. As exogenous variables of the causal model, their effects on the interface structure and on cold chain performance will be analyzed first before turning to the effects of the interface structure. Furthermore, the first order and second order models will be analyzed sequentially, to enhance comprehensiveness.

First order model

In the final model, "asset specificity" has been measured with five indicators. Table 35 shows the loading and complete formulation of each indicator:

Table 35: Relevance of indicators for the construct "asset specificity"

ID	Indicator	Loading
Spec1	*We have made significant investments in cooling and monitoring equipment dedicated to our relationship with this partner*	.778
Spec2	*This partner has some unusual technological/managerial processes and standards, which have required adaptation on our part*	.855
Spec3	*Training and qualifying this partner has involved substantial commitment of time and money*	.783
Spec4	*Our logistics system has been tailored to fit the particular products/services of this partner*	.811
Spec5	*Our information system has been tailored to meet the requirements of dealing with this partner*	.663

The reason why Spec6 had to be excluded is presumably that in contrast to the indicators above, it asked for the *necessity* for specific investments, which is not the same as the extent of investments *realized.* This might explain why the answers of respondents to the sixth indicator did not correspond sufficiently with the other five indicators, resulting in poor loading on the construct. Of the remaining indicators, Spec2 loads highest, suggesting that where specific investments were taken, most were concerned with training employees to deal with new processes, or to apply different decision-making criteria. However, the degree of instructions seems to remain equal, as no significant influence of "asset specificity" on "level of detail" or "preciseness" has been detected. Therefore, it seems likely that one work prorgamme has been replaced with another one, without increasing the complexity of tasks.

In total, "asset specificity" has a significant effect on three variables of the first order model, namely "durability", "range of addressees", and "logistics performance". The first one, namely "durability" has been measured with three indicators:

Table 36: Relevance of indicators for the construct "durability"

ID	Indicator	Loading
Dur2	*The procedures for product and document exchange have already been in use for a long time*	.863
Dur3	*The procedures to exchange information were developed a long time ago*	.919
Dur4	*We expect the procedures for the exchange of products and documents to endure for a long time*	.627

As can be seen, Dur2 and Dur3 have the highest loadings on the construct, implying that the two items referring to the past duration are most important for the construct. Since predictions about the future involve a certain degree of uncertainty, the higher loadings of already witnessed facts seems to be comprehensive. “Asset specificity” has a significant negative effect on “durability” (- .4427**), which indicates firstly that the temporal stability of procedures for exchange processes is indeed influenced by the specificity of the transaction partner. Secondly, the direction of relation implies that the more specific investments have been carried out, the less durable become procedures for coordinating product and information flows. This effect can be explained by a higher need for the transaction partners to adapt to each other, which has also been claimed by transaction cost theory (Williamson 2002). From this point of view, the more specific investments become, the higher is dependency on the partner, wherefore the structure and processes of the own company are altered to cope with the new assets and requirements by the partner. Hence, compared to the general procedures in place, these procedures might appear to more recent.

This is also consistent with the importance of Spec2 for “asset specificity”: if processes are adapted to meet the requirements by the partner, they are presumably in place for less time than general processes and standards. At the same time, due to the dependency on the partner, the future retention of these procedures might be less certain, if the stability of partnership cannot be predicted accurately. Thus, temporal generalization of exchange procedures is reduced if partner-specific adaptations of equipment and operations take place. Therewith, Proposition 14.1 can be specified into a hypothesis with a concrete assumption on the effect direction. However, as this relation has been observed in a specific case, namely when processes where not realized as planned, this hypothesis is not necessarily valid for all cases. Therefore, the proposition is not only specified regarding the effect, but also regarding its situational validity:[143]

hypothesis 2 In case of disruptions, if asset specificity increases, then durability of exchange procedures decreases

Apart from this negative path coefficient, “asset specificity” also shows two significant positive path coefficients. The first one relates “asset specificity” to “range of addressees” (+ .3125*) and can be understood as an increase in socio-spatial validity of procedures for interaction with rising partner-specific assets. “Range of addressees” was thereby operationalized as follows:

Table 37: Relevance of indicators for the construct “range of addressees”

ID	Indicator	Loading
RoA2	*Procedures for information exchange are available to guide everyone involved*	.834
RoA3	*Procedures exist for everyone involved in the exchange processes*	.989

[143] Therewith, universality of validity is reduced, which decreases information content of statements (see section 1.2). At the same time, determinateness of the statement is increased, which increases information content and falsifyability of hypotheses Popper (1973).

Even though only two indicators remained after the quality evaluations or "range of addressees", both indicators load highly on the construct. Considering the effects of specific assets on optimal governance structures, Williamson (1981) argues that products requiring specific assets can most likely not be passed through standard channels, as people supposed to handle the product require special knowledge and abilities. This has also been affirmed in this research, especially by the high loadings of Spec2 and Spec3. Additionally, respondent no. 110 for instance stresses the importance of "*dedicated teams from A to Z*" and respondent no. 48 suggests "*follow up your employees with education and relevant information*". Hence, when products and partners become more specific, employees of all parties involved in the logistics processes must be in possession of tailored instructions, increasing therewith the "range of addressees". Especially in case cold chain logistics, supply chain partners tend to specialize in the provision of these services (Aertsen 1993). To assure temperature maintenance end-to-end, the involved parties consequently all have to adhere to specific requirements, wherefore the emergence of specialized networks can be assumed. In consequence, this leads to a specification based on the general undirected assumptions of Proposition 15.1:

hypothesis 3 In case of disruptions, if asset specificity increases, then the range of addressees of exchange procedures also increases

Furthermore, apart from these effects on dimensions of the interface structure, "asset specificity" has a direct connection to one dimension of disruptions, namely "logistics performance, which has been operationalized as:

Table 38: Relevance of indicators for the construct "logistics performance"

ID	Indicator	Loading
LP1	*Punctuality*	.822
LP2	*Accuracy of documents*	.932
LP3	*Completeness of documents*	.922
LP4	*Adherence to preferred transport route*	.840

The construct "asset specificity" showed a significant positive relation to "logistics performance" (+ .2894*). That infrastructure, equipment and processes which have been tailor-made to fit the requirements by the transaction partner lead to better maintenance of logistical requirements seems to be logical. Thereby, the risks associated with an increased dependency on a specific transaction partner are juxtaposed to the benefits of better service quality and may reduce potential hazards (Williamson 2008). At the same time, it is intriguing that "product quality" does not benefit from higher specificity of assets in these cases. This finding leads to the deduction of the following hypothesis based on Proposition 6:

hypothesis 4 In case of disruptions, if asset specificity increases, then logistics performance also increases

Apart from characterizing transactions by the type of assets employed, the frequency of interaction was also hypothesized to have an impact on the interface design. This hypothesis is supported by four significant paths between "frequency" and elements of the interface structure, as well as of the supply chain performance. Since frequency is a manifest variable, it has been operationalized as:

Table 39: Operationalization of "frequency" of transactions

ID	Indicator	Scale
Freq	*In comparison to other transaction partners, how frequent are transactions with this partner?*	*1 (very frequent) – 5 (very infrequent)*

The first significant path links "frequency" to "level of detail" (+ .4313**) and can be understood as an increase in the extensity of procedures with increasing frequency of transactions. "Level of detail" was thereby operationalized as follows:

Table 40: Relevance of indicators for the construct "level of detail"

ID	Indicator	Loading
Det1	*We have a wide range of procedures to consider for all aspects of the information exchange*	.921
Det3	*There are procedures on the entire range of tasks concerned with the exchange of products and documents*	.803

Hence, it is assumed that more frequent transactions with the same transaction partner lead to a wider range of procedures, which have been defined between the parties. This can be again explained with the help of transaction cost theory, which postulates that more measures are taken to assure both parties' compliance with the agreed-upon contract, if parties move away from spot-market transactions to repeated collaboration and long-term contractual agreements (Williamson 1971). To assure that the partner knows exactly how exchange processes have to be conducted and that no misinterpretation occurs, more detailed procedures would then be established. With detailed agreements on how to interact with each other, both parties might try to prevent opportunistic behaviour, as ties become closer and dependency increases. Hence, the general assumption that frequency of transactions does not have an effect on the interface structure can be rejected and reformulated as:

hypothesis 5 In case of disruptions, if frequency of transactions increases, then the level of detail of exchange procedures also increases

Regarding potential direct effects on product and logistics performance, both of the paths are positive and significant at the .05 level. The effect on "logistics performance" (+ .296*) is thereby smaller and slightly less significant than the effect on "product performance" (+ .321*). "Product performance" has thereby been operationalized as:

Table 41: Relevance of the indicators for the construct "product performance"

ID	Indicator	Loading
PP1	*Temperature maintenance*	.718
PP2	*Product quality*	.925
PP3	*Integrity of packaging*	.595

As already mentioned in section 4.5, indicator PP4, "accuracy of product quantity" was eliminated due to its relatively poor loading of .313 on the construct. A possible reason might be that it is less affected by process performance, as the quantity is fixed before the process starts and less variable as e.g. temperature. Furthermore, spoilage is not necessarily detected or controlled for at every stage in the supply chain, as such manual handling is in case of food products normally only done after harvest and later on at a DC (Hülsmann & Brenner 2011). In the case of pharmaceuticals, inaccurate product quantity might even play a more insignificant role as products are not simply thrown away if unfit for use (WHO 1999). Other reasons for wrong quantity at the end of the logistics process, such as theft, might be less common than the issues reported above. The highest loading has "product performance", whereas "integrity of packaging" is comparatively low.

Both positive effects can be explained by the development of routines for exchange procedures, if transactions with the same partner occur more frequently and results are consistent with other empirical research in supply chains (e.g. Spekman & Kamauff 1998; Fearne 1998; Artz 1999). From a decision theory perspective, the individuals receive the same stimulus repeatedly, wherefore less problem solving is required, facilitating correct decision making.[144] This might also imply that they know how to react to process deviations in such a way that comparatively less damage is incurred. Additionally, for the case of identification by individuals with a group, March & Simon (1958) state that the more frequent interactions are between an individual and other group members, the greater is the identification with the group and the group's goals. Hence, for the case of interactions at interfaces, individuals may change their priorisation of tasks and put more efforts on compliance with the instructions received for transactions occurring more frequently. Thereby, the importance of frequent transactions with the same partner is highlighted and Proposition 5 decomposed into two hypotheses:

hypothesis 6 **In case of disruptions, if frequency of transactions increases, then logistics performance also increases**

hypothesis 7 **In case of disruptions, if frequency of transaction increases, then product performance also increases**

The last variable of the transaction type regarded here is uncertainty. "Volume uncertainty" has been operationalized based on Walker & Weber (1987) as:

---

144 See section 3.4.3.

Table 42: Relevance of indicators for the construct "volume uncertainty"

ID	Indicator	Loading
Un1	*With this partner, to what extent are significant fluctuations in the monthly shipping volume requirements expected?*	.933
Un2	*With this partner, to what extent are shipping volumes considered to be uncertain?*	.890

In this case, none of the path coefficients were significant at the .05 level, wherefore Proposition 4 seems to hold true for the case of disruptions. This finding contradicts transaction cost theory and decision theory, which postulate both a negative effect of uncertainty. An explanation might be that natural fluctuations are considerable for the entire sector, due to e.g. seasonal demand and difficulties to forecast production volumes (Vega 2008). In this case, volume uncertainties might be prevalent in all transactions alike and not only with respect to one specific partner. Furthermore, volume uncertainty might be less pronounced in the segment of LSPs, as part of their business model is to combine shipments of different partners to optimally use their capacities (Aertsen 1993). Hence, the LSP might not experience volume uncertainties to such an extent as for instance the producer.

Starting also alphabetically, "durability" has a significant negative effect on "product performance" (- .2773*). At first sight, this effect seems unexpected, considering that from a decision theoretic point of view, one could assume that errors are reduced if activities are more routinized (March & Simon 1958). However, as has been highlighted in section 3.2.3, routinized behaviour might also lead to lower aspiration levels. These may in turn lead to the application of learned solutions to new stimuli, which might require different solutions, and therewith to errors of commission.[145] Since products might differ substantially regarding shipping requirements, once defined procedures might not always be appropriate once and for all. In the case where for example the product is already out of the adequate temperature range, it might require additional cooling or should not be accepted at all. In this case, predefined procedures might be inadequate if they do not consider exceptions from the norm. This is also supported by respondent no. 110 who claims that "*SOPs, Procedures, etc.... will not help if people don't know how to handle*". Hence, the defined procedures might require additional interpretation, to identify the *intended* outcome, and adapt the procedures accordingly. Proposition 2.1 is therefore specified as:

hypothesis 8 In case of disruptions, if durability of exchange procedures increases, then product performance decreases

The changing nature of product requirements would also explain why "durability" has a positive relation to "logistics performance", even though it is only significant at the .1 level (+ .2784). Hence, whereas procedures would have to be adapted to changing requirements by products, long-term validity of procedures would benefit logistics quality due to routinized

145 See section 3.4.2.

activities. However, for the case of disruptions, the impact of "durability" on "logistics performance" cannot be affirmed at the significance levels regarded.

Apart from "durability", the constructs "preciseness" and "range of addressees" also show significant paths to "product performance". Thereby the effect of "preciseness" on "product performance" is highly significant and negative (- .4867**). The construct has been operationalized as:

Table 43: Relevance of indicators for the construct "preciseness"

ID	Indicator	Loading
Prec2	*In important matters, procedures are very clear for checking products and documents*	.779
Prec3	*There are exact procedures on how to exchange information*	.972

One possible explanation would be a mental overload posed on employees for how to conduct exchange processes. In this line of thought, respondent no. 48 suggests: "*Keep it simple and be practical. Do not implement procedures that cannot be followed in practice. Follow up your employees with education and relevant information*".[146] This is supported on the one hand by Remer (1989) who stresses the limits of instructions for reasons of practicability, and on the other hand by decision theory, which assumes limited cognitive capacities of individuals. Another explanation would be that intensively predefined procedures cannot be realized in practice, as the complexity of the situation is not taken into account. Interestingly, the indicator referring to the information flow loads higher on the construct as the indicator for the product flow, which might be a hint at that procedures are less precise for the exchange of products and documents. In this context, Remer (1989) stresses that precise and detailed programming only makes sense, if the contextual parameters can be adequately foreseen. Given the complex operations at interfaces, where several exchanges might take place at the same time, it might be less sensible to define as precise procedures as for the information flow, which is more on a metaphysical level and which might be more identical for different shipments as the physical handling requirements. In the case of deviations, precise instructions could thereby mislead employees to execute their tasks as prescribed by procedures, instead of trying to counteract the deviation by handling the product differently. In consequence, Proposition 1.2 can be specified to:

hypothesis 9 In case of disruptions, if preciseness of exchange procedures increases, then product performance decreases

The other significant path concerns the "range of addressees", which in turn is positive (+ .4211*). Interpreting the path, the quality of the product becomes better if agreed procedures exist for everyone involved in the logistics processes. This is supported by several respondents in the survey. For instance, respondent no. 139 requests "*involvement of all parties*

146 An overview on the comments is provided in Appendix 15.

in the supply chain... [who A/N.] should agree on defined processes before they go live" and respondent no. 81 states that "*everyone must follow the agreed procedures*". From a decision theoretic point of view, the complexity of decision making for the individual is reduced, as the aspiration level and the way to achieve this level are clearly defined, which is why March & Simon (1958) favour objectives that can be easily operationalized for the context of the individual. Furthermore, referring back to the explanation of why specific assets seem to favour a large range of addressees, the involved parties might belong to a supply chain network specialized on certain product groups, wherefore each individual knows better how to protect the products in case of deviations. Therewith, it becomes easier for the individual to make optimal decisions as it possesses the knowledge required. Therefore, Proposition 3.1 is reformulated as:

hypothesis 10 In case of disruptions, if the range of addressees of exchange procedures increases, then product performance also increases

Subsuming the results of the first order model, some significant relations have been identified between transaction type and interface structure, between transaction type and disruptions, and between interface structure and disruptions. However, whereas "asset specificity" and "frequency" both showed several significant effects, "volume uncertainty" revealed no significant effects at all. With regards to its operationalization, its measurement does not reveal any violations of the defined quality criteria, and since an established scale has been used, it can be assumed that no measurement-specific errors result in lacking significance of paths. Furthermore, its items were identified by industry experts as being more important as other indicators of uncertainty, wherefore also its relevance seems to be established. Notwithstanding these attempts to enhance the validity of measurement, it might be possible that either the indicators were not appropriately formulated, or that volume uncertainty is much less relevant as other kinds of uncertainty in the context of cold chain logistics. Nevertheless, the importance stipulated by transaction cost theory of volume uncertainty cannot be confirmed in this research, as it does not affect the interface structure or performance to a significant degree. Based on the findings presented above, Figure 48 shows the resulting first order causal model for the case where disruptions occurred.

Figure 48: Validated first order causal model on effects of interface design on disruptions

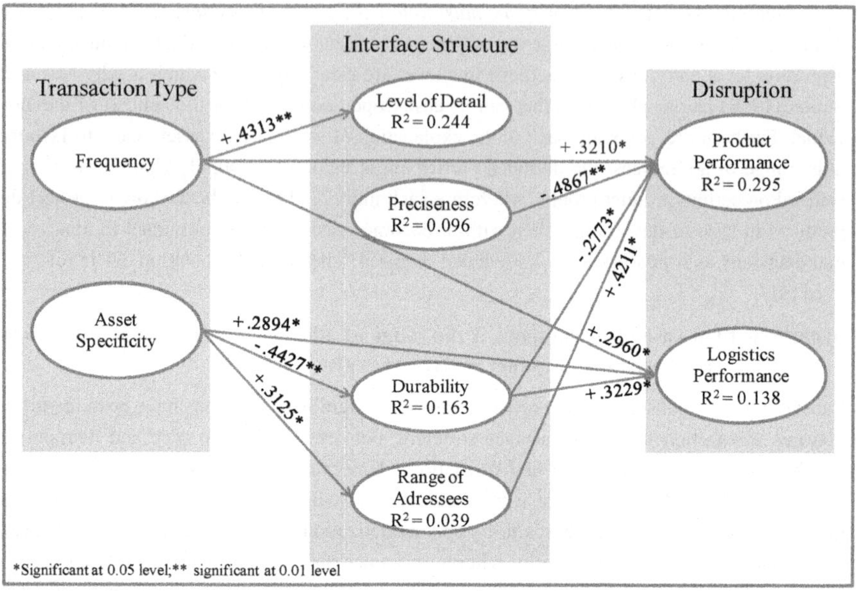

Another interesting point is that the direction of effects is not always the same between the constructs of interface structure and the two constructs of disruptions. Hence, apparently "logistics performance" and "product performance" are not always changing in the same direction, whereby important causal relations might be hidden if all indicators of both constructs were taken as equal representations of disruptions in operational performance. This highlights the importance of defining disruptions as two different constructs. This has also been shown by the disruption profiles in section 4.5 and might result in different effects in the successful transaction scenario. However, also between the first order model and the second order model for the case of disruptions differences have been observed, wherefore the findings of the second order model will be presented first. To avoid redundancies, only those findings will be presented, which refer to changed relations, or new relations, in comparison to the first order model.

Second order model

As already indicated by the strong relation between "asset specificity" and "durability" in the first order model, the relation to "standardization" in the second order model is negative and highly significant (- .4402**). This effect can be interpreted as: with more specific investments into a partnership, exchange procedures become less standardized to accommodate the more specific needs of the respective partner. Based on transaction cost theory, this could be explained by the need to design monitoring and control measures more carefully, as assets cannot be redeployed without incorporating sunk costs in case of preliminary termination of the partnership (Williamson 2008). Therewith, procedures which are sufficient for less specific partnerships do not meet the level of expectation and need for reassurance required here, and have to be replaced by tailor-made solutions. These findings are also supported by previous research results by Artz (1999), who found that investments in specific assets of both parties increase collaboration and commitment. Thereby, transaction partners move away from market transactions and create interdependencies in their working relationships (Heide & John 1990). At the same time, they assure their ability to adapt to contingencies in their bilateral contracts Artz (1999). Therewith, adaptability is enhanced, while standardization of procedures is reduced. Thus, Proposition 14 is specified for the case of disruptions as:

hypothesis 11 In case of disruptions, if asset specificity increases, then the standardization of exchange procedures decreases

At this point, the hitherto lacking relevancy of "asset specificity" to "product performance" can finally be observed: when regarding the total effects, "asset specificity" is positively correlated with "product performance" (+.2908*).[147] According to Hair et al. (2014), the direct effect and the total effect differ, if another variable mediates the relationship, which can only be the case, if both paths between the exogeneous variable, the mediator, and the endogeneous variable are significant. Here, as the path between "asset specificity" and "standardization" is considerably significant and negative, while the path between "standardization" and "product performance" is less significant, but still negative, specific assets seem to increase product-related performance by reducing standardized interactions. This is consistent with the findings of Heide & John (1990) and Artz (1999) on the advantages of adaptability of collaborative partnerships, where both parties engage in specific investments. At the same time, this interpretation of asset specificity seems to be more positive compared to transaction cost theory, where such investments are rather regarded as trigger for safeguards or vertical integration (Williamson 1971). Therewith, it falls rather in line with evolutionary and co-evolutionary theories, which have already been applied for instance to the fresh produce industry, where considerable positive outcomes of co-evolution were observed (Wilson & Hynes 2009). Therewith, Proposition 6 can be respecified as:

hypothesis 12 In case of disruptions, if asset specificity increases, then product performance also increases through reduction of standardization

The same development emerges for "frequency" of transactions: the positive and significant path for "level of detail" results in a highly significant positive relation between "frequency" and "degree" (+ .3369**). This indicates that more elaborate procedures are agreed upon by partners in frequent exchange relationships, which can again be explained by transaction cost theory and the tendency to draft more carefully the exchange relationships in recurrent trans-

147 For the total effects see Appendix 13.

actions (Wathne & Heide 2004). Respondent no. 112 states in this context: "*The first step is to sign a good Quality Assurance Agreement (QAA A/N.). The QAA must describe all the technical processes and also the organisational framework including the information pathways between both companies. The QAA should be extensive and accurate, providing no room for misunderstanding*". Hence, breadth as well as depth of the agreement is considered to be important to avoid misunderstandings between both partners. The rising transaction costs caused by more carefully designed agreements can then be amortized through a larger amount of transactions. At the same time, the causal relation might also be the other way round: because of the need to describe exchange procedures extensively, transaction partners prefer to execute transactions more frequently with the same partner, to avoid additional costs and efforts. Nevertheless, given that transaction partners firstly have to decide to work together before drafting any agreements, it seems more probable that the decision to engage in frequent collaboration comes first. In consequence, Proposition 10 is respecified as:

hypothesis 13 In case of disruptions, if frequency of transactions increases, then the degree of programming exchange procedures also increases

However, whereas in the first order model, the path between "frequency" and "logistics performance" as well as "product performance" were positive and significant, they are not significant any longer. Apparently, the "degree" of programming fully mediates the relations between "frequency" and "product performance", as well as "logistics performance".[148] Thereby, positive effects prevalent on the first order construct level diminish, due to apparently stronger negative effects of the second order construct. Hence, the positive effects by "frequency" on performance are superposed by the simultaneous positive effects on "preciseness" and "level of detail", which in turn have negative effects on performance in case of disruptions. The positive effect of "frequency" on "degree" confirms the assumptions made in section 3.5.1, namely that setup costs of transactions can be distributed over more transactions, which justifies more elaborate programs. However, as March & Simon (1958, p. 187) notice, the motivation experienced during program development decreases considerably when it comes to program execution, and the individual turns into an "*orderly bureaucrat*". Additionally, they stress that decisions made during program development are frequently not reconsidered during program execution, which may in case of deviations also lead to inferior performance, as decisions are not adapted to the actual situation. In this context, further research should consider not only the extent of programs, but also the actual compliance with these in daily operations. However, for the current research, the following hypothesis can be deduced:

hypothesis 14 In case of disruptions, more frequent transactions do not increase process performance, if the degree of programming the exchange procedures also increases

---

148 According to Baron & Kenny (1986, p. 1173), a variable has a mediator function, if it "*represents the generative mechanism through which the focal independent variable is able to influence the dependent variable of interest*".

The construct "standardization" in turn has a significant relation to both, "logistics performance" and "product performance". However, whereas the effect on "logistics performance" is positive (+ .2751*), the effect on "product performance" is nearly the same in magnitude, but negative (- .2769*). This supports the impression already gained from the first order model that the two constructs of process performance fall apart in the case of disruptions. The positive effect on "logistics performance" can be explained by the development of routines, which reduce the complexity of decision making for the individual. However, whereas the dimension "durability" was already significant in the first order model, "invariability" showed no significant paths. Based on the quality evaluation, it has been operationalized as:

Table 44: Relevance of the indicators of the construct "invariability"

ID	Indicator	Loading
Invari1	*We agreed that under all circumstances, the procedures for exchanging products and documents are the same*	.547
Invari3	*Our exchange procedures do not vary a lot*	.995

As can be seen, the two indicators differ substantially in their loadings, and since only two indicators remained, an explanation for the lack of significant paths might be high measurement errors. Nevertheless, whereas in the first order model none of the two dimensions loaded highly on "logistics performance", in the second order model this path indeed is significant, indicating that both dimensions reinforce each other and lead to a positive influence.

Even though the products might change, the logistical activities seem to remain similar enough to allow for a high standardization of exchange procedures, wherefore few errors and therewith little deviations in "logistics performance" occur. This is also confirmed by respondent no. 44 who states "*I will strongly recommend that procedures and standards must be in place for each process. Flexibility can be exercised but continuous deviations must have some penalties or disadvantage*".[149] Standardization of processes thus increases the efficient execution of tasks, as more activities can be executed rather automatically instead of requiring problem-solving capacities. The goal to optimize resource utilization and increase efficiency by reducing variations can be found for example in the use of Six Sigma or lean management principles, which also try to optimize the distribution of products (Arnheiter & Maleyeff 2005). This leads to the re-specification of Proposition 2:

hypothesis 15 In the case of disruptions, if standardization of exchange procedures increases, then logistics performance also increases

However, the increasing standardization of processes to optimize the outcome also has some drawbacks. For instance, the use of lean management principles might reduce the adaptibility of processes to such an extent that unforeseen events cannot be handled appropriately. In this context, Engle (2011) reports on the drawbacks of lean supply chains in the face of natural

[149] See section 3.4.2.

disasters, where companies are not able to cope with breakdowns at supplier facilities, as safety buffers have been eliminated. This would explain why in the case of "product performance", "standardization" has a negative effect. If processes have been standardized to such an extent that no alternative handling of products requiring special care is considered, the efficiency of processes is enhanced at the expense of product quality. At the same time, the problem does not necessarily reside within the system, but may also be caused by individual decision making. If the individual does not possess the required level of knowledge on how to handle the product, it might simply assume that no special actions have to be taken (i.e. pattern recognition). As a result, hypothesis 16 can be deduced as:

hypothesis 16 In case of disruptions, if standardization of exchange procedures increases, then product performance decreases

A considerable change in comparison to the first order model is the effect of the construct "formalization" opposed to the effects of "rigidity" and "range of addressees". While the first order constructs did not show any significant influences, "formalization" significantly affects "logistics performance" and "product performance". The effect on "logistics performance" is thereby negative (- .2417*), whereas the effect on "product performance" is highly significant and positive (+ .218**). This indicates that whereas both first order constructs were associated too weakly with disruptions, they reinforce each other on the level of the second order construct. "Rigidity" has been operationalized here as:

Table 45: Relevance of the indicators for the construct "rigidity"

ID	Indicator	Loading
Rig1	*The agreement contains penalties if procedures for the exchange of products and documents are not followed*	.610
Rig2	*Procedures for information exchange are considered to be the law*	.721
Rig4	*Violations of procedures for exchanging products and documents are normally tolerated (R)*	.793

The negative effect on "logistics performance" may be explained by comparing the two first order constructs regarding path coefficients and t-statistics. Thereby, it becomes apparent that "rigidity" is more influential than the socio-spatial dimension "range of addressees". Considering that "logistics performance" involves a temporal dimension (i.e. punctuality), which was rated worse than all other indicators for the construct in the case of disruptions, then an explanation would be that with more rigid exchange procedures, the exchange takes more time, resulting in less punctual shipments.

In contrast, "product performance" was affected positively, with "range of addressees" having the largest impact, which can be explained with a more careful treatment of the products by everyone involved. As has been shown in section 4.4.3, the extent of third party involvement had a significant negative impact on "product performance". This can be explained by transaction cost theory, as the adherence to agreed upon contracts cannot be observed directly, wherefore the risk of opportunism is increased (Williamson 2008). This is also supported by decision theory, as individuals tend to be satisficing, implying that not more efforts are taken as necessary (Simon 1979). However, if predefined exchange procedures become binding for all parties involved in the shipping process, everyone is forced to comply with the requirements to avoid the incurrence of repercussions. This leads to the re-specification of Proposition 3:

hypothesis 17 In case of disruptions, if formalization of exchange procedures increases, then logistics performance decreases

hypothesis 18 In case of disruptions, if formalization of exchange procedures increases, then product performance also increases

Comparing the two models, the causal relations have been affirmed in the case of "standardization". Further evidence on the importance of constructs was found for the case of "formalization", whereas the relevance of the dimensions of "degree" decreased upon combination. Furthermore, "logistics performance" and "product performance" seem to develop in opposed directions when disruptions occur or at least are not affected by the interface structure in the same way. Figure 49 shows the resulting causal model for the second order constructs:

Figure 49: Validated second order model on effects of interface design on disruptions

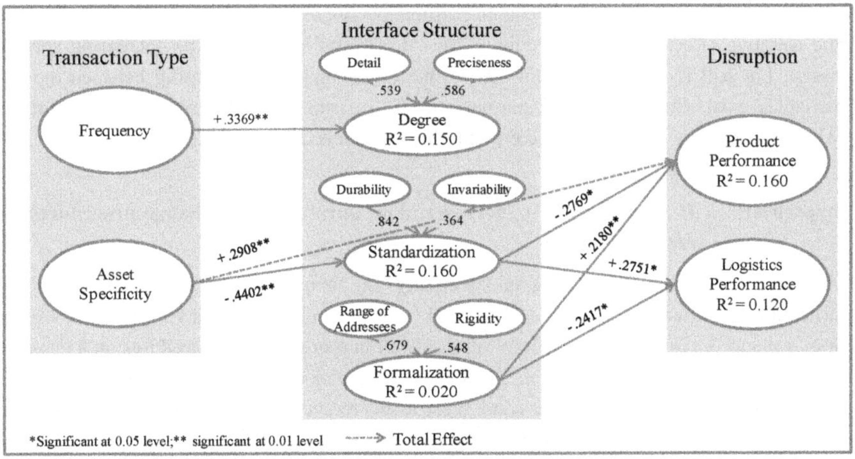

In conclusion of the findings above, it seems as if the hypothesized organizational causes of disruptions indeed have substantial influence. Even though not all constructs were found to be relevant, the majority revealed some interesting causal relations. However, the question arises, whether these relations are only significant in the case of disruptions, or can be generalized to impacts of organizational design on cold chain performance. Therefore, section 4.5.3 will juxtapose the findings of causal relations in the case of disruptions with those of the case where the logistics processes performed as planned.

4.5.3 Effects of Interface Design on the Susceptibility to Disruptions

Whereas the objective of the previous section was to identify organizational causes of disruptions, the objective of this section is to identify general causal relations between the design of interfaces and operational process performance in cold chains. Thereby, it shall be assessed whether the factors that were identified to result in extremely bad performance have an absolute bad influence or whether their influence depends on their degree and/or the context. Furthermore, those factors resulting in better performance in the case of disruptions shall be analyzed to see whether this positive influence holds true also for regular cold chain performance, to identify which factors indeed increase the susceptibility to disruptions, and which reduce susceptibility to disruptions. Therefore, the significant path coefficients for the best case will be analyzed and compared to the worst case.

First order model

Comparing in turn the effects of "asset specificity" on interface structure in the worst case and the best case, the general patterns are quite similar, even though to different extents. For "durability" for instance, the influence of "asset specificity" is reduced and less significant (-.2586*). As the extent of investments in partner-specific assets is higher,[150] this indicates that the negative effect of "asset specificity" on "durability" decreases with increasing specific assets, but still remains significant, hence that an asymptotic relationship between the two variables exist. Considering that partner specific investments can theoretically be infinite, whereas durability has a natural zero point, this form of relation seems to be logic. Hence, hypothesis 2 can be generalized to:

hypothesis 2.1 If asset specificity increases, then durability of exchange procedures decreases

At the same time, the effect of "asset specificity" on "invariability" grows from being insignificant to significant at the .05 level (- .3131*). This would imply that with processes working as planned, rising asset specificity would result in more flexible procedures, in a temporal *and* situative sense. On the one hand, this could be explained by higher service levels offered for strategic partners. On the other hand, these assets might be in place for products with more demands, where procedures cannot be standardized as for other products. From a transaction cost theory point of view, the dependency on one or few suppliers of a specific product increases the extensity of contractual agreements and the investments to assure that all parties comply with the contract (Williamson 1971). This is confirmed by respondent no. 44 who states "*one is tempted to have different procedures for different partners under the guise of*

150 See comparison of means can be found in the explanation volume..

tailor-made, but in reality it is designed to suit once dependence on that partner". Hence, as has already been highlighted in section 4.5.2, where dependency in a partnership is high, the parties adapt their agreements to cope with contingencies and to become more competitive as strategic partners. Thus, Proposition 14.2 can be specified into a directed hypothesis for the case where operational processes can be realized as planned:

hypothesis 19 In case of regular operational processes, if asset specificity increases, then invariability of exchange procedures decreases

Furthermore, as this causal relation has not been confirmed for the case where disruptions occurred, one could assume that one cause of disruptions lies herein: if specific assets are employed but the procedures are invariable, the probability of disruptions would become higher. The need for adaptation has been stressed by Aertsen (1993) for the outsourcing of logistics services, who states that the logistics service provider has to adapt to the formal and informal procedures of its client to comply with its demands. From a decision theoretic point of view, a lack of adaptation of work processes by the service provider would lead to errors of commission, if unadjusted procedures would be applied to new processes. Therewith, the risk of mismatch between transaction type and interface structure would increase, resulting in more errors and deviations from process plans. Hence, based on the comparison of both cases, the following hypothesis is deduced:

hypothesis 20 If asset specificity increases and invariability of exchange procedures does not decrease, then susceptibility to disruptions increases

Also the even more pronounced and highly significant path coefficient to "level of detail" (+ .4017**) could be explained along this line of thought, as it has been significant via the total effects and negative in the case of disruptions. Considering that these partners are adapting processes, equipment, or infrastructure to each other, a rise in the level of detail of procedures seems to be logical, since employees have to be instructed on how to adapt their work processes. Decision theory explains the need for instructions to two different kinds of stimuli. In the first case, a stimulus evokes an activity which has been learned and routinized through repetitive stimuli without much effort. In the second case, a stimulus involves to some extent problem-solving activities, to find an appropriate activity as an answer.[151] Hence, detailed procedures in the case of newly implemented assets help employees to reduce their problem-solving efforts and assure that activities are carried out as required. This finding falls in line with the analysis of agricultural supply chain agreements by Loader (1997), who reports on advantages of close agreements between suppliers and UK retailers when specific assets are employed. Consequently, Proposition 13.1 is specified for this case as:

hypothesis 21 In case of regular operational processes, if asset specificity increases, then the level of detail of exchange procedures also increases

[151] See March & Simon (1958).

The effect of "frequency" on "level of detail" is less significant though still positive (+ .2306*), while the hitherto not significant effect on "preciseness" is now significant, too (+ .2244*). Thereby, the strength of path nearly is the same as in the case of disruptions, but the significance increases from the .1 level to the 0.5 level, implying that the extent of preciseness varied less than in the other case. Both effects are similar in size and magnitude, which indicates that in the successful case, more frequent transactions had more detailed *and* more precise exchange procedures. Considering that in the other case, frequent transactions were only associated with detailed procedures, the possitive association also with precise procedures might result in more balanced instructions, which provide the individual with all information required on the range of tasks, as well as on the exact content of tasks. Therewith, firstly, hypothesis 5 can be generalized to:

hypothesis 5.1 If frequency of transaction increases, then the level of detail of exchange procedures also increases

However, "preciseness" was not that much affected by more frequent transactions in the case of disruptions. Comparing the mean values of "frequency" for both cases, transactions reported for the inferior case occurred slightly less frequent. This might be an indicator for an asymptotic relationship between both variables, where at the high end of transaction frequency, the accuracy of instructions is increasing considerably. This seems comprehensible, since the number of partners at a certain level of partnership is presumably decreasing the more one moves away from market transactions to vertical integration. Hence, instead of focussing on precise agreements with the bulk of partners, only those partners receive special treatment, which are considered as strategic partners, what Williamson (2002, p. 183) terms "*credible contracting*". Hence, Proposition 10.2 is replaced for the case of regular performance by:

hypothesis 22 If frequency of transactions increases, then preciseness of exchange procedures also increases

Furthermore, the path to "logistics performance" is in the best case similar to the path in the worst case, namely positive and significant (+ .2459*). This indicates that the higher the frequency of transaction, the better is the process performance regarding logistics quality, no matter if disruptions occurred or transactions are realized as planned. Hence, hypothesis 6 can be generalized to:

hypothesis 6.1 If frequency of transactions increases, then logistics performance also increases

The hitherto significant path to "product performance" in turn is not significant anymore, which seems to indicate that more frequent transactions help to avoid the worst damage to food and pharmaceuticals, but does not lead to extraordinary performance.

Another similarity to the worst case is that volume uncertainty does not reveal any significant path coefficients to the constructs of interface structure or process performance. This finding opposes the assumptions made by transaction cost theory, where especially significant paths to the constructs "rigidity" and "range of addressees" would be expected (Hobbs 1996). However, this might also explain why both constructs are nearly not explained at all by the causal model.

Regarding the components of interface structure, "durability" shows two significant paths to the variables of process performance. The path to "logistics performance" again is positive, and this time highly significant (+ .4980**). At the same time, the path to "product performance" is also highly significant, but now, it is positive (+ .3059**). Hence, the effect of "durability" differs substantially between the worst case and the best case, even though its mean value is approximately the same. The effect on "logistics performance" can again be explained as in the previous section with routinized activities and relatively predictable and stable requirements.[152] Hence, a general causal relation between "durability" of exchange procedures and "logistics performance" seems to exist, indicating that the more enduring the exchange procedures, the better is logistics quality. At the same time, the strength of relation is reduced substantially with higher deviations from process plans, wherefore "durability" rather seems to facilitate optimal performance, rather than preventing inferior performance. Therefore, the following hypothesis is stipulated:

hypothesis 23 In case of regular operational processes, if durability of exchange procedures increases, then logistics performance also increases

The reversed effect on "product performance" seems to imply that in transactions where processes are executed as planned, long-term exchange procedures foster the ability of employees to take the right decisions and to perform the required activities, enhancing the maintenance of product quality even more. At the same time, such durable procedures are detrimental in case of deviations. This could be explained by decision theory, if individuals base decision making on pattern recognition instead of seeking alternative solutions resulting in errors of commission, or low aspiration levels, which lead to errors of omission.[153]

This trade-off between assuring excellent product quality if plans can be realized and preventing even worse product quality in case of disruptions, can also be observed for "preciseness" of exchange procedures, where the effect also changes from being negative to positive, if processes are realized as planned (+ .3857*). March & Simon (1958) argue that a crucial aspect of the effectiveness of rewards systems is dependent on how precise performance standards are formulated. In a similar fashion it can be argued that the more precise the program is, the easier it becomes for the individual to identify the aspiration level and to control its performance against this level.

This is also supported by respondent no. 48 by referring to "*relevant information*" and by respondent no. 115, stating that "*very clear procedures are extremely important*". Respondent

152 See section 4.5.2.
153 See section 3.4.2.

no. 43 even refers explicitly to the performance criteria by stating that most important is "*clear and transparent communication of requirements for transportation (time, temperature, routing, volumes)*". For the case where processes are realized as planned, the following hypothesis can be deduced:

hypothesis 24 In case of regular operational processes, if preciseness of exchange procedures increases, then product performance also increases

One explanation for these two controversial effects is that the predefined procedures do not match product requirements in certain situations and that if being followed nevertheless product quality is becoming even worse. To recognize where exchange procedures might not be appropriate for maintenance of product quality in turn would require that employees firstly, can identify initial deviations, and secondly that they know how to avoid further damage to the product. In consequence, product quality would have to be constantly monitored and the data exchanged between partners. The fact that such equipment is not in place is highlighted by respondent no. 66 who explains "*the key in the supply chain for temperature sensitive products is to identify the weak spots, normally the escalation points where the product is handed over from one to the other party. This process should be harmonized, as currently this is still not done. The fear factor of taking ownership of any liability in this process and the fact that transparency is still a curse in our industry,* [results in that A/N.] *we as an industry fail to improve the complete supply chain*". This is also supported by respondent no. 69 who demands for "*visibility through integrated IT systems*". Thereby, the increase in transparency would have two effects: on the one hand, as mentioned by respondent no. 66, parties would have to assume responsibility, if processes were not realized as planned. Especially if only one of the parties is dependent on the partner, higher transparency might be regarded as a risk, raising either the demands by the partner, or the claims incurred. On the other hand, individuals would have more guidance in their decision making, if they can rely on technological support. Hence, whereas on the organizational level, from a transaction cost point of view, higher transparency might be undesirable, from the individual level and decision theory, higher transparency might be favourable. Therewith, a kind of trade-off seems to exist between increasing performance by preventing errors, and avoiding penalties because of inferior performance.

In order to account for these insights based on the comparison of both models, further determinants thus seem to play a role in explaining why some supply chains for food and pharmaceuticals might be more susceptible to disruptions than others. Therefore, additional hypotheses are derived for further empirical research. Based on the argumentation above, the following hypothesis is derived:

hypothesis 25 If transparency of operational processes increases, then susceptibility to disruptions decreases

The other requirement for preventing further damage is that employees have the know how to deal with these special goods, demanding for more investments in the human resource base. In the case of food products, the reciprocally stimulating increase of ripening gas and temperature (Mercantila Publishers 1989) could for instance be interrupted, if the product is actively cooled down again before the transport continues, which might require a deviation from regular processes. The need to handle actively such deviations is also stressed by the respondents in the survey. For instance, respondent no. 112 states: "[The Quality Assurance Agreement, A/N] *must include procedures for handling* [...] *deviations and change control. However, the best QAA doesn't help, if it is not implemented*". This is also stressed by respondent no. 107 who states: "*Establishing the complete process, ensuring all involved are in agreement and trained, monitoring adherence, evaluating deviations and putting CAPAs* [Corrective and Preventive Action, A/N] *in place*". Hence, the existing procedures for exchanges processes for regular operations have to be completed by additional procedures for cases where deviations from process plans occur. The decision on which procedures are applicable have to be taken by the employees, resulting in more cognitive demands and therewith requiring more skilled employees. These considerations lead to the following hypothesis:

hypothesis 26 If specialization of employees increases, then susceptibility to disruptions decreases

Based on the findings for the second sample where processes were realized as planned, Figure 50 shows the resulting adapted and validated causal model.

Figure 50: Validated first order model on effects of interface design on performance

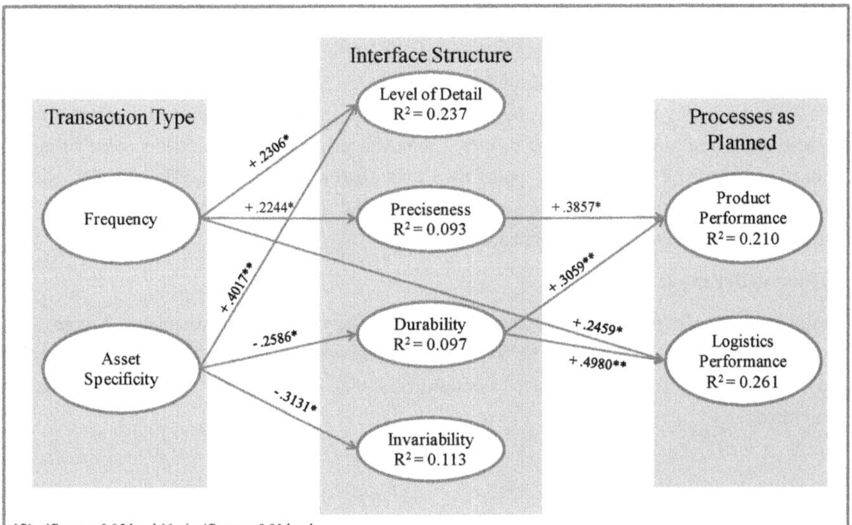

*Significant at 0.05 level;** significant at 0.01 level

Summarizing the findings on how "product performance" and "logistics performance" become extraordinarily good, "frequency" of transactions, "durability" of exchange procedures, and "preciseness" of exchange procedures increase process performance directly, while "asset specificity" reduces the quality indirectly through the reduction of "durability" of exchange procedures. In contrast, in the case of disruptions, "frequency" of transactions is the only determinant, which improves both, product and logistics quality, while "range of addressees" at least improves "product performance". However, this variable in turn does not seem to be relevant in the case where processes are realized as planned, even though many participants in the survey stressed the importance of having all parties involved to agree and comply with the same procedures.[154] One explanation could be that the absolute number of parties involved differed more in the sample of the worst case, so that in those cases where less parties were involved, the relative range of addressees was larger as in those cases with more parties. This explanation is partly supported by the fact that the extent of third party involvement was found to have a detrimental effect on "quality performance". Additionally, the mean value of third party involvement was higher in the worst case, as well as the standard deviation, indicating a greater variance in the sample between different observations.[155] This would imply that whereas the absolute range of addressees did not change between both samples, the relative range of addressees did and would stress the importance of further investigations into third party involvement.

Furthermore, when comparing the two causal models, there are differences in the variables for which causal relations have been observed. Whereas the transaction type in both cases is the same, with "frequency" and "asset specificity" as determinants of interface structure and supply chain performance, the variables of the interface structure partly change. This implies that those aspects of the interface structure determining performance during normal operations are not all the same as those determining performance in case of disruptions. Furthermore, the effects of variables partly change between both cases. Hence, the cause and effect patterns underlying disruptions seem to be different than those of regular operations, confirming the choice of analyzing two opposite poles as a first approach to the analysis of organizational causes of disruptions. Also for the second order model differences were observed, as will be illustrated in the following paragraphs.

Second order model

In the second order model, the effect of "asset specificity" on "standardization" becomes less significant (- .302*), which can be explained by the reduced effect on "durability" and its higher importance for the construct "standardization".[156] Nevertheless, hypothesis 11 can be generalized to:

---

154 See Appendix 14.
155 The mean values can be found in the explanation volume.
156 See the correlation matrix in section 4.4.3.

hypothesis 11.1 If asset specificity increases, then standardization of exchange procedures decreases

Furthermore, the construct has a significant effect on "degree" (+ 2977*), which can be explained by the highly significant path to "level of detail". Therewith, Proposition 13 is specified to:

hypothesis 27 In case of regular operational processes, if asset specificity increases, then the degree of programming exchange procedures also increases

The relationship between "frequency" and "degree" is also confirmed (+ .2622*) and therefore hypothesis 13 replaced by:

hypothesis 13.1 If frequency of transactions increases, then the degree of programming exchange procedures also increases

As indicated by the first order model, the path coefficient between "standardization" and "logistics performance" becomes more significant (+ .3860**), indicating that if processes can be realized as planned, standardization is favourable for the achievement of expected logistics performance. Therewith, hypothesis 15 can also be generalized to:

hypothesis 15.1 If standardization of exchange procedures increases, then logistics performance also increases

However, this general relation cannot be confirmed for "product performance", as indicated by and reasoned for the first order model. In contrast to the second order model of the worst case, "standardization" has a highly significant positive effect on "product performance" in the best case (+ .2488**). In case of a stable environment, March & Simon (1958) argue that standardized procedures support optimal individual decision making by providing stable decision rules. If the environment is not stable however, they stress that organizations require a repertory of programs, so that short-term adaptiveness is assured by deciding on which program to apply. Hence, standardized procedures only seem to be favourable if any deviations can be excluded, which explains the controversial effects on "product performance". Therefore, the following hypothesis can be deduced:

hypothesis 28 In case of regular operational processes, if standardization of exchange procedures increases, then product performance also increases

The last interesting observation when comparing both cases is that "formalization" becomes irrelevant when logistics processes are realized as planned. Thus, formalized exchange procedures seem to help to prevent the worst process outcomes in terms of product quality, but do not facilitate excellent performance. This might also explain why some respondents are rather against formalized exchange procedures. For instance, respondent no. 50 prefers "*open line communication with a goal to achieving improvement and not penalties*", while respondent no. 61 states that in the fruit and vegetable sector, "*business is mainly done by gentlemen's agreement*". These opinions also provide reason for the overall lack of significance of "rigidity" as determinant for process performance. Hence, compared to the second order model of the disruption scenario, some differences become obvious, which can be also seen by comparing Figure 48 with the following Figure 51:

Figure 51: Validated second order model on effects of interface design on performance

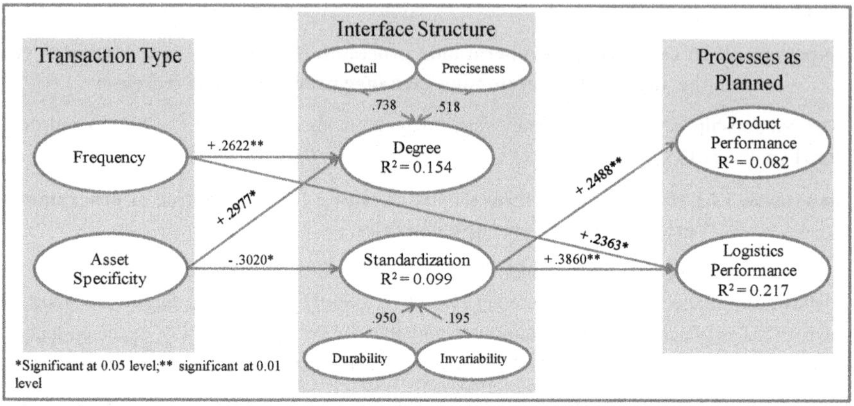

Comparing the two models, it becomes obvious that again, the variables of the transaction type relevant for this research do not change between cases. However, whereas in the case of disruptions, "frequency" did not reveal an effect on "logistics performance", in the best case, the path coefficient is significant at the 0.05 level.[157] Hence, the mediating effect of "degree" in the case of disruptions does not hold true for the best case scenario, presumably because the effect direction of "preciseness" also changes. Thereby, "level of detail" and "preciseness" show now opposite effects, reducing the importance of "degree". This seems to confirm the assumptions made in section 4.5.2 regarding the adequacy of programs: only if procedures are not perturbed by environmental conditions, extensive programming does not have a negative impact on performance.

The variables of the interface structure in turn are firstly not all the same in both samples, and secondly have partly different causal relations. This indicates that one has to differentiate between several objectives in the design of interfaces: *firstly*, the objective to foster excellent performance if processes can be realized as planned, *secondly*, the objective to mitigate deviations before they turn into disruptions, and *thirdly*, the objective to prevent disruptions. All three may require different approaches to interactional programming and are not in all cases complementary, but rather controversial, as for instance durable procedures. Furthermore, the findings indicate that decisions taken during the interface design stage do not necessarily match the subsequent situation during execution of transactions, as precise or durable programming do not necessarily yield optimal performance, but even may have detrimental ef-

157 See Appendix 9.

fects. Even though standardization fosters logistics performance in both cases analyzed, the question emerges whether the design of alternative programs would not increase the short-term adaptiveness as stipulated by March & Simon (1958) and result also in better product performance when deviations occur.

This observation also leads to the next finding of the comparison of both cases: if the aim of transaction partners is to achieve the best performance in terms of logistics, they should be aware of potential trade-offs with respect to product quality. The provision of alternative programs to actively counteract deviations may result in more complex decision making for individuals, but at the same time prevent disruptions from developing to the full extent.

Furthermore, the positive effects of frequent transactions on performance can only be realized, if transaction partners do not only consider the feasibility of extensive programs, but also their usefulness. Thereby, the practicability of extensive programs needs to be taken into account, as well as the cognitive abilities of individuals executing these programs, to avoid loss of adaptability of procedures to assure optimal performance.

Apart from these findings concerning the performance, the comparison of the constructs of the interface structure and their correlations reveal further insights. First of all, in both cases, if significant correlations existed, these were positive. This indicates that increasing manifestations of one construct is associated with increasing manifestations of several other constructs. Hence, whereas different dimensions of interactional programming are available for the design of interfaces, they cannot be regarded as completely separated from one another, even though they might belong to different second order constructs. However, these correlations were not identical between the two cases, indicating that few generally persisting patterns exist in the design of interfaces in cold chains.

The only construct, which showed relatively similar correlations for both cases, is "durability", which seems to be closely linked to all other constructs except "level of detail". The more pronounced each of the other constructs is, the more durable the programming seems to become. From a decision theoretic point of view, tailoring instructions for interactions poses more burdens on the cognitive capacities of the individuals. This burden could then be compensated by learning, if a sufficiently large time frame is provided. Also from a transaction cost theoretic point of view, investments in tailoring instructions would have to be compensated, which can be done if these investments can be amortized during a longer period of use. Nevertheless, the partially considerable differences in correlations between the interface structures of the two samples indicates that the range of combinatorial possibilities is indeed not limited to a few typical structures, even though the transitions seem to be flexible.

Based on these exploratory findings, further research requirements can be depicted, as will be done in section 5.4. Such future research can now build on the specific hypotheses derived and concentrate on relevant variables of the interface design as determinants of susceptibility to disruptions. However, since two scenarios were considered, in which different causal effects were identified, it is now possible to concretize three causal models for future research. In the figure below, the dotted lines show the assumed relations resulting from the comparison of both cases and reflect either an increase or decrease of susceptibility to disruptions in either the product performance or the logistics performance.

Figure 52: Proposal of causal models for further research on supply chain performance

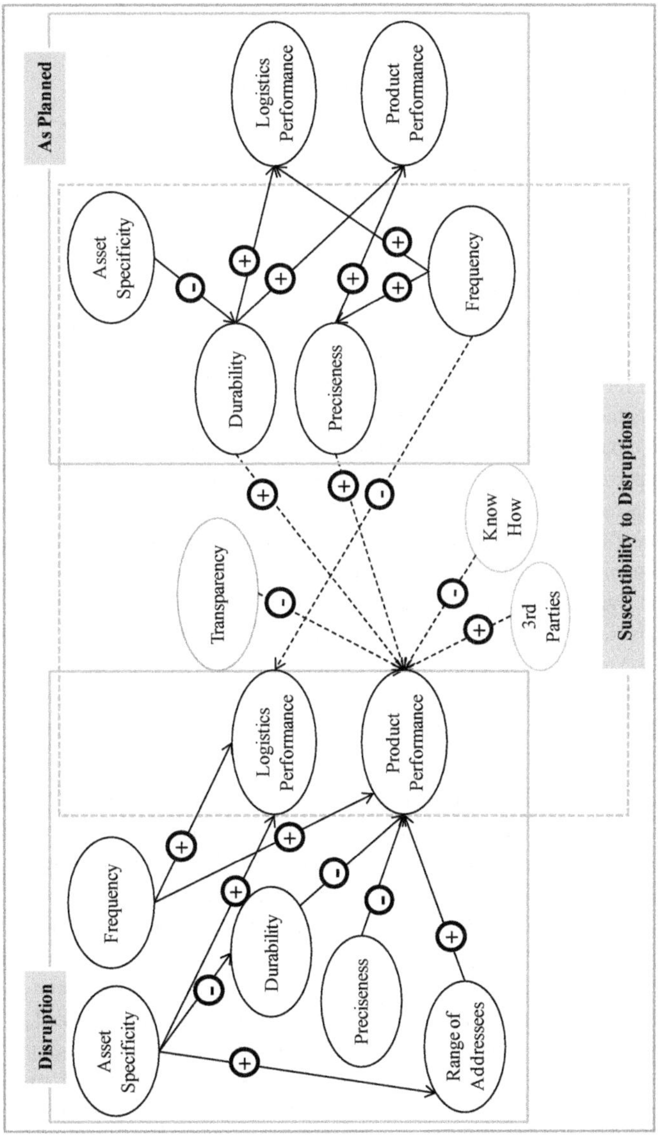

As has been shown, the organizational design indeed seems to have considerable influence on the performance of cold chains at interfaces. Several determinants have been identified that lead to considerable differences in performance during disruptions, in the case where processes are realized as planned, or that have an influence in general. Furthermore, potential determinants of susceptibility of cold chains to disruptions have been identified. The interpretation of the findings regarding theoretical and practical implications as the final step of empirical research as postulated by Diekmann (2002) will be subject to section 5.

4.6 Interim Conclusion

The purpose of section 4 was to plan, prepare, and execute the empirical analysis and to analyze its results. To this purpose, **section 4.1** depicted the proceeding in the section. **Section 4.2** was concerned with planning the empirical analysis in a step-wise concretization of the research design. Therefore, in **section 4.2.1** the target population was specified. Thereby, the scope of analysis was broadened to supply chains for temperature sensitive food products and pharmaceuticals. Based on this specification, the internationality of these supply chains, and the resource constraints limiting the choice of methods, an online survey among cold chain managers was selected for the data collection. With the choice of method, the operationalization of latent constructs had to meet the requirements of survey-based research, and to be interpretable by the participants. Therefore, in **section 4.2.2** transaction type and disruptions as deviations of process performance were operationalized. For the transaction type, specificity of transactions was operationalized as "asset specificity" based on evaluation of practical relevancy and theoretical quality of existing scales. Similarly, uncertainty of transaction was operationalized as "volume uncertainty". Disruptions have thereby been operationalized based on suggestions by cold chain experts and based on the developed understanding of disruptions, as disruptions in "logistics performance" and disruptions in "product performance". Subsequently, in **section 4.2.3** all scales of the interface structure were newly developed to fit the terminological framework based on Remer. Wherever possible, existing scales were taken as starting points for the construction of new scales. In the end, six new scales to measure the constructs of the interface structure were developed.

However, before new scales can be used in empirical analysis, first of all, they have to be pretested to assure their validity and reliability (Kromrey 2009). This was part of **section 4.3**, which comprised the description of all empirical analyses. The pre-tests were described in **section 4.3.1** and based on the results the scales were adapted for the main survey. Thereby, the methodology proposed by Anderson & Gerbing 1991 was applied, and indicators showing insufficient proportions of substantive agreement as well as coefficients of substantive validity were deleted from the scales. Based on tests with experts from organizational research and practice, the newly developed scales for all variables of interface structure were purified and validated. Apart from testing the measurement models, another pre-test concerns the questionnaire (Schnell, Hill & Esser 2011), which was described in **section 4.3.2**. Based on the comments received by research experts as well as cold chain experts, the questionnaire was refined and prepared for the main survey. The execution of the main survey was described in **section 4.3.3.** In total about 350 potential participants were contacted via mail and received a link to the survey. Of those, 96 participated, resulting in a response rate of 28.4%.

The description and analysis of the data was part of **section 4.4**. However, before the start of analysis, firstly, decision criteria to assess the validity and reliability of measurements had to be illustrated in **section 4.4.1**. This resulted in a list of quality criteria for the analysis of raw data, indicators, and measurement models, as well as a four step procedure for the following analysis. The sample, its composition and initial overviews on similarities and differences between sub-groups were presented in **section 4.4.2**. After the data set had been cleaned, the sample contained 61 data sets for the subsequent analysis. Furthermore, this section revealed partly considerable differences in the performance ratings by different sub-groups, especially for ratings by different handling specialists. The description of results from the analytical statistic procedures were part of **section 4.4.3**. Thereby, the results showed nine significant paths for the first order model and six significant paths for the second order model in the case of disruptions, which supports the assumption that the interface design indeed has a considerable effect on disruptions.

In **section 4.5**, the results of the empirical analysis on causes of disruptions in cold chains were analyzed. In order to gain a deeper understanding of disruptions, **section 4.5.1** firstly compared the performance indicators for both cases. The substantial differences observed support the understanding of disruptions as substantial negative deviations from the process plans. Furthermore, disruption profiles of several sub-groups revealed differences in disruptions in food and pharmaceutical cold chains and a more substantial deviation of product quality than of logistics quality. This finding supports the operationalization of disruptions as two constructs and had also implications for the analysis of findings on disruptions presented in **section 4.5.2**. In this section, the first order model and the second order model for the case of disruptions were analyzed. Detrimental impacts were thereby identified for the "durability" and "preciseness" of exchange procedures, while positive effects emerged from the "frequency" of transactions, and the "range of addressees". To find out whether these effects are consistent across scenarios, **section 4.5.3** compared the findings to the other case, where logistics processes were realized as planned. Thereby, "durability" and "preciseness" showed opposite effects on the performance, indicating that mechanisms of action are not the same if disruptions occur. At the same time, "frequency" was again found to have a positive effect on performance, showing that the effect of transaction types is consistent across scenarios, while the effects of interface structure are not. The implications of these findings will be elaborated in the next section.

5 Conclusions

5.1 Synopsis of the Main Findings

The main findings can be illustrated in analogy to the research objectives into descriptive, analytical, and pragmatic constraints.

Descriptive contributions: In section 2, the literature review on disruptions and similar terms resulted in the definition and separation of the phenomenon, which can now be described and identified unambiguously. Therewith, this thesis provides a terminological basis for the investigation of disruptions. Furthermore, the literature analysis helps to embed the phenomenon contextually, as well as to identify some of their causes and effects. Based on this definition and explanation of disruptions, the comprehensiveness of the phenomenon increases, and further research requirements are revealed.

Furthermore, the development of a classification framework for disruptions based on a systematic decomposition provides the possibility to differentiate between types of disruptions, allowing for the analysis of commonalities and differences in their structure, determinants, and consequences. By selecting the terminology of Remer for the classification of disruptions, consistency with the following description of interface structures is enhanced. Furthermore, the framework has therewith been expanded to the detailed description of operational planning, which has not been accomplished in the original work by Remer.

The scoring model developed in this thesis could be used for a systematic deduction of performance indicators for the prevalence of disruptions in food chains. Therewith, disruptions could be measured, misperceptions reduced, weak points identified, and countermeasures prioritized. Furthermore, the analysis of causal relations and efficacy of countermeasures is enhanced. Thereby, robustness of food chains might be increased and disruptions prevented or mitigated more effectively. Another advantage of the tool is the ability to use the same methodology for other supply chain contexts, such as for the pharmaceutical industry, which has already been developed elsewhere (see: Brenner & Hülsmann 2013). This shows that the methodology can be transferred and adapted, which increases the generalizability of the tool. Based on this scoring model, a generic foundation for the identification and analysis of disruptions in supply chains is facilitated.

In section 3.3, this thesis contributes to the systematic description of interfaces by applying Remer's terminological framework of organizational structures to interfaces in supply chains. Therewith, a systematic terminology for the description of interfaces has been provided, which can also be expanded to the systematic description of supply chains in general, as has been shown elsewhere (see: Brenner, Cordes & Hülsmann 2013). Since the focus of analysis shifts from company-centred management and performance to supply chain-centred management and performance (Beamon 1999), interfaces require a more thorough investigation and consideration as a natural part of organizational structures in supply chains. The thesis provides to this purpose a basis for describing and analyzing interfaces in more detail, which may foster the depth of insights on optimal configurations. At the same time, it shows the variety of options to alter the structure of interfaces, which can be used to manage exchange processes between companies.

Analytical contributions: As has been noted for instance by Dunn, Seaker & Waller (1994), empirical tests and validation of hypotheses on latent variables are scarce in logistics research. They attribute this lack to the abundance of abstract and complex concepts in this research area, and the difficulties to develop operational measures for these constructs. In this respect, this thesis provides some useful insights and measures for further applications in logistics research. This includes firstly that the methodology of pre-testing indicators by Anderson & Gerbing (1991) can be applied in cases where large sample pre-tests are not possible. Thereby, the preparation and execution of hypotheses-testing surveys in logistics settings becomes easier and fewer resources in terms of potential participants of the main survey are required ant therewith used up for pre-tests.

Additionally, the phenomenon of disruptions was substantiated with indicators for investigations in cold chains. The resulting disruption profiles provide valuable insights on how exactly disruptions affect operational performance and in which respect the sub-groups differ in their susceptibility to disruptions. Therewith, tailor-made measures might be deduced and implemented and the understanding of disruptions enhanced.

Another important aspect is the possibility to compare decent performance with unsatisfactory performance in the same setting. The comparison helps to identify more exactly the contexts to which the findings can be applied, indicating which findings are only applicable to a certain kind of situtation, and which ones can be generalized to a larger extent. Hence, apart from the content-wise insights, also the quality of findings can be better evaluated and more informative statements can be drawn.

Furthermore, this thesis provides measures for analyzing how transaction partners coordinate exchange processes on the product and information flow level, which has gained a lot of interest in research on supply chain management (Sahin & Robinson 2002). Therewith, it makes an important contribution to substantiate research on supply chain management, by facilitating empirical testing and validation of hypotheses in a field, where currently case-studies and simulation-based research prevails (Dunn, Seaker & Waller 1994). Additionally, it provides a basis for measuring and analyzing performance in supply chains on an operational level, by considering different dimensions of performance. Hereby, supply chain performance as a latent construct is concretized, which enhances falsifyability of hypotheses.

Finally, apart from the findings on the application context, contributions to the organization literature can be identified. Even though not at the center of interest, the correlations between organizational structure variables, as well as their interplay with the transaction type, shed more light on apparent interdependencies and organizational design options. Furthermore, the findings substantiate the assumptions of organizations theory that the choice of organizational structures affects the performance of systems.

Pragmatic contributions: In section 4, insights on cold chain management in practice and organizational performance drivers are provided. Thereof, further research requirements can be deduced, but also suggestions for how to configure exchange processes for *firstly*, avoiding disruptions, *secondly*, mitigating disruptions, and *thirdly*, enhancing excellence in cold chain performance. Therewith, cold chain managers can be equipped with additional adjusting screws and decision foundations, to increase robustness of supply chains and quality of services and products. Furthermore, these findings might also be useful to other kinds of supply chains, as they show the general goal conflict between increasing efficiency and assuring robustness of supply networks.

Since this research is presumably the first attempt to discover performance drivers in cold chains, it lays the foundation for further analyses regarding theoretic and descriptive bases, and provides already measures and hypotheses for further investigations. Figure 53 shows the main contributions of this thesis in analogy to the illustration of research aims in section 1.

Figure 53: Contributions of this thesis

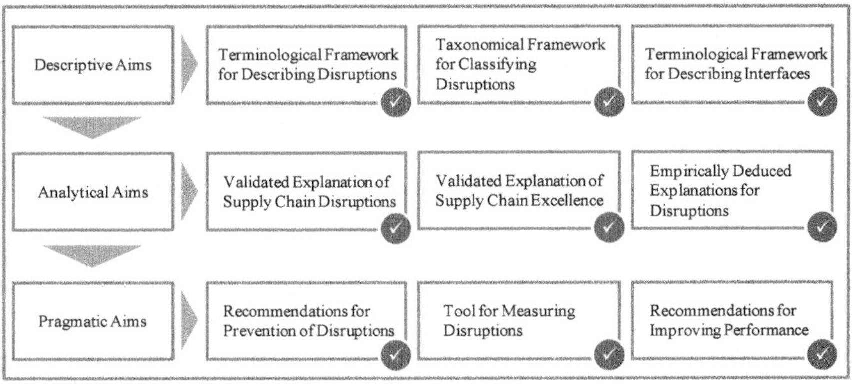

Comparing the achievements of this thesis as illustrated above with the originally pursued research aims, some differences can be observed. On the one hand, more contributions have been made to research on organizational determinants of supply chain performance as expected in the beginning. On the other hand, these achievements may in some points not be as complete as originally intended due to several limitations, which will be illustrated in the next section.

5.2 Critical Reflection of the Proceeding and Results

As with every research, several limitations can be observed also in this context. The major drawbacks shall be outlined in the following, to increase interpretability of this research and its findings. Thereby, the limitations of this research can be distinguished in analogy to the research objectives into descriptive, analytical, and pragmatic constraints.

Descriptive constraints: the *first* point to be mentioned here is the definition of supply chain disruptions developed in this thesis, which is not necessarily coherent with the understanding by other researchers. Gaonkar & Viswanadham (2004, p. 2700) for instance understand disruptions as "*radical transformations*", which contradicts the understanding developed here, as it also incorporates less radical events. This difference in understandings may lead to misinterpretations and non-transferability of research results (Kromrey 2009). Furthermore, not every publication on supply chain disruptions may have been discovered in the literature review. Thereby, a bias in understanding might occur, if those publication not included would focus on other aspects of disruptions.

The *second* point is the developed classification framework of disruptions, which also includes the scoring model for measuring disruptions.[158] Thereby, the classes of objects and directions are very broad and schematic, but may at the same time result in the exclusion of other important classes. To be named are for example the choice of product characteristics and logistics processes as basic unit of classification. Other classes, such as deployed equipment, or information characteristics are not considered explicitly and run the risk of omission. Another point of critique is that classes may appear to be unbalanced. For instance, whereas the process step MAKE differentiates several types of primary production, it does not differentiate between types of processing. Thus, whereas during primary production, disruptions could be further differentiated into sub-classes, all disruptions occurring during processing would belong to the same class, increasing thereby its relative importance and leading potentially to biased empirical analyses. Furthermore, the development of indicators is based on what is considered to be important. In consequence, the scoring model builds to a great extent on expert opinion and experience, which may result in the omission of indicators relevant to low-likelihood, high-impact events, which are a class of disruptions on their own (Oke & Gopalakrishnan 2009).

However, not only the definition of indicators poses the risk of biased results. Another constraint is that the scoring model depicts the actual situation and relies on historical data. For instance, thresholds established are based on data and experience from the past, which may not reflect new developments, such as increasing robustness towards high temperatures due to more effective packaging solutions. At the same time, in cases where no prior data exists, reference has to be made to similar cases, which reduces the exactness of thresholds. Even though a prediction of disruptions may be possible for recurring processes under the same specifications, no prediction can be done for – from the current point of view – highly improbable disruptions. Additionally, even though quantification of measures increases transparency, discrete measures do not allow for a prediction of negative process changes, but only

[158] Regarding the limitations of the scoring model, see also: Brenner, Hülsmann & Cordes (2013).

ex-post observation (Dietrich & Schulze 2005). Consequently, the tool needs to be constantly updated and adapted, to assure that it reflects the current situation. To counteract path dependencies in the assessment of vulnerabilities in supply chains, one might work with a scenario technique (Murray, Matisziw & Grubesic 2008), to obtain a more holistic picture.

The *third* point to be mentioned is the use of the terminological framework by Remer. One drawback of this framework is that it is very general and abstract, which leaves an ample space for interpretation and logic errors. Especially inter-subjective identical interpretation seems to be at risk, considering firstly that it is translated, which leaves room for misinterpretation. Secondly, between the description of its main objects and its operationalization in an industry-specific context, many transformation steps have to be conducted, wherefore much bias can be introduced between conceptualization and empirical analysis. Indeed, its application in this research might be considered as being still on a relatively abstract level, where more tailoring to the empirical research might be desirable to avoid that the methodology dictates the content of research. One crucial point here is that an empirical validation of the model is not possible, due to its conceptual and descriptive nature. At the same time, other important variables of organizational structure might receive less attention, or might be omitted altogether, as the selection of dimensions depends always on the perspective and the scope of conceptualization (Kieser & Walgenbach 2007).

Analytical constraints: limitations regarding the objective to deduce true and informative statements are *firstly*, that the classification of research on disruptions based on its science theoretic foundation bears the risk of excluding important findings, which could have led to a different scope of analysis. To be named here is for instance the exclusion of simulations of process plans, which could result in the attribution of too much importance on interactional programming, rather than on intra-actional programming. Furthermore, the focus on interfaces in cold chains results in the exclusion of company-internal causes of disruptions, which could also have an impact on performance at the interface itself. In this context, Remer (1989) stresses that a position is only completely covered by regarding both, differentiation and programming. By reducing the scope of analysis to the degree, standardization and formalization of interactional programming, important influences might be overlooked. The choice of dimensions is therefore a critical step in research on organizations, as therewith a pre-cut of reality is effected, which determines the focus of the following analysis. Characteristics of real organizations, which have been excluded in this step, cannot be considered anymore in the following and therewith their potential effects are neglected (Kieser & Walgenbach 2007). Apart from company-internal causes of disruptions, also the organizational structure at interfaces is not entirely covered in this research. For instance, the role of vertical coordination at interfaces is neglected, which might lead to different explanations of why disruptions occur.

Secondly, apart from the choice of analytical scope, the choice of theories to explain causal relations might also lead to constraints. Transaction cost theory for instance can lead to an over-accentuation of opportunism and problems of transactions as causal explanation, omitting that companies might have other reasons for close cooperation, such as convenience. Furthermore, the focus on three basic determinants of types of transactions, which are not necessarily on the same level of analysis or control of companies, results in a schematic depiction of transactions, which omits other important aspects, such as strategic decisions. Also the assumptions of decision theory should be adopted with caution: as Chmielewicz (1979) remarks, bounded rationality might be rather a normative judgement, as only because an external observer does not understand the motives for a decision, they might be completely rational to the decision maker. In this point, decision theory might contradict itself, as the concept of satisficing behaviour already is an explanation for taking decisions, which do not maximize the overall outcome but personal utility, and is therewith also rational, though from an individual's point of view. Another point of critique regarding the application of decision theory is that it can be basically used for arguments in opposite directions. For example, the reasons for errors can either be mental overload of individuals, or insufficient workload, depending on the individual, the situation, and the task at hand. Therewith, a falsification of hypotheses becomes challenging, if it cannot fail in practice as demanded by Popper (1973). This problem is not exclusive to decision theory, but an issue, which has not yet been resolved in social science theory (Schnell, Hill & Esser 2011).

Thirdly, the preparation and execution of the empirical analysis involves several critical decisions and contextual constraints, which have to be mentioned. The first one is the decision to conduct a survey-based analysis. Some limitations of surveys are that the interview or response situation, the behaviour of the interviewee, as well as the conceptualization and form of the survey may have an effect on the answers provided by the respondent (Diekmann 2002). Even though the importance of the role of the interviewee has been tried to be controlled by conducting an online survey, online surveys as such represent challenges on their own as for instance reported by Roberts (2007). To be named are a lack of control on the research setting, technological limitations, and poor response rates. However, a more critical aspect seems to be the reliance on individuals as source of information. This may result in biases due to a tendency of respondents to answer questions in a socially desirable way, to misinterpretations, or stereo-type kinds of answers (Bortz & Döring 1995). Especially when asking respondents about such relatively abstract constructs as the design of procedures for exchange processes, accuracy of answers might be imperilled. This problem has been also acknowledged by Remer (2005), who favours therefore observations as method of choice, even though he recognizes its limitations regarding feasibility.

The second problem associated with the empirical analysis is the development of indicators and measurements. Even though the pre-test methodology applied in this research has been tested and accepted in practice (e.g. Anderson & Gerbing 1991; Mathwick, Malhotra & Rigdon 2001; Müller-Martini 2008), it is up to discussion whether it can replace a complete exploratory factor analysis. Consequently, the validity and reliability of indicators might be compromised due to a lack of large sampling pre-tests.

Another issue are measurement theoretical problems of rating scales. There is an ongoing discussion among researchers whether rating scales can be assumed to be interval-scaled or not, which has also an impact on the statistical procedures which can be applied (Kromrey 2009). Furthermore, rating scales may result in errors of evaluation, caused by influences by the survey situation (Bortz & Döring 1995), which have been reported above. Therefore, the values reported should not be misinterpreted as hard facts and the analysis of findings evaluated with caution.

According to Buch (2007), causal analysis can be understood as an eclectic methodology, which is dependent on its parametrical preconditions and the methods incorporated. Hence, the analysis of causal relationships depends on the design of measurement models and the operationalization of constructs. In this context, Diamantopoulos & Siguaw (2006), Jarvis, MacKenzie & Podsakoff (2003), and others stress the importance of correct specification of indicators as formative or reflective measurements, which can result in the wrong choice and therewith lack of accuracy of results. As no previous operationalizations of Remer's framework were encountered, and existing operationalizations of organizational structure as understood here lacking, little previous findings could be incorporated, which may reduce reliability of the measurement models.

This is also supported by Peter (1981) who states that a single study does not establish construct validity and that whether empirical findings support or invalidate a measure depends on the research context. This seems especially true for those constructs, which have only been measured by two indicators, as these measurements do not represent the strongest evidence and may lead to identification problems if parameter estimates are not unidimensional (Chin 1998). At the same time, Hair et al. (2014) state that in cases of small populations, even single items might be used as a pragmatic solution, wherefore measuring each construct with two indicators seems to be not that problematic. Additionally, even though it has been tried to substantiate validity of the model by applying it to two situations, no final quality evaluation can take place without application to another independent sample. However, as has already been remarked by Diekmann (2002, p. 210) empirical research design is always a "*trade-off between additional research efforts and potential quality improvements of the measurement*".

An additional issue arises regarding the transformation of the first order models into second order models. According to Bagozzi & Yi (2012), second order formative constructs only make sense, if there is high multicollinearity between their indicators, and if these indicators can be considered to be dimensions of the higher order construct. Even though the two first order constructs are considered as being dimensions of the second order constructs, high multicollinearity was only observed for "formalization" and "standardization" in the best case scenario, whereas the other constructs were nearly completely different. This indicates either that the operationalizations did not tab sufficiently well the constructs. However, this should have become obvious in the quality evaluation of the worst case, too. Another explanation would be that the terminological framework does not adequately cover organizational structures in practice, at least in this case. Therefore, the results of the second order model should be interpreted with caution, and further analyses should regard and measure both models separately.

However, apart from analytical constraints caused by measurement-theoretic constraints, also other influencing factors on the interpretability of results should be considered. For instance, the reversed effect of "preciseness" and "durability" in both cases could also have other reasons as non-suitability to the situation. As a matter of fact, the *compliance* with the established procedures cannot be verified, as actual behaviour is not directly observed. In consequence, procedures might have been adequate, but simply not applied.

Additional limitations can be identified regarding the execution of analysis. Firstly, representativeness of the sample is an issue, as the basic population can only be identified qualitatively. Thereby, no comparisons can be executed between the sample and the basic population regarding equality of means, for instance regarding company size, geographic coverage, etc, wherefore equality between sample structure and basic population cannot be asserted. This has also a direct impact on the β-error of the analysis, hence the acceptance of a wrong null hypothesis, as the size of the β-error can only be determined by comparing the sample to the basic population (Bortz & Döring 1995; Diekmann 2002). This inability stresses again the exploratory nature of this research, whereby requirements such as selection of respondents from a basic population become rather obsolete (Bortz & Döring 1995).

Pragmatic constraints: the pragmatic constraints of this thesis do not only include suggestions on how to use the findings of the empirical part in practice, but also the developed tool for measuring disruptions in section 2.4. The application of this tool requires firstly that it is adapted to the context in which it shall be used. Even though it has been shown elsewhere that by the same logic, also disruptions in pharmaceutical supply chains can be measured (see: Brenner & Hülsmann 2013), it may require considerable adaptation to be useful in a specific supply chain setting. Furthermore, the development of indicators might be laborious in the beginning, if disruptions shall be identified in their entirety. The question thereby results, whether the resulting scoring model will be inter-subjectively comprehensive and whether normative decisions on e.g. thresholds, weightings, etc. can be controlled to such an extent that the tool can be transferred and applied by different people and in changing settings. Thus, it stands to reason that the tool is feasible and useful and therewith the empirical validation is still lacking.

Last but not least the empirical findings cannot be generalized to supply chains as such, due to the constraints reported above. Hence, whereas some patterns seem to be persistent across product groups, supply chain segments, or countries, the exploratory nature and lacking representativeness of the sample negates the possibility to apply the lessons from the findings to other supply chains or even organizations involved in cold chain logistics. For instance, as some European countries are comparatively overrepresented, there might be cultural, regulatory, or infrastructural biases in the sample, which would lead to false claims if suggestions would be generalized to other geographic regions. Furthermore, deducing exact suggestions seems to be difficult, given that most of the measures build on Likert scales, and therewith on subjective assessments (Bortz & Döring 1995). As with empirical social research in general, it has to be kept in mind that the explanations provided for how consrtucts might be causally related are only an excerpt of possible explanations, which can only be suuported by experience and further research (Zetterberg 1973).

Given all the constraints pointed out above, it becomes obvious that on the one hand, results of this research should be interpreted with caution, but on the other hand, that there are many findings, from which lessons can be learned. These shall be depicted in the following section.

5.3 Theoretical and Practical Implications of the Findings

Based on the contributions and limitations of this thesis as depicted in the previous sections, the question rises, what can be learned from the findings?

The first point regarding the **theoretical implications** of this research can be made with reference to the literature review on disruptions. Thereby, it became obvious that the majority of publications did not mention how disruptions are understood by the researchers. To increase comprehensiveness and accuracy of research, relevant terms should be defined at the beginning of each publication, to avoid such fragmented and inconsistent understandings, as has been found here for disruptions. Furthermore, the share of research including theory-based hypotheses and their empirical testing was found to be quite low. Due to the relevance of disruptions in practice, efforts in this respect should be increased to provide practitioners with aid for the avoidance and mitigation of disruptions. At the same time, the scarcity of research findings offers a large variety of opportunities for further research, as will be shown in the next section.

What became apparent during the deduction of hypotheses is the ambivalence in interpreting transaction cost theory and decision theory. That the direction of influence of a variable may indeed depend on its particular manifestation was confirmed in section 4.5.3 and stresses the importance of examining the assumptions of the theories from different points of view. However, it also shows that their applicability and interpretability should be reflected critically and should be completed by descriptive methodologies to decompose the phenomenon under study to explain gradual changes. However, at the same time, transaction cost theory was found to be not only applicable to make-or-buy decisions, but also to explain how companies design their transactions without changing the institutional setting. This has already been highlighted by Aertsen (1993) and increases the range of configurations, transaction cost theory can explain. Nevertheless, for further theory building, the assumptions of transaction cost theory and decision theoy should be rendered more precisely, so that they become falsifyable as demanded for instance by Popper (1973).

The lacking importance of rigid procedures both, in the design of interface structures as well as in the operational performance supports theories focussing on the positive aspects of inter-organizational relationships. The costs, risks, and drawbacks of such relationships, as for example stressed by the principal agent approach or in transaction cost theory, did not seem to be as important, since the safeguards, which rigid contracts are expected to provide did not show any significant impacts. Instead, the assumptions of co-evolutionary theories about positive effects of close collaboration on joint competitiveness (Wilson & Hynes 2009) find support in the positive effects of frequent transactions and specific assets employed. Hence, research on supply chain management should continue to focus on advantages of specialized supply networks and strategic collaboration.

The measurement of interface structures in both cases provided some interesting insights on structural patterns. It also showed that these abstract constructs used on organizational theory cannot be completely separated from one another in empirical research. Researchers should therefore be careful regarding the interpretability of results and the accuracy of indicators used to measure such constructs, as interaction effects might result in measurement bias of organizational structures.

The prevalent approach to research in supply chain performance is up to now still to focus on the more abstract level, where companies and their interactions are the major unit of analysis (e.g. Spekman & Kamauff Jr 1998; Ngai, Lai & Cheng 2004; van Aramyan et al. 2007). However, as shown in this research, breaking it down to processes and people working in these processes offers many explanations for differences in performance, as well as starting points for the improvement of performance. Therefore, the micro perspective should neither be neglected in analyzing and explaining supply chain performance, nor in the development of unambiguous performance indicators.

Additionally, the scarcity of empirical research based on SEM and operationalizations of latent variables in logistics research has already been criticised by Dunn, Seaker & Waller (1994). Even though this kind of research requires a lot of careful preparation and is complicated by the heterogeneity of supply chain agents, it allows for a more holistic perspective on supply chain management and logistics processes, resulting in more realistic constraints and assumptions.

The **practical implications** can be differentiated depending on the objectives of the decision maker. These can be *firstly*, to foster excellence in supply chain management, *secondly*, to mitigate disruptions, and *thirdly*, to prevent disruptions.[159]

Regarding the *first* objective, standardization of exchange procedures was found to increase the performance in terms of logistics and products alike. Especially logistics quality can be enhanced considerably by the use of durable procedures, resulting in punctual shipments, adherence to preferred transport routes, as well as complete and accurate documents. Nevertheless, also product quality was found to be more optimally maintained if procedures were du-

[159] However, it should be kept in mind that the findings are exploratory in nature, wherefore their applicability should be thoroughly reflected in each case.

rable and more precise. Therefore, if the objective is to become better in regular performance, transaction partners in cold chains should reduce the amount of partner-specific investments, increase the frequency of transactions with each other, and base exchange processes on precise and durable procedures. These findings can also be interpreted in a more general supply chain or production system context: higher repetition of process steps, longer duration and exact definition of work programs are associated with higher efficiency, supporting therewith the school of thought by Taylor and others.[160]

Regarding the *second* objective, the strategy becomes less unambiguous. Even though standardization was found to be fostering logistics quality if a disruption occurred, product quality was affected negatively. Here, a trade-off between the two performance criteria emerges, wherefore supply chain partners would have to decide which criterion to prioritize. This highlights the inequality of objectives and consequential need of differentiation of weights for different criteria, which has already been considered during the development of the scoring model in section 2.4. Therefore, transaction partners should agree on what is considered to be more important and should be aware of trade-offs in achieving both objectives. In the case where mitigation of disruptions in logistics quality is deemed more important, the same strategy as above applies. However, in the case where mitigation of disruptions in product quality is more important, procedures have to be adaptive and less precise regarding how tasks should be executed. This may require more training of employees in product specific handling, but also smarter technology, which supports correct decision making and correction of potentially critical deviations. Additionally, procedures should apply to everyone involved in the logistics processes, so that in latter steps, agents do not have to mitigate the deviations caused by others in the supply chain. Therewith, risk management is linked across companies and results in a holistic supply chain risk management.

In the case of the *third* objective, hence the prevention of disruptions, a mixture of the two previous strategies with some additional elements seems to be advantageous. Hence, exchange processes should be frequent, with standardized and precise instructions provided, but at the same time, employees should possess expert knowledge on the requirements of products, to adapt the processes if deviations occur. This implies at the same time that employees are provided with instruments for the evaluation of the status-quo of product quality, for example with temperature monitoring devices and optical reference tools. The deviation from procedures as required can be understood as active disruption prevention, and should be part of cold chain management instruments. Indeed, in some cases, as for example the implementation of CAPA in pharmaceutical supply chains, such instruments are already in use. In these cases, the individual is equipped with two alternative sets of rules and has to decide upon which one is appropriate in a certain situation. This change of procedures falls in line with emergency plans in production contexts, which are highlighted for example in the Business Continuity Management philosophy and seems to be a logical expansion of these concepts in

---

[160] See section 3.2.1.

risk management. Therewith, risk management is linked across companies and results in a holistic supply chain risk management.

Furthermore, preliminary results indicate that as much of the logistics processes should be executed by either one of the partners as possible, avoiding numerous interfaces and influence of other agents. However, before starting the actual operations, decision makers should be aware that variables may not be omitted for the design of interfaces just because they were not identified as drivers of excellence. Rather, they are part of the design options and therefore require attention.

Subsuming the strategies above, the only factor which leads to higher performance in any one of the cases, is the frequency of transactions. This highlights the importance of stable and close partnerships in cold chains for the improvement of logistics quality and avoidance of product losses. Therefore, wherever possible, producers, retailers, and logistics service providers should strive for a reduction of partners, to increase the performance of cold chains.

Figure 54 shows the suitable measures for the different strategies regarded.

Figure 54: Strategic choices and measures to improve supply chain performance

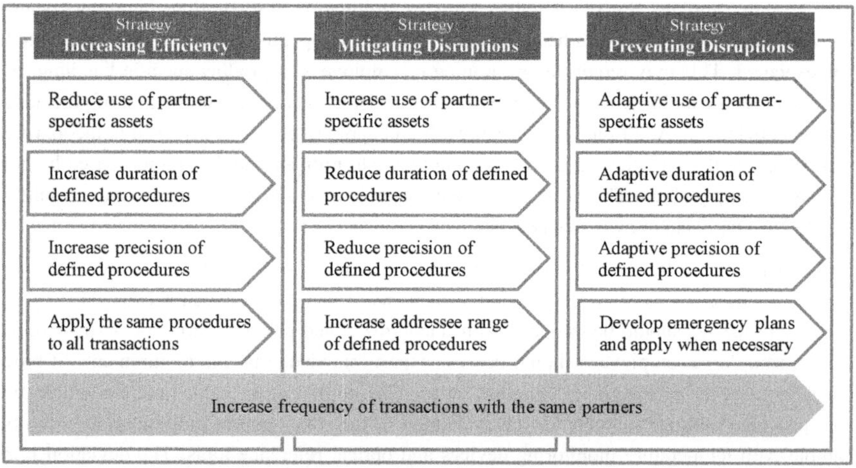

As the figure above indicates, the deduced measures are not necessarily limited to applications in cold chain specific contexts. Even though the indicators for product-related performance are tailored to this specific sector, at least the measures referring to logistics-related performance might be transferable to other applications as well.

However, also in other kinds of supply chains, the same logic can be applied: if products have been handled in a wrong way to the point where continuing the journey as planned would put the shipment at risk, agents have the choice between adhering to the logistic goals *or* the product goals. In case the latter is preferred, products might require e.g. repair or repackaging to protect them from damage, which requires time and additional efforts not planned for in preparation. Instead, plans may also include buffers or alternatives, which could render supply chains more robust to disruptions.

5.4 Outlook for Further Research

As has been shown in sections 2.2 and 2.3 of this thesis, research on disruptions in supply chains, and in particular in food chains is still in an early stage and rather fragmented. Especially empirical findings are scarce, which could be used to better prevent and mitigate disruptions. Apart from the content-wise opportunities for further research, the terminological and conceptual deficits in research on disruptions could be reduced, if a common understanding and terminology would be developed. Thereby, quality, transferability and comparability of research results could be enhanced and robustness of supply chains increased.

Furthermore, even though transaction cost theory and its main components are well established in research in supply chain management (e.g. Loader 1997; Hobbs 1996; Banterle & Stranieri 2008; Heide & John 1988), variations from those components could be useful to derive more facets of transactions. Especially volume uncertainty did not show any significant effect in the empirical analysis conducted here, which might hint at other factors being more important, being either other forms of uncertainty, or changes of perspective. For example, some of the respondents pointed out at the importance of information sharing, which can be considered as a countermeasure of uncertainty.[161]

As has been stated by e.g. Kromrey 2009, the usefulness of indicators always depends on the purpose of empirical research. The same holds true for the usefulness of the scoring model and the indicators developed therein. Hence, the scoring model could be amended regarding the scope of measurement. For instance, in analogy to Remer 1989 and Remer 2005, there could be adaptations with respect to the products considered in the degree, type or form – hence changing its preciseness or the range of products, shifting to other product groups or processing stages. The same applies to the activities regarded – hence changing the preciseness of activities, their range, type (e.g. action vs. prevention) or form (e.g. instruction-oriented vs. goal-oriented). Additionally, empirical tests may reveal that the decision rules for weighting and aggregating have to be adapted. Prioritization for instance can follow different purposes, such as reducing waste or reducing financial losses. Furthermore, the tool could be linked to other dimensions of supply chains, such as the structural or institutional dimension. Therewith, relations between logistics processes and organizational structures could be analyzed and conflicts of goals identified – both, regarding conflicts between structure and process, but also in between organizations or departments. Finally, the predictive ability of the scoring model could be enhanced, for example by taking into consideration scenario techniques, simulations, and findings of evolutionary and complexity theory.[162]

161 See Appendix 14.
162 See also Brenner, Hülsmann & Cordes (2013).

Starting from the description of the terminological framework by Remer in sections 3.3.2 and 3.3.3, the scope of analysis had been narrowed down in section 3.4.1 to interactional programming of positions. In consequence, the analysis of dimensions of organizational structure could be expanded again to cover more dimensions of the framework and to learn more about organizational causes of disruptions. For instance, the comparison of intra-actional and interactional programming of positions could provide insights for the question, whether similar design of both types of programming results in lower probability of errors, or whether both types have to be balanced to provide incentives to employees.

Even though the scales developed for the measurement of interface structure showed to be consistent across two samples, these samples were not completely independent from one another, nor extremely large. Therefore, the scales should be re-tested for more and larger samples, in other supply chain contexts, and with respondents from other organizational levels, to assure model reliability. This would also allow comparing the results between application fields and to identify similarities and differences in interface structures. Additionally, since some of the scales remained after quality evaluation only with two indicators these should be amplified to enhance their reliability and validity. For instance, the "range of addressees" should involve apart from relative statements also statements which allow quantifying the actual range of partners and employees involved. By more extensive testing and application of the measurement models, synergies could be created as research results would become transferable and comparable. The measurement models and research findings could then be integrated into a tool for optimizing interface design.

The two dimensions of disruptions put into focus in this thesis could also be used as a starting point for measuring disruptions in their entirety. Disruptions could then be constructed as second order formative constructs, provided that all relevant dimensions can be identified. Hence, a larger number of cold chain experts should be involved in the identification of further relevant dimensions, to include for example regulatory and financial aspects in the range of dimensions considered. An optimal amendment would be to follow a multiple indicators multiple causes (MIMIC) approach (Jarvis, MacKenzie & Podsakoff 2003), to increase unambiguous identification of disruptions. Thereby, the inclusion of quantitative indicators should be considered as a way to avoid normative evaluation of disruptions. The resulting model could then be used to substantiate the hitherto relatively heterogeneous and evidence-lacking research on supply chain disruptions in general, and in cold chains in particular.

Altogether, the empirical analysis undertaken in this thesis could be conducted in more breadth and depth across different geographic regions, product groups, supply chain segments, etc. Even though there is already a considerable body of research on e.g. advantages of partnerships in supply chains,[163] these partnerships normally take quite different forms, and explicit consideration of exchange procedures is lacking as well as their effects on disruptions.

Thereby, for example the question could be answered, which types of exchange procedures yield optimal performance, when product and logistics quality attributes are changing in importance.

However, also the exchange procedures were found to explain to a considerable extent changes in logistics and product quality, other determinants should be considered to further increase explicability as well as predictability of disruptions. This may include for instance the more explicit modelling of human behaviour according to such models as illustrated in

Figure 16 in section 1. In this context, Frese, Graumann & Theuvsen 2012 for instance stress the importance of motivation for the decision making of individuals. One possibility to consider motivation could be the integration of the incentive system in the analysis, to see whether different payment schemes may boost performance. Another determinant might be the use of managerial practices and cold chain-related technologies, for which those practices and technologies reported here may serve as a starting point.[164] In fact, these could be used as a starting point for an exploratory factor analysis to identify indicators for the technological and managerial sophistication of supply chains, which might also be an explanation for disruptions. In this context, one of the respondents of the survey suggested the integration of financial determinants, whereas another one suggested focusing in further research also on the role of regulatory requirements between countries as source of disruptions.[165]

In total, there are many options for expanding the causal models depicted in Figure 52, which provide a starting point for not only investigating disruptions, but also supply chain performance in general, as well as the topic of this thesis, namely organizational determinants for the susceptibility to disruptions. Such research results might help to reduce wasteful resource usage along supply chains, increase resilience to disruptions and may contribute to close cooperation between research and practice. At the same time, rethinking how supply chains and other production systems are designed might become necessary, as striving for more efficiency reduces the possibility to individualize processes, which has been shown to increase the susceptibility to disruptions.

---

163 See e.g. Ketzenberg & Ferguson (2008); Custódio & Oliveira (2006); Spekman & Kamauff (1998); Trienekens & Willems (2007).

164 See Appendix 2 and Appendix 3.

165 See Appendix 15.

Bibliography

Abad, E, Palacio, F, Nuin, M, Zárate, AG de, Juarros, A, Gómez, J & Marco, S 2009, 'RFID smart tag for traceability and cold chain monitoring of foods: Demonstration in an intercontinental fresh fish logistic chain', *Journal of Food Engineering*, vol. 93, no. 4, pp. 394–399.

Aertsen, F 1993, 'Contracting out the Physical Distribution Function: A Trade-off between Asset Specificity and Performance Measurement', *International Journal of Physical Distribution & Logistics Management*, vol. 23, no. 1, pp. 23–29.

Ahmed, S & Sahinidis, NV 1998, 'Robust Process Planning under Uncertainty', *Industrial & Engineering Chemistry Research*, vol. 37, no. 5, pp. 1883–1892.

Aidoo, KE 1993, 'Post-harvest storage and preservation of tropical crops', *International Biodeterioration & Biodegradation*, vol. 32, 1–3, pp. 161–173.

Aiken, M, Bacharach, SB & French, JL 1980, 'Organizational Structure, Work Process, and Proposal Making in Administrative Bureaucracies', *The Academy of Management Journal*, vol. 23, no. 4, pp. 631–652.

Albers, S, Klapper, D, Konradt, U, Walter, A & Wolf, J (eds.) 2009, *Methodik der empirischen Forschung,* Gabler, Wiesbaden.

Albino, V, Garavelli, A & Okogbaa, O 1998, 'Vulnerability of production systems with multi-supplier network: A case study', *International Journal of Production Research*, vol. 36, no. 11, pp. 3055–3066.

Alchian, A & Demsetz, H 1972, 'Production, Information Costs, and Economic Organization', *The American Economic Review*, vol. 62, no. 5.

Alchian, AA 1965, 'The Basis of Some Recent Advances in the Theory of Management of the Firm', *The Journal of Industrial Economics*, vol. 14, no. 1, pp. 30–41.

Alessi, L de 1969, 'Implications of property rights for government investment choices', *The American Economic Review pp. 13-24*, vol. 59, no. 1, pp. 13–24.

Alessi, L de 1987, 'Property Rights and Privatization', *Proceedings of the Academy of Political Science*, vol. 36, no. 3, pp. 24–35.

Alfaro, J & Rabade, L 2009, 'Traceability as a strategic tool to improve inventory management: A case study in the food industry', *International Journal of Production Economics*, vol. 118, no. 1.

Alfred Dupont Chandler 1977, *The visible hand: the managerial revolution in American business,* Belknap Press, Cambridge, Mass. [et al.].

Allen, D & Lueck, D 1992, 'Contract Choice in Modern Agriculture: Cash Rent versus Crop-share', *Journal of Law and Economics*, vol. 35, no. 2, pp. 397–426.

Anderson, J & Gerbing, D 1982, 'Some Methods for Respecifying Measurement Models to Obtain Unidimensional Construct Measurement', *Journal of Marketing Research*, vol. 19, no. 4, pp. 453–460.

Anderson, JC & Gerbing, DW 1988, 'Structural equation modeling in practice: A review and recommended two-step approach', *Psychological Bulletin*, vol. 103, no. 3, pp. 411–423.

Anderson, JC & Gerbing, DW 1991, 'Predicting the performance of measures in a confirmatory factor analysis with a pretest assessment of their substantive validities', *Journal of Applied Psychology*, vol. 76, no. 5, pp. 732–740.

Anderson, R & Vastag, G 2004, 'Causal modeling alternatives in operations research: Overview and application', *European Journal of Operational Research*, vol. 156, pp. 92–109.

Andler, N 2011, *Tools for project management, workshops and consulting. A must-have compendium of essential tools and techniques,* Publicis, Weinheim.

Ansoff, HI & Brandenburg, RG 1971, 'A Language for Organization Design: Part II', *Management Science*, vol. 17, no. 12, pp. B717-B731.

Arnheiter, ED & Maleyeff, J 2005, 'The integration of lean management and Six Sigma', *The TQM Magazine*, vol. 17, no. 1, pp. 5–18.

Aronson, E 1969, 'The Theory of Cognitive Dissonance: A Current Perspective' in *Advances in experimental social psychology,* ed L Berkowitz, Academic Press, New York, pp. 2–32.

Artz, KW 1999, 'Buyer-Supplier Performance: The Role of Asset Specificity, Reciprocal Investments and Relational Exchange', *British Journal of Management*, vol. 10, no. 2, pp. 113–126.

Ash, RC & Smith-Daniels, DE 2004, 'Managing the impact of customer support disruptions on new product development projects', *Project Management Journal*, vol. 35, no. 1, pp. 3–10.

Ashie, INA, Smith, JP, Simpson, BK & Haard, NF 1996, 'Spoilage and shelf-life extension of fresh fish and shellfish', *Critical Reviews in Food Science and Nutrition*, vol. 36, 1-2, pp. 87–121.

Axelrod, R 2007, 'Simulation in Social Sciences' in *Handbook of research on nature-inspired computing for economics and management / Jean-Philippe RennardVol. 1. Chapters I - XXVI,* ed J Rennard, Idea Group Reference, Hershey, Pa. [et al.], pp. 90–100.

Ayarkwa, J, Hirashima, Y & Sasaki, Y 2001, 'Predicting Modulus of Rupture of Solid and Finger-Jointed Tropical African Hardwoods Using Longitudinal Vibration', *Forest Products Journal*, vol. 51, no. 1, p. 85.

Backhaus, J 1983, 'Competition, innovation and regulation in the pharmaceutical industry', *Managerial and Decision Economics*, vol. 4, no. 2, pp. 107-121.

Backhaus, K 2011, *Fortgeschrittene multivariate Analysemethoden. Eine anwendungsorientierte Einführung,* Springer, Berlin [et al.].

Backhaus, K, Erichson, B, Plinke, W & Weiber, R 2011, *Multivariate Analysemethoden. Eine anwendungsorientierte Einführung,* Springer, Berlin [et al.].

Badke-Schaub, P, Hofinger, G & Lauche, K 2008, 'Human Factors' in *Human Factors. Psychologie sicheren Handelns in Risikobranchen,* eds P Badke-Schaub, G Hofinger & K Lauche, Springer Medizin Verlag Heidelberg, Berlin, Heidelberg, pp. 4–18.

Bagozzi, R & Yi, Y 1988, 'On the evaluation of structural equation models', *Journal of the Academy of Marketing Science*, vol. 16, no. 1, pp. 74-94.

Bagozzi, R & Yi, Y 2012, 'Specification, evaluation, and interpretation of structural equation models', *Journal of the Academy of Marketing Science*, vol. 40, no. 1, pp. 8-34.

Bagozzi, RP 1981, 'Evaluating Structural Equation Models with Unobservable Variables and Measurement Error: A Comment', *Journal of Marketing Research*, vol. 18, no. 3, pp. 375–381.

Bailey, KD 1994, *Typologies and taxonomies. An introduction to classification techniques,* Sage, Thousand Oaks, Calif. [et al.].

Bakshi, N & Kleindorfer, P 2009, 'Co-opetition and Investment for Supply-Chain Resilience', *Production and Operations Management*, vol. 18, no. 6, pp. 583–603.

Ballou, RH, Gilbert, SM & Mukherjee, A 2000, 'New Managerial Challenges from Supply Chain Opportunities', *Industrial Marketing Management*, vol. 29, no. 1, pp. 7–18.

Bamber, GJ & Lansbury, RD 1988, 'Management Strategy and New Technology in Retail Distribution: A Comparative Case Study', *Journal of Management Studies*, vol. 25, no. 3, pp. 197–216.

Banbury, S & Berry, DC 1998, 'Disruption of office-related tasks by speech and office noise', *British Journal of Psychology*, vol. 89, no. 3, p. 499.

Banterle, A & Stranieri, S 2008, 'The consequences of voluntary traceability system for supply chain relationships. An application of transaction cost economics', *Food Policy*, vol. 33, no. 6.

Baron, RM & Kenny, DA 1986, 'The moderator–mediator variable distinction in social psychological research: Conceptual, strategic, and statistical considerations', *Journal of Personality and Social Psychology*, vol. 51, no. 6, pp. 1173–1182.

Barroso, C, Carrión, G & Roldán, J 2010, 'Applying Maximum Likelihood and PLS on Different Sample Sizes: Studies on SERVQUAL Model and Employee Behavior Model' in *Handbook of Partial Least Squares,* eds V Esposito Vinzi, WW Chin, J Henseler & H Wang, Springer Berlin Heidelberg, pp. 427–447.

Batchelor, GK 1999, *An introduction to fluid dynamics,* Cambridge University Press, Cambridge, New York.

Bea, F & Haas, J 2001, *Strategisches Management,* Lucius & Lucius, Stuttgart.

Beamon, B 1999, 'Measuring supply chain performance', *International Journal of Operations & Production Management*, vol. 19, no. 3, pp. 275–292.

Bechini, A, Cimino, M, Marcelloni, F & Tomasi, A 2008, 'Patterns and technologies for enabling supply chain traceability through collaborative e-business', *Information and Software Technology*, vol. 50, no. 4.

Beckmann, C & Specht, G 1996, *F & E-Management,* Schäffer-Poeschel, Stuttgart.

Beidernikl, G & Kerschbaumer, A 2007, 'Sampling in Online Surveys' in *Handbook of research on electronic surveys and measurements,* eds RA Reynolds, R Woods & JD Baker, Idea Group Reference, Hershey, PA, pp. 90–96.

Bell, KN, Hogue, CJR, Manning, C & Kendal, AP 2001, 'Risk Factors for Improper Vaccine Storage and Handling in Private Provider Offices', *PEDIATRICS*, vol. 107, no. 6, pp. e100.

Ben-Ner, A, Kong, F & Lluis, S 2011, 'Uncertainty, task environment, and organization design: An empirical investigation', *Journal of Economic Behavior and Organization*, vol. 82, no. 1, pp. 281–313.

Bentrup, H 1969, *Der europäische Kühlverkehr auf Straße und Schiene,* thesis, University of Düsseldorf, Düsseldorf.

Berman, O, Krass, D & Menezes, MBC 2009, 'Locating Facilities in the Presence of Disruptions and Incomplete Information', *Decision Sciences*, vol. 40, no. 4, pp. 845–868.

Berndt, ER 2002, 'Pharmaceuticals in U.S. Health Care: Determinants of Quantity and Price', *The Journal of Economic Perspectives*, vol. 16, no. 4, pp. 45–66.

Berschet, K 2009, 'Innovative Logistikinstrumente in der Arzneimittel-Supply-Chain: das SCOR-Modell', *Arzneimittel-Supply-Chain / Thomas Wilke,* pp. 175 OP 185.

Beulens, AJ, Broens, D, Folstar, P & Hofstede, GJ 2005, 'Food safety and transparency in food chains and networks', *Food Control*, vol. 16, no. 6, pp. 481–486.

BfR 2011, *Bedeutung von EHEC O104:H4 in Bockshornkleesamen, die zu anderen Lebensmitteln als Sprossen und Keimlingen weiterverarbeitet werden. - Aktualisierte Stellungnahme Nr. 031/2011 des BfR vom 26. Juli 2011.* Available from: http://www.bfr.bund.de/cm/343/bedeutung_von_ehec_o104_h4_in_bockshornkleesamen_die_zu_anderen_lebensmitteln_als_sprossen_und_keimlingen_weiterverarbeitet_werden.pdf. [05 January 2012].

Bichou, K, Kee-Hung Lai, Lun, YHV & Cheng, TCE 2007, 'A Quality Management Framework for Liner Shipping Companies to Implement the 24-Hour Advance Vessel Manifest Rule', *Transportation Journal (American Society of Transportation & Logistics Inc)*, vol. 46, no. 1, pp. 5–21.

Blackhurst, J, Craighead, CW, Elkins, D & Handfield, RB 2005, 'An empirically derived agenda of critical research issues for managing supply-chain disruptions', *International Journal of Production Research*, vol. 43, no. 19, pp. 4067–4081.

Blackhurst, J, Dunn, KS & Craighead, CW 2011, 'An Empirically Derived Framework of Global Supply Resiliency', *Journal of Business Logistics*, vol. 32, no. 4, pp. 374–391.

Blain, I 1964, *Structure in management. A study of different forms and their effectiveness,* National Institute of Industrial Psychology no. 17, London.

Blau, PM 1954a, 'Co-operation and Competition in a Bureaucracy', *American Journal of Sociology*, vol. 59, no. 6, pp. 530–535.

Blau, PM 1954b, 'Patterns of Interaction Among a Group of Officials in a Government Agency', *Human Relations*, vol. 7, no. 3, pp. 337–348.

Blau, PM, Falbe, CM, McKinley, W & Tracy, PK 1976, 'Technology and Organization in Manufacturing', *Administrative Science Quarterly*, vol. 21, no. 1, pp. 20–40.

Blunch, NJ 2008, *Introduction to structural equation modelling using SPSS and AMOS,* Sage, Los Angeles, London.

Bode, C, Wagner, S, Petersen, K & Ellram, L 2011, 'Understanding Responses to Supply Chain Disruptions: Insights from Information Processing and Resource Dependence Perspectives', *Academy of Management Journal*, vol. 54, no. 4, pp. 833–856.

Bogataj, M, Bogataj, L & Vodopivec, R 2005, 'Stability of perishable goods in cold logistic chains', *International Journal of Production Economics*, 93-94, pp. 345–356.

Böing, A & Schwarz, C 2005, 'Mehr als nur Hilfsfunktion - Logistik verbessert Wettbewerbsfähigkeit in der Ernährungsindustrie', *F+H Fördern und Heben* 2005, pp. 670–671.

Bollen, K & Lennox, R 1991, 'Conventional wisdom on measurement: A structural equation perspective', *Psychological Bulletin*, vol. 110, no. 2, pp. 305–314.

Bolstorff, PA, Rosenbaum, RG & Poluha, RG 2007, *Spitzenleistungen im Supply Chain Management. Ein Praxishandbuch zur Optimierung mit SCOR,* Springer, Berlin [et al.].

Bortz, J & Döring, N 1995, *Forschungsmethoden und Evaluation,* Springer, Berlin [et al.].

Bourlakis, MA & Weightman, PWH 2004, 'Introduction to the UK food supply chain' in *Food Supply Chain Management,* eds MA Bourlakis & PWH Weightman, Blackwell, Oxford [et al.], pp. 1–10.

Braimah, N & Ndekugri, I 2006, 'The Link Between Planning and Programming Practice and the Analysis of Delay and Disruption Claims', *AACE International Transactions,* pp. 19.1.

Brandt, A, Fröhlingsdorf, M, Klawitter, N, Koch, J, Loeckx, M & Ludwig, U, 'Schmierige Geschäfte', *Der Spiegel,* pp. 32–36. Available from: http://www.spiegel.de/spiegel/print/d-76229467.html [02 December 2013]

Brecht, J, Chau, K, Fonseca, S, Oliveira, F, Silva, F, Nunes, F & Bender R.J. 2003, 'Maintaining optimal atmosphere conditions for fruits and vegetables throughout the postharvest handling chain', *Postharvest Biology and Technology*, vol. 27, no. 1, pp 87-101.

Brenner, V & Hülsmann, M 2013, 'Proposal of a Disruption Scoring Model for Pharmaceutical Supply Chains', *Pharmaceutical Outsourcing*, vol. 14, no. 3, pp. 38–43.

Brenner, V, Cordes, P & Hülsmann, M 2013, 'Identifying Logistics Structures - A Holistic Framework for the Analysis of Structural Design Options for Supply Chains'. In: Pawar, KS, Lalwani, CS [eds.]: *Proceedings of 18th International Symposium on Logistics (ISL).* Vienna, Austria, 7th – 10th July 2013.

Brenner, V, Hülsmann, M & Cordes, P 2013, 'Measuring Supply Chain Disruptions'. In: Pawar, KS, Lalwani, CS [eds.]: *Proceedings of 18th International Symposium on Logistics (ISL).* Vienna, Austria, 7th – 10th July 2013.

Bridges, AM & Jones, DM 1996, 'Word Dose in the Disruption of Serial Recall by Irrelevant Speech: Phonological Confusions or Changing State?', *The Quarterly Journal of Experimental Psychology A*, vol. 49, no. 4, pp. 919–939.

Brockhoff, K 1989, *Schnittstellen-Management. Abstimmungsprobleme zwischen Marketing und Forschung und Entwicklung,* Poeschel, Stuttgart.

Brockhoff, K & Hauschildt, J 1993, 'Schnittstellen-Management. Koordination ohne Hierarchie' in *Zeitschrift Führung + Organisation,* pp. 396–403.

Brown, L 1983, *Managing conflict at organizational interfaces,* Addison-Wesley Publ, Reading/Mass. [et al.].

Buch, S 2007, *Strukturgleichungsmodelle - ein einführender Überblick,* ESCP-EAP, Europ. School of Management, Berlin.

Buckley, W 1958, 'Social Stratification and the Functional Theory of Social Differentiation', *American Sociological Review*, vol. 23, no. 4, pp. 369–375.

Bundesamt für Verbraucherschutz und Lebensmittelsicherheit 2007, *Sicherheit und Kontrollen: Nationale Berichterstattung Pflanzenschutzmittel - Rückstände 2007. Zusammenfassung der Ergebnisse des Jahres 2007 aus der Bundesrepublik Deutschland.* Available from: http://www.bvl.bund.de/nn_493682/DE/01__Lebensmittel/01__Sicherheit__Kontrollen/05__NB__PSM__Rueckstaende/01__nb__psm/nbpsm__2007/nbpsm__Bericht__2007.html> [25 August 2010].

Buzby, JC, Wells, H, Axtman, B & Mickey, J 2009, *Supermarket Loss Estimates for Fresh Fruit, Vegetables, Meat, Poultry, and Seafood and Their Use in the ERS Loss-Adjusted Food Availability Data,* US Dep. of Agriculture ERS, Washington, DC.

BWV 2011, *BWV-Gutachten: Organisation des gesundheitlichen Verbraucherschutzes (Schwerpunkt Lebensmittel),* Bonn.

Cadogan, JW, Diamantopoulos, A & Mortanges, CP de 1999, 'A Measure of Export Market Orientation: Scale Development and Cross-Cultural Validation', *Journal of International Business Studies*, vol. 30, no. 4, pp. 689–707.

Cai, J, Liu, X, Xiao, Z & Liu, J 2009, 'Improving supply chain performance management: A systematic approach to analyzing iterative KPI accomplishment', *Decision Support Systems*, vol. 46, no. 2, pp. 512–521.

Canavari, M, Fritz, M, Hofstede, GJ, Matopoulos, A & Vlachopoulou, M 2010, 'The role of trust in the transition from traditional to electronic B2B relationships in agri-food chains', *Computers and Electronics in Agriculture*, vol. 70, no. 2, pp. 321–327.

Cardello, A 1995, 'Food Quality: Relativity, Context and Consumer Expectations', *Food Quality and Preference*, vol. 6, no. 3, pp. 163–170.

Cavinato, JL 2004, 'Supply chain logistics risks: From the back room to the board room', *International Journal of Physical Distribution & Logistics Management*, vol. 34, no. 5, pp. 383–387.

Chalmers, AF 2007, *Wege der Wissenschaft. Einführung in die Wissenschaftstheorie,* Springer, Berlin [et al.].

Chandra, P & Fisher, M 1994, 'Coordination of production and distribution planning', *European Journal of Operational Research*, vol. 72, no. 3, pp. 503–517.

Chase, RB & Tansik, DA 1983, 'The Customer Contact Model for Organization Design', *Management Science*, vol. 29, no. 9, pp. 1037–1050.

Cheke, RA & Ward, AR 1998, 'A model for evaluating interventions designed to reduce post-harvest fish losses', *Fisheries Research*, vol. 35, no. 3, pp. 219–227.

Chen, H & Yao, DD 1992, 'A Fluid Model for Systems with Random Disruptions', *Operations Research,* vol. 40, no. 3, p. 239.

Cheng Piao & Groom, L 2010, 'Residual Strength and Stiffness of Lumber from Decommissioned Chromated Copper Arsenate -- Treated Southern Pine Utility Poles', *Forest Products Journal*, vol. 60, no. 2, pp. 166–172.

Cheng, JLC 1984, 'Organizational Coordination, Uncertainty, and Performance: An Integrative Study', *Human Relations*, vol. 37, no. 10, pp. 829–851.

Cheung, GW & Lau, RS 2008, 'Testing Mediation and Suppression Effects of Latent Variables: Bootstrapping With Structural Equation Models', *Organizational Research Methods*, vol. 11, no. 2, pp. 296–325.

Chien, A, Tateshima, S, Castro, M, Sayre, J, Cebral, J & Viñuela, F 2008, 'Patient-specific flow analysis of brain aneurysms at a single location: comparison of hemodynamic characteristics in small aneurysms', *Medical & Biological Engineering & Computing*, vol. 46, no. 11, pp. 1113–1120.

Chin, WW 1998, 'Commentary: Issues and Opinion on Structural Equation Modeling', *MIS Quarterly*, vol. 22, no. 1, pp. vii.

Chmielewicz, K 1979, *Forschungskonzeptionen der Wirtschaftswissenschaft*, Poeschel, Stuttgart.

Chopra, S & Sodhi, MS 2004, 'Managing Risk To Avoid Supply-Chain Breakdown', *MIT Sloan Management Review*, vol. 46, no. 1, pp. 53–62.

Chou, C & Bentler, P 1995, 'Estimates and Tests in Structural Equation Modeling' in *Structural equation modeling. Concepts, issues, and applications*, ed RH Hoyle, Sage Publ, Thousand Oaks [et al.], pp. 37–55.

Christopher, M & Lee, H 2004, 'Mitigating supply chain risk through improved confidence', *International Journal of Physical Distribution & Logistics Management*, vol. 34, no. 5, pp. 388–396.

Christopher, M & Peck, H 2004, 'Building the Resilient Supply Chain', *The International Journal of Logistics Management*, vol. 15, no. 2, pp. 1–14.

Christopher, M & Rutherford, C 2004, 'Creating supply chain resilience through agile six sigma', *Critical Eye*, June-August, pp. 24–28.

Christophersen, T & Grape, C 2009, 'Die Erfassung latenter Konstrukte mit Hilfe formativer und reflektiver Messmodelle' in *Methodik der empirischen Forschung*, eds S Albers, D Klapper, U Konradt, A Walter & J Wolf, Gabler, Wiesbaden, pp. 103–118.

Churchill, GA, JR. 1979, 'A Paradigm for Developing Better Measures of Marketing Constructs', *Journal of Marketing Research*, vol. 16, no. 1, pp. 64–73.

Clarke, DL, Gouveia, J, Thomson, SR & Muckart, DJJ 2008, 'Applying Modern Error Theory to the Problem of Missed Injuries in Trauma', *World Journal of Surgery*, vol. 32, no. 6, pp. 1176–1182.

Clegg, C 2000, 'Sociotechnical principles for system design', *Applied Ergonomics*, vol. 31, no. 5, pp. 463–477.

Closs D. & McGarrell, E 2004, *Enhancing Security Through the Supply Chain*, IBM Center for the Business of Government Special Report Series, April 2004.

Coase, RH 1937, 'The Nature of the Firm', *Economica*, vol. 4, no. 16, pp. 386-405.

Cochran, EB, Patz, AL & Rowe, AJ 1978, 'Concurrency and Disruption in New Product Innovation', *California Management Review*, vol. 21, no. 1, pp. 21–34.

Codex Alimentarius Commission *Codex alimentarius. Food hygiene. Basic texts* 2009, World Health Organization; Food and Agriculture Organization of the United Nations, Rome.

Codex Alimentarius Commission 2013, *Codex Alimentarius. International Food Standards*. Available from: http://www.codexalimentarius.org [18 August 2013].

Cohen, MD, March, JG & Olsen, JP 1972, 'A Garbage Can Model of Organizational Choice', *Administrative Science Quarterly*, vol. 17, no. 1, pp. 1–25.

Cohen, SG & Bailey, DE 1997, 'What Makes Teams Work: Group Effectiveness Research from the Shop Floor to the Executive Suite', *Journal of Management*, vol. 23, no. 3, pp. 239–290.

Cole, S 2010, 'The regional portfolio of disruptions, protection, and disasters', *Annals of Regional Science*, vol. 44, no. 2, pp. 251–272.

Collins English dictionary 2000, Collins, London.

Cook, C, Heath, F & Thompson, RL 2000, 'A Meta-Analysis of Response Rates in Web- or Internet-Based Surveys', *Educational and Psychological Measurement*, vol. 60, no. 6, pp. 821–836.

Cook, R, Woods, D & McDonald, J 1991, *Human Performance in Anesthesia: A Corpus of Cases,* Columbus.

Cooper, KG, Reichelt, KS & Moore, J 2004, 'Quantifying Disruption through Simulation and Heuristics', *AACE International Transactions,* pp. EST.8.1-EST.8.9.

Cooper, MC & Ellram, LM 1993, 'Characteristics of Supply Chain Management and the Implications for Purchasing and Logistics Strategy', *The International Journal of Logistics Management*, vol. 4, no. 2, pp. 13–24.

Cooper, MC, Lambert, DM & Pagh, JD 1997, 'Supply Chain Management: More Than a New Name for Logistics', *The International Journal of Logistics Management*, vol. 8, no. 1, pp. 1–14.

Cordeiro, C, Machás, A & Neves, MM 2010, 'A Case Study of a Customer Satisfaction Problem: Bootstrap and Imputation Techniques' in *Handbook of Partial Least Squares,* eds V Esposito Vinzi, WW Chin, J Henseler & H Wang, Springer Berlin Heidelberg, pp. 279–287.

Cordes, P 2013, *Dynamic Capabilities in Organisations between Chaos and Order. A Meta-Analysis on Effects of Organisational Structures on the Evolvement of Knowledge-based Dynamic Capabilities,* Palgrave Macmillan.

Coronado Mondragon, A, Coronado Mondragon, E & Coronado Mondragon, C 2009, 'Innovative Information and Communication Technology for Logistics: the case of road transportation feeding port operations and Direct Short Range Communication Technology' in *Supply Chain Management and Knowledge Management,* eds A Dwivedi & T Butcher, Palgrave Macmillan, Basingstoke, pp. 254–268.

Coton, M, Denis, C, Cadot, P & Coton, E 2011, 'Biodiversity and characterization of aerobic spore-forming bacteria in surimi seafood products', *Food Microbiology*, vol. 28, no. 2, pp. 252–260.

Coughlan, A & Narasimhan, C 1992, 'An Empirical Analysis of Sales-Force Compensation Plans', *The Journal of Business*, vol. 65, no. 1, pp. 93–121.

Cover, TM 1991, *Elements of Information Theory,* Wiley-Interscience.

Craighead, CW, Blackhurst, J, Rungtusanatham, M & Handfield, RB 2007, 'The Severity of Supply Chain Disruptions: Design Characteristics and Mitigation Capabilities', *Decision Science*, vol. 38, no. 1, pp. 131–156.

Curado, E & Tsallis, C 1991, 'Generalized statistical mechanics: connection with thermodynamics', *Journal of Physics A: Mathematical and General*, vol. 24, no. 2, pp. L69-L72.

Custódio, A & Oliveira, R 2006, 'Redesigning distribution operations: a case study on integrating inventory management and vehicle routes design', *International Journal of Logistics*, vol. 9, no. 2, pp. 169–187.

Czaja, S & Nair, S 2006, 'Human Factors Engineering and Systems Design' in *Handbook of human factors and ergonomics,* ed G Salvendy, John Wiley, Hoboken, N.J, pp. 32–49.

Danish Food Information 2012, *LanguaL™ - the International Framework for Food Description*. Available from: http://www.langual.org/ [12 March 2013].

David, RJ & Han, S 2004, 'A Systematic Assessment of the Empirical Support for Transaction Cost Economics', *Strategic Management Journal*, vol. 25, no. 1, pp. 39–58.

Davidson, R & MacKinnon, JG 2000, 'Bootstrap tests: how many bootstraps?', *Econometric Reviews*, vol. 19, no. 1, pp. 55–68.

Dean, JM 1995, 'Market Disruption and the Incidence of VERS under the MFA', *Review of Economics & Statistics*, vol. 77, no. 2, pp. 383–388.

Dekker, S 2003, 'Illusions of explanation: a critical essay on error classification', *International Journal of Aviation Psychology*, vol. 13, no. 2, pp. 95–106.

Dempster, AP, Laird, NM & Rubin, DB 1977, 'Maximum Likelihood from Incomplete Data via the EM Algorithm', *Journal of the Royal Statistical Society. Series B (Methodological)*, vol. 39, no. 1, pp. 1–38.

Demski, JS & Feltham, GA 1978, 'Economic Incentives in Budgetary Control Systems', *The Accounting Review*, vol. 53, no. 2, pp. 336–359.

Der Spiegel, 'Futtermittelindustrie gegen Kontrollen', *Der Spiegel,* p. 62. Available from: http://wissen.spiegel.de/wissen/image/show.html?did=79973986&aref=image049/2011/08/13/CO-SP-2011-033-0062-0062.PDF&thumb=false [04 January 2012].

Desai, VM 2011, 'Mass Media and Massive Failures: Determining Organizational Efforts to Defend Field Legitimacy Following Crises', *Academy of Management Journal*, vol. 54, no. 2, pp. 263–278.

Dethloff, J 2001, 'Vehicle routing and reverse logistics: the vehicle routing problem with simultaneous delivery and pick-up', *OR Spektrum*, no. 23, pp. 79–96.

Dhillon, B 2007, *Human reliability and error in transportation Systems,* Springer, London.

Diamantopoulos, A & Siguaw, JA 2006, 'Formative Versus Reflective Indicators in Organizational Measure Development: A Comparison and Empirical Illustration', *British Journal of Management*, vol. 17, no. 4, pp. 263-282.

Diamantopoulos, A & Winklhofer, H 2001, 'Index Construction with Formative Indicators: An Alternative to Scale Development', *Journal of Marketing Research*, vol. 38, no. 2, pp. 269–277.

Dian-Qing Yang, Xiang-Ming Wang & Hui Wan 2010, 'Optimizing Manufacturing Conditions for Durable Composite Panels with Eastern White Cedar and Aspen Strands', *Forest Products Journal*, vol. 60, no. 5, pp. 460–464.

Diekmann, A 2002, *Empirische Sozialforschung. Grundlagen, Methoden, Anwendungen,* Rowohlt-Taschenbuch-Verl, Reinbek bei Hamburg.

Dietrich, E & Schulze, A 2005, *Statistische Verfahren zur Maschinen- und Prozessqualifikation. Mit 61 Tabellen,* Hanser, München [et al.].

Dolan, C & Humphrey, J 2000, 'Governance and trade in fresh vegetables. The impact of UK supermarkets on the African horticulture industry', *The journal of development studies*, vol. 37, no. 2, pp. 147–176.

Dorndorf, U, Jaehn, F, Chen Lin, Hui Ma & Pesch, E 2007, 'Disruption management in flight gate scheduling', *Statistica Neerlandica*, vol. 61, no. 1, pp. 92–114.

Dörner, D 1992, *Die Logik des Misslingens. Strategisches Denken in komplexen Situationen,* Rowohlt, Reinbek bei Hamburg.

Douglas J. Thomas & Paul M. Griffin 1996, 'Coordinated supply chain management', *European Journal of Operational Research*, vol. 94, no. 1, pp. 1–15.

Drewry Shipping Consultants 1990, *Reefer container market. Progress in the containerised transport of perishable commodities 1987-2000,* Drewry Shipping Consultants, London.

Dreyer, A 1975, *Nutzwertanalyse als Entscheidungsmodell bei mehrfacher Zielsetzung. Eine Untersuchung zu Grundlagen und Durchführung der Nutzwertanalyse*. Thesis, University of Hamburg, Hamburg.

Driesen, DM & Popp, D 2010, 'Meaningful Technology Transfer for Climate Disruption', *Journal of International Affairs*, vol. 64, no. 1, pp. 1–15.

Droge, C, Vickery, SK & Jacobs, MA 2012, 'Does supply chain integration mediate the relationships between product/process strategy and service performance? An empirical study', *International Journal of Production Economics*, vol. 137, no. 2, pp. 250–262.

Duarte, PA & Raposo, ML 2010, 'A PLS Model to Study Brand Preference: An Application to the Mobile Phone Market' in *Handbook of Partial Least Squares,* eds V Esposito Vinzi, WW Chin, J Henseler & H Wang, Springer Berlin Heidelberg, pp. 449–485.

Dunn, SC, Seaker, RF & Waller, MA 1994, 'Latent variables in business logistics research: scale development and validation', *Journal of Business Logistics*, vol. 15, no. 2, pp. 145–172.

Ebers, M & Gotsch, W 2006, 'Institutionenökonomische Theorien der Organisation' in *Organisationstheorien,* eds A Kieser & M Ebers, Kohlhammer, Stuttgart, pp. 247–308.

Eisenführ, F & Weber, M 2010, *Rationales Entscheiden,* Springer, Berlin [et al.].

Eisenhardt, KM 1989, 'Agency Theory: An Assessment and Review', *The Academy of Management Review*, vol. 14, no. 1, pp. 57–74.

Elifoglu, IH, Fitzsimons, AP & Lange, GA 2010, 'SEC Proposes Rules to Better Track Market Trades, Monitor Market Activity and Prevent Market Disruptions', *Bank Accounting & Finance (08943958)*, vol. 23, no. 5, pp. 41–45.

Elkins, D, Handfield, RB, Blackhurst, J & Craighead, CW 2005, '18 ways to guard against disruption', *Supply Chain Management Review, V. 6, NO. 4 (JULY/AUG. 2002), P. 52-61*, vol. 9, no. 1, pp. 46–53.

Elliott, MA 1941, 'Comment', *American Sociological Review*, vol. 6, no. 3, pp. 316–319.

El-Sharif, Y 2011, 'Dioxin Fund: der nächste Skandal kommt bestimmt', *SpiegelOnline* 14 January. Available from: http://www.spiegel.de/wirtschaft/soziales/0,1518,739480,00.html [05 January 2012].

Embrey, S, Remais, JV & Hess, J 2012, 'Climate Change and Ecosystem Disruption: The Health Impacts of the North American Rocky Mountain Pine Beetle Infestation', *American Journal of Public Health*, vol. 102, no. 5, pp. 818–827.

Enders, CK 2010, *Applied missing data analysis,* Guilford Press, New York.

Engelhardt, D 2005, *Administrativ-handelsrechtliche Vorgaben bei der Handhabung von Getreide und die dafür erforderlichen technologisch-logistischen Maßnahmen und bautechnischen Ausstattungen für den Getreideumschlag,* Gießen.

Engle, P 2011, 'The other side of lean', *Industrial Engineer: IE*, vol. 43, no. 7, p. 20.

Engström, R & Carlsson-Kanyama, A 2004, 'Food losses in food service institutions Examples from Sweden', *Food Policy,* vol. 29, no. 3, pp. 203–213.

Esposito Vinzi, V, Trinchera, L & Amato, S 2010, 'PLS Path Modeling: From Foundations to Recent Developments and Open Issues for Model Assessment and Improvement' in *Handbook of Partial Least Squares,* eds V Esposito Vinzi, WW Chin, J Henseler & H Wang, Springer Berlin Heidelberg, pp. 47–82.

European Commission *Regulation (EC) No 178/2002 of the European Parliament and of the Council of 28 January2002 laying down the general principles and requirements of food law, establishing the European Food Safety Authority and laying down procedures in matters of food safety* 2002.

European Commission *Regulation (EC) No 852/2004 of the European Parliament and of the Council of 29 April 2004 on the hygiene of foodstuffs* 2004.

Fama, E 1980, 'Agency Problems and the Theory of the Firm', *The Journal of Political Economy,* vol. 88, no. 2, pp. 288–307.

Fearne, A 1998, 'The evolution of partnerships in the meat supply chain: insights from the British beef industry', *Supply Chain Management: An International Journal*, vol. 3, no. 4, pp. 214–231.

Fearne, A & Hughes, D 2000, 'Success factors in the fresh produce supply chain: insights from the UK', *Supply Chain Management: An International Journal*, vol. 4, no. 3.

Festinger, L 1962, *A theory of cognitive dissonance,* Stanford Univ. Pr, Stanford/Calif.

Flin, R, O'Connor, P & Mearns, K 2002, 'Crew resource management: improving team work in high reliability industries', *Team Performance Management: An International Journal*, vol. 8, 3/4, pp. 68–78.

Fornell, C & Bookstein, FL 1982, 'Two Structural Equation Models: LISREL and PLS Applied to Consumer Exit-Voice Theory', *Journal of Marketing Research*, vol. 19, no. 4, pp. 440–452.

Fornell, C & Larcker, DF 1981, 'Evaluating Structural Equation Models with Unobservable Variables and Measurement Error', *Journal of Marketing Research*, vol. 18, no. 1, pp. 39–50.

Foss, NJ & Laursen, K 2005, 'Performance pay, delegation and multitasking under uncertainty and innovativeness: An empirical investigation', *Journal of Economic Behavior & Organization*, vol. 58, no. 2, pp. 246–276.

Foster, J & Hölzl, W 2004, *Applied evolutionary economics and complex systems,* Edward Elgar, Cheltenham, UK, Northhampton, MA.

Freight Best Practice 2006, *Key Performance Indicators for the Food Supply Chain*, UK. Available from: www.freightbestpractice.org.uk/kpis-for-food-supply-chain [02 December 2013].

Frese, E 1992, *Organisationstheorie. Historische Entwicklung, Ansätze, Perspektiven,* Gabler, Wiesbaden.

Frese, E & Beecken, T 1995, 'Dezentrale Unternehmensstrukturen' in *Handbuch Unternehmungsführung. Konzepte - Instrumente - Schnittstellen,* eds H Corsten & M Reiß, Gabler, Wiesbaden, pp. 133–145.

Frese, E, Graumann, M & Theuvsen, L 2012, *Grundlagen der Organisation. Entscheidungsorientiertes Konzept der Organisationsgestaltung,* Gabler, Wiesbaden.

Fricker, RD & Schonlau, M 2002, 'Advantages and Disadvantages of Internet Research Surveys: Evidence from the Literature', *Field Methods*, vol. 14, no. 4, pp. 347–367.

Frith, J 1991, *The transport of perishable foodstuffs,* Shipowners Refrigerated Cargo Research Association, revised ed.

Fritz, M & Schiefer, G 2009, 'Tracking, tracing, and business process interests in food commodities: A multi-level decision complexity', *International Journal of Production Economics*, vol. 117, no. 2, pp. 317–329.

Fritz, W 1995, *Marketing-Management und Unternehmenserfolg. Grundlagen und Ergebnisse einer empirischen Untersuchung,* Schäffer-Poeschel, Stuttgart.

Fulponi, L 2006, 'Private voluntary standards in the food system: The perspective of major food retailers in OECD countries', *Food Policy*, vol. 31, no. 1.

Furubotn, E & Pejovich, S 1972, 'Property Rights and Economic Theory: A Survey of Recent Literature', *Journal of Economic Literature*, vol. 10, no. 4.

Fynes, B, Voss, C & Burca, S de 2005, 'The impact of supply chain relationship quality on quality performance', *International Journal of Production Economics*, vol. 96, no. 3, pp. 339–354.

Gang Yu, Gao Song, Argüello, M, McCowan, SM & White, A 2003, 'A New Era for Crew Recovery at Continental Airlines', *Interfaces*, vol. 33, no. 1, pp. 5–22.

Gaonkar, R & Viswanadham, N 2004, 'A conceptual and analytical framework for the management of risk in supply chains'. *Robotics and Automation, 2004. Proceedings. ICRA '04. 2004 IEEE International Conference on, title=A conceptual and analytical framework for the management of risk in supply chains,* pp. 2699–2704.

Geary, S, Childerhouse P & Towill, D 2002, 'Uncertainty and the Seamless Supply Chain', *Supply Chain Management Review, V. 6, NO. 4 (JULY/AUG. 2002), P. 52-61*, vol. 6, no. 4, pp. 52–61.

Gefen, D & Straub, D 2005, 'A practical guide to factorial validity using PLS-Graph: Tutorial and annotated example', *Communications of the Association for Information Systems*, vol. 16, no. 1, p. 109.

Geiger, GR 1953, 'Dewey and the Experimental Attitude in American Culture', *American Journal of Economics & Sociology*, vol. 12, no. 2, pp. 111–121.

Georgiadis, P, Vlachos, D & Iakovou, E 2005, 'A system dynamics modeling framework for the strategic supply chain management of food chains', *Journal of Food Engineering*, vol. 70, no. 3, pp. 351–364.

Gerbing, DW & Anderson, JC 1988, 'An Updated Paradigm for Scale Development Incorporating Unidimensionality and Its Assessment', *Journal of Marketing Research*, vol. 25, no. 2, pp. 186–192.

Germanischer Lloyd *Cool Chain Quality Indicator Standard (CCQI)* 2009.

Giaccotto, BC, Santerre, RE & Vernon JA 2005, 'Drug Prices and Research and Development Investment Behavior in the Pharmaceutical Industry', *Journal of Law and Economics*, vol. 48, no. 1, pp. 195–214.

Glick, R & Taylor, AM 2010, 'Collateral Damage: Trade Disruption and the Economic Impact of War', *Review of Economics & Statistics*, vol. 92, no. 1, pp. 102–127.

Gordon, LA & Narayanan, VK 1984, 'Management accounting systems, perceived environmental uncertainty and organization structure: An empirical investigation', *Accounting, Organizations and Society*, vol. 9, no. 1, pp. 33–47.

Gorton, M, Dumitrashko, M & White, J 2006, 'Overcoming supply chain failure in the agrifood sector: A case study from Moldova', *Food Policy*, vol. 31, no. 1, pp. 90–103.

Götz, O & Liehr-Gobbers, K 2004, 'Analyse von Strukturgleichungsmodellen mit Hilfe der Partial-Least-Squares(PLS)-Methode', *Die Betriebswirtschaft*, vol. 64, no. 6, pp. 714–738.

Götz, O, Liehr-Gobbers, K & Krafft, M 2010, 'Evaluation of Structural Equation Models Using the Partial Least Squares (PLS) Approach' in *Handbook of Partial Least Squares,* eds V Esposito Vinzi, WW Chin, J Henseler & H Wang, Springer Berlin Heidelberg, pp. 691-711.

Götze, U 2006, *Investitionsrechnung. Modelle und Analysen zur Beurteilung von Investitionsvorhaben,* Springer, Berlin [et al.].

Grandori, A & Soda, G 2006, 'A Relational Approach to Organization Design', *Industry & Innovation*, vol. 13, no. 2, pp. 151–172.

Greving, B 2009, 'Messen und Skalieren von Sachverhalten' in *Methodik der empirischen Forschung,* eds S Albers, D Klapper, U Konradt, A Walter & J Wolf, Gabler, Wiesbaden, pp. 65–78.

Grochla, E & Welge, MK 1978, 'Zur Problematik der Effizienzbestimmung von Organisationsstrukturen' in *Elemente der organisatorischen Gestaltung,* ed E Grochla, Rowohlt, Reinbek bei Hamburg, pp. 191–210.

Grochla, E (ed.) 1978, *Elemente der organisatorischen Gestaltung,* Rowohlt, Reinbek bei Hamburg.

Gross, E 1953, 'Some Functional Consequences of Primary Controls in Formal Work Organizations', *American Sociological Review*, vol. 18, no. 4, pp. 368–373.

Grube, C, Schaper, N & Graf, BM 2002, 'Man at Risk', *Der Anaesthesist*, vol. 51, no. 4, pp. 239–247.

Gruner, R & Homans, GC 1978, *Theorie der sozialen Gruppe,* Westdt. Verl, Opladen.

Gupta, G, Yan, N & Feng, MW 2011, 'Effects of Pressing Temperature and Particle Size on Bark Board Properties Made from Beetle-Infested Lodgepole Pine (Pinus contorta) Barks', *Forest Products Journal*, vol. 61, no. 6, pp. 478–488.

Gurau, C 2007, 'The Ethics of Online Surveys' in *Handbook of research on electronic surveys and measurements,* eds RA Reynolds, R Woods & JD Baker, Idea Group Reference, Hershey, PA, pp. 112–119.

Gustavsson, J, Cederberg, C, Sonesson, U, van Otterdijk, R & Meybeck, A 2011, *Global food losses and food waste,* Rome.

Hackman, J 1970, 'Tasks and task performance in research on stress' in *Social and psychological factors in stress,* ed JE McGrath, Holt, Rinehart and Winston, New York [et al.], pp. 202–237.

Hage, J, Aiken, M & Marrett, CB 1971, 'Organization Structure and Communications', *American Sociological Review*, vol. 36, no. 5, pp. 860–871.

Hahn, P & Pichhardt, K 2008, *Lebensmittelsicherheit. Haftung, Rückruf, Rückverfolgbarkeit,* Behr, Hamburg.

Hair, JF, Hult, GTM, Ringle, CM & Sarstedt, M 2014, *A primer on partial least squares structural equations modeling (PLS-SEM),* Sage, Los Angeles.

Hair, JF, Sarstedt, M, Ringle, CM & Mena, J 2012, 'An assessment of the use of partial least squares structural equation modeling in marketing research', *Journal of the Academy of Marketing Science*, vol. 40, no. 3, pp. 414-433.

Hale, T. & Moberg, C, R, 2005, 'Improving supply chain disaster preparedness: A decision process for secure site location', *International Journal of Physical Distribution & Logistics Management*, vol. 35, no. 3, pp. 195–207.

Hall, RE 1997, 'Potential disruption from the move to a consumption tax', *American Economic Review*, vol. 87, no. 2, p. 147.

Hall, RH 2002, *Organizations. Structures, processes, and outcomes,* Prentice Hall, Upper Saddle River, N.J.

Halsband, E & Stölzle, W 2005, 'Das Supply-Chain Operations Reference (SCOR)-Modell', *Controlling*, vol. 17, 8/9, pp. 541 OP 543.

Handfield, RB & Nichols, EL 2008, *Introduction to supply chain management,* Prentice Hall, Harlow.

Hardman, P, Darroch, M & Ortmann, G 2002, 'Improving cooperation to make the South African fresh apple export value chain more competitive', *Journal on Chain and Network Science*, vol. 2, no. 1, pp. 61–72.

Harland, CM 1996, 'Supply Chain Management: Relationships, Chains and Networks', *British Journal of Management*, vol. 7, pp. S63-S80.

Hart, O & Moore, J 1990, 'Property Rights and the Nature of the Firm', *Journal of Political Economy*, vol. 98, no. 6, pp. 1119–1158.

Hasselmann, G 2008, 'Temperaturgeführte Transporte' in *Handbuch Logistik,* eds D Arnold, H Isermann, A Kuhn, H Tempelmeier & K Furmans, Springer, Berlin [et al.], pp. 570–579.

Hayek, FA von 1983, *Knowledge, evolution, and society,* ASI (Research), London.

Hayes, AF 2009, 'Beyond Baron and Kenny: Statistical Mediation Analysis in the New Millennium', *Communication Monographs*, vol. 76, no. 4, pp. 408–420.

Hegazy, SS & Aref, IM 2010, 'Suitability of Some Fast-Growing Trees and Date Palm Fronds for Particleboard Production', *Forest Products Journal*, vol. 60, 7/8, pp. 599–604.

Heide, JB & John, G 1988, 'The role of dependence balancing in safeguarding transaction-specific assets in conventional channels', *Journal of marketing / American Marketing Association*, vol. 52, no. 1, pp. 20–35.

Heide, JB & John, G 1992, 'Do Norms Matter in Marketing Relationships?', *The Journal of Marketing*, vol. 56, no. 2, pp. 32–44.

Held, M & Nutzinger, HG 2006, 'Perspektiven einer Allgemeinen Institutionenökonomik' in *Ökonomischer und soziologischer Institutionalismus: interdisziplinäre Beiträge und Perspektiven der Institutionentheorie und -analyse,* eds M Schmid & A Maurer, Metropolis-Verl, Marburg, pp. 117–137.

Helderman, F, Manoch, IJ, Breeuwer, M, Kose, U, Schouten, O, Sambeek, MRM, Poldermans, D, Pattynama, PTM, Wisselink, W, Steen, AFW & Krams, R 2008, 'A numerical model to predict abdominal aortic aneurysm expansion based on local wall stress and stiffness', *Medical & Biological Engineering & Computing*, vol. 46, no. 11, pp. 1121–1127.

Helmreich, R 2000, 'Culture and error in space: Implications from analog environments', *Aviation, Space, and Environmental Medicine*, vol. 71, 9-11, pp. 133–139.

Helmreich, R, Klinect, J & Wilhelm, J 2001, *System Safety and Threat and Error Management: The Line Operational Safety Audit (LOSA),* Austin.

Hendricks, K & Singhal, V 2005a, 'Association between Supply Chain Glitches and Operating Performance', *Management Science*, vol. 51, no. 5, pp. 695–711.

Hendricks, KB & Singhal, VR 2003, 'The effect of supply chain glitches on shareholder wealth', *Journal of Operations Management*, vol. 21, no. 5, pp. 501–522.

Hendricks, KB & Singhal, VR 2005b, 'An Empirical Analysis of the Effect of Supply Chain Disruptions on Long-Run Stock Price Performance and Equity Risk of the Firm', *Production & Operations Management*, vol. 14, no. 1, pp. 35–52.

Hendricks, KB & Singhal, VR 2008, 'The effect of supply chain disruptions on shareholder value', *Total Quality Management & Business Excellence*, vol. 19, 7/8, pp. 777–791.

Hendrickx, M, Ludikhuyze, L, van den Broeck, I & Weemaes, C 1998, 'Effects of high pressure on enzymes related to food quality', *Trends in Food Science & Technology*, vol. 9, no. 5, pp. 197–203.

Hennessy, JL & Patterson, DA 1998, *Computer organization and design. The hardware/software interface,* Morgan Kaufmann Publishers, San Francisco, Calif.

Hennig-Thurau, T, Walsh, G & Schrader, U 2004, 'VHB-JOURQUAL: Ein Ranking von betriebswirtschaftlich-relevanten Zeitschriften auf der Grundlage von Expertenurteilen', *Zeitschrift für betriebswirtschaftliche Forschung*, vol. 56, no. 9, pp. 520-545.

Herzberg, F, Mausner, B & Snyderman, BB 1959, *The motivation to work,* Wiley, New York [et al.].

Hickson, DJ, Pugh, DS & Pheysey, DC 1969, 'Operations Technology and Organization Structure: An Empirical Reappraisal', *Administrative Science Quarterly*, vol. 14, no. 3, pp. 378–397.

Hill, C 1990, 'Cooperation, Opportunism, and the Invisible Hand: Implications for Transaction Cost Theory', *The Academy of Management Review*, vol. 15, no. 3, pp. 500–513.

Hill, W, Fehlbaum, R & Ulrich, P 1994, *Organisationslehre 1:. Ziele, Instrumente und Bedingungen der Organisation sozialer Systeme,* Haupt, Bern [et al.].

Ho, C, Chi, Y & Tai, Y 2005, 'A Structural Approach to Measuring Uncertainty in Supply Chains', *International Journal of Electronic Commerce*, vol. 9, no. 3, pp. 91–114.

Hobbs, J, Fearne, A & Spriggs, J 2002, 'Incentive structures for food safety and quality assurance: an international comparison', *Food Control*, vol. 13, no. 2, pp. 77–81.

Hobbs, JE 1996, 'A transaction cost approach to supply chain management', *Supply Chain Management: An International Journal*, vol. 1, no. 2, pp. 15–27.

Hoffmann, E 1980, 'Defining information: An analysis of the information content of documents', *Information Processing & Management*, vol. 16, no. 6, pp. 291–304.

Hofmann, DA & Frese, M 2011, 'Errors, Error Taxonomies, Error Prevention, and Error Management: Laying the Groundwork for Discussing Errors in Organizations' in *Errors in organizations,* eds DA Hofmann & M Frese, Psychology Press, New York, pp. 1–43.

Hofmann, M 2008, *Lernen aus Katastrophen. Nach den Unfällen von Harrisburg, Seveso und Sandoz,* thesis, Free University of Berlin, Berlin.

Holden, RR & Jackson, DN 1979, 'Item subtlety and face validity in personality assessment', *Journal of Consulting and Clinical Psychology*, vol. 47, no. 3, pp. 459–468.

Holl, A, Pardo, R & Rama, R 2010, 'Just-in-Time Manufacturing Systems, Subcontracting and Geographic Proximity', *Regional Studies*, vol. 44, no. 5, pp. 519–533.

Hollnagel, E (ed.) 2008, *Resilience engineering. Concepts and precepts,* Ashgate, Aldershot [et al.].

Holt, JB 1940, 'Holiness Religion: Cultural Shock and Social Reorganization', *American Sociological Review*, vol. 5, no. 5, pp. 740–747.

Holt, JE, Schoorl, D & Muirhead, IF, 'Post-harvest quality control strategies for fruit and vegetables', *Agricultural Systems*, vol. 10, no. 1, pp. 21–37.

Homans, GC & Merton, RK 1961, *Social behavior. Its elementary forms,* Harcourt, Brace, New York.

Houlihan, JB 1987, 'International Supply Chain Management', *International Journal of Physical Distribution & Logistics Management*, vol. 17, no. 2, pp. 51–66.

Huang, H, Chou, Y & Chang, S 2009, 'A dynamic system model for proactive control of dynamic events in full-load states of manufacturing chains', *International Journal of Production Research*, vol. 47, no. 9, pp. 2485–2506.

Huber, N & Michael, K 2007, 'Vendor Perceptions of How RFID can Minimize Product Shrinkage in the Retail Supply Chain'. *RFID Eurasia, 2007 1st Annual,* pp. 1–6.

Hulland, J 1999, 'Use of partial least squares (PLS) in strategic management research: a review of four recent studies', *Strategic Management Journal*, vol. 20, no. 2, pp. 195-204.

Hülsmann, M 2002, *Management im Orientierungsdilemma,* Dt. Univ.-Verl, Wiesbaden, Bremen.

Hülsmann, M 2005, 'Ad-hoc-Krise - eine begriffliche Annäherung' in *Management von Ad-hoc-Krisen. Grundlagen, Strategien, Erfolgsfaktoren,* eds C Burmann, J Freiling & M Hülsmann, Gabler, Wiesbaden, pp. 35–57.

Hülsmann, M & Brenner, V 2011, *Causes and effects of cold chain ruptures. Performance of fragmented versus integrated cold chains,* Jacobs Univ., School of Engineering and Science, Internat. Logistics, Systems Management, Bremen.

Hülsmann, M & Grapp, J 2006, 'Monitoring of Autonomous Cooperating Logistic Processes in International Supply Networks'. *Proceedings of 11th International Symposium on Logistics,* eds K Pawar & et. al., pp. 113–120.

Hülsmann, M, Grapp, J & Li, Y 2008, 'Strategic adaptivity in global supply chains—Competitive advantage by autonomous cooperation. Special Section on Competitive Advantage through Global Supply Chains', *International Journal of Production Economics*, vol. 114, no. 1, pp. 14–26.

Hülsmann, M, Scholz-Reiter, B, Austerschulte, L, Beer, C de & Grapp, J 2007, 'Autonomous Cooperation - a Capable Way to Cope with External Risks in International Supply Networks?'. *Proceedings of the 12th International Symposium on Logistics (12th ISL),* eds K Pawar, C Lalwani, J de Carvalho & M Muffatto, Loughborough, United Kingdom.

Hülsmann, M, Windt, K, Wycisk, C, Philipp, T, Grapp, J & Böse, F 2006, 'Identification, evaluation and measuring of autonomous cooperation in supply networks and other logistic systems'. *Proceedings of the 4th International Logistics and Supply Chain Congress,* ed T Baltacioglu, pp. 216–255.

Hunt, SD, Sparkman, RD, JR. & Wilcox, JB 1982, 'The Pretest in Survey Research: Issues and Preliminary Findings', *Journal of Marketing Research*, vol. 19, no. 2, pp. 269–273.

Hwang, H 2002, 'Design of supply-chain logistics system considering service level', *Computers & Industrial Engineering*, vol. 43, 1–2, pp. 283–297.

Iakovou, E, Vlachos, D & Xanthopoulos, A 2010, 'A stochastic inventory management model for a dual sourcing supply chain with disruptions', *International Journal of Systems Science*, vol. 41, no. 3, pp. 315–324.

Ibbs, W & Liu, M 2005, 'System Dynamic Modeling of Delay and Disruption Claims', *Cost Engineering*, vol. 47, no. 6, pp. 12–15.

International Food Standard *IFS Logistics* 2012.

Imsirovic, B 2009, *Logistikprozesse für temperaturgeführte Lebensmittel,* Igel-Verl, Hamburg.

Jaffee, S & Masakure, O 2005, 'Strategic use of private standards to enhance international competitiveness: Vegetable exports from Kenya and elsewhere', *Food Policy*, vol. 30, no. 3, pp. 316–333.

Jain, R, Sahu, AK, Tewari, S, Malik, N, Singh, S, Khare, S & Bhatia, R 2003, 'Cold chain monitoring of OPV at transit levels in India: correlation of VVM and potency status', *Biologicals*, vol. 31, no. 4, pp. 237–244.

James, LR & Jones, AP 1980, 'Perceived Job Characteristics and Job Satisfaction: an Examination of Reciprical Causation', *Personnel Psychology*, vol. 33, no. 1, pp. 97–135.

Jansen, K, Corley, K & Jansen, B 2007, 'E-Survey Methodology' in *Handbook of research on electronic surveys and measurements,* eds RA Reynolds, R Woods & JD Baker, Idea Group Reference, Hershey, PA, pp. 1–8.

Janssen, J 2012, *Statistische Datenanalyse mit SPSS. Eine anwendungsorientierte Einführung in das Basissystem und das Modul Exakte Tests,* Springer.

Jarvis, CB, MacKenzie, SB & Podsakoff, PM 2003, 'A Critical Review of Construct Indicators and Measurement Model Misspecification in Marketing and Consumer Research', *Journal of Consumer Research*, vol. 30, no. 2, pp. 199–218.

Jedermann, R, Behrens, C, Westphal, D & Lang, W 2006, 'Applying autonomous sensor systems in logistics—Combining sensor networks, RFIDs and software agents', *Sensors and Actuators A: Physical*, vol. 132, no. 1, pp. 370–375.

Jennings, DF & Seaman, SL 1994, 'High and Low Levels of Organizational Adaptation: An Empirical Analysis of Strategy, Structure, and Performance', *Strategic Management Journal*, vol. 15, no. 6, pp. 459–475.

Jensen, M & Meckling, W 1976, 'Theory of the firm: Managerial behavior, agency costs and ownership structure', *Journal of Financial Economics*, vol. 3, no. 4, pp. 305–360.

Jetzke, S 2007, *Grundlagen der modernen Logistik. Methoden und Lösungen,* Carl Hanser Verlag, München.

John, G & Weitz, B 1988, 'Forward Integration into Distribution: An Empirical Test of Transaction Cost Analysis', *Journal of Law, Economics, & Organization*, vol. 4, no. 2, pp. 337–355.

John, G & Weitz, B 1989, 'Salesforce Compensation: An Empirical Investigation of Factors Related to Use of Salary versus Incentive Compensation', *Journal of Marketing Research*, vol. 26, no. 1, pp. 1–14.

Jones, DM, Macken, WJ & Mosdell, NA 1997, 'The role of habituation in the disruption of recall.', *British Journal of Psychology*, vol. 88, no. 4, p. 549.

Jüttner, U 2005, 'Supply chain risk management: Understanding the business requirements from a practitioner perspective', *International Journal of Logistics Management, The*, vol. 16, no. 1, pp. 120–141.

Juwan Jin & Chunping Dai 2010, 'Characterizing Variability of Commercial Oriented Strandboard: Bending Properties', *Forest Products Journal*, vol. 60, no. 4, pp. 373–381.

Kader, A 2005, 'Increasing Food Availability by Reducing Postharvest Losses of Fresh Produce'. *Proceedings of the Fifth International Symposium,* eds F Mencarelli & P Tonutti, pp. 2169–2176.

Kerr, S & Jermier, JM 1978, 'Substitutes for leadership: Their meaning and measurement', *Organizational Behavior and Human Performance*, vol. 22, no. 3, pp. 375–403.

Ketzenberg, M & Ferguson, ME 2008, 'Managing Slow-Moving Perishables in the Grocery Industry', *Production and Operations Management*, vol. 17, no. 5, pp. 513–521.

Kieser, A & Ebers, M (eds.) 2006, *Organisationstheorien,* Kohlhammer, Stuttgart.

Kieser, A & Walgenbach, P 2007, *Organisation,* Schäffer-Poeschel, Stuttgart.

Kim, S, Lewis, M & White, C 2005, 'Optimal Vehicle Routing With Real-Time Traffic Information', *IEEE Transactions on Intelligent Transportation Systems*, vol. 6, no. 2, pp. 178–188.

Kingdon, JW 1995, *Agendas, alternatives, and public policies,* Longman, New York.

Kjellen, U 2000, *Prevention of accidents through experience feedback,* Taylor & Francis, London; New York.

Kleinbaum, DG, Kupper, LL, Muller, KE & Kleinbaum, DG 2007, *Applied regression analysis and other multivariable methods,* Brooks/Cole, Australia, Belmont, CA.

Kleindorfer, PR & Saad, GH 2005, 'Managing Disruption Risks in Supply Chains', *Production & Operations Management*, vol. 14, no. 1, pp. 53–68.

Kletz, T 1998, *What went wrong? Case histories of process plant disasters,* Gulf Publishing, Houston, Tex.

Klinect, J, Wilhelm, J & Helmreich, R 1999, 'Threat and error management: data from Line Operations Safety Audits'. *Proceedings of the Tenth International Symposium on Aviation Psychology,* ed OTOSU Columbus, pp. 683–688.

Kornmeier, M 2007, *Wissenschaftstheorie und wissenschaftliches Arbeiten. Eine Einführung für Wirtschaftswissenschaftler : mit 3 Tabellen,* Physica-Verl., Heidelberg.

Kosiol, E 1962, *Organisation der Unternehmung,* Gabler, Wiesbaden.

Kosiol, E 1964, 'Betriebswirtschaftslehre und Unternehmensforschung. Eine Untersuchung ihrer Standorte und Beziehungen auf wissenschaftstheoretischer Grundlage', *Zeitschrift für Betriebswirtschaft*, vol. 34, no. 12, pp. 743–762.

Kosiol, E 1971, *Organisation der Unternehmung,* Gabler, Wiesbaden.

Kosiol, E 1978, 'Aufgabenanalyse und Aufgabensynthese' in *Elemente der organisatorischen Gestaltung,* ed E Grochla, Rowohlt, Reinbek bei Hamburg, pp. 66–84.

Kovács, G & Tatham, P 2009, 'Responding to Disruptions in the Supply Network - From Dormant to Action', *Journal of Business Logistics*, vol. 30, no. 2, pp. 215–229.

Koyanagi, J, Kiyota, G, Kamiya, T & Kawada, H 2004, 'Prediction of creep rupture in unidirectional composite: Creep rupture model with interfacial debonding and its propagation', *Advanced Composite Materials*, vol. 13, 3-4, pp. 199–213.

Krippendorff, K 1986, *Information theory. Structural models for qualitative data,* Sage, Beverly Hills, Calif. [et al.].

Kromrey, H 2009, *Empirische Sozialforschung. Modelle und Methoden der standardisierten Datenerhebung und Datenauswertung,* Lucius & Lucius, Stuttgart.

Krystek, U 1980, 'Organisatorische Möglichkeiten des Krisen-Managements', *Zeitung für Organisation*, vol. 49, no. 2, pp. 63–71.

Krystek, U 1987, *Unternehmungskrisen. Beschreibung, Vermeidung und Bewältigung überlebenskritischer Prozesse in Unternehmungen,* Gabler, Wiesbaden.

Kuckartz, U, Ebert, T, Rädiker, S & Stefer, C 2009, 'Evaluation online. Internetgestützte Befragung in der Praxis', *Evaluation online*.

Küppers, M 2002a, 'Die Glieder der Kühlkette' in *Handbuch temperaturgeführte Logistik,* eds J Peilnsteiner & G Truszkiewitz, Behr, Hamburg, pp. 19–21.

Küppers, M 2002b, 'Grundsätze der Kühl- und Tiefkühllogistik' in *Handbuch temperaturgeführte Logistik,* eds J Peilnsteiner & G Truszkiewitz, Behr, Hamburg, pp. 15–18.

Kwasniewski, N 2011, 'Hohe Verluste: Bauern fordern Millionen für Ehec-Schäden', *SpiegelOnline* 19 July. Available from: http://www.spiegel.de/wirtschaft/soziales/0,1518,775379,00.html [05 January 2012].

Laatz, W 1993, *Empirische Methoden. Ein Lehrbuch für Sozialwissenschaftler,* Deutsch, Thun [et al.].

Lai, K, Ngai E.W.T. & Cheng, TCE 2004, 'An empirical study of supply chain performance in transport logistics', *International Journal of Production Economics*, vol. 87, no. 3, pp. 321–331.

Lambert, DM, Emmelhainz, MA, & Gardner, JT 'Developing and Implementing Supply Chain Partnerships', *The international journal of logistics management.* - Bradford: Emerald.

Lam, SK, Ahearne, M, Hu, Y & Schillewaert, N 2010, 'Resistance to Brand Switching When a Radically New Brand Is Introduced: A Social Identity Theory Perspective', *Journal of Marketing*, vol. 74, no. 6, pp. 128–146.

Lang, M 2007, 'Dual-Mode Electronic Survey Lessons and Experiences' in *Handbook of research on electronic surveys and measurements,* eds RA Reynolds, R Woods & JD Baker, Idea Group Reference, Hershey, PA, pp. 65–75.

Lange, S & Nienhoff, M 2007, 'IFS Logistic Anforderungskatalog "Transport"' in *IFS Logistic Standard. Sicherheit der Lebensmittel auf dem Weg vom Hersteller zum Handel,* ed S Lange, Behr, Hamburg, pp. 73–80.

Larsen, JD & Baddeley, A 2003, 'Disruption of verbal STM by irrelevant speech, articulatory suppression, and manual tapping: Do they have a common source?', *The Quarterly Journal of Experimental Psychology Section A*, vol. 56, no. 8, pp. 1249–1268.

Laurin, É, Nunes, MCN, Émond, J & Brecht, JK 2006, 'Residual effect of low-pressure stress during simulated air transport on Beit Alpha-type cucumbers: Stomata behavior', *Postharvest Biology and Technology*, vol. 41, no. 2, pp. 121–127.

Law, KS, Wong, C & Mobley, WH 1998, 'Toward a Taxonomy of Multidimensional Constructs', *The Academy of Management Review*, vol. 23, no. 4, pp. 741–755.

Lawrence, PR & Lorsch, JW 1967, 'Differentiation and integration in complex organizations', *Administrative science quarterly / Samuel Curtis Johnson Graduate School of Management, Cornell University*, vol. 12, no. 1, pp. 1 OP 47.

Lebow, P, Lebow, S & Nelson, W 2010, 'Effect of Treatment Pressure on Treatment Quality and Bending Properties of Red Pine Lumber', *Forest Products Journal*, vol. 60, no. 5, pp. 447–452.

Leontief, W 1977, 'Natural Resources, Environmental Disruption, and the Future World Economy', *Journal of International Affairs*, vol. 31, no. 2, p. 267.

Leopold, H 2004, *Rücklauf bei Online Befragungen im Online Access Panel,* Hamburg.

Levine, S & White, PE 1961, 'Exchange as a Conceptual Framework for the Study of Interorganizational Relationships', *Administrative Science Quarterly*, vol. 5, no. 4, pp. 583–601.

Levy, DM 1997, 'Lean Production in an International Supply Chain', *Sloan Management Review*, vol. 38, no. 2, pp. 94–102.

Lindsey, R 1989, 'Import disruptions, exhaustible resources, and intertemporal security of supply', *Canadian Journal of Economics*, vol. 22, no. 2, p. 340.

Lister, C 1992, *Regulation of food products by the European Community,* Butterworths, London [et al.].

Littek, F 2005, *Kühltransport. Temperaturgeführte Logistik und Transporttechnik,* Agrimedia, Bergen/Dumme.

Little, RJA 1988, 'A Test of Missing Completely at Random for Multivariate Data with Missing Values', *Journal of the American Statistical Association*, vol. 83, no. 404, pp. 1198–1202.

Loader, R 1997, 'Assessing transaction costs to describe supply chain relationships in agrifood systems', *Supply Chain Management Review, V. 6, NO. 4 (JULY/AUG. 2002), P. 52-61*, vol. 2, no. 1, pp. 23–35.

Lodge, GC 1966, 'Revolution in Latin America', *Foreign Affairs*, vol. 44, no. 2, pp. 173–197.

Löhneysen, G von 1982, *Die rechtzeitige Erkennung von Unternehmungskrisen mit Hilfe von Frühwarnsystemen als Voraussetzung für ein wirksames Krisenmanagement*. Thesis, University of Göttingen.

Long, D 2004, *International logistics: global supply chain management,* Kluwer Academic Publ, Norwell, Mass. [et al.].

Longford, NT 2008, 'Missing Data' in *Handbook of multilevel analysis,* eds J de Leeuw & E Meijer, Springer Science+Business Media, LLC, New York, NY, pp. 377–400.

Lopez Jaquero, V, Montero Simarro, F, Molina Masso, JP & Vanderdonckt, J (eds.) 2009, *Computer-Aided Design of User Interfaces VI,* Springer-Verlag London, London.

Louw, A, Vermeulen, H, Kirsten, J & Madevu, H 2007, 'Securing small farmer participation in supermarket supply chains in South Africa', *Development Southern Africa*, vol. 24, no. 4, pp. 539–551.

Lubliner, J 1972, 'On the thermodynamic foundations of non-linear solid mechanics', *International Journal of Non-Linear Mechanics*, vol. 7, no. 3, pp. 237–254.

Ludwig Von Bertalanffy 1972, 'The History and Status of General Systems Theory', *The Academy of Management Journal*, vol. 15, no. 4, pp. 407–426.

Lumsden, J 2007, 'Online-Questionnaire Design Guidelines' in *Handbook of research on electronic surveys and measurements,* eds RA Reynolds, R Woods & JD Baker, Idea Group Reference, Hershey, PA, pp. 44–64.

Lundqvist, J, Fraiture, C de & Molden, D 2008, *Saving Water: From Field to Fork - Curbing Losses and Wastage in the Food Chain,* SIWI Policy Brief.

Luning, PA & Marcelis, WJ 2006, 'A techno-managerial approach in food quality management research', *Trends in Food Science & Technology*, vol. 17, no. 7, pp. 378–385.

Luning, PA & Marcelis, WJ 2007, 'A conceptual model of food quality management functions based on a techno-managerial approach', *Trends in Food Science & Technology*, vol. 18, no. 3, pp. 159–166.

Luo, Y 2010, *When Apology and Product Recall Is Not Enough: A Study of News Coverage of Mengniu Dairy Crisis Management Strategies In The 2008 Chinese Milk Scandal*. Thesis, University of Miami.

Luthans, F 2005, *Organizational behavior,* McGraw-Hill/Irwin, Boston, Mass. [et al.].

Lyson, T & Raymer, A 2000, 'Stalking the wily multinational: Power and control in the US food system', *Agriculture and Human Values*, vol. 17, pp. 199–208.

Ma, Q & McCord, M 2007, 'Web Survey Design' in *Handbook of research on electronic surveys and measurements,* eds RA Reynolds, R Woods & JD Baker, Idea Group Reference, Hershey, PA, pp. 9–18.

Macharzina, K 1977, 'Führungstheorien und Führungssysteme' in *Personalmanagement. Mitarbeiterführung und Führungsorganisation,* eds K Macharzina & W Oechsler, Gabler, Wiesbaden, pp. 19–54.

Macharzina, K 2010, *Unternehmensführung. Das internationale Managementwissen ; Konzepte, Methoden, Praxis,* Gabler, Wiesbaden.

MaCken, W, Tremblay, S, Alford, D & Jones, D 1999, 'Attentional Selectivity in Short-term Memory: Similarity of Process, Not Similarity of Content, Determines Disruption', *International Journal of Psychology*, vol. 34, 5-6, pp. 322–327.

MacMaoláin, C 2007, *EU food law. Protecting consumers and health in a common market,* Hart, Oxford [et al.].

MacPherson, A 2008, 'The Impact of the U.S. Bio-Terrorism Act upon Canadian Exporters of Food Products to the United States: A Firm-Level Analysis', *The International Trade Journal*, vol. 22, no. 1, pp. 17–38.

Majone, G 2000, 'The Credibility Crisis of Community Regulation', *JCMS: Journal of Common Market Studies*, vol. 38, no. 2, pp. 273-302.

Malik, F & Probst, GJB 1982, 'Evolutionary Management. Cybernetics and Systems', *Cybernetics and Systems*, vol. 13, no. 2, pp. 153–174.

Manalili, N, Dorado, M & van Otterdijk, R 2011, *Appropriate Food Packaging Solutions for Developing Countries,* Rome.

Manthou, V, Matopoulos, A & Vlachopoulou, M 2005, 'Internet-based applications in the agri-food supply chain: a survey on the Greek canning sector', *Journal of Food Engineering*, vol. 70, no. 3.

Manuj, I & Mentzer, JT 2008, 'Global supply chain risk management strategies', *International Journal of Physical Distribution & Logistics Management*, vol. 38, no. 3, pp. 192–223.

March, JG & Simon, HA 1958, *Organizations,* Wiley [et al.], New York [et al.].

Mao, A, Shi, SQ & Steele, P 2011, 'Flakeboard Bonded with Polymeric Diphenylmethane Diisocyanate/Bio-Oil Adhesive Systems', *Forest Products Journal*, vol. 61, no. 3, pp. 240–245.

Marquart, M 2011, *Ein Geschäft, viele Profiteure*. Available from: http://www.spiegel.de/wirtschaft/service/futtermittelbranche-ein-geschaeft-viele-profiteure-a-738001.html. [05 January 2011].

Marradi, A 1990, 'Classification, typology, taxonomy', *Quality & Quantity*, vol. 24, no. 2, p. 129.

Marsh, HW, Hau, K, Balla, JR & Grayson, D 1998, 'Is More Ever Too Much? The Number of Indicators per Factor in Confirmatory Factor Analysis', *Multivariate Behavioral Research*, vol. 33, no. 2, pp. 181–220.

Marucheck, A, Greis, N, Mena, C & Cai, L 2011, 'Product safety and security in the global supply chain: Issues, challenges and research opportunities', *Special Issue: Product Safety and Security on the Global Supply Chain*, vol. 29, 7–8, pp. 707–720.

Maslow, AH 1978, *Motivation und Persönlichkeit (Motivation and personality, dt.),* Walter-V, Olten.

Mathwick, C, Malhotra, N & Rigdon, E 2001, 'Experiential value: conceptualization, measurement and application in the catalog and Internet shopping environment☆', *Journal of Retailing*, vol. 77, no. 1, pp. 39–56.

Matthias, DM, Robertson, J, Garrison, MM, Newland, S & Nelson, C 2007, 'Freezing temperatures in the vaccine cold chain: A systematic literature review', *Vaccine*, vol. 25, no. 20, pp. 3980–3986.

Mayo, E 1977, *The social problems of an industrial civilization,* Arno Pr, New York.

McKinnon, A 2006, 'Life without Trucks: The Impact of a Temporary Disruption of Road Freight Tansport on a National Economy', *Journal of Business Logistics*, vol. 27, no. 2, pp. 227–250.

Meier, T 1979, *Probleme des temperaturgeführten Verkehrs aus der Sicht der Transportunternehmer*. Thesis, University of Bremerhaven.

Ménard, C & Klein, P, 'Organizational Issues in the Agrifood Sector: Toward a Comparative Approach', *American Journal of Agricultural Economics*, vol. 86, no. 3.

Mercantila Publishers 1989, *Guide to food transport. Fruit and vegetables,* Mercantila Publ, Copenhagen.

Merschmann, U & Thonemann, UW 2011, 'Supply chain flexibility, uncertainty and firm performance: An empirical analysis of German manufacturing firms', *International Journal of Production Economics*, vol. 130, no. 1, pp. 43–53.

Miller, D 1996, 'Configurations Revisited', *Strategic Management Journal*, vol. 17, no. 7, pp. 505–512.

Min, S, Roath, AS, Daugherty, PJ, Genchev, SE, Chen, H, Arndt, AD & Richey, RG 2005, 'Supply chain collaboration: what's happening?', *The international journal of logistics management*, vol. 16, no. 2, pp. 237–256.

Mintzberg, H 1980, 'Structure in 5's: A Synthesis of the Research on Organization Design', *Management Science*, vol. 26, no. 3, pp. 322–341.

Misumi, J, Wilpert, B & Miller, R 1998, *Nuclear Safety. A Human Factors Perspective,* CRC Press, London.

Mobley, RK 2000, *Fluid power dynamics,* Newnes, Boston, Mass. [et al.].

Moes, JE 1966, 'Foreign Exchange Policy and Economic Union in Central Africa', *Economic Development & Cultural Change*, vol. 14, no. 4, p. 471.

Moon, C, Kim, J & Hur, S 2002, 'Integrated process planning and scheduling with minimizing total tardiness in multi-plants supply chain', *Computers & Industrial Engineering*, vol. 43, 1-2, pp. 331–349.

Morrison, EW 2002, 'Newcomers' Relationships: The Role of Social Network Ties during Socialization', *The Academy of Management Journal*, vol. 45, no. 6, pp. 1149–1160.

Mortimore, S & Wallace, C 2000, *HACCP. Die praktische Umsetzung,* Behr, Hamburg.

Moskow, MH 2000, 'Disruptions in global financial markets: The role of public policy', *Economic Perspectives*, vol. 24, no. 3, p. 2.

Mowat, A & Collins, R 2000, 'Consumer behaviour and fruit quality: supply chain management in an emerging industry', *Supply Chain Management: An International Journal*, vol. 5, no. 1.

Mowrer, E 1938, 'The Trend and Ecology of Family Disintegration in Chicago', *American Sociological Review*, vol. 3, no. 3, pp. 344–353.

Mühlenfeld, H 2004, *Der Mensch in der Online-Kommunikation. Zum Einfluss webbasierter, audiovisueller Fernkommunikation auf das Verhalten von Befragten,* Wiesbaden.

Müller, M & Gaudig, S 2011, 'An empirical investigation of antecedents to information exchange in supply chains', *International Journal of Production Research*, vol. 49, no. 6, pp. 1531–1555.

Müller-Martini, M 2008, *Kundenkompetenzen als Determinanten der Kundenbindung. Eine empirische Kausalanalyse am Beispiel der TV-Versorgung von Privatkunden,* Wiesbaden.

Murray, AT, Matisziw, TC & Grubesic, TH 2008, 'A Methodological Overview of Network Vulnerability Analysis', *Growth and Change*, vol. 39, no. 4, pp. 573–592.

Nair, A & Vidal, JM 2011, 'Supply network topology and robustness against disruptions - an investigation using multi-agent model', *International Journal of Production Research*, vol. 49, no. 5, pp. 1391–1404.

Neugebauer, M, Gasteiger, R, Beuing, O, Diehl, V, Skalej, M & Preim, B 2009, 'Map Displays for the Analysis of Scalar Data on Cerebral Aneurysm Surfaces', *Computer Graphics Forum*, vol. 28, no. 3, pp. 895–902.

Newell, A & Simon, HA 1976, 'Problemlösung' in *Organisationstheorie,* ed E Grochla, Poeschel, Stuttgart, pp. 409–425.

Nitzl, C 2010, *Eine anwenderorientierte Einführung in die Partial Least Square (PLS)-Methode*. Working Paper, Institute of Industrial Management, University of Hamburg.

Norfleet, DA 2005, 'Loss of Learning in Disruption Claims', *Cost Engineering*, vol. 47, no. 11, pp. 10–14.

Norrman, A & Jansson, U 2004, 'Ericsson's proactive supply chain risk management approach after a serious sub-supplier accident', *International Journal of Physical Distribution & Logistics Management*, vol. 34, no. 5, pp. 434–456.

North, DC 1993, 'What Do We Mean by Rationality?', *Public Choice*, vol. 77, no. 1, pp. 159–162.

Nourse, EG 1960, 'Some Questions Emerging under the Employment Act', *American Economic Review*, vol. 50, no. 2, pp. 130–144.

Nunes, M, Brecht, JK, Morais, AMMB & Sargent, SA 1995a, 'Physical and chemical quality characteristics of strawberries after storage are reduced by a short delay to cooling', *Postharvest Biology and Technology*, vol. 6, pp. 323-328.

Nunes, M, Emond, J & Brecht, J 2006, 'Brief deviations from set point temperatures during normal airport handling operations negatively affect the quality of papaya (Carica papaya) fruit', *Postharvest Biology and Technology*, vol. 41, no. 3, pp. 328–340.

Nunes, M, Emond, J, Rauth, M, Dea, S & Chau, K 2009, 'Environmental conditions encountered during typical consumer retail display affect fruit and vegetable quality and waste', *Postharvest Biology and Technology*, vol. 51, no. 2, pp. 232–241.

Nunes, M, J. K. Brecht, S. A. Sargent & A. M. M. B. Morais 1995b, 'Effects of delays to cooling and wrapping on strawberry quality (cv. Sweet Charlie)', *Food Control*, vol. 6, no. 6.

Oke, A & Gopalakrishnan, M 2009, 'Managing disruptions in supply chains: A case study of a retail supply chain', *International Journal of Production Economics*, vol. 118, no. 1, pp. 168–174.

Oliveira, N 2012, *Automated Organizations. Development and Structure of the Modern Business Firm,* Physica-Verlag HD, Heidelberg.

Olorunnisola, Pitman & Mansfield-William 2005, 'Strength properties and potential uses of rattan–cement composites', *Journal of Bamboo and Rattan*, vol. 4, no. 4, pp. 343–352.

Ornitz, BE & Champ, MA 2002, *Oil spills first principles. Prevention and best response,* Elsevier, Amsterdam; New York.

Ortmann, F 2005, *Modelling the South African fresh fruit export supply chain*. Thesis, University of Stellenbosch, South Africa.

Oulanov, A 2008, 'Business administration students' perception of usability of the Business Source Premier database: A case study', *The Electronic Library*, vol. 26, no. 4, pp. 505–519.

Özilgen, M 2011, *Handbook of food process modeling and statistical quality control. With extensive MATLAB applications,* CRC Press, Boca Raton, FL.

Palazuelos, E & García, C 2008, 'China's energy transition: features and drivers', *Post-Communist Economies*, vol. 20, no. 4, pp. 461–481.

Parfitt, J, Barthel, M & Macnaughton, S 2010, 'Food waste within food supply chains: quantification and potential for change to 2050', *Philosophical Transactions of the Royal Society B: Biological Sciences*, vol. 365, no. 1554, pp. 3065–3081.

Parkinson, D 1992, *Risk: analysis, perception and management,* Royal Society, London.

Parmar, D, Wu, T, Callarman, T, Fowler, J & Wolfe, P 2010, 'A clustering algorithm for supplier base management', *International Journal of Production Research*, vol. 48, no. 13, pp. 3803–3821.

Patnayakuni, R, Rai, A & Seth, N 2006, 'Relational Antecedents of Information Flow Integration for Supply Chain Coordination', *Journal of Management Information Systems*, vol. 23, no. 1, pp. 13–49.

Paul, J 2008, 'Supply Chain Disruption: Risk and Management', *SCMS Journal of Indian Management*, vol. 5, no. 1, pp. 109–112.

Paull, R 1999, 'Effect of temperature and relative humidity on fresh commodity quality', *Postharvest Biology and Technology*, vol. 15, no. 3, pp. 263–277.

Peck, H 2005, 'Drivers of supply chain vulnerability: an integrated framework', *International Journal of Physical Distribution & Logistics Management*, vol. 35, no. 4, pp. 210–232.

Peck, H & Jüttner, U 2000, 'Strategy and Relationships: Defining the Interface in Supply Chain Contexts', *The International Journal of Logistics Management*, vol. 11, no. 2, pp. 33–44.

Peck, H 2005, 'Drivers of supply chain vulnerability: an integrated framework', *International Journal of Physical Distribution & Logistics Management*, vol. 35, no. 4, pp. 210–232.

Pennington, J 1993, 'Food Classification and Terminology Systems'. *Quality and Accessibility of Food-Related Data. Proceedings of the First International Food Data Base Conference,* ed H Greenfield, AOAC International, Arlington, pp. 85–98.

Perrow, C 1967, 'A Framework for the Comparative Analysis of Organizations', vol. 32, no. 2, pp. 194–208.

Perrow, C 1999, *Normal accidents. Living with high-risk technologies,* Princeton University Press, N.J.

Perrow, C 2006, 'The limits of safety: the enhancement of a theory of accidents' in *Key Readings in Crisis Management. System and structures for prevention and recovery,* eds D Smith & D Elliott, Routledge, Oxon, pp. 15–28.

Peter, JP 1981, 'Construct Validity: A Review of Basic Issues and Marketing Practices', *Journal of Marketing Research*, vol. 18, no. 2, pp. 133–145.

Picot, A 1981, 'Der Beitrag der Theorie der Verfügungsrechte zur ökonomischen Analyse von Unternehmensverfassungen'. *Unternehmungsverfassung als Problem der Betriebswirtschaftslehre,* ed K Bohr, Schmidt, Berlin, pp. 153-197.

Picot, A & Schneider, D 1988, 'Unternehmerisches Innovationsverhalten, Verfügungsrechte und Transaktionskosten' in *Betriebswirtschaftslehre und Theorie der Verfügungsrechte,* eds D Budäus, E Gerum, G Zimmermann & W Braun, Gabler, Wiesbaden, pp. 91-118.

Picot, A, Dietl, H & Furubotn, E 2008, *Organisation. Eine ökonomische Perspektive,* Schäffer-Poeschel, Stuttgart.

Plaggenhoef, Wv 2007, *Integration and self regulation of quality management in Dutch agrifood supply chains. A cross-chain analysis of the poultry meat, the fruit and vegetable and the flower and potted plant chains,* Wageningen Academic Publishers, The Netherlands.

Podsakoff, PM & MacKenzie, SB 1994, 'An examination of the psychometric properties and nomological validity of some revised and reduced substitutes for leadership scales', *Journal of Applied Psychology*, vol. 79, no. 5, pp. 702–713.

Podsakoff, PM, MacKenzie, SB, Podsakoff, NP & Lee, JY 2003, 'The mismeasure of man(agement) and its implications for leadership research', *The Leadership Quarterly*, vol. 14, no. 6, pp. 615–656.

Polderijk, JJ, Vogels, J, Demkers, R & van Dyk, FE 2006, 'Fruitful: Integrated supply-chain information system for fruit produce between South Africa and the Netherlands' in *The agrofood chains and networks for development,* eds R Ruben, M Slingerland & H Nijhoff, Springer, Dordrecht, the Netherlands, pp. 129–140.

Popper, KR 1973, *Logik der Forschung,* Mohr, Tübingen.

Popper, KR 1980, 'Was ist Dialektik?' in *Logik der Sozialwissenschaften,* eds E Topitsch & P Payer, Verlagsgruppe Athenäum, Hain, Scriptor, Hanstein, Königstein/Ts, pp. 262–290.

Porter, ME 1998, *Competitive advantage. Creating and sustaining superior performance,* Free Press, New York.

Porter, ME & Millar, V 1985, 'How information gives you competitive advantage', *Harvard Business Review*, July-August, pp. 149–160.

Powell, TC 1996, 'How Much Does Industry Matter? An Alternative Empirical Test', *Strategic Management Journal*, vol. 17, no. 4, pp. 323–334.

Proctor, RW & van Zandt, T 2008, *Human factors in simple and complex systems,* CRC Press, Boca Raton, Fla. [et al.].

Puerta, A 2009, 'The Mecano Project: Comprehensive and Integrated Support for Model-Based Interface Development' in *Computer-Aided Design of User Interfaces VI,* eds V Lopez Jaquero, F Montero Simarro, JP Molina Masso & J Vanderdonckt, Springer-Verlag London, London, pp. 19–36.

Pugh, DS & Hickson, DJ 1979, *The Aston programme,* Saxon House, Farnborough (Hants).

Qi, L, Shen, ZM & Snyder, LV 2009, 'A Continuous-Review Inventory Model with Disruptions at Both Supplier and Retailer', *Production & Operations Management*, vol. 18, no. 5, pp. 516–532.

Ramamoorthy, N & Flood, PC 2004, 'Gender and Employee Attitudes: The Role of Organizational Justice Perceptions', *British Journal of Management*, vol. 15, no. 3, pp. 247–258.

Ramsey, NF 1956, 'Thermodynamics and Statistical Mechanics at Negative Absolute Temperatures', *Physical Review*, vol. 103, no. 1, pp. 20–28.

Rasmussen, J & Vicente, K 1989, 'Coping with human errors through system design: implications for ecological interface design', *International Journal of Man-Machine Studies*, vol. 31, no. 5, pp. 517–534.

Raspor, P 2008, 'Total food chain safety: how good practices can contribute?', *Trends in Food Science & Technology*, vol. 19, no. 8.

Ratick, S, Meacham, B & Aoyama, Y 2008, 'Locating Backup Facilities to Enhance Supply Chain Disaster Resilience', *Growth and Change*, vol. 39, no. 4, pp. 642–666.

Real, JC, Roldán, JL & Leal, A 2012, 'From Entrepreneurial Orientation and Learning Orientation to Business Performance: Analysing the Mediating Role of Organizational Learning and the Moderating Effects of Organizational Size', *British Journal of Management,* pp. n/a.

Reason, J 1990, *Human error,* Cambridge University Press, Cambridge et al.

Reason, J 1995, 'Understanding adverse events: human factors', *Quality in Health Care*, vol. 4, pp. 80–89.

Reason, J 1997, *Managing the risks of organizational accidents,* Ashgate.

Reason, J 2000, 'Human error: models and management', *BMJ*, vol. 320, March, pp. 768–770.

REFA : Lehrgang Arbeits- und Zeitstudien 1. Einführung in das Arbeitsstudium s.d., Studiengemeinschaft Kamrath Darmstadt, [S.l.].

Reiß, M & Corsten, H 1995, 'Schnittstellenfokussierte Unternehmensführung' in *Handbuch Unternehmungsführung. Konzepte - Instrumente - Schnittstellen,* eds H Corsten & M Reiß, Gabler, Wiesbaden, pp. 5–18.

Remer, A 1982, *Instrumente unternehmenspolitischer Steuerung. Unternehmensverfassung, formale Organisation und personale Gestaltung,* de Gruyter, Berlin [et al.].

Remer, A 1989, *Organisationslehre. Eine Einführung,* de Gruyter, Berlin [et al.].

Remer, A 2004, *Management. System und Konzepte,* REA-Verl. Managementforschung, Bayreuth.

Remer, A 2005, *Organisation : Struktur und Prozess,* REA-Verl, Bayreuth.

Remer, A & Hucke, P 2007, *Grundlagen der Organisation,* Kohlhammer, Stuttgart.

Rice Jr, JB 2011, 'Only as Strong as the Weakest Link', *Mechanical Engineering*, vol. 133, no. 6, pp. 26–31.

Rice, J & Caniato, F 2003a, 'Building a secure and resilient supply network', *Supply Chain Management Review, V. 6, NO. 4 (JULY/AUG. 2002), P. 52-61*, vol. 7, no. 5, pp. 22–30.

Rice, J & Caniato, F 2003b, 'Supply chain response to terrorism: Creating resilient and secure supply chains', *Report by MIT Center for Transportation and Logistics*.

Richter, R & Furubotn, E 2003, *Neue Institutionenökonomik: eine Einführung und kritische Würdigung,* Mohr Siebeck, Tübingen.

Riechey, J 2008, 'Dauerhafte Kooperationen — ein Grenzmanagementproblem' in *Kontinuitätsorientierte Koordination dynamischer Kooperationen,* ed M Hülsmann, Gabler Verlag / GWV Fachverlage GmbH, Wiesbaden, Wiesbaden, pp. 159–286.

Ringle, C, Wende, S & Will, A 2010, 'Finite Mixture Partial Least Squares Analysis: Methodology and Numerical Examples' in *Handbook of Partial Least Squares,* eds V Esposito Vinzi, WW Chin, J Henseler & H Wang, Springer Berlin Heidelberg, pp. 195–218.

RKI 2011, *Abschließende Darstellung und Bewertung der epidemiologischen Erkenntnisse im EHEC O104:H4 Ausbruch,* Robert Koch Institut, Berlin. Available from: http://www.rki.de/cln_226/nn_205760/DE/Content/InfAZ/E/EHEC/EHEC-Abschlussbericht,templateId=raw,property=publicationFile.pdf/EHEC-Abschlussbericht.pdf [05 January 2012].

Robert, D 1979, 'What is the right organization structure? Decision tree analysis provides the answer', *Organizational Dynamics*, vol. 7, no. 3, pp. 59–80.

Roberts, L 2007, 'Oppoertunities and Constraints of Electronic Research' in *Handbook of research on electronic surveys and measurements,* eds RA Reynolds, R Woods & JD Baker, Idea Group Reference, Hershey, PA, pp. 19–27.

Röder, R 2001, *Kooperation an Schnittstellen. Eine empirische Untersuchung,* Frankfurt am Main [et al.].

Rodriguez-Bermejo, J, Barreiro, P, Robla, J & Ruiz-Garcia, L 2007, 'Thermal study of a transport container', *Journal of Food Engineering*, vol. 80, no. 2.

Roethlisberger, FJ & Dickson, WJ 1961, *Management and the worker. An account of a research program conducted by the Western Electric Company, Hawthorne works, Chicago,* [s.n.], Cambridge [et al.].

Rosenberger, JM, Johnson, EL & Nemhauser, GL 2003, 'Rerouting Aircraft for Airline Recovery', *Transportation Science*, vol. 37, no. 4, pp. 408–421.

Rosenberger, JM, Schaefer, AJ, Goldsman, D, Johnson, EL, Kleywegt, AJ & Nemhauser, GL 2002, 'A Stochastic Model of Airline Operations', *Transportation Science*, vol. 36, no. 4, p. 357.

Ross, DF 2011, *Introduction to supply chain management technologies,* CRC Press/Taylor & Francis, Boca Raton.

Ruiz-Garcia, L, Steinberger, G & Rothmund, M 2010, 'A model and prototype implementation for tracking and tracing agricultural batch products along the food chain', *Food Control*, vol. 21, no. 2.

Russell, B & Purcell, J 2009, *Online research essentials. Implementing and designing research studies,* Jossey-Bass, San Francisco.

Saaty, TL 1982, *Decision making for leaders. The analytical hierarchy process for decisions in a complex world,* Lifetime Learning Publ, Belmont, Cal. [et al.].

Sacilik, K, Keskin, R & Elicin, AK 2006, 'Mathematical modelling of solar tunnel drying of thin layer organic tomato', *Journal of Food Engineering*, vol. 73, no. 3, pp. 231–238.

Sahin, F & Robinson, EP 2002, 'Flow Coordination and Information Sharing in Supply Chains: Review, Implications, and Directions for Future Research', *Decision Sciences*, vol. 33, no. 4, pp. 505–536.

Salvendy, G (ed.) 2006, *Handbook of human factors and ergonomics,* John Wiley, Hoboken, N.J.

Saraph, JV, Benson, PG & Schroeder, RG 1989, 'An Instrument for Measuring the Critical Factors of Quality Management', *Decision Sciences*, vol. 20, no. 4, pp. 810-829.

Sarathy, R 2006, 'Security and the Global Supply Chain', *Transportation Journal (American Society of Transportation & Logistics Inc)*, vol. 45, no. 4, pp. 28–51.

Schaefer, AJ, Johnson, EL, Kleywegt, AJ & Nemhauser, GL 2005, 'Airline Crew Scheduling Under Uncertainty', *Transportation Science*, vol. 39, no. 3, pp. 340–348.

Schaefer, DR & Don A. Dillman 1998, 'Development of a Standard E-Mail Methodology: Results of an Experiment', *The Public Opinion Quarterly*, vol. 62, no. 3, pp. 378–397.

Schafer, JL & Graham, JW 2002, 'Missing data: Our view of the state of the art', *Psychological Methods*, vol. 7, no. 2, pp. 147–177.

Scherer, AG 2006, 'Kritik der Organisation oder Organisation der Kritik? Wissenschaftstheoretische Bemerkungen zum kritischen Umgang mit Organisationstheorien' in *Organisationstheorien,* eds A Kieser & M Ebers, Kohlhammer, Stuttgart, pp. 1–37.

Scherer, FM 1993, 'Pricing, Profits, and Technological Progress in the Pharmaceutical Industry', *The Journal of Economic Perspectives*, vol. 7, no. 3, pp. 97–115.

Scherm, E & Pietsch, G 2007, *Organisation. Theorie, Gestaltung, Wandel ; mit Aufgaben und Fallstudien,* Oldenbourg, München [et al.].

Schieck, A 2008, *Internationale Logistik. Objekte, Prozesse und Infrastrukturen grenzüberschreitender Güterströme,* Oldenbourg, München.

Schmitt, AJ & Singh, M 2012, 'A quantitative analysis of disruption risk in a multi-echelon supply chain', *International Journal of Production Economics,* vol. 139, no. 1, pp. 22-32.

Schnell, R, Hill, P & Esser, E 2011, *Methoden der empirischen Sozialforschung,* Oldenbourg, München.

Schreyögg, G 1999, *Organisation. Grundlagen moderner Organisationsgestaltung; mit Fallstudien,* Gabler, Wiesbaden.

Schulenburg, N 2008, *Entstehung von Unternehmenskrisen. Eine evolutionstheoretische Erklärung,* Wiesbaden.

Schulte-Zurhausen, M 1999, *Organisation,* Vahlen, München.

Schulte-Zurhausen, M 2004, 'Schnittstelle Marketing und Organisation' in *Absatzorganisation,* ed W Pepels, Peter Lang, Frankfurt am Main, pp. 23–53.

Schulte-Zurhausen, M 2010, *Organisation,* Vahlen, München.

Schumpeter, JA 1947, *Capitalism, socialism, and democracy,* Harper, New York [et al.].

Scott, WR 1987, 'The Adolescence of Institutional Theory', *Administrative Science Quarterly*, vol. 32, no. 4, pp. 493–511.

Seuring, S 2004, 'Integrated chain management and supply chain management comparative analysis and illustrative cases', *Journal of Cleaner Production*, vol. 12, 8-10, pp. 1059–1071.

Seuring, S 2009, 'The product-relationship-matrix as framework for strategic supply chain design based on operations theory', *International Journal of Production Economics*, vol. 120, no. 1, pp. 221–232.

Shah, J 2009a, 'Supply Chain Risk Management: Academic Perspective', *IIMB Management Review (Indian Institute of Management Bangalore)*, vol. 21, no. 2, pp. 149–157.

Shah, J 2009b, 'Supply Chain Risk Management: Discussion'. *IIMB Management Review (Indian Institute of Management Bangalore) : IIMB Management Review (Indian Institute of Management Bangalore),* Indian Institute of Management Bangalore, pp. 158–167.

Shannon, CE & Weaver, W 1976, *Mathematische Grundlagen der Informationstheorie,* R. Oldenbourg, München.

Sharp, R & Timme, L 1986, 'Effects of Storage Time, Storage Temperature, and Packaging Method on Shelf Life of Brown Rice', *Cereal Chem.*, vol. 63, no. 3, pp. 247–251.

Sheehan, KB 2001, 'E-mail Survey Response Rates: A Review', *Journal of Computer-Mediated Communication*, vol. 6, no. 2, p. 0.

Sheffi, Y 2005, 'Preparing for the big one [supply chain management]', *Manufacturing Engineer*, vol. 84, no. 5, p. 12.

Sheffi, Y & Rice, J 2005, 'A supply chain view of the resilient enterprise.', *Sloan Management Review*, vol. 47, no. 1, pp. 41–48.

Shelanski, HA & Klein, PG 1995, 'Empirical Research in Transaction Cost Economics: A Review and Assessment', *Journal of Law, Economics, & Organization*, vol. 11, no. 2, pp. 335–361.

Shen, W, Wang, L & Hao, Q 2006, 'Agent-based distributed manufacturing process planning and scheduling: a state-of-the-art survey', *IEEE Transactions on Systems, Man and Cybernetics, Part C (Applications and Reviews)*, vol. 36, no. 4, pp. 563–577.

Shook, CL, Ketchen, DJ, Hult, GTM & Kacmar, KM 2004, 'An assessment of the use of structural equation modeling in strategic management research', *Strategic Management Journal*, vol. 25, no. 4, pp. 397–404.

Shrivastava, S, Sonpar, K & Pazzaglia, F 2009, 'Normal Accident Theory versus High Reliability Theory: A resolution and call for an open systems view of accidents', *Human Relations*, vol. 62, no. 9, pp. 1357–1390.

Siebel, L 2000, *Food Logistics. Lebensmittel via Internet ; Trends, Konzepte und logistische Probleme,* Symposion Publishing, Düsseldorf.

Simon, HA, 'Birth of an Organization: The Economic Cooperation Administration', *Public Administration Review*, vol. 13, no. 4, pp. 227–236.

Simon, HA 1959, 'Theories of Decision-Making in Economics and Behavioral Science', *The American Economic Review*, vol. 49, no. 3, pp. 253–283.

Simon, HA 1978a, 'On How to Decide What to Do', *The Bell Journal of Economics*, vol. 9, no. 2, pp. 494–507.

Simon, HA 1978b, 'Rationality as Process and as Product of Thought', *The American Economic Review*, vol. 68, no. 2, pp. 1–16.

Simon, HA 1979, 'Rational Decision Making in Business Organizations', *The American Economic Review*, vol. 69, no. 4, pp. 493–513.

Smith, A 1791, *An inquiry into the nature and causes of the wealth of nations: By Adam Smith,* printed [by J. J. Tourneisen] for J. J. Tourneisen; and J. L. Legrand, Basil.

Smith, C, Jennings, C & Castro, N 2005, 'Model for Assessing Adaptive Effectiveness Development', *Journal of Contingencies and Crisis Management*, vol. 13, no. 3, pp. 129–137.

Smith, D & Sparks, L 2004, 'Temperature controlled Supply Chains' in *Food Supply Chain Management,* eds MA Bourlakis & PWH Weightman, Blackwell, Oxford [et al.], pp. 179–198.

Smith, GE, Watson, KJ, Baker, WH & Pokorski II, JA 2007, 'A critical balance: collaboration and security in the IT-enabled supply chain', *International Journal of Production Research*, vol. 45, no. 11, pp. 2595–2613.

Smith, JH & Blau, PM 1962, *Formal organizations. A comparative approuch,* Routledge & Kegan Paul, London.

Spekman, R & Kamauff Jr, J 1998, 'An empirical investigation into supply chain management: a perspective on partnerships', *Supply Chain Management: An International Journal*, vol. 3, no. 2, pp. 53–67.

Spencer, F 2000, 'Human Error in Hospitals and Industrial Accidents: Current Concepts', *Journal of the American College of Surgeons*, vol. 191, no. 4, pp. 410–418.

Staehle, WH 1999, *Management. Eine verhaltenswissenschaftliche Perspektive,* Vahlen, München.

Stan, V & Saporta, G 2010, 'Conjoint Use of Variables Clustering and PLS Structural Equations Modeling' in *Handbook of Partial Least Squares,* eds V Esposito Vinzi, WW Chin, J Henseler & H Wang, Springer Berlin Heidelberg, pp. 235–246.

Statistisches Bundesamt 2008, *Structure of the Classification of Economic Activities, Edition 2008 (WZ 2008),* Wiesbaden.

Steckel, JH, Gupta, S & Banerji, A 2004, 'Supply Chain Decision Making: Will Shorter Cycle Times and Shared Point-of-Sale Information Necessarily Help?', *Management Science*, vol. 50, no. 4, pp. 458–464.

Stevens, GC 1989, 'Integrating the Supply Chain', *International journal of physical distribution and materials management*, vol. 19, no. 8, pp. 3–8.

Stoner, JAF, Freeman, RE & Gilbert, DR 1996, *Management,* Pearson, New Delhi.

Strassnig, B 2009, 'Einblicke in Online-Research — Das Internet als Medium zur Datenerhebung' in *Gesundheit und Neue Medien,* ed S Kryspin-Exner, Springer Vienna, pp. 277-296.

Subramani, M 2004, 'How do suppliers benefit from information technology use in supply chain relationships?', *MIS Quarterly*, vol. 28, no. 1, pp. 45–73.

Subramani, MR & Venkatraman, N 2003, 'Safeguarding Investments in Asymmetric Interorganizational Relationships: Theory and Evidence', *The Academy of Management Journal*, vol. 46, no. 1, pp. 46–62.

Subramaniam, V, Raheja, AS & Rama Bhupal Reddy, K 2005, 'Reactive repair tool for job shop schedules', *International Journal of Production Research*, vol. 43, no. 1, pp. 1–23.

Sufian, F & Habibullah, MS 2012, 'Developments in the efficiency of the Malaysian banking sector: the impacts of financial disruptions and exchange rate regimes', *Progress in Development Studies*, vol. 12, no. 1, pp. 19–46.

Supply Chain Council 2010, *Supply Chain Operations Reference (SCOR) model.* Available from: https://supply-chain.org/f/SCOR-Overview-Web.pdf [02 December 2013].

Sydow, J & Windeler, A 1998, 'Organizing and Evaluating Interfirm Networks: A Structurationist Perspective on Network Process and Effectiveness', *Organization Science*, vol. 9, no. 3, pp. 265–284.

Szczesniak, A 1962, *Classification of Textural Characteristics,* Miami Beach, Florida.

Tang, C & Tomlin, B 2008, 'The power of flexibility for mitigating supply chain risks', *International Journal of Production Economics*, vol. 116, no. 1, pp. 12–27.

Tang, CS 2006, 'Perspectives in supply chain risk management', *International Journal of Production Economics*, vol. 103, no. 2, pp. 451–488.

Taylor, FW 1977, *Die Grundsätze wissenschaftlicher Betriebsführung. The principles of scientific management,* Beltz, Weinheim, Basel.

Teece, DJ 1984, 'Economic Analysis and Strategic Management', *California Management Review*, vol. 26, no. 3, pp. 87–110.

Teevs, C 2011, 'Nach Kritik: Aigner verspricht effizientere Lebensmittelkontrollen', *SpiegelOnline* 22 November. Available from: http://www.spiegel.de/wirtschaft/soziales/0,1518,799290,00.html [05 January 2012].

Temme, D, Kreis, H & Hildebrandt, L 2010, 'A Comparison of Current PLS Path Modeling Software: Features, Ease-of-Use, and Performance' in *Handbook of Partial Least Squares,* eds V Esposito Vinzi, WW Chin, J Henseler & H Wang, Springer Berlin Heidelberg, pp. 737–756.

Thomas, E & Petersen, L 2003, 'Measuring Errors and Adverse Events in Health Care', *Journal of General Internal Medicine*, vol. 18, no. 1, pp. 61–67.

Thomeczek, C & Ollenschläger, G 2006, 'Fehlermeldesysteme – aus jedem Fehler auch ein Nutzen?', *Rechtsmedizin*, vol. 16, no. 6, pp. 355–360.

Transport Intelligence 2011, *Global Pharmaceutical Logistics Report 2012,* UK.

Trienekens, J & Willems, S 2007, 'International Food and Agribusiness Management Review', *IAMA International Food and Agribusiness Management Review*, vol. 10, no. 4, pp. 42–63.

Trienekens, J & Zuurbier, P 2008, 'Quality and safety standards in the food industry, developments and challenges', *International Journal of Production Economics*, vol. 113, no. 1, pp. 107–122.

Trist, E 1977, 'A Concept of Organizational Ecology', *Australian Journal of Management*, vol. 2, no. 2, pp. 161–175.

Turner, CF, Ku, L, Rogers, SM, Lindberg, LD, Pleck, JH & Sonenstein, FL 1998, 'Adolescent Sexual Behavior, Drug Use, and Violence: Increased Reporting with Computer Survey Technology', *Science*, vol. 280, no. 5365, pp. 867–873.

US Food and Drug Association *Current Good Manufacturing Practice in Manufacturing, Packing, or Holding Human Food. 21 CFR Part 110.*

Upson, J, Ketchen, D & Ireland, R 2007, 'Managing Employee Stress:: A Key to the Effectiveness of Strategic Supply Chain Management', *Organizational Dynamics*, vol. 36, no. 1, pp. 78–92.

Vahrenkamp, R & Siepermann, C 2005, *Logistik. Management und Strategien,* Oldenbourg, München.

van Aramyan, L, Oude Lansink, A, Vorst, J & Kooten, O 2007, 'Performance measurement in agri-food supply chains: a case study', *Supply Chain Management: An International Journal*, vol. 12, no. 4, pp. 304–315.

van Baalen, P, Bloemhof-Ruwaard, J & van Heck, E 2005, 'Knowledge Sharing in an Emerging Network of Practice: The Role of a Knowledge Portal', *European Management Journal*, vol. 23, no. 3, pp. 300–314.

van de Ven, AH & Ferry, DL 1980, *Measuring and assessing organizations,* Wiley, New York.

van der Vorst, J, Beulens, A, Wit, W de & van Beek, P 1998, 'Supply chain management in food chains: improving performance by reducing uncertainty', *International transactions in operational research*, vol. 5, no. 6, pp. 487–499.

van der Vorst, J, Beulens, AJ & van Beek, P 2005, 'Innovations in Logistics and ICT in Food Supply Chain Networks' in *Innovation in agri-food systems. Product quality and consumer acceptance,* eds W Jongen & M Meulenberg, Wageningen Academic Publishers, pp. 245–299.

van der Vorst, JG & Beulens, AJ 2002, 'Identifying sources of uncertainty to generate supply chain redesign strategies', *International Journal of Physical Distribution & Logistics Management*, vol. 32, no. 6, pp. 409–430.

van der Vorst, JGAJ, van Kooten, O, Marcelis, WJ, Luning, PA & Beulens, AJ 2007, *Quality Controlled Logistics in Food Supply Chain Networks: Integrated Decision-Making on Quality and Logistics to Meet Advanced Customer Demands,* Ankara, Turkey.

van Dyk, FE & Maspero, E 2007, 'An analysis of the South African fruit logistics infrustructure', *ORiON: The Journal of ORSSA*, vol. 20, no. 1, pp. 55-72.

van Hoek, RI 1999, 'Postponement and the reconfiguration challenge for food supply chains', *Supply Chain Management: An International Journal*, vol. 4, no. 1, pp. 18–34.

Vandenberg, RJ, Richardson, HA & Eastman, LJ 1999, 'The Impact of High Involvement Work Processes on Organizational Effectiveness: A Second-Order Latent Variable Approach', *Group & Organization Management*, vol. 24, no. 3, pp. 300–339.

Vedres, B & Stark, D 2010, 'Structural Folds: Generative Disruption in Overlapping Groups', *American Journal of Sociology*, vol. 115, no. 4, pp. 1150–1190.

Vega, H 2008, 'Air cargo, trade and transportation costs of perishables and exotics from South America', *Journal of Air Transport Management*, vol. 14, no. 6.

Vermeulen, H, Jordaan, D, Korsten, L & Kirsten, J 2006, *Private Standards, Handling and Hygiene in Fruit Export Supply Chains: A Preliminary Evaluation of the Economic Impact of Parallel Standards.*

Vicente, K & Rasmussen, J 1992, 'Ecological interface design: theoretical foundations', *IEEE Transactions on Systems, Man, and Cybernetics*, vol. 22, no. 4, pp. 589–606.

Vicente, KJ 2002, 'Ecological Interface Design: Progress and Challenges', *Human Factors: The Journal of the Human Factors and Ergonomics Society*, vol. 44, no. 1, pp. 62–78.

Vonderembse, M, Uppal, M, Huang, S & Dismukes, J 2006, 'Designing supply chains: Towards theory development', *International Journal of Production Economics*, vol. 100, no. 2, pp. 223–238.

Wagner, SM & Bode, C 2006, 'An empirical investigation into supply chain vulnerability. Conference 2006, the Fourth Worldwide Symposium in Purchasing & Supply Chain Management', *Journal of Purchasing and Supply Management*, vol. 12, no. 6, pp. 301–312.

Wagner, SM & Bode, C 2008, 'An Empirical Examination of Supply Chain Performance Along Several Dimensions of Risk', *Journal of Business Logistics*, vol. 29, no. 1, pp. 307-325.

Waldheim, C & Berger, A 2008, 'Logistics Landscape', *Landscape Journal*, vol. 27, no. 2, pp. 219–246.

Walgenbach, P & Meyer, RE 2008, *Neoinstitutionalistische Organisationstheorie,* Kohlhammer, Stuttgart.

Walker, G & Weber, D 1987, 'Supplier Competition, Uncertainty, and Make-or-Buy Decisions', *Academy of Management Journal*, vol. 30, no. 3, pp. 589–596.

Waters, D 2009, *Supply chain management. An introduction to logistics,* Palgrave Macmillan, Basingstoke.

Wathne, KH & Heide, JB 2004, 'Relationship Governance in a Supply Chain Network', *The Journal of Marketing*, vol. 68, no. 1, pp. 73–89.

Weber, M 2005, 'Bureaucracy' in *Classics of organization theory,* ed JM Shafritz, Thomson Wadsworth, Belmont, Calif. [et al.], pp. 73–78.

Weber, M & Winckelmann, J 1976, *Wirtschaft und Gesellschaft. Grundriss der verstehenden Soziologie,* Mohr, Tübingen.

Weick, G 2012, 'Incoterms 2010. Ein Beispiel für die "neue lex mercatoria"', *Zeitschrift für das juristische Studium*, vol. 5, no. 5, pp. 584–592.

Weimer, H 1926, *Fehlerbehandlung und Fehlerbewertung*, Klinkhardt, Leipzig.

Weingardt, M 2004, *Fehler zeichnen uns aus. Transdisziplinäre Grundlagen zur Theorie und Produktivität des Fehlers in Schule und Arbeitswelt,* Klinkhardt, Bad Heilbrunn/Obb.

Weinkauf, K, Hölzle, K, Högl, M & Gemünden, H 2005, 'Zusammenarbeit zwischen organisatorischen Gruppen: ein Literaturüberblick über die Intergroup Relations-, Schnittstellen- und Boundary- Spanning-Forschung', *Journal für Betriebswirtschaft / Eigentümer: Wirtschaftsuniversität Wien*, vol. 55, no. 2, pp. 85–111.

White, D 1995, 'Application of systems thinking to risk management: a review of', *Management Decision*, vol. 33, no. 10, pp. 35–45.

WHO 1999, *Guidelines for the Safe Disposal of Unwanted Pharmaceuticals in and after Emergencies. Interagency Guidelines*. Available from: http://apps.who.int/medicinedocs/en/d/Jwhozip51e/ [02 December 2013].

Wiktorowicz, ME 2003, 'Emergent Patterns in the Regulation of Pharmaceuticals: Institutions and Interests in the United States, Canada, Britain, and France', *Journal of Health Politics, Policy and Law*, vol. 28, no. 4, pp. 615–658.

Wild, Y 2005, *Containerhandbuch: Fachinformationen der Deutschen VersicherungswirtschaftBd. 3. Kühlcontainer und CA-Technik,* Gesamtverband der Deutschen Versicherungswirtschaft, Berlin.

Wilding, R & Humphries, AS 2006, 'Understanding collaborative supply chain relationships through the application of the Williamson organisational failure framework', *International Journal of Physical Distribution & Logistics Management*, vol. 36, no. 4, pp. 309–329.

Wilhelm, WE, Som, P & Carroll, B 1992, 'A model for implementing a paradigm of time-managed, material flow control in certain assembly systems', *International Journal of Production Research*, vol. 30, no. 9, p. 2063.

Williams, R 2004, *What a Waste!* Available from: http://www.abc.net.au/radionational/programs/scienceshow/what-a-waste/3433276#transcript [19 August 2013].

Williamson, HP 1945, 'The Functions of States in American Government', *American Journal of Economics & Sociology*, vol. 4, no. 2, pp. 213–226.

Williamson, O 1979, 'Transaction-Cost Economics: The Governance of Contractual Relations', *Journal of Law and Economics*, vol. 22, no. 2, pp. 233–261.

Williamson, O 1981, 'The Economics of Organization: The Transaction Cost Approach', *The American Journal of Sociology*, vol. 87, no. 3, pp. 548–577.

Williamson, OE 1971, 'The Vertical Integration of Production: Market Failure Considerations', *The American Economic Review*, vol. 61, no. 2, pp. 112–123.

Williamson, OE 1985, *The economic institutions of capitalism. Firms, markets, relational contracting,* Free Press [et al.], New York, NY [et al.].

Williamson, OE 1990, *Die ökonomischen Institutionen des Kapitalismus. Unternehmen, Märkte, Kooperationen,* Mohr, Tübingen.

Williamson, OE 1991, 'Comparative Economic Organization: The Analysis of Discrete Structural Alternatives', *Administrative Science Quarterly*, vol. 36, no. 2, pp. 269–296.

Williamson, OE 2002, 'The Theory of the Firm as Governance Structure: From Choice to Contract', *Journal of Economic Perspectives*, vol. 16, no. 3, pp. 171–195.

Williamson, OE 2008, 'Outsourcing: Transaction Cost Economics and Supply Chain Management', *Journal of Supply Chain Management*, vol. 44, no. 2, pp. 5-16.

Williamson, OE 2010, 'Transaction Cost Economics: The Natural Progression', *American Economic Review*, vol. 100, no. 3, pp. 673–690.

Wilson, J 2000, 'Fundamentals of ergonomics in theory and practice', *Applied Ergonomics*, vol. 31, no. 6, pp. 557–567.

Wilson, J & Hynes, N 2009, 'Co-evolution of firms and strategic alliances: Theory and empirical evidence', *Technological Forecasting and Social Change*, vol. 76, no. 5, pp. 620–628.

Wing, SL & Greenwood, DR 1993, 'Fossils and Fossil Climate: The Case for Equable Continental Interiors in the Eocene', *Philosophical Transactions: Biological Sciences*, vol. 341, no. 1297, pp. 243–252.

Wolf, J 2005, *Organisation, Management, Unternehmensführung. Theorien und Kritik,* Gabler, Wiesbaden.

Wolf, J 2008, *Organisation, Management, Unternehmensführung. Theorien, Praxisbeispiele und Kritik,* Gabler, Wiesbaden.

Woodward, J 1975, *Management and technology,* H.M.S.O., London.

Woolthuis, R, Lankhuizen, M & Gilsing, V 2005, 'A system failure framework for innovation policy design', *Technovation*, vol. 25, no. 6, pp. 609–619.

Wu, F, Yeniyurt, S, Kim, D & Cavusgil, ST 2006, 'The impact of information technology on supply chain capabilities and firm performance: A resource-based view', *Industrial Marketing Management*, vol. 35, no. 4, pp. 493–504.

Yafang Yin, Xiaomei Jiang, Lijuan Wang & Mingming Bian 2011, 'Predicting Wood Quality of Green Logs by Resonance Vibration and Stress Wave in Plantation-Grown Populus Xeuramericana', *Forest Products Journal*, vol. 61, no. 2, pp. 136–142.

Yang Zhang & Zhiming Yu 2011, 'Effects of Vertical Density Profiles on Bending Properties of Fiberboard with a "Bowl-Shaped" Vertical Density Profile', *Forest Products Journal*, vol. 61, no. 7, pp. 510–516.

Yang, B & Yang, Y 2010, 'Postponement in supply chain risk management: a complexity perspective', *International Journal of Production Research*, vol. 48, no. 7, pp. 1901–1912.

Yin, RK 2009, *Case study research. Design and methods,* Sage Publications, Los Angeles, Calif.

Yossi Sheffi 2001, 'Supply Chain Management under the Threat of International Terrorism', *International Journal of Logistics Management,* vol. 12, no. 2, pp. 1–11.

Young, MP 2002, 'Confessional Protest: The Religious Birth of U.S. National Social Movements', *American Sociological Review*, vol. 67, no. 5, pp. 660–688.

Zäpfel, G 2004, 'Sukzessive und simultane Formen der Koordinierung der Material- und Warenflüsse in Lieferketten durch Supply-Chain-Planung' in *Entwicklungen im Produktionsmanagement,* eds H Corsten & A Braßler, Vahlen, München, pp. 183–202.

Zetterberg, H 1973, 'Theorie, Forschung und Praxis in der Soziologie' in *Handbuch der empirischen Sozialforschung / hrsg. von René König Bd. 1. Geschichte und Grundprobleme der empirischen Sozialforschung,* ed R König, Dt. Taschenbuch-Verl., München [et al.], pp. 103–160.

Zhang, G 1997, *Optimierung der Verteilungskette von gekühlten und gefrorenen Lebensmitteln in der Bundesrepublik Deutschland,* Hamburg.

Zsidisin, GA & Wagner, SM 2010, 'Do Perceptions become Reality? The MOderating Role of Supply Chain Resiliency on disruption Occurrence', *Journal of Business Logistics*, vol. 31, no. 2, pp. 1–20.

Zsidisin, GA, Melnyk, SA & Ragatz, GL 2005, 'An institutional theory perspective of business continuity planning for purchasing and supply management', *International Journal of Production Research*, vol. 43, no. 16, pp. 3401–3420.

Zucker, LG 1977, 'The Role of Institutionalization in Cultural Persistence', *American Sociological Review*, vol. 42, no. 5, pp. 726–743.

Appendix

Appendix 1: Comparison of effect of third party involvement in logistics segment for both cases

	Path Coefficient		Standard Deviation		Standard Error		T Statistics	
Third Party Involvement -> Logistics Performance	0,1734	0,1572	0,1804	0,1804	0,1691	0,1691	0,9608	0,9295
Third Party Involvement -> Product Performance	0,375**	0,231	0,1301	0,1301	0,136	0,136	2,8815	1,6998

Appendix 2: Use of cold chain-specific technologies in different sub-groups

		never	1-25%	25-50%	50-75%	75%-100%	Total	Mean
Temperature Monitoring	Food	0	7	2	2	**17**	28	3,1
	Pharma	0	1	2	3	**8**	14	
	Mix	1	1	3	4	**10**	19	
Active Packaging Solutions	Food	5	**9**	3	2	5	24	1,8
	Pharma	3	**4**	2	**4**	0	13	
	Mix	2	**5**	3	**5**	3	18	
Location Monitoring	Food	3	**9**	2	2	8	24	2,0
	Pharma	2	**6**	4	0	1	13	
	Mix	3	**5**	2	3	**5**	18	
Online Access	Food	8	**9**	6	1	2	26	1,8
	Pharma	0	4	3	0	**5**	12	
	Mix	3	4	**5**	2	**5**	19	
Humidity Monitoring	Food	**9**	6	5	3	2	25	1,2
	Pharma	4	**6**	0	0	1	11	
	Mix	**7**	6	1	1	2	17	
Thermal Protection	Food	2	**13**	6	2	2	25	1,8
	Pharma	0	**5**	4	**5**	0	14	
	Mix	2	3	**8**	2	2	17	
Active Cooling	Food	0	2	1	2	**23**	28	2,9
	Pharma	0	4	**5**	4	1	14	
	Mix	0	**9**	0	3	6	18	
Gas Monitoring	Food	**12**	7	1	2	0	22	0,5
	Pharma	**8**	1	0	0	0	9	
	Mix	**9**	4	1	0	0	14	
Passive Cooling	Food	5	**14**	3	1	0	23	1,4
	Pharma	1	3	**7**	2	0	13	
	Mix	4	3	**7**	2	2	18	

Appendix 3: Use of cold chain-specific managerial practices in different sub-groups

		never	1-25%	25-50%	50-75%	75%-100%	Total	Mean
Tailor-made SOP	Food	2	6	5	3	**8**	24	2,4
	Pharma	1	1	4	2	**5**	13	
	Mix	0	5	5	**7**	2	19	
Complaint Handling Practices	Food	1	7	3	3	**7**	21	2,6
	Pharma	0	2	0	1	**11**	14	
	Mix	2	**7**	2	3	5	19	
Informal Communication	Food	3	**12**	4	4	2	25	1,8
	Pharma	1	**6**	2	3	2	14	
	Mix	0	**9**	4	4	2	19	
Formal Communication	Food	1	**10**	3	6	3	23	2,1
	Pharma	0	4	2	**5**	3	14	
	Mix	0	**9**	4	2	4	19	
Cold Chain Standards	Food	1	4	1	3	**16**	25	3,1
	Pharma	0	0	3	1	**10**	14	
	Mix	0	4	3	**6**	**6**	19	
Training & Qualifying Partners	Food	2	**10**	3	3	7	25	2,5
	Pharma	0	1	2	1	**10**	14	
	Mix	1	**6**	3	2	**6**	18	
Continuous Quality Improvement	Food	5	6	2	3	**9**	25	2,3
	Pharma	0	2	2	3	**5**	12	
	Mix	2	**6**	4	5	2	19	
Audits of Partners	Food	0	10	1	3	**11**	25	2,6
	Pharma	0	0	2	2	**9**	13	
	Mix	3	**5**	**5**	3	3	19	
Private Quality Management Standards	Food	1	7	5	2	**12**	27	2,5
	Pharma	0	2	2	3	**5**	12	
	Mix	3	4	**5**	2	4	18	

Appendix 4: Quality evaluation of the adapted first order model applied to the best case scenario

Construct	Indicator	Loading > 0.4	AVE > 0.5	Composite Reliability > 0.7	Cronbach Alpha > 0.6	R2
Asset Specificity	Spec1	.788	.612	.887	.842	-
	Spec2	.792				
	Spec3	.729				
	Spec4	.829				
	Spec5	.770				
Volume Uncertainty	Un1	.783	.760	.863	.714	-
	Un2	.952				
Level of Detail	Det1	.926	.784	.879	.733	.237
	Det2	.843				
Preciseness	Prec2	.995	.533	.631	.536	.093
	Prec3	.273				
Durability	Dur2	.839	.618	.829	.703	.097
	Dur3	.729				
	Dur4	.787				
Invariability	Invari1	.742	.739	.848	.698	.113
	Invari3	.964				
Range of Addressees	RoA2	.826	.835	.909	.863	.066
	RoA3	.994				
Rigidity	Rig1	.487	.530	.763	.662	.037
	Rig2	.835				
	Rig4	.808				
Logistics Performance	LP1	.666	.650	.880	.818	.261
	LP2	.896				
	LP3	.848				
	LP4	.795				
Product Performance	PP1	.879	.649	.845	.726	.210
	PP2	.872				
	PP3	.643				

Appendix 5: Discriminant validity of the reflective measurement models in the best case scenario

	Spec	Dur	Freq	Det	LQ	Prec	PQ	RoA	Rig	Invar	Un
Asset Specificity	**0,612**										
Durability	0,072	**0,618**									
Frequency	0,004	0,030	**1,000**								
Level of Detail	0,092	0,008	0,012	**0,739**							
Logistics Quality	0,148	0,002	0,037	0,090	**0,784**						
Preciseness	0,003	0,177	0,063	0,001	0,005	**0,649**					
Product Quality	0,028	0,020	0,058	0,000	0,018	0,005	**0,533**				
Range of Addressees	0,003	0,059	0,001	0,021	0,001	0,230	0,074	**0,649**			
Rigidity	0,000	0,116	0,049	0,002	0,003	0,002	0,153	0,001	**0,835**		
Invariability	0,022	0,025	0,009	0,003	0,007	0,000	0,035	0,005	0,062	**0,529**	
Volume Uncertainty	0,000	0,001	0,004	0,003	0,035	0,020	0,014	0,012	0,021	0,007	**0,758**

Appendix 6: Correlations between first order constructs in the best case scenario

Correlations							
		Detail	Durability	Preciseness	Range of Addressees	Rigidity	Invariability
Detail	Pearson Correlation	1	-,046	-,074	,038	,072	-,101
Durability		-,046	1	,391**	,264*	,293*	,981**
Preciseness		-,074	,391**	1	,490**	-,008	,379**
Range of Addressees		,038	,264*	,490**	1	-0,020	,224
Rigidity		,072	,293*	-,008	-,020	1	,304*
Invariability		-,101	,981**	,379**	,224	,304*	1
							$*\alpha = 0.05; **\alpha = 0.01;$

Appendix 7: Quality evaluation of the second order model applied to the best case scenario

Construct	Indicator	Weight	Correlation < 0.9	VIF < 10
Degree of interactional programming	Level of Detail	.738	-0.074	1.006
	Preciseness	.518		
Standardization of interactional programming	Durability	.950	.981**	1.024
	Invariability	.195		
Formalization of interactional programming	Range of Addressees	.628	-0.020	26.612
	Rigidity	.645		
				$*\alpha = 0.05; **\alpha = 0.01$

Appendix 8: Correlations between second order constructs in the best case scenario

Correlations				
		Degree	Standardization	Formalization
Degree	Pearson Correlation	1	-,070	,359**
Standardization		-,070	1	,125
Formalization		,359**	,125	1
				$*\alpha = 0.05; **\alpha = 0.01;$

Appendix 9: Results on causal relations for the first order model in the best case scenario

	Path Coefficients	Standard Deviation	Standard Error	T Statistics
Asset Specificity -> Durability	**-0,2586***	**0,1178**	**0,1178**	**2,1957**
Asset Specificity -> Invariability	**-0,3131***	**0,1416**	**0,1416**	**2,2116**
Asset Specificity -> Level of Detail	**0,4017****	**0,1009**	**0,1009**	**3,981**
Asset Specificity -> Logistics Quality	0,1374	0,13	0,13	1,0569
Asset Specificity -> Preciseness	-0,1563	0,1736	0,1736	0,9002
Asset Specificity -> Product Quality	0,0848	0,1474	0,1474	0,5754
Asset Specificity -> Range of Addressees	0,0226	0,1128	0,1128	0,2007
Asset Specificity -> Rigidity	0,1422	0,1564	0,1564	0,9094
Durability -> Logistics Quality	**0,498****	**0,0883**	**0,0883**	**5,639**
Durability -> Product Quality	**0,3059****	**0,109**	**0,109**	**2,8053**
Frequency -> Durability	0,1569	0,1103	0,1103	1,422
Frequency -> Invariability	-0,1311	0,0887	0,0887	1,4781
Frequency -> Level of Detail	**0,2306***	**0,0922**	**0,0922**	**2,5003**
Frequency -> Logistics Quality	**0,2459***	**0,0991**	**0,0991**	**2,482**
Frequency -> Preciseness	**0,2244***	**0,0914**	**0,0914**	**2,4565**
Frequency -> Product Quality	-0,0576	0,1003	0,1003	0,5746
Frequency -> Range of Addressees	0,2141	0,1076	0,1076	1,99
Frequency -> Rigidity	-0,0913	0,1387	0,1387	0,6581
Invariability -> Logistics Quality	0,0293	0,0994	0,0994	0,2942
Invariability -> Product Quality	-0,1725	0,1115	0,1115	1,5464
Level of Detail -> Logistics Quality	-0,1232	0,1245	0,1245	0,9897
Level of Detail -> Product Quality	-0,0973	0,15	0,15	0,6489
Preciseness -> Logistics Quality	0,0407	0,1292	0,1292	0,3148
Preciseness -> Product Quality	**0,3857***	**0,1562**	**0,1562**	**2,47**
Range of Addressees -> Logistics Quality	-0,2363	0,1346	0,1346	1,755
Range of Addressees -> Product Quality	-0,2254	0,1268	0,1268	1,7771
Rigidity -> Logistics Quality	0,1235	0,1209	0,1209	1,0216
Rigidity -> Product Quality	-0,0482	0,1357	0,1357	0,3551
Volume Uncertainty -> Durability	0,0227	0,1244	0,1244	0,1826
Volume Uncertainty -> Invariability	0,0666	0,0969	0,0969	0,6869
Volume Uncertainty -> Level of Detail	-0,208	0,1187	0,1187	1,7517
Volume Uncertainty -> Logistics Quality	0,103	0,1059	0,1059	0,9728
Volume Uncertainty -> Preciseness	0,1056	0,1444	0,1444	0,7314
Volume Uncertainty -> Product Quality	-0,1344	0,1145	0,1145	1,1746
Volume Uncertainty -> Range of Addressees	0,1304	0,1793	0,1793	0,7271
Volume Uncertainty -> Rigidity	0,0889	0,1547	0,1547	0,5749
				*α = 0.05;***α = 0.01;

Appendix 10: Results on causal relations for the second order model in the best case scenario

	Path Coefficients	Standard Deviation	Standard Error	T Statistics
Asset Specificity -> Degree	**0,2977***	**0,1124**	**0,1124**	**2,6497**
Asset Specificity -> Formalization	0,095	0,0985	0,0985	0,9638
Asset Specificity -> Logistics Quality	0,0896	0,1077	0,1077	0,8319
Asset Specificity -> Product Quality	-0,0116	0,1196	0,1196	0,0974
Asset Specificity -> Standardization	**-0,302***	**0,1166**	**0,1166**	**2,5908**
Degree -> Logistics Quality	-0,0567	0,1109	0,1109	0,5117
Degree -> Product Quality	0,1332	0,1245	0,1245	1,0698
Formalization -> Logistics Quality	-0,0524	0,1166	0,1166	0,4495
Formalization -> Product Quality	-0,0982	0,124	0,124	0,7918
Frequency -> Degree	**0,2622****	**0,0801**	**0,0801**	**3,2728**
Frequency -> Formalization	0,0705	0,095	0,095	0,7415
Frequency -> Logistics Quality	**0,2363***	**0,1005**	**0,1005**	**2,3523**
Frequency -> Product Quality	-0,0351	0,0962	0,0962	0,3647
Frequency -> Standardization	0,0614	0,0729	0,0729	0,8419
Standardization -> Logistics Quality	**0,386****	**0,0816**	**0,0816**	**4,7312**
Standardization -> Product Quality	**0,2488****	**0,0932**	**0,0932**	**2,6698**
Volume Uncertainty -> Degree	-0,0928	0,1044	0,1044	0,8887
Volume Uncertainty -> Formalization	0,1235	0,0927	0,0927	1,3316
Volume Uncertainty -> Logistics Quality	0,1132	0,0893	0,0893	1,2676
Volume Uncertainty -> Product Quality	-0,1037	0,0962	0,0962	1,0784
Volume Uncertainty -> Standardization	0,0365	0,0978	0,0978	0,373
				N= 60; *α = 0.05;**α = 0.01;

Appendix 11: Total effects of the first order model in the worst case scenario

	Path Coefficients	Direct Effects	Total Effects
Asset Specificity -> Logistics Quality	**0,2894**	**2,0927**	**2,1511**
Asset Specificity -> Product Quality	-0,0605	0,4288	0,435
Frequency -> Logistics Quality	**0,296**	**2,4986**	**2,5269**
Frequency -> Product Quality	**0,321**	**2,618**	**2,5984**
Volume Uncertainty -> Logistics Quality	0,0029	0,0239	0,0237
Volume Uncertainty -> Product Quality	0,0289	0,2717	0,265

Appendix 12: Total effects of the first order model in the best case scenario

	Path Coefficients	Direct Effects	Total Effects
Asset Specificity -> Logistics Quality	0,1374	1,0569	0,3667
Asset Specificity -> Product Quality	0,0848	0,5754	0,4123
Frequency -> Logistics Quality	0,2459	**2,482**	**2,348**
Frequency -> Product Quality	-0,0576	0,5746	0,3346
Volume Uncertainty -> Logistics Quality	0,103	0,9728	1,1624
Volume Uncertainty -> Product Quality	-0,1344	1,1746	1,09

Appendix 13: Total effects of the second order model in the worst case scenario

	Path Coefficients	Direct Effects	Total Effects
Asset Specificity -> Logistics Quality	0,1629	1,3131	0,4301
Asset Specificity -> Product Quality	0,1951	1,8219	**2,6687**
Frequency -> Logistics Quality	0,174	1,5295	1,6948
Frequency -> Product Quality	0,0552	0,5047	0,2113
Volume Uncertainty -> Logistics Quality	-0,12	0,9812	1,0008
Volume Uncertainty -> Product Quality	-0,2129	1,8418	1,912

Appendix 14: Total effects of the second order model in the best case scenario

	Path Coefficients	Direct Effects	Total Effects
Asset Specificity -> Logistics Quality	0,0896	0,8319	0,44
Asset Specificity -> Product Quality	-0,0116	0,0974	0,4812
Frequency -> Logistics Quality	0,2363	**2,3523**	**2,4398**
Frequency -> Product Quality	-0,0351	0,3647	0,0865
Volume Uncertainty -> Logistics Quality	0,1132	1,2676	1,3851
Volume Uncertainty -> Product Quality	-0,1037	1,0784	1,3441

Appendix 15: Comments by respondents

lfdn	According to you, what is most important in achieving seamless processes at interfaces between companies? Do you have any suggestions for future research?
43	Clear and transparent communications of requirements for transportation (Time, Temperature, Routing, Volumes)
44	I will strongly recommend that procedures and standards must be in place for each process. Flexibility can be exercised but continuous deviations must have some penalties or disadvantage. One is tempted to have different processes for different partners under the guise of tailor-made, but in reality it is designed to suit once dependence on that partner. The more dependent we are on the partner the less we apply strict processes.
45	Yes, we are in the supply chain service industry for the export of perishables - mainly fruit. This involves many parties from the farm to the fork starting with the grower, packhouse, cold store, packaging supplier, transporter, shipping line, forwarding agent etc. In South Africa once deregulation occurred it became very important for various fruit industry bodies to be formed in order to manage the best interests of these industries based mainly on the differing fruit types i.e. stone fruit, grapes, citrus, pomes, subtropicals. Also because of the wide range of products we require many different variances within the same basic temperature controlled chain for optimum shipment of goods from A to B. We also have a unique governing body called the PPECB (Perishable Products Export Control Board) who gives guidance, sets rules, polices that these are adhered to & has the status to accept or reject all fruit for export. The rules both within South Africa (as harbours/systems/protocols are updated) & in receiving countries (Europe, Far East, Middle East - HACCP, Fair Trade etc. or various product sterilization or pest inspection or chemical spraying restrictions) are fast changing & therefore impacting more & more on a fairly stable/standard operating environment that is now having to adapt - both in terms of procedures & information flow/deadlines. So what I am saying is that given your questions it is very difficult to explain the above except to say that most of the time we manage the supply chain in South Africa in a very controlled environment but times are changing - can the drive to lower costs create problems in trying to manage an ever increasing sophisticated safety first global food market?

48	Keep it simple and be practical. Do not implement procedures that cannot be followed in practice. Follow up your employees with education and relevant information. Take them seriously and listen to good advices. Follow up irregularity reports. Keep your suppliers updated at all times.
50	Open line communication with a goal to achieving improvement and not penalties.
60	to rely on third parties when providing logistics services for temp. sensitive goods is not a good idea. Toleration to mistakes varies from companies to companies, unfortunately when handling perishables goods there is not room for mistakes. Normally the mistakes are fatal and Customers don't tolerate then.
61	We mainly cooperate with specialized transport companies on existing supply chains based on long term relations on both suppliers as clients. In Fresh Fruit and Veg all transport is refrigerated and main damage exists when cooling is interrupted. In our trade business is mainly done by gentlemen's agreement, using many certificates as HACCP, ISO, BRC, IFS, etc.
66	Every supply chain has companies linking in with each other, both on an operational- and a communication level. The key in the supply chain for temperature sensitive products is to identify the weak spots, normally the escalation points, where the products are handed over from one to the other party. This process should be harmonized, as currently this is still not done. The fear factor of taking ownership of any liability in this process and the fact that transparency is still a curse in our industry, we as an industry fail to improve the complete supply chain. Exchanging best practice cases, sharing own experiences on how to overcome issues on a global level, would help our industry tremendously. At this moment in time the supply chain in our industry is being dominated by local heroes, not the big multinationals of this world.
68	Clear contractual agreements defining roles and responsibilities including communication.
69	visibility though integrated IT systems
71	1. the end goal of the whole process plan must be defined clearly 2. the process must be flexible enough to endure uncertainties in other parts of the chain 3. the process must frequently undergo a live audit and improved and updated accordingly
77	Universal process / procedure and documents. Clear definition of terminology and required information.
81	(1) Everyone must follow the agreed procedures, and (2) financial penalties enforce compliance to the procedures.
86	Collaboration, alignment, knowhow
100	As so much activity in transportation is managed by third parties (forwarder / airline / trucking company / customs broker - plus shipper / consignee), communication is critical. All processes, whether operational or EDI should be documented.
103	most important: - seamless transition of data from one IT system to another - try to reduce manual input of data
105	ROI the first part answers could be duplicated for the second part
107	Establishing the complete process, ensuring all involved are in agreement and trained, monitoring adherence, evaluating deviations and putting CAPAs in place.
109	Standard Operating Procedures covering physical handling and information exchange for all parties involved in the supply/cool chain
110	Awareness and Training and dedicated teams from A to Z Too many changes on the suppliers lead to mistakes SOPS, Procedures etc. will not help if people don't know how to handle ...

112	The first step is to sign a good Quality Assurance Agreement. The QAA must describe the technical processes and also the organizational framework including the information pathways between both companies. The QAA should be extensive and accurate, providing no room for misunderstanding. It must include procedures for handling with deviations and change control. However, the best QAA doesn't help, if it is not implemented: A system must be established to assure regular re-qualification and/or Audit of the Partner. It is also important to hold regular Meetings or Telephone conferences with the Partner.
114	Most important is the accuracy of received data. Pre-notification is also a part of success in this process.
115	Very clear procedures are extremely important. These procedures have to be implemented in the whole supply chain. Also pre and post shipment. The ideal model goes from tree to shelf in the supermarket at destination - all controlled by an independent and transparent supply chain service provider who needs to monitor the whole process.
116	Clear expectations and an efficient Claims and CAPA system are key to a successful relationship. Depending on the industry, the toll for not being effective might have a considerable financial and/or P.R. impact.
117	Setting up quality systems and aligning the procedures with all different partners is a challenge even though the relationships have been formalized in Contracts and SLA's and/or QA's.
121	Complete transparency on the requirements and expectations from the customer to the supplier.
122	Important: using agreed, industry-wide standards; immediately iron out appearing issues
124	Clearly defined procedures and expectations
126	Very important for achieving seamless processes at interfaces between companies are exactly defined requirements on processes, interfaces, IT, dealing with deviations Solutions based on the defined requirements defined temperature monitoring online data availability of all temperature devices
128	The requirements, stakeholders involved, facilities, equipment, packaging material etc. change quite often. This provides new opportunities as well as challenges. Market knowledge and drive for continuous improvement are important to achieve the best result and avoid surprises. Furthermore accurate training of staff and complaint management combined with CAPA analyses are important to maintain and improve existing procedures. For future research the weakest link in the airfreight could be interesting. What are the airport facility and service expectations with regards to conditioned storage and handling and would it be possible to define standards?
133	The capabilities of the partners especially regarding the adherence of temperature (cold chain)
139	Involvement of all parties in the supply chain, Shipper, Forwarding Agent, Handling Agent, Airline, CNEE, should all agree on defined processes before they go live
141	Communication lines must be defined and frequent meetings are required to keep on track
142	It is very hard to work with truck drivers. Most of the time we discuss with them regarding the rules.
144	Standard IDOCS and processes

Printed by Printforce, the Netherlands